THE MASTER
ARCHITECTS

THE MASTER ARCHITECTS

Building the United States
Foreign Service
1890-1913

Richard Hume Werking

The University Press of Kentucky

The papers of Francis M. Huntington Wilson are quoted
by permission of Myrin Library, Ursinus College

ISBN: 0–8131–1342–3

Library of Congress Catalog Card Number: 76–9509

Copyright © 1977 by The University Press of Kentucky

A statewide cooperative scholarly publishing agency
serving Berea College, Centre College of Kentucky,
Eastern Kentucky University, The Filson Club,
Georgetown College, Kentucky Historical Society,
Kentucky State University, Morehead State University,
Murray State University, Northern Kentucky University,
Transylvania University, University of Kentucky,
University of Louisville, and Western Kentucky University.

Editorial and Sales Offices: Lexington, Kentucky 40506

to Judith
and
to Mary and Woody Werking

Among the many reasons given above . . . we should also include the most significant failure of all organizational theory: the failure to see society *as adaptive to* organizations. . . . *Parts of the "environment" are seen as affecting organizations, but the organization is not seen as defining, creating, and shaping its environment.*

Charles Perrow, Complex Organizations: A Critical Essay

CONTENTS

PREFACE

This book began with my intention to examine United States foreign policy in the period before World War I by studying the attitudes of individuals who made or conducted that policy. I was interested, however, in finding more concrete evidence of their thinking than could be inferred merely from their writings and speeches, however sincere these were. I wanted to observe the relationship between their beliefs and their behavior, to discover whether their attitudes were translated into policy and action, and if so, how.

One way of approaching the issue would have been to study the official relations of the United States with another country or group of countries. Focusing on official relations is, after all, the usual method of diplomatic history. This approach tends toward the particular, toward relations with specific countries or regions. On the basis of these particulars, generalizations can frequently be made about the basic guidelines and principles informing policy.

A different avenue appealed to me because of its broader scope and its relative neglect by historians. I became interested in examining institutions connected with foreign policy and foreign relations. By studying one or more such institutions, with special emphasis upon the attitudes and assumptions of the persons who operated them, I hoped to glean some insights into the general direction of foreign policy over a particular span of years. I especially wanted to obtain a clearer understanding of the relative importance of foreign and domestic factors affecting United States foreign policy. Were overseas developments, particularly crisis events, pulling the United States onto the world's stage, or were domestic forces pushing it into greater activity?

Previous accounts of the foreign affairs bureaucracy have provided valuable information about its historical development, a topic once almost exclusively the province of foreign service officers and political scientists.[1] Yet this study is the first attempt to present an extensive analysis, based on a variety of published and unpublished sources, of the organization and reorganization of the foreign affairs machinery between the 1890s and World War I.

The "foreign service" is defined here in two ways. As used throughout the book the term refers to the State Department proper, the diplomatic service, and the consular service. This definition is broader than the most common usage, which has generally limited the term to that arm of the State Department located abroad. (The usual definition stresses the physical location; mine stresses the function, as contemporary descriptions often did.) On a second level, no discussion of an American "foreign service" in this period should ignore the Department of Commerce and Labor. Together with the State Department's organization, it was a key element in the federal government's program of assistance to the nation's business community. Moreover, State Department personnel correctly believed that the Commerce and Labor Department, in building its own foreign service, posed a threat to them and their institution.

This account of foreign affairs institutions consists of four principal elements. The simplest is the structure as it might have existed on an organization chart, that is, the "anatomy" of the American foreign service. For example, it is important, though not widely known, that the State Department possessed a commercial office from the mid-1850s onward. Furthermore, a study of the organization permits correction of some errors in standard accounts of foreign service development, minor in themselves but major in their implications. According to some accounts, for instance, neither the Commerce Department's field foreign service nor the State Department's training school for foreign service officers existed until the 1920s. In fact, both began during the first years of this century.[2]

A second and more important element is the functioning of the organization, its "physiology," covering such matters as the activities of the State Department's new geographic divisions and the working relationship between the State Department and the Department of Commerce and Labor. The organization and functioning of the government's apparatus for making foreign policy and conducting foreign relations can be an excellent clue to the nature of government policy.

Examination of those two elements, organization and function, indicates that the pre–World War I foreign service was first and foremost an instrument for the nation's commercial expansion. It not only held open the door to equal opportunity for American exports (ensuring *protection* for American trade), but it increasingly attempted to shove American businessmen through the open door (*promoting* foreign trade). As the foreign service improved its facilities for conducting official relations with other countries, it also developed its system for communicating with America's merchants and manufacturers, placing domestic producers in contact with foreign customers.

But to describe only the structure and functioning of the foreign affairs machinery is not enough. Even more important are the interrelated questions of how and why it developed as it did. These questions relate chiefly to two additional ingredients: the attitudes of government officials (toward their individual work, their institution's purpose, and their country's world role) and the dynamics of *re*organization. The attitudes and personal concerns of the reorganizers and the tactical considerations in the process of reorganization were key determinants of why the system evolved as it did.

The "master architects" themselves were the men chiefly responsible for planning and building the modern foreign service.[3] Their ranks included several department clerks and bureau chiefs, a secretary of state and an assistant secretary of state, a businessman-lawyer, and perhaps one or two others. Almost all were in the executive branch of the government, principally in the middle-echelon positions that historians have usually neglected. A common characteristic of these men was a horizon that extended to the world—not just to the edge of a city, state, or even the nation. They believed that the United States had to play a larger role in world affairs and that it lacked the modern machinery with which to do it. Most of them also saw their own careers, their own spheres of usefulness, tied closely to the service of a nation increasingly active in the world. To describe the interaction of their personal ambitions with their hopes for their country—and to recount their efforts to create a structure that would accommodate both—is a major purpose of this book.

A heuristic model useful for studying foreign service reform is a modification of the schema outlined by Robert Merton, Samuel Hays, Thomas McCormick, and others, which helps explain social behavior by placing individuals within what Hays calls the "community-society continuum." The "cosmopolitans" in this arrangement are persons whose horizons extend far beyond the space they occupy and who attempt to come to terms with the functioning of the whole society. They are frequently system-builders, and it is often the society-polity that serves as the arena for their mental gymnastics or the exercise of their talents. "Locals," as the name implies, are interested chiefly in their own community, defined spatially. The community, not the larger society, provides both locus and focus for their mental and physical interaction. Between these two types are the "functionals," persons organized on the basis of occupational function, such as members of labor unions or businessmen's associations. The size and geographic extent of the functional groups may vary, but the focus within each involves common goals and often common means.[4]

Such categories are most useful when considered to be flexible and not necessarily mutually exclusive. The handful of individuals spearheading reform of the State Department and its field branches were cosmopolitans, whose geographic horizons and daily concerns were worldwide. Their outlook often blended trends within and outside the United States. Most of these men thought deeply about what was happening in American society, and they expected the United States, principally as a result of economic forces, to play a more active role on the world's stage. Their desire for a reorganized foreign service reflected these concerns and beliefs.

But with the exception of Secretary of State Elihu Root, the movement's leaders were younger men who were also working to satisfy more immediate group and individual needs that related to the work function. In these respects they behaved like members of an interest group as well as like more detached cosmopolitans. Their concern with foreign markets as essential to domestic well-being, and their belief in the necessity of a foreign service oriented principally toward marketplace expansion, meshed neatly with their desires for enhancing their organization and for doing useful and stimulating work that brought personal recognition. Their attempts to awaken others to foreign trade opportunities and to the utility of a reorganized foreign service reflected a fusion of their cosmopolitan and functional concerns.

Because it was necessary to obtain appropriations and enabling legislation from a Congress whose horizons and daily concerns were more local, foreign service reform was difficult and only gradual. Reorganization lagged far behind the hopes of State Department personnel. Even after World War I, with the foundations of the modern foreign service securely in place, attempts at further reorganization and the annual struggle for appropriations were often difficult for the State Department. Thus foreign service officers from the nineteenth century to the present have bemoaned the public's narrow horizons and preoccupation with local matters, its general indifference to foreign affairs, and the consequent congressional parsimony toward their organization.

Finally, this is also a study in institution-building, which implicitly addresses itself to questions about mobilizing public support in American society. In a thought-provoking essay on the New Deal, William Leuchtenburg has observed the propensity of government leaders to rely on the rhetoric of the Great War, conveying a sense of shared crisis, to mobilize public opinion behind their programs.[5] An even greater war and subsequent lesser ones have continued to demonstrate this tendency among individuals and groups advocating programs national in scope, whether involving participation in combat (current or pending), education, or the conquest of poverty. But how were reformers to gain widespread public support for their programs before the precedent of national mobilization during World War I? This was the problem faced by those who wished to remake the foreign service, and the historical record is replete with their frustrations as well as their triumphs.

ACKNOWLEDGMENTS

My greatest obligation is to my wife, Judith Keneipp Werking. She has furnished indispensable support throughout the undertaking, and her numerous suggestions have considerably improved the final product. I am heavily indebted as well to John DeNovo, professor of history at the University of Wisconsin, Madison, who supervised an earlier version of this work as a Ph.D. dissertation. From the beginning, Professor DeNovo exhibited the combination of insight and great painstaking that his students have come to know as his trademark. In addition, Tom Fiddick at the University of Evansville first awakened my interest as an undergraduate in American foreign relations, and Robert Freeman Smith spurred that interest during the course of a master's seminar at the University of Wisconsin.

Other scholars have read all or part of the manuscript and made helpful recommendations. They include· Michael Berry, Paul Conkin, John Cooper, Paul Glad, Stanley Kutler, Diane Lindstrom, Thomas McCormick, and Morton Rothstein, all of the Department of History, University of Wisconsin; Fred Carstensen of the Department of History, University of Virginia; and Paul Hirsch of the Graduate Business School, University of Chicago. Lewis Gould, of the Department of History, University of Texas, read the manuscript twice and offered many useful suggestions. I alone, of course, am responsible for whatever errors or shortcomings remain.

Considerations of space allow me to mention only a few of the many archivists and librarians who aided my research. At the National Archives in Washington, I received much assistance from Milton Gustafson and Sandra Rangel in Diplomatic Records, Suzanne Harris in Commerce Department Records, and Charles South in

Legislative Records. Kate Stewart, Carolyn Sung, and Charles Cooney provided similar help at the Division of Manuscripts, Library of Congress, as did Ellen Burke and John Peters at the State Historical Society of Wisconsin Library. I would also like to thank the librarians and archivists at the following institutions: Bucknell University; Cornell University; Duke University; Georgetown University; Harvard Business School; Harvard University; Historical Society of Pennsylvania; Hoover Institution on War, Revolution, and Peace; Johns Hopkins University; Massachusetts Historical Society; Minnesota State Historical Society; Organization of American States, Records Management Center; Pan American Union; Princeton University; Stanford University; State Historical Society of Wisconsin; University of California, Berkeley; University of Chicago; University of Rochester; University of Vermont; Ursinus College; United States Civil Service Commission, Washington, D.C.; United States Department of State, Historical Office and the Records Management Center; and Yale University.

I am grateful to the following persons and institutions for permission to quote from unpublished writings in personal manuscript collections: Bucknell University Archives; Mrs. Pitt F. Carl, Jr.; Cornell University Libraries; Duke University Library; The Historical Society of Pennsylvania; The Houghton Library, Harvard University; Philip C. Jessup; Henry Cabot Lodge; Frank G. MacMurray; the National Civil Service League; Eleanor Hunt O'Donoghue and Mary Hunt Power; Paul V. Siggers; The Stanford University Libraries; The State Historical Society of Wisconsin; The University of Rochester Library; Ursinus College Library; Yale University Library.

In addition, I would like to express appreciation for the many manuscript collections whose literary property rights have been dedicated to the public.

1 THE UNITED STATES FOREIGN SERVICE

From the beginning of George Washington's presidency, the foreign service of the United States consisted of three parts. The diplomatic and consular services were separate entities, whose members represented the United States abroad and were theoretically responsible to the third section —the Department of State. By the end of the nineteenth century, serious defects existed in all three branches.

THE CONSULAR SERVICE

The commercial and maritime character of the United States Consular Service during the nineteenth century reflected centuries of tradition in the Western world. Six hundred years before the birth of Christ, according to Herodotus, the Egyptians granted to a community of Greeks established at Naucratis the right to select from their ranks a magistrate who would apply to them the laws of the mother country. Well over a millennium later, in the Mediterranean world of the Middle Ages, merchants from Genoa, Pisa, Venice, Marseilles, and Barcelona established mercantile agencies in Syria, Egypt, and Palestine. The merchants were unwilling to have their disputes judged according to Saracen law and consequently were allowed to choose a magistrate from their number who would arbitrate in such cases and also present their grievances to the local authorities. The magistrate was called baile or consul, and he obtained his jurisdiction from the Muslim princes by treaty. As set forth in the regulations of Barcelona in 1266, a consul was required to "order, govern, cite, regulate, punish and take any other action with respect to persons who voyage from our shores to places across the sea and establish their residence in those ports."[1]

As monarchies and the European state system evolved, the nation-state began to appoint consuls to represent the interests of its nationals in foreign lands. In Europe and then throughout most of the world consuls lost some jurisdiction over their own countrymen, since newly self-conscious sovereignties were no longer willing to surrender the prerogative of dispensing justice within their borders—when they could avoid it. At the same time, countries began to exchange permanent embassies that were distinct from consulates. Consuls were thus relieved of most political and diplomatic functions, and commercial duties took most of their time.[2]

In 1790, Secretary of State Thomas Jefferson issued the first general instruction to American consular officers, requiring them to send periodic reports of American ships entering or clearing their respective ports, to report on military preparations at their ports and notify American merchants and vessels if war threatened, and to supply political and commercial information of interest to the United States. Other responsibilities, added by Congress two years later, included receiving protests from or against United States citizens, giving aid to American seamen in distress, performing notarial tasks for their countrymen, and settling the estates of American citizens who died abroad without a legal representative. For several decades the primary function of the consular corps continued to be aiding Americans engaged in maritime commerce.[3]

During the nineteenth century consuls assumed additional duties. They notified Washington of epidemics in their districts and issued bills of health to ships leaving their ports for the United States. They visaed, and sometimes issued, passports. They examined ships' lists of emigrants to the United States, seeking to exclude Chinese laborers, most contract laborers, idiots, paupers, criminals, prostitutes, and polygamists. In certain non-Christian countries where the western powers exercised "extraterritoriality," or legal jurisdiction over their own citizens, consular functions included the most traditional task; by the end of the nineteenth century, treaties gave United States consuls jurisdiction over cases involving American citizens in China, Turkey, Borneo, Siam, Persia, the Barbary States, Madagascar, and Maskat. Beginning in 1818 an increasingly important duty, designed to protect Treasury revenues, was to verify invoices of goods about to be shipped to the United States: the consul certified to customs collectors at United States ports of entry that the value of the merchandise was stated correctly and not undervalued to secure a lower import duty. After the destruction of the American merchant marine during the Civil War and the consequent reduction in American ocean shipping, invoice certification was easily the single most important consular function. Finally, in the mid-nineteenth century consuls began to make regular reports to Washington about commercial conditions in their districts.[4]

To perform these tasks throughout the world, the United States government maintained a large number of consular offices. In 1890 there were 238 consulates and 38 consulates-general, whose incumbents were appointed by the president with the Senate's consent. Ten years later they numbered 248 and 43. Consuls-general theoretically supervised the consuls within a country, to the slight degree that supervision could be maintained by correspondence. Actually it amounted to virtually nothing. Within the jurisdiction of many consular districts, but not in the same town as the consulate, were consular agencies, 437 of them in 1890 and 395 in 1900. These were established in localities that offered some consular business but not enough for a full-fledged consulate. Consular agents were appointed by the State Department on the consul's recommendation (rather than by the president) and functioned under the consul's supervision. Most were foreigners (three-quarters in 1900), and they were paid with a portion of the fees they collected.[5]

Employed at each consulate or consulate-general in addition to the principal officer were a vice-officer, authorized to assume charge in the absence of his superior, and, sometimes, another deputy. Both subordinate officials normally performed clerical duties, and there were often additional clerical personnel. Like consular agents, these men were appointed by the State Department on the consul's recommendation. Including deputy and vice-consuls, other clerks, consular agents, consuls and consuls-general, and a few miscellaneous officers, the United States Consular Service in 1900 numbered well over a thousand men, distributed among some seven hundred cities and towns.[6]

A little more than a century passed between the establishment of the service and its inspection in 1896–1897. Robert S. Chilton, Jr., chief of the Consular Bureau, was less than delighted with what he discovered. The consul-general at Shanghai was misusing funds, and his office was generally "in an unsatisfactory condition and in need of a general overhauling." In Mexico a consular agent had set up shop in the same room with the consul (instead of working in another part of the consular district as the regulations demanded) and was doing most of the consul's work under a fee-splitting arrangement. That same consul's son was employed full-time during business hours as a clerk in the local railroad office while simultaneously drawing pay from the United States government as the sole clerk in the consulate, where it was evident to Chilton that his services were only nominal. In England the bureau chief discovered that consuls were paying local commissioners a small wage to certify invoices, while pocketing the fees in violation of regulations. The consul at Liverpool cleared at least six or seven thousand dollars annually from this scheme, and those at Bradford and Manchester about five thousand each. Chilton characterized the arrangement as "demoralizing and mischievous in the extreme."[7]

Had some of Chilton's findings been made public, they would only have confirmed the low public image of American consular officers—an image that officials in the foreign service knew was often close to the mark. Many years afterward, Wilbur Carr, the "father of the foreign service," was thankful that the American consul could no longer "be truthfully pictured sleeping under the proverbial palm tree with his bottle beside him." Consul-General Eugene Seeger, after investigating consulates in Brazil, concluded that only "degenerates" had occupied a particular post over the previous ten years; the incumbent was a heavy drinker, and it was commonly rumored in the city that he had "recently endangered his life by trying to rape his landlady, whose husband had not sufficiently mistrusted him."[8]

Yet notwithstanding recurring comments about hard-drinking, tobacco-chewing consuls, and despite the presence in the service of a large number of men obviously unfit to hold their positions, the question of the individual consul's personal fitness was only the most visible of many problems. Chilton himself, and many others acquainted with the situation, stressed that even more at fault was the system itself—"our very faulty system," as Chilton put it.[9] Many of its features made for poor public officers.

Consular regulations prescribed that each new appointee was to undergo a thirty-day instruction period in Washington to become acquainted with his duties and responsibilities, but the department made no provision for any real instruction. The "training period" was often no more than a one-day stop for some general advice, good wishes, and a copy of the consular regulations. The neophyte frequently left for his post without even visiting Washington. Consul-General Frank H. Mason, probably the most highly regarded officer in the service, complained that most of the appointee's instruction period was normally spent "in arranging his private affairs and in attending farewell festivities given in his honor by his neighbors and friends."[10]

Although by 1900 most of the consulates were salaried positions, those salaries were generally low, and the consul's financial troubles by no means ended there.[11] They were required to pay their own transportation to and from their posts; once there they had to operate their offices on meager governmental allowances. Some consuls had to contribute from their own pockets for clerk hire, and most of them were obliged to dig even deeper to help pay for office rent, supplies, and other contingent expenses.[12]

On the other hand, additional remuneration came in the form of fees. Consuls charged fees for a number of services, including certifying invoices for shippers, authenticating other kinds of documents, and settling estates. Since 1856, salaried consuls had been required to send all their official fees to the Treasury, submit quarterly reports of their official receipts, and post the fee schedule in the consulate. But it was difficult for the State Department to determine the veracity of those reports (much less to know whether the correct schedule was prominently posted), and consuls frequently charged what the traffic would bear. They sometimes competed with their colleagues in neighboring districts for the privilege of certifying invoices and, to attract more business, allowed the shipper to undervalue his merchandise and thus pay a lower duty when the goods and false invoice reached the United States.[13]

A variety of notarial services brought in unofficial fees, and the consuls kept all of these. Although necessary in many places because of low or nonexistent salaries, unofficial fees created additional problems. At some posts they far exceeded official fees. A State Department officer guessed in 1900 that the consulates-general at London and Paris each took in more than $20,000 annually from this source. According to another estimate, the consulate at Amoy was worth $40,000 in fees to its incumbent, and the one at Liverpool $60,000. Thus while some consuls languished at posts with few fees, some of their prosperous colleagues argued against placing the entire service on a salaried basis. Robert Chilton's successor as head of the Consular Bureau remarked in 1902 that the unofficial fee system was "the most demoralizing element in our service."[14]

The fee system also helped prompt the appointment of unfit subordinates to the service. Until 1898 a consular agent and his supervising consul were permitted to split the fees collected by the agency. The consul in Mexico whom Chilton discovered farming out an appointment as consular agent, in return for a special kickback arrangement, was by no means the only offender. Secretary of State William R. Day concluded that the "tendency of the practice is to impair the efficiency of the service, through the appointment of unfit men as consular agents."[15]

A principal reason for the frequently inadequate salaries—and itself another major problem—was the outdated classification of the consulates. This arrangement of the posts into grades according to their importance was based on earlier conditions, since the only reclassifications had occurred no more recently than 1856 and 1874. Not only had the cost of living increased substantially at many posts, but changes had taken place both in trade routes and consular practices, rendering the previous overhaulings meaningless by the turn of the century. The 1874 reclassification had itself occurred because of the obsolescence of the 1856 arrangement. Congressman Godlove S. Orth of Indiana, an advocate of reclassification in 1874, argued that the American consular system "has been so far merely patchwork," and he well described the haphazard methods of determining a post's importance: "A consulate was created at one session of Congress and a salary fixed for it, and at another session another consulate was created at some point and a different salary fixed there, and thus it has continued from year to year without any attempt at equalization or at reducing it to anything like a system." Unfortunately, the same procedure continued after the 1874 reclassification. A former consular officer remarked to Chilton in 1899 that "the matter of consular salaries is still in the same chaotic condition in which it has been since time immemorial." He was distressed that the consul at the Bavarian capital of Munich received a salary of $2,000, while a colleague at Nuremberg, a less important town in the same kingdom, and with one-third the population, received $3,000.[16]

Some posts had been established at commercial centers and seaports whose importance had since diminished. Others were located in inland towns and cities principally to certify invoices of goods bound for the United States. Chilton was particularly disturbed by the unnecessary proliferation of consulates in Canada, which he attributed to the law requiring consular certificates accompanying the invoices, and he urged that the American consulates in Canada and Mexico be reduced to eight or ten offices at the principal cities.[17] By the late 1890s there had also emerged a related and growing concern that the United States had far too many consulates in the more developed countries to certify invoices and was not establishing them where they were most needed—in the less-developed areas where they could foster America's growing export trade. Since the State Department had traditionally estimated the importance of a consulate by the reported amount of fees it collected, the European posts received the highest salaries. Not surprisingly, the higher salaries and greater business (and consequently more official and unofficial fees) at those offices attracted the best officers of the lot. The service was worst in the non-European countries where, generally, less business meant lower salaries and fewer supplementary fees to attract competent men. One official complained in 1899 that the United States was spending almost as much on consular salaries in a small area of Germany, in order to certify invoices, as "in our great market of the future Brazil and four times as much as we spend in either Chile or Argentine Republic."[18]

Since the classification was virtually meaningless, there could be no system for orderly promotion in the service from one post to a higher one. The result was a situation in which, as Secretary of State Elihu Root put it, "each consulate was a separate office by itself, having no relation to any other office." Without hope of promotion, there was little to motivate the consul to do good work.[19]

The separateness of the posts was part of an overall conception, embedded in American practice for over a century, which failed to consider either the consular or the diplomatic service as a unity. Appointments were made to specific posts, not to the service.

If the president wished to transfer an officer to a higher or lower post or even to one of the same relative importance, a new nomination had to go to the Senate. Moreover, the individual consulates were institutionally isolated from the State Department as well as from one another. An official in the Consular Bureau in the 1890s advised new officers that "the really efficient consul doesn't bother the Department very much."[20]

No regular system of inspection existed to bind the field force closer to the State Department and keep it informed about what was going on at the posts. In the 1880s, Secretary of State Thomas Bayard repeatedly, and unsuccessfully, asked Congress to appropriate for inspectors of consulates. "There are now serious complaints lodged against several consuls," Bayard explained to a congressional committee. "It is not fair to strike a man in the dark without a hearing, and I have no means of hearing him." One horror story told of a newly appointed consul who arrived at his office in a large European city and attempted for several days, without telling the staff at the consulate who he was, to see the man he was replacing. After being put off repeatedly, the visitor revealed his identity and demanded to see the consul so that he could take over. The clerk in charge informed the appointee that his predecessor had been insane for three years and could be found tied to a chair upstairs.[21] Although probably apocryphal, the tale nevertheless illustrates that more than physical distance separated the department from the field; a corps of inspectors would have helped to bridge the gap.

Another problem was the appointment of foreigners at some posts. Following the practice of European nations, the United States had appointed as consuls commission merchants established in trade in foreign ports. These merchant-consuls could be found at offices with no salaries and few fees—posts not eagerly sought by Americans. Most of the appointees desired the positions to gain prestige for their local businesses. Often they used the office to aid their own establishments at the expense of other merchants in the port, a practice that did little to advance American interests. In 1894 there were more than twenty such officers in charge of consular posts. Consul-General Robert Peet Skinner once told of a local citizen entering a large American consulate and, noticing an unfamiliar face, asking who the stranger was. Informed that it was the new consul, the inquirer exclaimed: "You don't say so; why he looks like an American."[22]

The other group of foreigners in the consular service was the large number serving as consular agents, subordinate officers, and clerks. They too desired the positions for the prestige they gained in their local communities, and some American consuls were disturbed by their presence. If unsatisfactory work was found even among Americans, Consul-General Charles M. Dickinson at Constantinople asked, were matters likely to improve with employees who were "mostly foreigners or tainted with Levantine leaven, who accept these posts primarily for the honor and prestige with which they are clothed?" Many United States officials feared that these foreigners were in a position to certify invoices falsely and to work against the extension of America's export trade. Consul-General John M. Crawford remarked in 1890 that of fourteen occupants of American consular positions in Russia, only three actually were Americans, and that in some cases "the only apparent interest of the Consul is to use his office to further the schemes of dishonest exporters."[23]

The principal obstacle to an efficient consular service was not the quality of the appointees, their lack of initial training, or any of the other matters mentioned above. Despite all the problems, after three or four years at their posts some of the consuls managed to acquire a modicum of efficiency and suitability for their jobs. Even after uncovering many weak spots on his inspection tour, Robert Chilton could still write Assistant Secretary of State William Rockhill that "as a whole our Consular service in those countries that I have visited is faithful and efficient," and he expressed hope that the government would retain those who had demonstrated their fitness. But this was precisely the overriding problem, and Chilton's fears were realized early in 1897 when the incoming McKinley administration began firing a large number of the consuls appointed by Grover Cleveland and appointing many new and inexperienced men in their places. Between March 3, 1897, and November 1, 1898, changes among the principal consular officers in grades of $1,000 and above numbered 238 out of a total of 272.

Consul-General Frank Mason in Frankfort thought the new men he had seen were "very good material indeed." The problem was their inexperience; they were "as yet only good material out of which it is to be hoped good consuls can be made."[24]

McKinley was not breaking with tradition by his action. During the first months of the Cleveland administration four years earlier, Assistant Secretary of State Josiah Quincy had wielded the hatchet in what some observers termed a "debauch" of the service. In less than ten months, 30 consuls-general out of 35 and 133 consuls of the first class out of 183, along with the great majority of the lower-ranking officers, were thrown out to make way for deserving Democrats. The final turnover was about 90 percent. According to a survivor, it was "a regular orgy of decapitations."[25]

Both actions highlighted the major problem with the consular service—the very real possibility that any presidential election might change the political party represented in the White House and thus result in a wholesale removal of experienced consuls. The consular service, in short, was not really in the hands of the State Department, but under the control of the spoils system. Because the Civil Service Act of 1883 and subsequent extensions had shut off substantial numbers of government jobs to political hacks, the pressure was increased upon those portions of the government service still open to purely political appointments, such as the consular branch. Senator John Sherman, later a secretary of state, referred to "the great pressure for consular positions," and John Hay as secretary found that same pressure "almost indescribable." Hay once told a friend how the senators from Kansas had brought a client to the president's attention. "He was represented," Hay confided, "not only as the best possible man personally for such a post, but his appointment was distinctly referred to as the salvation of the Republican party in Kansas." And in 1898 when the American consul-general at Berlin died, politicians from nearly every state in the union had claimed the position before the funeral.[26]

The political nature of consular appointments was complex, involving more than simply presidential accession to humble pleas for the return of a political favor. The constitution provides that consuls and diplomats are to be appointed by the president with the Senate's consent; thus the senators could refuse to confirm presidential nominations made against their advice. Members of the House of Representatives could hold up appropriations and other legislation desired by the administration. A sympathetic John Hay contended that the president was not to blame. "The pressure is so cruel that he must use these offices to save his life."[27]

Moreover, the spoils system did not operate solely for congressional benefit. So long as the practice lasted, even reform-minded presidents like Theodore Roosevelt, bound to the system's network of reciprocal political obligations, found the consular service a useful source of political rewards. And like the White House, the top echelons of the executive departments were deeply involved with partisan concerns. Then (as now) they were staffed with persons who had earned their party spurs and who looked for opportunities to use government patronage for the advancement of the party's interests. It was in this spirit that Perry Heath, assistant postmaster-general and secretary of the Republican National Committee, urged favorable consideration for a consul who had worked with him on the committee. Heath asked Assistant Secretary of State David Jayne Hill that if the opportunity should arise, "I would thank you to personally interest yourself in Professor Diederich on account of his personal merit and the political influence his advancement would have upon our interests."[28]

Because of the political nature of the consular service, Elihu Root could accurately describe it as a place "to shelve broken down politicians and to take care of failures in American life whose friends were looking for some way to support them at Government expense." But even when good men were appointed, as they sometimes were, the probability of being thrown out of office after the next presidential election, coupled with the absence of any system for promotion, discouraged them from extending their efforts past the minimum amount of routine labor. As Root put it, they had "no hope for the future, no enthusiasm in their calling, and rather resented the idea that they were expected to do anything." Consequently, few men if any entered the consular service hoping seriously to make it a career. They sought appointment to draw the salary or fees, and, by their own testimony, to do literary work, get a rest at one of the more pleasant posts, or for "mental enlargement."[29]

The dominance of the spoils system also resulted in a large congressional role in the administration of the consular corps and a weak control by the State Department, reflecting the power balance in the federal government during the late nineteenth century. Aware of where the power lay, consuls would appeal to members of Congress (perhaps the same ones who originally had secured their appointments) for higher salaries or more money for the operating expenses of the consulates. State Department officials were anxious to avoid making enemies of the legislators, and they often approved requests such as that made by Senator Robert J. Gamble on behalf of a consul with whom he had been acquainted for many years. "I believe he is rendering most efficient service in behalf of the government, and that the increase is warranted," Gamble wrote Assistant Secretary of State David J. Hill, who might have been in a better position than the senator to gauge the consul's efficiency. Gamble enclosed memoranda furnished by the consul who, like many of his colleagues, evidently believed that his chances were better if he petitioned a member of Congress instead of his superiors in the department.[30]

It was next to impossible for persons interested in changing the service to get the necessary legislation through Congress. Congress traditionally has exhibited little sustained interest in foreign affairs; moreover, congressmen and senators had a stake in retaining the system's political nature as it was. While not preventing attempts at change, such a situation discouraged reformers and helped delay for many years the State Department's active involvement in reform efforts.

THE DIPLOMATIC SERVICE

There were important differences between the diplomatic and consular branches of the foreign service. For centuries, diplomatic positions have required much entertaining and social activity, and until recently only people of independent means could afford the expense. Since the performance of diplomatic duties seldom involved fees, graft and other problems associated with the combination of low salaries and fee collection were absent from the administration of the service. Also there were no "merchant-diplomats" corresponding to the merchant-consuls and no situations in which native employees could defraud the United States Treasury of import revenues.

By 1900 the diplomatic service represented the United States government in forty-two foreign capitals. In addition to the principal envoy (an ambassador or minister), each mission was assigned one or more diplomatic secretaries. These were mostly younger men, some of whom had gotten started in diplomacy as private secretaries to ambassadors or ministers. They transcribed correspondence into permanent record books, issued passports, had custody of the seal, cipher, and archives, and functioned temporarily as *charges d'affaires* in the absence of the principal officer. In the more traveled capitals they helped important visiting Americans in their contacts with local society.[31]

Although relatively well-to-do, many of the ambassadors and ministers were not extremely wealthy. Consequently they were unable to afford the kind of quarters they and a few of their countrymen considered appropriate for a representative of one of the world's leading powers.[32] Several European nations normally purchased embassies, intending them as symbols of the country's representation regardless of who was ambassador. The location and nature of the American embassy or legation, on the other hand, depended largely on the wealth of the particular appointee. Lloyd Griscom, Ambassador Thomas F. Bayard's private secretary and later an ambassador himself, recalled that while "a rich envoy rented a mansion . . . a comparatively poor man like Mr. Bayard had to find something he could afford."[33]

Such a state of affairs, diplomats believed, was injurious to America's dignity. Henry White, while secretary of the embassy in London, commiserated with a colleague having house-hunting woes. "It is an outrage," he wrote the minister to Portugal, "that our Government should not own houses in all the Capitals of the world for its diplomatic representatives." When White was ambassador to Italy a few years later, he was having his own housing troubles. He complained to Secretary of State Root that it was "really ignominious for the representative of a Great Power to be at a local landlord's mercy—especially an Italian landlord."[34]

It is doubtful, however, that such lamentations received a

sympathetic hearing from most Americans. While the consuls were frequently portrayed as rum-soaked tobacco chewers, criticism centered on their unfitness for the positions, not on the usefulness of the positions themselves. A business culture could understand duties such as certifying invoices, dealing with ships' masters and seamen, reporting on trade conditions, and other commercial tasks. But the responsibilities of diplomats were rather amorphous and difficult to understand.[35] Historically removed from the cockpit of Europe, the United States seemingly had not been forced to rely on negotiation—the primary and distinguishing function of diplomacy—for its security and well-being. Washington's entrapment of Cornwallis at Yorktown and Jackson's stunning victory at New Orleans over the conquerors of Napoleon obscured the vital contributions made by the negotiators of the treaties that ended two wars with Great Britain. It could easily appear to Americans that during the nineteenth century a continent had been conquered, rebellion broken and crushed, and an overseas empire acquired, all by force of arms and without any skills at the negotiating table.[36]

As a result, it was difficult for Americans to comprehend the function of diplomacy, which Elihu Root succinctly described as keeping the country "out of trouble." After all, "trouble" was thousands of miles across the Atlantic in Europe. Even Lloyd Griscom's father, owner of a large international steamship line, considered diplomats "among the parasites of society." Woodrow Wilson's assessment was only slightly less critical when, in 1905, he tried to discourage a former student from entering the diplomatic corps. "There is little," wrote the president of Princeton University, "of serious importance to do; the activities are those of society rather than those of business; the unimportant things are always at the front."[37]

Reinforcing this antipathy toward diplomacy and diplomats was the poor quality of many officers. Stories circulated that matched any of those about the comic-opera antics of consuls. One minister rented a legation room to a revolutionary leader in order to make some extra money. Another, the American envoy in Vienna, shocked the court ladies by trying to drum up some business among them for his dentist son.[38]

Like the consuls, the diplomats received presidential appointments and were at the mercy of the spoils system. The result was an organization staffed by what British diplomat Sir Harold Nicolson labeled "a constant succession of temporary amateurs" who were at a disadvantage when dealing with foreign diplomats. Some good men were in the service, such as Dr. Horace N. Allen, who combined the positions of minister and consul-general at Seoul, Korea. But again, as in the consular service, no system existed to help ensure quality appointments. One diplomatic secretary who worked with Allen thought the minister was "another example of the fact that our haphazard methods of appointment were often luckier than they deserved to be."[39]

Perhaps because there were far fewer diplomatic than consular positions, the senators had an even greater voice in these appointments. As usual, the State Department had little to say about who represented the United States abroad. John Hay admitted to David J. Hill that he had "pretty well despaired of ever seeing an important appointment go to a man in whom neither the President nor Senators are vitally interested." In 1897, Assistant Secretary of State William Rockhill sought a ministerial appointment and, although a strong advocate of foreign service reform, resembled other would-be reformers in his willingness to play the game by existing rules. "My God, what a tiresome, nasty business it all is!" Rockhill wrote a friend, as he used more than half a dozen senators to support his application for the position.[40]

Political hiring meant political firing, with a discouraging effect on getting good people into the lower ranks of the service. Like the consuls, the diplomatic secretaries had no reason to hope for a foreign service career. Nevertheless, perhaps because their positions required independent means, the rate of political turnover among the diplomatic secretaries was less than for the consular positions.[41]

THE DEPARTMENT OF STATE

The third branch of the foreign service, the State Department in Washington, was also handicapped by inadequate organization. The spoils system, bête noire of the field foreign service, was not so much a problem at the department. By the early 1890s, the clerical force had been brought successfully under the civil service regulations. The bureau chiefs were sometimes removed with a political change in the White House, but this was no hunting ground for the spoilsmen. There were only seven of these positions, which paid salaries of $2,100 and provided important continuity of experience for the politically appointed incoming secretary and assistant secretaries. During the 1890s when new bureau chiefs were appointed, they usually came from other positions within the department.[42]

The difficulties lay rather with the obsolescent methods in the State Department, the American foreign office responsible for directing the rest of the service. As late as 1906, diplomat Huntington Wilson complained, the department's "antiquated organization remained pitifully inadequate for the conduct of foreign relations, in sorry contrast to the other great powers, our commercial competitors." Wilson himself experienced firsthand the department's inefficiency early in his own diplomatic career. He showed up at his first post only to find that the man he was replacing had not been notified "until my unwelcome face appeared at the Chancery door and I showed him my commission."[43]

Among the department's problems was its haphazard system of record keeping. There was almost no specialization in classifying the correspondence, which was filed by kind and not by subject. The major categories were diplomatic, consular, and miscellaneous. The diplomatic correspondence was arranged in four series: instructions to United States diplomats, dispatches from them, notes to foreign embassies or legations in the United States, and notes from them. The consular correspondence was arranged in four similar series: instructions to United States consular officers, dispatches from them, and notes to and from foreign consuls. The diplomatic correspondence was bound chronologically by country. Consular dispatches were filed chronologically by consulate; the other three consular series were arranged chronologically regardless of consulate. The miscellaneous correspondence was simply arranged chronologically as outgoing or incoming. As the State Department's chief clerk told a congressional committee in 1897, the lack of a subject classification was a considerable hindrance to the department's efficient operation:

We have heavy books now, ledgers; and the consular correspondence outgoing and incoming is indexed in a set of consular books; also the diplomatic correspondence and some miscellaneous correspondence. The system is as perfect as that kind of a system can be, but if the House wants information, say on the Cuban question, and particulars covering all correspondence between the Department of State and Spain, and between the Department of State and the consul-general and consuls in Cuba we would go to the index bureau and ask for the information, and they will begin to go back and take the books and go over those books and would take from this page and that page, and when the work was completed, if that word can be used, there would be no virtual certainty as to the correctness of the brief because you know by experience in the turning of page after page, and hunting up a vast number of indexes there is a liability of error.

Huntington Wilson discovered that the "archaic" methods of handling correspondence in the diplomatic and consular services were no worse than in the department itself. When he later served in Washington, Wilson once had to rummage around John Hay's cellar to find some notes of important oral assurances given by a Russian representative, of which no official record had been made.[44]

Other major problems involved the isolation of the field force from the department and of the individual posts from one another. Root's description of the consulates as isolated entities held true for each unit in the foreign service. The occasional interchange of personnel between the department and the field was sporadic and unsystematic.[45] No procedures existed for bringing consuls or diplomats from the field on a regular basis to share their expertise with departmental officers, perhaps because they were in the service too briefly to acquire much expertise.

This lack of purposeful interchange between the department and the field was detrimental to good administration. One casualty was the morale of the officers at the posts; neither Huntington Wilson in Japan nor Lloyd Griscom in Persia expected the department to read the reports they sent to Washington. In Wilson's opinion such a separation of duties also worked against the efficient departmental direction of the diplomatic and consular services. When he came to the State Department in 1906, he and Chief Clerk Charles Denby were the only officers there who had recently been in either the diplomatic or consular service, "and thus seen the work from the foreign end."[46]

The organization of the Diplomatic and Consular bureaus reflected both this lack of specialization and isolation from the field. Those two important bureaus handled all the incoming and outgoing correspondence of the field service. Huntington Wilson was appalled to find in 1906 that the countries of the world were divided among clerks in the Diplomatic Bureau according to alphabetical order, rather than by geographic specialization. The same clerk handled diplomatic correspondence for China and Cuba, and neither clerks nor bureau chiefs had served abroad. Furthermore, the tasks of the clerks in both bureaus were quite routine, partly because the bureaus lacked geographic specialization and partly because the salaries were too low to attract better personnel. As early as 1881, Secretary of State William Evarts pleaded with Congress for greater flexibility in paying clerical salaries. Money saved on salaries for more menial work could then be used to obtain the services of "persons of intellectual capacity and education" to help prepare correspondence and reports. Evarts was unsuccessful and the clerical salaries remained fixed, as policy questions and the important drafting work continued to fall on the increasingly overloaded secretary and assistant secretaries.[47]

The department's administrative isolation from the posts was a particularly severe problem in the diplomatic stations, since their principal function involved representing United States government policy to foreign governments. The American legation in Korea tried to keep abreast of official policy by reading American newspapers, which arrived six weeks to two months late. In this fashion, Secretary of Legation William Sands observed, the diplomats guided their actions "by what the editors might think European nations seemed to be doing to each other." Not only were the missions sometimes left in the dark about government policy toward their host country, but no system kept them informed about developments elsewhere that related to their own work. If, for example, the State Department received from the legation in Tokyo information that might have a bearing on American policy in the Far East and hence relations with the other major powers having interests in that region, there was no guarantee that the information would be forwarded to American envoys in European capitals. Discussing this problem and others many years later, Huntington Wilson summed up the department's woes: "The efforts of the able men in various bureaus and offices were handicapped . . . by haphazard ways."[48]

Huntington Wilson, Robert Chilton, and their contemporaries were not the first public officials who sought to correct deficiencies in the foreign service. During most of the nineteenth century some secretaries of state and even a few congressmen had urged reform, particularly in the consular branch. Their efforts were partially rewarded in 1856 by legislation that graded portions of the consular and diplomatic services, provided salaries instead of official fees for some of the consular positions, and forbade consuls above a certain salary to engage in trade. But the new law had a minimal effect, since it was not followed by additional legislation, presidential executive orders, or vigorous administration within the department itself.[49]

After the Civil War, supported by periodicals such as the *Nation*, a few reformers continued to agitate for salaries at all consular posts and for a more effective classification. They also began to propose a system of civil service appointments, removals, and promotions, envisioning a consular career for ambitious and competent men. From time to time, recommendations were offered, bills and amendments to bills introduced, decisions of congressional committees reported. Yet Congress usually did not act, and the organization did not improve.[50] Never the object of any systematic or sustained reorganization, the American foreign service at the turn of the century was ill equipped to meet the demands already being made upon it, much less those some observers saw lying ahead. What changed the pattern of unsuccessful reform activity was a combination of factors that came together for the first time in the 1890s.

2 REFORM IN THE 1890s

THE ECONOMIC SETTING

When Walter Raleigh, Humphrey Gilbert, and Richard Hakluyt were prodding English officialdom into establishing settlements in North America, they had a clear conception of the proper commercial relationship between those settlements and the mother country. They anticipated that the new world would supply the metropolis with raw products that could not conveniently be produced in England, taking in exchange finished manufactured goods. From the early years of Virginia, the outline of their vision held true for over two and a half centuries. Raw goods like tobacco, and then fish and wheat, provided the leading exports of those colonies which later became the United States. About 1815, cotton replaced tobacco as the principal export item of an extractive economy.[1]

Despite the large volume of agricultural products and other raw materials sent abroad, during most of the nineteenth century the United States experienced an unfavorable balance of trade. But after 1874 the trade balance became favorable, and from then until the 1970s the value of American exports almost always exceeded that of imports. In 1878 United States exports of domestic goods surpassed those of France and remained ahead; after 1889 they regularly surpassed Germany's. In 1898 and 1901 they exceeded even Great Britain's. Thus in some years the United States was, despite its vast home market, the world's leading exporter of domestic products.[2]

Another major change in the foreign commerce of the United States during the late nineteenth century was the steady growth of manufactured products as a component in the export trade, reflecting a shift in domestic production. After the mid-nineteenth century, manufacturing overtook agriculture as the economy's chief income generator; by 1900 the value of manufactured goods produced annually had more than doubled that of agricultural products. In 1860 the United States manufactured fewer articles than Great Britain, Germany, or France; American manufacturing output in 1900 almost equaled their combined total. By 1913 the United States was turning out more than one-third of the world's industrial products. From less than $8 million in 1820, the value of exported manufactures (excluding manufactured foodstuffs) increased to $48.5 million in 1860, $122 million in 1880, and $179 million in 1890, then soared to $485 million by 1900 and to $1.2 billion by 1913.[3] Thus the 1890s saw a huge surge that highlighted the long-range trend, not only in the amounts of manufactured goods exported, but also in their increased percentage of total exports. In 1892, when exports of manufactures totaled $183 million, they formed 18 percent of the United States export trade; five years later they accounted for $311 million and 30 percent of American exports. That year also was the first in which the United States exported more manufactures than it imported. By 1913 manufactured goods (still excluding manufactured foodstuffs) amounted to 49 percent of all domestic exports.[4]

During the same years that manufactured goods rose from 18 to 30 percent of total exports, the United States was enduring the most socially and economically wrenching depression it had yet experienced. According to one historian, the depression triggered by the panic of 1893 "vividly dramatized the failures of industrialism" and spawned "an atmosphere of restless and profound questioning which few could escape." Millions lost their jobs, and government troops clashed with Pullman strikers the same year Jacob Coxey's "army" and other groups marched on Washington. Secretary of State Walter Q. Gresham confided to John Bassett Moore in 1894 that the outlook was grave; in Moore's words, it seemed to Gresham "to portend revolution." Alexander D. Noyes, who experienced every panic from 1874 to 1933, remarked many years afterward that "talk of 'the country being done for,' of American prosperity being gone forever" occurred much sooner after the panic of 1893 than on "any similar occasion of our time." The census of 1890 had reported the end of the nation's frontier, and suddenly it seemed as if the future was closing in, that the United States was not immune from European social ills. Ever since the seventeenth century, the physical presence of the frontier had served as a symbolic gate of escape for many Americans, and now the gate had slammed shut.[5]

The searing experience of the 1890s helped convince some businessmen and, more important for foreign policy, a number of government officials that exporting manufactured products to foreign markets was a way to secure prosperity and social peace through fuller production and employment. The steadily growing production of manufactured goods appeared certain to outrace the capacity of the domestic market to absorb them. "A world market and the power to protect it have become the essentials of a prosperous people," Assistant Secretary of State David Jayne Hill remarked. Senator William P. Frye of Maine told a convention of manufacturers in 1898 that four years before, the nation had received a "new teacher"—the depression—which had taught Americans to make "a determined advance and march upon the foreign market." Frederic Emory, chief of the State Department's own Bureau of Foreign Commerce, referred to "the growing importance of foreign trade as the balance wheel of our industrial mechanism, even in times of great domestic prosperity." Senator Knute Nelson of Minnesota warned that without "greater markets abroad, industrial stagnation and congestion, superinduced by too rapid production . . . will not only bring an economic convulsion, but will also raise serious social problems, difficult to meet and adjust." Senator Henry Cabot Lodge of Massachusetts reminded Secretary of State William Day that foreign markets were essential to increase the country's wealth and "wage fund," if America did not wish to be "visited by declines in wages and by great industrial disturbances, of which signs have not been lacking." The Senate Committee on Commerce decided that there was "no subject more deserving of serious public consideration, or of more engrossing interest concerning our national welfare, than the extension and development of our export trade." Even Senator Eugene Hale, who disagreed with this view, demonstrated its popularity during an argument with Ohio's Senator Mark Hanna when he disparaged "what is rather a commonly accepted fad at the present day, that we shall go into a decline if we do not capture the trade of the world."[6]

It is perhaps Emory's "balance-wheel" metaphor that is most instructive. To be effective, such a balancing mechanism had to help stabilize the economy by providing enough additional demand to match supply. The adherents of the overproduction (or underconsumption) view of the economy feared a future glut of manufactures in the domestic market because supply was about to outstrip effective demand. If this happened, they warned, prices would drop, and lower wages or unemployment would result. The wider the market area, the greater the likelihood that products could be sold somewhere if demand declined closer to home. The National Association of Manufacturers, founded in January 1895, was one group that perceived an imbalance affecting the economy and saw in foreign markets the means to produce greater uniformity of demand. John Kirby, the organization's president, wrote that it was "wise forethought in manufacturing and merchandising to cultivate as broad a field as is practicable, in order to be prepared for local or transitory changes, which at one time or another will be affecting the particular or local markets of every industry."[7]

But selling American manufactured goods in foreign markets would require considerable effort. Since the earliest days of European settlement, America had sent abroad its raw products. They generally had found ready markets, particularly in the more economically advanced European countries. When it came to manufactured goods, however, the United States faced stiff competition from western European nations. European manufacturers not only had advantages in their home markets, but they were generally more experienced than Americans in producing specifically for foreign consumers. Although Secretary of State John Hay expressed confidence that in the commercial battle with western European powers the United States would "bring the sweat to their brows," it would have to expend some sweat of its own. From Russia, Ambassador E. A. Hitchcock warned that while the development of Russia and China offered the United States markets for its surplus, "from England, Germany, France and Belgium we must expect the hottest competition in all directions—because of their over production." And from the State Department itself Frederic Emory pointed to "a more strenuous competition" from the other industrial powers, which might "check our progress in the world's markets, unless we equip ourselves in the meantime for the ultimate phases of the struggle."[8]

If American manufacturers and exporters were going to compete successfully in world markets, they would require more than good fortune or reliance on solely individual resources. Too much was at stake. Public officials as well as businessmen believed that the national government should lend a hand, as the European governments were aiding their own exporters. Since the views of policy makers and bureaucrats were shaped largely within a context of classical economics, they did not assign to government a significant role in enlarging domestic demand to keep pace with rapidly growing supplies. But when it came to opportunities in foreign fields, there was a growing willingness to break with tradition.[9]

Short of selling their goods for them, what could the federal government do for manufacturers and merchants? It could facilitate the foreign sale of products by subsidizing a merchant marine to carry them; it could encourage the expansion overseas of American branch banks to help finance their sale; it could lower tariffs so that other countries could more easily send their goods in exchange. These and other measures were widely and heatedly discussed in the late nineteenth and early twentieth centuries, but with little result. Despite the general agreement about the desirability of foreign markets, the apparent consensus often broke down in Congress when legislators from different sections and representing different interests confronted the question of how to attain the objective.

The United States Industrial Commission pointed to another, more politically feasible service when it observed that "the opening of foreign markets depends upon accurate commercial intelligence regarding the needs of those markets."[10] The leading industrial nations, including the United States, were seeking ways of getting such information to their exporters, in order to link domestic producers with foreign consumers. "Small as the world is becoming," former diplomat Truxtun Beale wrote in 1897, "buyers and sellers in it are still groping for each other in the dark." Supplying information was a government service that would threaten fewer politically powerful interest groups than proposals to subsidize shipbuilders or certain bankers, or to lower the tariff. In the mid-

1890s a commercial museum was established at Philadelphia to promote foreign trade, and in 1898 it received a $350,000 grant from Congress to hold an international exposition. Manufactured products from other countries were placed on display "in order," the museum's list of objectives stated, "that our manufacturers may be properly informed concerning all markets which they ought to enter or control."[11] Portions of the federal government's executive branch likewise became increasingly involved in dispensing commercial information. During the 1890s and early 1900s the State Department and, after 1903, the new Department of Commerce and Labor steadily enlarged their facilities for this purpose.

Although impending overproduction was the verity most popular among advocates of government assistance to the export trade, some foreign affairs officials saw an additional reason for greater exports of manufactures. They reasoned that with the end of the westward movement and with the shift of population from farms to towns and cities, American factories and industrial labor would increasingly consume domestic surpluses of raw materials and foodstuffs.[12] In this fashion the city would, as historian Fred Shannon later concluded it did, serve as a safety valve for agricultural overproduction and rural discontent. It was a process well under way, government officials thought, as raw products formed a declining share of exports. In their eyes, at the same time that the export trade in manufactures helped maintain industrial employment by siphoning off excess goods, it would also help retain a favorable trade balance, which was imperative for a debtor nation like the United States. Robert P. Skinner, the highly regarded consul-general at Hamburg, remarked that "our prosperity is dependent to a great extent upon bringing into this country of ours, by means of the sale abroad of our manufactured products, that steady stream of payments which formerly came to us by the sale of natural products which we now consume at home."[13]

The relative indifference toward exports of unfinished goods among officials at the Department of State and the Department of Commerce and Labor reflected a pronounced metropolitan outlook. These men did not share the concerns of policy makers in more recent decades who either wanted to preserve the family farm as a social institution or were indebted to agricultural pressure groups, or both, and thus were compelled to deal with continuing farm surpluses. When the agrarians captured control of the Democratic party in 1896, metropolitan Democrats abandoned the party in droves. At least some Democrats in the State Department backed McKinley, despite his identification with high tariffs. One important Democratic official, hitherto a fierce partisan, even wrote anonymous articles on McKinley's behalf.[14]

Some of the metropolitan emphasis also involved application of the "value-added" theory to exports. Officials observed that exports of raw materials, involving less labor or capital, contributed less to the nation's wealth than did semifinished or finished goods. Bureaucrats at the Department of Commerce and Labor (C & L) furnished an example of this neomercantilistic outlook in 1908:

> Manufactured exports must shortly take the place of raw farm products in order to continue the credit balance of trade so necessary to the welfare of the nation. As it is true of the farm that it is more profitable, for example, to sell the corn in the form of fattened live stock, so also is it true that it would prove more profitable in a national sense to convert our annual $50,000,000 exports of corn into preserved meat exports worth several times as much. To carry the point further, it would again multiply the profits of the country to furnish home mechanics with the meat, and through their skill transform its vital force into high-priced manufactured products for export.[15]

Another important element was the general belief of officials at State and C & L that American raw products sold themselves and that finished manufactures did not.[16] As one ranking State Department officer instructed the diplomats and consuls, raw materials like cotton and grain found "ready sale abroad, because they are needed and cannot elsewhere be procured so favorably as from this country." Consequently, Huntington Wilson continued, it was "to the development of a demand for finished manufactures that increasing attention should be given by the foreign service."[17]

As a corollary to the proposition that raw goods needed little help to secure foreign markets was the belief that relatively little

could be done to promote their sale anyway.[18] Prices of the principal agricultural staples depended on current supply and demand.
According to the State Department's Frederic Emory, industrial nations sought food supplies and raw materials because of crop failures, depressions, and other circumstances beyond the control of
the United States.[19]

Moreover, an extensive international information network
already existed for the major raw products, communicating the
ever-changing prices to agricultural businessmen along the chain
from producer to retailer. During the nineteenth century,
produce-exchanges had been formed as an integral part of this mar-
keting mechanism. The great majority of American manufacturers,
on the other hand, were accustomed to producing solely for a
domestic market, often a local one. With a few exceptions they did
not have extensive foreign sales operations and, if interested in developing foreign markets, they might find government-supplied information useful.[20]

Besides the steady growth of exports in general and manufactured exports in particular, the commercial statistics around the
turn of the century documented another important trend. The percentage of American exports bound for Europe began gradually to
decline, while increasing for the non-European world. Finished
manufactures naturally formed a higher percentage of the products
imported by these less developed countries than they did of the
goods imported by the western European nations. During the 1890s
United States exports to Asia grew by some 233 percent (including
221 percent to China and Hong Kong, 456 percent to Japan), and
those to Central America, Mexico, and the Caribbean by 73 percent. Simon Newton Dexter North, member of the United States
Industrial Commission and later director of the Census Bureau, saw
this development as part of a larger movement of the industrialized
West into the rest of the world. Industrialism, he believed, "is producing goods too fast for civilized people to keep up with the output.
It has become necessary to corral the barbarians, and compel them
to become civilized, in order to increase the markets for the manufactured goods of civilization."[21]

By the late 1890s, foreign affairs officials were looking mainly
toward regions outside western Europe as the most promising mar-

kets for the future. Although the increase slowed for Asia after 1905, United States exports there even declining sharply for several years, the optimism remained. Government leaders and bureaucrats continued to believe that their country was on the threshold of a new era of commercial expansion into Latin America and Asia.[22] That those areas were poor and required development through capital investment was increasingly obvious to certain observers; particularly during the "dollar diplomacy" era from 1909 to 1913, officials frequently urged and aided American capital to undertake the work.[23] Meanwhile, however, greater trade did not have to await additional purchasing power and the resulting expansion of market size. Markets for manufactured goods were already there, supplied principally by the western European powers. Officials used export statistics to demonstrate the feasibility of increasing exports at the expense of other industrial powers. The undisputed fact that the United States held a small portion of many markets outside western Europe seemed to indicate their potential for American products. As one consul put it, because he rarely saw goods from America in the local shops, "It must be concluded that there are vast opportunities for our manufacturers and merchants." The first step for the United States was to increase its share of existing markets.[24]

The institution that many considered potentially the most important aid to American exporters was the consular service. Congressman Robert Adams insisted that "an intelligent extension of our commerce can only be effected through reliable information furnished by experienced observers," and he hoped that an improved consular service would supply the information. During his inspection tour, Robert Chilton wrote the State Department that America's intention to "keep pace with other nations in the struggle for foreign markets" demanded "the assistance of a competent, experienced Consular corps."[25]

The consular service was by no means indifferent to the export trade before the 1890s. After the Civil War, promotion of exports had gradually begun to play a larger role in the consuls' work. Consular reports supplied data about foreign tariffs and customs regulations, patent laws, packing and credit requirements, transportation facilities, currency, occasional crop shortages, local buying

habits, and general opportunities for the sale of American products.[26] In 1877 the State Department issued circular instructions to
consuls in Europe and Latin America, requiring them to supply information about the manufactured goods desired in their districts
and the ability of the United States to supply them. Three years
later, partly in response to requests from commercial interests
awakened to export possibilities by the depression of the 1870s, the
department began publishing consuls' commercial reports on a
monthly as well as an annual basis. Indeed, when Secretary of State
Frederick Frelinghuysen urged reorganization of the consular service in 1884, he felt that given the "plethora of production and the
prevalent competition everywhere, which the future will greatly
augment, the primary commercial usefulness of the American consul is . . . his agency in the enlargement of our export trade."[27]

As businessmen and government officials showed greater
interest in foreign markets, some members of the foreign service
were intent on demonstrating its utility as a vehicle of trade extension. An early example of this increasingly frequent and important
activity was Eugene Schuyler's work. Described as "our one trained
diplomatist," Schuyler in the early 1880s held the position of minister resident and consul-general to Greece, Serbia, and Rumania. A
gifted scholar, he had translated several works from the Russian and
was a respected author in his own right. In 1884 Congress failed to
appropriate for his post, retiring him to private life. He was soon
giving lectures at Cornell and Johns Hopkins universities to "explain
the actual workings of one department of our Government, about
which there seems to be much ignorance and misunderstanding,"
and to show how American diplomacy had been "practically useful
in furthering our commerce and navigation." Still stung by his in-
voluntary departure from the foreign service, he castigated Congress for its "annual tinkering" with the diplomatic and consular
services as well as for hampering the State Department's operations
"by niggardly appropriations." Schuyler's book based on his lectures
was given the title *American Diplomacy and the Furtherance of
Commerce*—one more indication of the growing connection between the foreign service and export trade promotion.[28]

But that connection was not paramount before the mid-
1890s. In spite of the expressed views and wishes of Secretary

Frelinghuysen, the primary duty (commercial or otherwise) of the consular corps in the 1880s was not the extension of America's export trade. More important was the certification of invoices to protect import revenues. In this respect the last quarter of the nineteenth century was a transition period. By the end of the century the expansion of exports was the principal function, and it would continue to increase in importance. The reason trade promotion did not hold this position in the 1880s was that the people who comprised the service thought otherwise; after the mid-1890s it did hold this rank, because those individuals began to think that it was more important and acted accordingly. In 1890, for example, the principal American consular officers stationed throughout Europe convened in Paris for a special conference with the chief of the Consular Bureau. Virtually all the discussion was devoted to the various problems relating to certifying invoices, while none of it centered on assisting exports. And in the early 1890s, when consuls discussed the importance of their posts (often in letters to congressmen, pleading for more money), the criteria they used consisted of the number of invoices or of American travelers, or the amount of the fees collected; they rarely stressed their value to the export trade.[29]

By the end of the decade, after several years of economic depression, the emphasis had changed. The highly respected consul-general at Frankfort, Frank H. Mason, did write Assistant Secretary of State William Day in 1897 that at most consulates "the first and most important duty is the examination and authentication of invoices of merchandise." Yet, he added, the productive capacity of the United States had "reached a point at which there is demanded a steady, systematic development of export commerce. . . . In this development, a properly organized, trained and managed consular corps can and should render services of inestimable value." Less than a year later, Consul-General Charles M. Dickinson at Constantinople classified invoice certification together with visaing passports as routine business, in contrast to "earnest and well directed efforts . . . to extend and improve our Commercial relations and push American interests at every point." By 1904, when R. J. Gross, vice-president of the American Locomotive Company, wrote the secretary of Commerce and Labor that the most important function consuls could perform was to act as "torch bearers in the advance guard of the conflicting forces" that were struggling "for the commercial supremacy of the world," businessmen and foreign service officers alike could agree with his meaning, if not his somewhat exaggerated language.[30] It was the growing importance of this consular function—and the perceived need of enhancing it—which brought new allies into the struggle for consular reform in the 1890s.

THE CONSULAR REFORM AGITATION

Boston had long been a home of reformers and agitators, and it was here that businessmen first became involved in consular reform. Late in 1892, after the November elections had ensured that for the third time in eight years political control of the White House would change hands, the Boston Merchants Association took up the issue of consular improvement. This group had for years been interested in foreign trade extension, particularly for manufactured goods. It had recommended reciprocal trade treaties with Canada and with South American nations, the continuance of the government's Commercial Bureau of American Republics, a federal department of commerce and manufactures, and an isthmian canal. On a December evening in 1892, the association's members assembled for their annual banquet. After addresses by an ex-consul and by Congressman Robert Roberts Hitt of Illinois, formerly a secretary of legation and an assistant secretary of state, the membership recommended that the consular corps be freed from the customary political turnover.[31]

In the spring of 1893, the Merchants Association instructed its executive committee to examine the Cleveland administration's handling of the service and determine whether the association's recommendations were being followed. Although the investigation was cut short when the panic of 1893 jolted the country and placed heavy burdens on the committee members, no such inquiry was necessary. These were the months when Josiah Quincy's purge of the consular branch was in full swing. Coinciding as it did with the beginnings of the depression, Quincy's action spurred a movement for consular reform. Reporting to the association's board of directors in November 1893, President Jonathan Abbot Lane could see one positive sign "in the midst of this disaster"—namely, that the people were so disgusted with the wholesale removals that "a most vigorous and hopeful reaction . . . has begun."[32]

The Merchants Association invited the support of additional organizations. First to join it was the Boston Chamber of Commerce, the other leading commercial group in town. In January 1894, responding to the appeal of the Merchants Association, the Chamber of Commerce petitioned Congress for a consular service based on "merit and permanency." A week later Lane went to Washington to lay his case before the annual convention of the National Board of Trade, on whose executive council he served. The board was an unwieldy and generally ineffective body, but it was the only association of trade organizations national in scope, and it provided a larger forum than Lane's own group.[33]

Lane told the assembled delegates that he was there "to solicit your aid and cooperation. We cannot go alone in an enterprise of so much magnitude as this." There was a great public desire, he declared, "to somehow or other take, what we may call this great commercial service, in which we are interested as commercial men, from the spoils system and place it on the basis of merit and permanency." Lane also appealed to the delegates' pride in their country: "We do not care to have our country, which stands foremost among the nations of the earth, an object of reproach any longer . . . and our consular service a matter of disrepute." The delegates rewarded Lane with a resolution commending the two Boston organizations, and they urged the board's constituent bodies to support consular reform regardless of party feeling or affiliation. They apparently considered Lane eminently qualified to head their new committee on consular reform; for the next several years at the board's annual meetings, it was he who reported on the state of the effort.[34]

By April 1894, a sympathetic journal could report that consular reorganization was "becoming a fruitful topic of discussion among business men everywhere." The subject naturally appealed most to the kinds of businessmen associated in chambers of commerce or boards of trade. These groups attracted the smaller and medium-sized firms, which often lacked large export departments and were more dependent than the major corporations upon government information about foreign markets. At its May meeting, the influential Chamber of Commerce of the State of New York, after considering the resolutions of the Boston Chamber of Commerce and the National Board of Trade, joined the movement. Convening in December, Congress was bombarded with petitions, memorials, and resolutions from business groups across the country.[35]

When Lane returned to Washington early in 1895 for the National Board of Trade's annual meeting, he could report substantial progress. Not only had numerous trade bodies responded, but other voices had joined the swelling chorus. Sometime diplomat Oscar Straus explained that the system's evils had "become more glaring than at any previous period of our history, because the party in control of the Government has changed three times, so that our Consuls have been on the march to and fro ever since." The substantial public outcry came from former consuls and diplomats who wrote articles advocating foreign service reorganization, the columns of some newspapers, and, according to Lane, "especially the National Civil Service Reform League."[36]

The group to which Lane drew special attention had been organized in 1881 at Newport, Rhode Island, from a number of local civil service associations; veteran reformer Carl Schurz introduced the resolution creating the new body. The National Civil Service Reform League perceived its chief duty as arousing public opinion in the tradition of the Sons of Liberty and the antislavery societies. But the league's reform was genteel, not one of the seemingly radical strains so much in evidence during the late nineteenth century. As its secretary once remarked to members of the New York Civil Service Association, the very word "reform" was "as distasteful to some of us as it probably is to you." Heartened by the passage of the Pendleton Act in 1883, the league pressed its efforts and in 1892 was strengthened by the consolidation of several local publications into a single journal, *Good Government*. The consular corps was a natural target for the civil service reformers; they believed that eradicating corruption there was even more important than in domestic branches of government, since an official could perpetrate frauds more easily when he was thousands of miles from public scrutiny.[37]

There were differences between the goals of organized businessmen and those of the civil service advocates. The businessmen's principal aim was efficiency in the consular service on a sound business basis. "We are a commercial body," Lane told the National

Board of Trade, "and the interests we are here to promote are largely the commercial interests of our country in their relations with
other lands." Harry Garfield, a Cleveland businessman and a leader
in consular reform, told a Senate committee that there was "absolutely no desire on our part to bring to you a civil-service measure,
because we are interested in civil service. All we want is a result."
He was equally candid with the league when he informed its members that the commercial bodies wanted to secure good businessmen for the consular corps by civil service methods or by any other
methods that would produce results.[38]

   The civil service reformers, on the other hand, had a different aim. One of them said that he and his colleagues were "seeking
efficiency only as a secondary or by-product" and desired chiefly to
deprive the party boss of the patronage "by which he controls cau-
cuses and conventions and holds our representatives responsible to
himself instead of to us." Although it would be a mistake to
dichotomize these two groups, the difference in emphasis is nota-
ble. It is unlikely that the business organizations would have agreed
with league secretary Elliot Goodwin that "the main evil of our
political life" was "commercialism in politics—a free government
fast turning into a business proposition." Like the businessmen, the
civil service proponents recognized the difference in emphasis between the two groups. When *Good Government* distinguished between "the organizations which are commercially interested, and
. . . the intelligent people at large who feel the disgrace of the present system," there was no doubt about where the journal placed its
readers.[39]

   Despite such differences, the two groups knew that removal
of the service from the spoils system would work toward satisfying
both sets of objectives. Each considered the other an ally in the fight
and invited the other's members to address its own constituents.
The speaker who followed Jonathan Lane the first time Lane addressed the National Board of Trade on consular reorganization was
a young civil service commissioner and historian who spoke on the
same subject. In a sense of combative self-righteousness, which future generations could recognize as a trademark, Theodore
Roosevelt told the delegates: "We want to make people understand
that if they shock the decent sense of the community, the decent

sense of the community will do more than whack their heads; that it will make them feel that their actions are actively disapproved of." Roosevelt suggested that the consular service be systematically reorganized into grades and that new appointees be required to enter at the lowest grade, after they had passed an examination stressing knowledge of foreign languages and foreign trade.[40]

Taking advantage of the interest stirred by the reform clamor, two or three young men employed as State Department clerks drafted a bill to reorganize the foreign service. It was principally the work of Francois S. Jones, later secretary of legation at Buenos Aires. Jones had studied the foreign services of other countries, especially that of France, and his bill was the result. To introduce the measure in Congress, he enlisted the services of his acquaintance John Tyler Morgan of Alabama, chairman of the Senate Foreign Relations Committee. The Democratic Morgan was one of the most ardent expansionists in Congress, a strong advocate of an isthmian canal, a powerful navy, and the increased commercial growth such projects would presumably bring. One reason for Morgan's interest in commercial expansion was probably the cotton industry's stake in the export trade. For decades raw cotton had been the principal export product of the United States, and finished cotton goods had also become an important trade item. The southern mills concentrated on producing cheaper textiles for foreign buyers, particularly for the China market. One Alabama mill sold its entire output to China in 1897.[41]

Morgan introduced the bill in April 1894. According to *Good Government*, it was the first "definite attempt" at consular legislation in many years. Indeed the measure provided for the improvement of the entire foreign service—State Department and diplomatic corps as well as the consular branch. To assist him in the reorganization, the president was authorized to appoint a commission consisting of the secretary of state, two senators from different political parties, and two congressmen, also from different parties. The reorganization would cover all department employees below the rank of assistant secretary of state (except the private secretaries to the three assistant secretaries, the mail clerk, messengers, and laborers) and all positions in the field foreign service except the two highest diplomatic ranks. Classification grades were created in each of the three branches and maximum numbers of officers specified for each grade. All notarial fees were to be considered official and therefore turned in to the Treasury.[42]

Only persons between the ages of twenty and fifty-five who had passed an examination would be eligible for appointment to the foreign service. The president would appoint a five-member board of examiners, consisting of the commissioner of education, two professors of public law, and two officials of the State Department. Two-thirds of the officers in the field foreign service would be recalled over three years to take the test, which would also be given to the departmental employees (except for the experienced Second Assistant Secretary Alvey Adee). The exam would cover general and American history, constitutional and international law, political economy, geography, arithmetic, the English language, and foreign language. Candidates passing the test would be eligible for appointment on the basis of the relative standing of their exam scores. Each appointee would serve a six months' probation in the State Department before receiving a permanent appointment, and he would serve six more months in the department before becoming eligible for assignment to the field. Removals or dismissals were to be made only for misconduct or inefficiency, as determined by a departmental board.[43]

Morgan's bill was referred to his own Foreign Relations Committee for consideration. The congressional session was nearing an end, and it was evident that the legislators would take no action until they reconvened in December. Meanwhile, Morgan was getting more advice from within the foreign service.

Henry White, former secretary of the London legation and a future ambassador under Republican administrations, sent the Alabama senator a detailed explanation of his views. For years White had been interested in service reform, and he must have seen this as a splendid opportunity to have his ideas implemented. He advised Morgan to drop the departmental and diplomatic portions for the time being, not because their improvement was unnecessary but because the bill's chances of passing would be better. The consular service, he wrote, "is better known by—and appeals more directly to the sympathies of—our people, than the other two." Quincy's actions of the year before had focused public attention on the consular branch, and reforming that portion of the foreign service would "affect directly the pockets of many thousands, indirectly those of millions, of our fellow citizens who are losers by the present vicious system." Unfortunately, he acknowledged, there was not as much sympathy for his own branch of the service, "about which the general public, I fear, know and care very little," or the department, where political removals were now so rare that reforming it was not an urgent matter. White also recommended modifying portions of the bill relating to examinations. The people presently in the service should be left there, partly to avoid enormous political pressure upon the secretary of state. Such pressure would mean that the people reappointed to the service after taking the examination would be those with the most political clout. The inefficient should be removed gradually, White argued, because it was "the only way whereby . . . a satisfactory and complete reform in the public service of any country has ever been accomplished."[44]

Morgan thanked White effusively, remarking that although he had received valuable information from individuals familiar with the consular and diplomatic branches, he had obtained "no suggestions more important or valuable than those in your letter." Frankly, he confessed to the diplomat, the interest in the bill was much greater than he had expected. He then admitted two more things, both of which would be characteristic of the reform movement over the following decades. First, the senator honestly confessed his own general lack of knowledge on the subject and his willingess to follow the guidance of the foreign service officer. "I am without any fixed opinions as to the best plan for inaugurating and conducting this reformation," he said, adding that he had "little besides zeal and the convictions of duty to sustain me in this new field of endeavor." And second, despite the wide-ranging bill he had introduced, Morgan was experienced enough in the ways of politics and legislation, and sufficiently conservative, to know that the reformers were not going to obtain at once all they desired. "I am concerned most," he told White, "in laying a foundation adapted to our government & people upon which a system can grow up and develop gradually and safely."[45]

Meanwhile, White sent his good friend Theodore Roosevelt a copy of his letter to Morgan. Roosevelt was impressed and promised to show the letter to their mutual friend Senator Henry Cabot Lodge, "who will be greatly interested in it." In December, Roosevelt made alterations in Morgan's bill and gave it to Lodge to introduce. Lodge also conferred with Morgan and on December 19 introduced his bill, which simplified the Jones/Morgan bill but still retained portions covering the diplomatic service.[46]

In February 1895, the Foreign Relations Committee gave the revised Morgan bill a favorable report. The measure had changed considerably since the previous April. The departmental portions had been dropped and the diplomatic provisions toned down. As Morgan told White when he sent him a copy of the committee's report, "if we include all now, we will get nothing." Morgan reiterated that the principal purpose of the bill was that it serve "as a structural foundation for future reforms."[47]

Once again the report came late in the session, and the bill could be offered only as an amendment to the diplomatic and consular appropriations bill. Morgan and Lodge collaborated to this end, but the Senate threw out their amendment on the point of order that substantive legislation could not be enacted through appropriations bills. Lodge reintroduced his own bill at the next session of Congress, and a favorable report again ventured out of the Foreign Relations Committee. But the Senate was insufficiently interested to take further action.[48]

In the midst of these legislative forays, the executive branch took its own action on behalf of consular reform. President Grover Cleveland had long been interested in the subject; as early as 1885 he had remarked in an official message that consular reorganization was "a matter of serious importance to our national interests." Although his resolve apparently had weakened by 1893, when his administration used the service as a source of political largess, it was revitalized after deserving Democrats were ensconced in their positions. Furthermore, after June 1895 he had a new secretary of state, former corporation lawyer and United States attorney-general Richard Olney. "He seems a very intelligent man," Henry White wrote his wife about Olney, "keen, rather rugged, and, unlike his predecessor, of ability and force."[49] In September 1895, after the revised Morgan bill had been thrown out and before Lodge reintroduced his own unsuccessful version, Olney and Cleveland collaborated on an executive order. Unlike legislation, an executive order is not binding on the administrations of succeeding presidents.

For several days the two men exchanged drafts and ideas about what Cleveland referred to as "our Civil Service scheme." On September 17, with the aid of a draft written by Consular Bureau chief Walter Faison, Olney sent a formal letter to the president enclosing a final draft of the order. Olney gave considerable weight to the arguments of the boards of trade and chambers of commerce, and he noted the bipartisan nature of the reform movement, as shown by the introduction into Congress of the Lodge and Morgan bills. He asked Cleveland to issue the order on the authority of an 1871 civil service act that gave the president power to prescribe regulations for admission into the federal civil service. Olney acknowledged that the machinery provided for in the Senate bills might be necessary to reform the service, but he warned that Congress had not yet acted and might never do so. Meanwhile, issuing the order might accomplish some good, and it was "at least a step in the right direction, and a step to be judged of not by the advance it itself makes but by the advance it may rightly be expected to inevitably lead to."[50]

Cleveland issued the order on September 20. Its provisions were simple. Any vacancy in a consulate with an annual compensation between \$1,000 and \$2,500 was to be filled in one of three ways: by transfer or promotion from some other position under the State Department; by appointment of a person having prior satisfactory service in the consular branch; or by appointment of an applicant who successfully passed an examination. The president would designate the person who was to take the examination, and the secretary of state would appoint three persons as a board to administer the test.[51]

Reaction among reformers was mixed. Roosevelt thought the order might do more harm than good, since it left administration of the measure with a State Department vulnerable to political pressures while it simultaneously persuaded people "that something had actually been done, and that therefore there was no further cause for agitation." More typical, probably, was the cautiously optimistic assessment of Third Assistant Secretary of State William Rockhill, who saw it as a step in the right direction and thought Roosevelt "narrow minded in refusing to recognize good in a half measure." Rockhill told Henry White that Cleveland believed executive orders were the only way to extend the examination system's coverage; he added that the president probably had his doubts about the constitutionality of all civil service legislation, because it limited the power of presidential appointment.[52]

Given its limitations, the order worked fairly well for the rest of Cleveland's term. During 1896, of the thirty-five appointments to the consular service, eight went to candidates who had successfully passed an examination; the examining board rejected five other candidates for failing to pass. The tests were not the competitive examinations of today's civil service. The president would select a man for a post, and if he was not already in the department or a former consul, and if the salary was between $1,000 and $2,500, he was sent to the department to take the examination and be graded on a pass/ fail basis.[53]

A third, less important accomplishment during Cleveland's second administration was the securing of an appropriation for consular inspection. Inspection of consulates was not completely new; in 1876 the chief of the consular branch had been sent to Europe to inspect the posts there, and from time to time consuls-general had made inspections in their districts. But the service needed both a regular system of inspection (rather than an occasional investigation) and inspection as part of other reforms. Congressman Robert R. Hitt wrote his friend Jonathan Lane about the problem. According to Hitt, consuls frequently entertained their inspectors in style, with the result that the inspector's "harmless reports simply made the innocent wonder how all the cardinal virtues had been secured at these posts for such low pay." But if a system of appointment, tenure, and promotion on the basis of merit were established, Hitt continued, *"the whole tested regularly and disciplined, I may say, by a thorough system of inspection*, it would immensely increase the value of the Service to our commercial interests, to the welfare of individual Americans in every part of the globe, and to the standing and power of the nation." Secretaries Frelinghuysen and Bayard had asked Congress for a corps of inspectors in the 1880s, and the 1890 convention of the principal consuls in Europe interrupted its discussions of invoices long enough to urge the same thing.[54]

In May 1894, a month after Morgan introduced the Jones bill in the Senate, he received a letter from Edwin F. Uhl, assistant secretary of state. Uhl asked the Foreign Relations chairman to add, as an amendment to the annual diplomatic and consular appropriations bill, a provision for a thorough inspection of the consulates. The purpose of the investigation was not only the usual detection of abuses in the service and the institution of more uniform methods, but also a "preparation for improved reorganization of the system." This proposition found the going no easier than would the Lodge and Morgan bills, and it was not even reported from Morgan's committee. But two years later, with some help from Lane, Hitt, and Olney, the amendment was reported favorably and passed. As a result, Chilton was sent on his inspection tour around the world, and areas he did not reach were covered by three other inspectors.[55]

Some observers felt that Chilton's inspection tour achieved moderately satisfactory results. Secretaries Olney and, years later, John Hay referred to the introduction of businesslike methods and the correction of irregularities as results of investigations by Chilton and others. No doubt the department received some valuable information about the consulates. But Chilton was still out inspecting when party control of the White House changed hands for the fourth time in a dozen years; once again, in Oscar Straus's words, the consuls were "on the march to and fro."[56] Most of the consuls whose mistakes Chilton had tried to correct did not remain on the job much longer. The consular service had a new crew.

In subsequent years, a few inspections were conducted by some of the consuls-general, who may well have been new to their own positions. George Murphy, later to become one of the leading officers in the reorganized service, was disgusted with the way inspections were handled. After examining an inspection report covering consulates in Norway and Sweden, he wrote Wilbur J. Carr in the Consular Bureau: "Another inspection of no value whatever. Everything perfect & all the Consuls have 'enviable reputations.' Not a single recommendation for the improvement of the service. Nothing but an appeal for increas-[ed] salaries for everybody." Even when the inspecting consul-general knew and cared what he was doing, the method itself had certain drawbacks. Frank Mason reported to the department that many consuls believed the consuls-general were prying and looking for grounds to criticize the work of the consuls placed loosely under their jurisdiction; the result was mutual distrust and friction.[57] The answer seemed to be, as Congressman Hitt had told Lane years earlier, a special corps of consular inspectors, coupled with a general reform of the service. But most of Hitt's colleagues in both houses of Congress had not served in legations at foreign capitals or as assistant secretaries of state, and they were considerably less interested than he in foreign service reform.

Lack of congressional enthusiasm for consular reform was also displayed by the treatment the reform bills received. After Lodge's second attempt failed in 1896, the focus shifted to the House. During that same session, a bill written principally by J. R. Leeson, Lane's successor as president of the Boston Merchants Association, was introduced by Congressman Samuel McCall of Massachusetts. It was referred to in the Foreign Affairs committee, there to be swallowed up in an omnibus measure proposed by committee member Robert Adams of Pennsylvania.[58]

Congressman Adams would be among the leading proponents of consular reform over the next few years. He had become vividly aware of the need for it in 1890 when, as minister to Brazil, he had inspected the United States consulates on the eastern coast of South America. Like Lodge and Morgan, the former diplomat helplessly saw his bills languish through congressional apathy or hostility, and because of the Speaker's unwillingness to bring them to the floor for debate and consideration. As a result, notwithstanding the petitions and resolutions of businessmen and civil service reformers, the vast expenditure of print and paper devoted to the topic, and the wishes of a few reform-minded officials in the executive and legislative branches of the federal government during the 1890s, legislation to improve the service was not forthcoming until well into the next decade.

Part of the cause may have been the discouragement resulting from President William McKinley's restaffing of the consular corps in 1897. In the process, McKinley largely ignored Cleveland's executive order, although he did not formally disavow it. His policy ran counter to the pleas of businessmen and others asking him to preserve and improve upon the initial step toward a merit system. Theodore Search, president of the young and vigorous National Association of Manufacturers, wrote McKinley that "the impairment of the efficiency of our Consular Service by the substitution of untrained men for tried and experienced efficiency, would mean enormous financial loss to those of our manufacturers who are interested in foreign trade." But the new president, like his predecessors and successors, had political obligations to repay. Even Cleveland had not issued his executive order until some two years after Republicans had been removed from the service and Democrats put into their places. Though the examination machinery created by Cleveland's order remained in effect, it was not especially rigorous in weeding out unfit applicants. Of the 112 candidates examined for appointment during the first year of the McKinley administration, only one failed. The secretary of the National Civil Service Reform League was hardly exaggerating when he remarked that "as a measure of reform, the plan in question cannot be taken seriously."[59]

A year after McKinley came into office, the consular reform movement of the 1890s, born in the aftermath of one of the recurring White House turnovers and vitalized by reaction to Quincy's "debauch" and to the depression, was dying. Passing resolutions and petitioning Congress was not getting results, and even this sort of activity lasted only a year or two, most of it taking place in the few months during the winter and spring of 1895. With an occasional exception, the interest of organized businessmen in consular reform was waning. Yet their support was essential to its success. Senator Lodge wrote Jonathan Lane, "If we are ever to get the bill into law we must have the ardent and active and continuous support of the business associations of the country."[60] Perhaps the return of domestic prosperity helped many businessmen forget the urgent necessity of foreign markets, with which they had seemed so concerned during the depression years.[61] Consequently, it was not this movement that led directly to the eventual reform of the consular service. A new kind of effort was needed, and it was soon forthcoming.

3 THE BUREAUCRAT AND THE BUSINESSMAN

The young clerk in the State Department had received a promotion and was anxious to share the news with his friend. "Hail to thee bright boy!" Gaillard Hunt wrote James Garfield in 1887. "I have been put into another Bureau where I rank next to the Chief and do work that any child of seven could perform if he only knew how to hold his tongue & not give away State Secrets." Hunt had entered the State Department only a few months earlier, at the age of twenty-four, and was currently employed in the Bureau of Indexes and Archives. He had previously worked as a tallyist in the Census Office and then as a clerk at the Pension Office. He combined an interest in history with a taste for writing, and in later years his publications would include biographies of John C. Calhoun and James Madison, two histories of the State Department, a book about the American passport, and numerous newspaper and magazine articles. His father had served as secretary of the navy in President James A. Garfield's cabinet, and Gaillard was a close friend of the two oldest Garfield boys, Harry and James.[1]

Hunt was anxious to find a sphere of activity that he could consider socially useful and that would simultaneously make use of his talents. He spent his adult life in the public service, writing Secretary of State Robert Lansing in 1916 that he considered "no occupation so high as that of being useful to the Government." Hunt strove repeatedly to bring his historical and literary interests into closer harmony with his day-to-day work, and on separate occasions he sought appointment as chief of the department's Bureau of Rolls and Library and as librarian at the Washington City Library. Although he received an offer in 1897 to become chief of the Manuscripts Division at the Library of Congress, he turned down that "congenial" position, he wrote, because "woe is me, the salary is only $1500"—$300 less than his State Department salary.[2]

Hunt's aspirations, whether for a promotion within the department or for satisfying work elsewhere, were often frustrated. He had entered the State Department as a civil service employee; yet it seemed that everywhere he looked he saw the spoils system operating in the federal government, bringing into office persons who lacked proper qualifications. In 1897 his ambitions to become head of the Diplomatic Bureau (a post he intended to use as a springboard to the Bureau of Rolls and Library) were thwarted when the position was awarded to the third assistant secretary's son-in-law, whom Hunt described as "unread, uncultured and altogether undesirable." A few days later he angrily reported another outrage to James Garfield: "O, it is heartrending, to see that our hopes of better government are mere will o' the wisps. Our Solicitor is to go. . . . His scalp has been taken by the spoilsmen. It almost makes me laugh to think that you and I built up any hopes that claims like mine should ever receive even a wink of recognition at this time." Disheartened by a public sentiment that tolerated the spoils system at the expense of people like himself, who wished to make public service a career, he once told James that the situation could be corrected only by a leader of the masses and concluded on a note that promised future activity: "You must believe it & act accordingly when the time comes for you—& all of us young fellows—to do something."[3]

But Hunt did not wait for any leader to emerge. Working in the State Department, and occasionally in the Consular Bureau itself, he had a bird's-eye view of how the spoils system dominated the consular service. During the 1890s he became a key figure in the movement for consular reorganization.

By undertaking reform, Hunt was in step with many men and women of his generation who, as one historian observes, "were brought to rebellion by pain experienced directly, by some setback to their own interest." Although there seems to be no evidence that Hunt wished to be a consul, he did desire a system that allowed competent and ambitious men like himself to find a niche in service to the national government, and he expected that a merit system would clear out political hacks who were clogging the paths of opportunity. When Francois Jones drew up his foreign service bill in the spring of 1894, Hunt gave him a little help. That was only the beginning. Late in 1896 he obtained renewed support from the Cleveland Chamber of Commerce.[4]

The Cleveland chamber had already contributed to the businessmen's agitation for consular reorganization. In February 1895, the same month in which Senator Morgan reported the revised Jones bill from committee, the chamber adopted resolutions strongly endorsing a reform measure on the grounds of furthering commercial expansion. Almost two years later, the chamber again passed resolutions, introduced at Hunt's request by his friend E. A. Angell, that specifically advocated congressional adoption of either the Lodge or the Morgan bill.[5]

Hunt's other contact in the Cleveland chamber was his close friend Harry Garfield, the oldest son of the assassinated president. Securing the organization's endorsement, Hunt explained to Garfield late in 1896, was part of his wider plan to enroll a large number of businessmen in the movement; he hoped it would have a snowballing effect and culminate in congressional action.[6] Although this particular scheme failed, Hunt's efforts helped bring into the movement a man who would be an enormous asset in the years ahead.

Harry Garfield was a lawyer prominent in Cleveland's industrial and financial affairs. He was an organizer, trustee, and vice-president of the Cleveland Trust Company, helped construct a railway system, and aided in reorganizing and financing the Conneaut Water Company. Garfield was also a strong advocate of municipal efficiency and helped organize and guide the policies of the Cleveland Municipal Association. Both he and his brother James were intensely involved with public service as a duty that able men owed their society. Harry was thus in hearty accord with Hunt's proposal to E. A. Angell in 1896 and helped draft the resolutions, but his own sustained interest in consular reform did not ignite for more than a year.[7]

In April 1898, the United States declared war on Spain and soon held a territorial empire in Asia and the Caribbean. In that same April, at the age of thirty-four Harry Garfield became president of the Cleveland Chamber of Commerce. He and Hunt shared the doubts of many Americans about the new direction their country seemed to be taking. Hunt bitterly opposed the acquisition of the Philippines, "those vile islands" as he called them. Harry also questioned the wisdom of acquiring the islands, but was more easily reconciled to their ultimate fate than was his friend in Washington. In July he met with other businessmen in New York to discuss the government's future policy regarding territorial expansion. "I am conservative," he wrote his brother, "but not unmindful of great changes and necessary modifications. What are the modifications, is the question?"[8]

The events of the spring and summer of 1898, particularly Commodore George Dewey's devastating victory at Manila Bay and the consequent speculation about the future of the Philippines, awakened a latent interest among American businessmen in using Manila as a springboard into the fabled China market. Such was the context of president Harry Garfield's address to his organization on May 17, in which he linked the work of the Cleveland Chamber of Commerce for the coming year with what the *Cleveland Plain Dealer* termed "the broad question of extension of the world trade of the United States." Hunt wrote Harry that he was "very much interested" in the speech and agreed that "the cue before us is extension of international trade. I suppose that means a peaceful gradual passing away of excessive tariff rates. It does not mean an extension of our territory in far distant quarters."[9]

During the spring and summer of 1898, therefore, Harry Garfield's horizons expanded to encompass greater geographic space as the result of wrestling with the issues growing out of the war with Spain. Already involved with reorganization and efficiency in private business and municipal government, he pictured the United States as an expanding moral and commercial force in the world. Garfield was also proud of his racial and paternal heritage, optimistic about man's ability to structure and control his environment, and driven by an appetite for useful activity. He displayed these elements in his account of sighting the English shore on a trip in 1899. "The land whereon mighty forces have contended for & won the supremacy of the world," he wrote his mother, "& we are of the same blood. Why shouldn't one be proud! Yes, proud & inflamed at once; that, pressing forward, we latest descendants of a noble race may prove the undying strength of that blood. Conquer,

conquer, conquer! Everywhere prove how terribly certain and triumphant man can be, if only he persist enough, & persist honestly."[10] Later that summer he and Hunt took up consular reform in earnest.

In August, Garfield wrote the State Department for a list of the commercial organizations that had sent resolutions to Washington favoring consular reform. The following month he brought up the subject with his chamber's board of directors, who, he told Hunt, were enthusiastic. As the board's report explained, the directors were interested in the subject because of Cleveland's "prominent position among the cities of this country in which goods for export are manufactured." And they believed that the time was ripe for action because of "the awakening of our people to international relations heretofore unthought of."[11]

After involving his own association, Garfield turned to Hunt for advice, as he frequently would during the next few years. The State Department clerk outlined for his friend the steps he ought to take: secure the cooperation of other chambers of commerce; visit the president in Washington and ask him to incorporate a statement in his annual message; once Congress has convened and a bill has been introduced, request a hearing before the committee handling the bill. The measure's principal provisions, Hunt suggested, should be appointment, promotion, and retention on merit. The service should be reorganized by classes, not individual places—"a vital point," which would make consuls as interchangeable as officers in the army or navy. (Sharing the prevailing view about diplomats' unimportance, Hunt was indifferent to obtaining good men for the subordinate diplomatic positions.) He stressed particularly the need for cooperation among chambers of commerce instead of the "disjointed actions" of the past. In November 1898, with a congressional session imminent, he advised Garfield that when he came to Washington, he must "be armed to speak not for yourself but for your organization and must magnify to the utmost the influences behind you." The next month he swallowed hard and demonstrated how much he wanted the movement to succeed. "There is no doubt that the Expansion idea is favorable to the reform," he observed. "It can be used as a means to push it. . . . Let us extract some good from so evil a thing."[12]

A newspaper article brought Garfield into contact with his other principal ally. Early in December 1898, he heard from Gustav Schwab, head of the American office of the North German Lloyd Steamship Company, chairman of the Committee on Foreign Commerce and the Revenue Laws of the New York State Chamber of Commerce, first vice president of the New York Merchants Association, and a member of the American Reciprocal Tariff League, the American Asiatic Association, and similar groups. Schwab's chamber of commerce committee had recently concluded an extensive study of commercial education, including the training given in European commercial schools to candidates for consular and diplomatic appointments. He had noticed in the *New York Evening Post* that the Cleveland chamber was advocating consular legislation, and he eagerly offered his assistance. Garfield welcomed Schwab's interest. The two men agreed that their own organizations should act as an executive committee to secure support from other commercial bodies. They planned to go to Washington and obtain a hearing on the reform bill, which had been introduced by Congressman Robert Adams of Philadelphia.[13]

Meanwhile, serious reservations were being expressed about the Adams bill. The provision for a congressional commission to help the president reorganize the service was particularly obnoxious to the critics, who thought there was already too much congressional interference in what should be an executive function. Consequently, Hunt began to draft a more satisfactory bill, which could be either incorporated into the Adams bill or submitted as a new measure. By late January 1899, it was evident to Garfield that the Speaker of the House was not going to allow Adams's bill to come up for consideration that session; the reformers would have to wait at least until the next session for favorable action. The intervening time could be spent mobilizing the interest of other commercial groups and arranging with Adams to introduce Gaillard Hunt's bill.[14]

After serving the Cleveland Chamber of Commerce as president for a year, Harry Garfield turned over the office to a successor. But his involvement in consular reform remained unabated. The chamber placed him in charge of its committee on the consular service and, with Gaillard Hunt's guidance and Gustav Schwab's assistance, he continued the fight. During the summer of 1899 Hunt drew up his bill and in November asked Garfield to see that it was first adopted by his chamber and then introduced in Congress—without divulging the identity of the author. Since Adams was attached to his own measure and was cool toward the new bill, part of Garfield's job would be to find congressional sponsors for Hunt's creation. Sending his friend a pep talk along with the bill, the State Department clerk wrote Garfield: "You can't escape this thing, Hal. It is of greater consequence than city affairs, altho' I would not belittle *them.* . . . From now on there should be no let up. It is just time to begin."[15]

Garfield began by traveling to Washington to meet with Hunt, Chilton, Assistant Secretary of State David J. Hill, and former Secretary of State John W. Foster, to obtain their comments on the new bill. Since the department officers regarded the Adams bill as unsatisfactory, they were glad to see a substitute, but they warned Garfield that the bill's prospects would be endangered if it were known that the State Department had approved it even before it was introduced.[16]

During December and early January the reformers deliberated over who should be asked to sponsor the bill in the House and the Senate. Congressman Theodore E. Burton and Senator Mark Hanna were members of the Cleveland Chamber of Commerce and had offered to help. If the Cleveland people had been acting alone, they might have accepted both offers, but since other organizations were also involved, Garfield preferred that one of the sponsors come from New York, Pennsylvania, or Massachusetts. Gustav Schwab favored Lodge of Massachusetts in the Senate, and Garfield agreed.[17] On January 23, 1900, Lodge and Burton introduced Hunt's bill into Congress.

Like the Jones and Adams bills, Hunt's measure established classes or grades for the service and prescribed maximum numbers for each. Incumbents were to be placed in the prescribed classes according to their current salaries or fees and would be recalled gradually over a two-year period for an examination, which would be administered by a board consisting of the secretary of state or his designee, a consul or consul-general selected by the president, and the civil service commissioners. Promotions to the higher grades were to be made from the lower. Public examinations would be given at stated times and places, and when vacancies that the president desired to fill occurred in the lowest rank, the board would certify to the secretary of state the names of the five applicants with the highest examination scores.[18] Only persons between the ages of twenty-one and forty-five could be appointed. The examination would test the candidate's fluency in French, German, or Spanish, as well as his acquaintance with the commercial resources of the United States, "especially with reference to the possibilities of increasing and extending the trade of the United States with foreign countries."[19] All fees, official and unofficial, would be turned in to the Treasury. A consul's first year would be a probationary period, during which he could be recalled at any time; thereafter he could not be dismissed from the service without due cause. An important departure from previous bills was the absence of any provision for a congressional commission to assist the president in reorganizing the service. No doubt the reformers reasoned that in the absence of a commission the president would rely on the State Department for advice.[20]

As provided in the Jones bill, consuls could be moved from one post to another within the same classification without the necessity of a new appointment. Hunt also continued Jones's emphasis on interchangeability between the department and the field. Anyone employed continuously for at least the preceding two years in the classified civil service of the State Department would be eligible for appointment to a consulship without having to take the examination. It worked the other way as well; any consul or consul-general who had served abroad two years continuously in a consular capacity could be assigned to duty, not exceeding one year at a time, in any bureau of the State Department, or on special duty in or for the department, or in any other department by arrangement with its chief. Such flexibility would make experience gained in the field available for the home office and vice versa. Also, under the phrase "on special duty in or for the Department," the State Department could bring consuls back to the United States to talk with manufacturers about how to increase their sales in foreign markets.[21]

Having found sponsors for their bill, Hunt, Garfield, and Schwab knew the work was only beginning. The whole course of the consular reform effort in the 1890s had made it clear, as Garfield expressed it, that "Congress seldom, if ever, initiates movements of this kind. It must first 'hear from the country.' "[22] During the winter of 1900 they worked to make the country speak and Congress listen.

In February Schwab and Garfield sent letters to the leading chambers of commerce and trade organizations, urging them to appoint delegates to appear before the Senate Foreign Relations Committee when it held hearings on the bill introduced by Senator Lodge. They also worked closely with Lodge to arrange a convenient time for the hearings. While attempting to mobilize business organizations to bring pressure on Congress, they also wrote letters to the important newspapers, providing a brief history of consular reform and enclosing a copy of Hunt's bill. Hunt himself wrote a short piece for the *Nation*, calling for consular reorganization on the grounds that the current system was injurious to foreign trade, placed in jeopardy the rights of individual Americans, lessened American prestige, and generally humiliated the United States. Garfield arranged with Hamilton Holt, editor of the *Independent*, to publish his "dry, argumentative" article on the consular service, which he intended for a particular purpose—to appear simultaneously with the businessmen's hearing before the Senate Foreign Relations Committee.[23]

Garfield and his colleagues concentrated on the Senate early in 1900, because if any bill was going to be reported from the House Foreign Affairs Committee it would probably be Adams's bill. Adams was a member of that committee and chairman of the subcommittee to which consular bills were referred for initial action. The reformers knew that he was bitter about Burton's bill and that they could not expect his endorsement of their measure. Even Burton urged Garfield to concentrate on the Senate; if Adams's bill did pass the House, Burton thought the details could be worked out in a conference committee.[24]

In mid-March, Garfield, Schwab, and other businessmen made their case before the Senate Foreign Relations Committee. "We are business men, or the associates and representatives of business men," Garfield told the committee in his opening remarks, "and it is through those associations that we have been led to take an interest in this subject. . . . Extension of trade is an undoubted fact. We must push forward, and by every worthy means at our command seize the markets of the world." Schwab agreed, adding: "I take it that we wish to extend our markets, and that is the chief reason we are anxious to have such a bill passed." Although certain that the proposed changes would weed many incompetents out of the service, Garfield insisted that the problem was not so much the consular personnel but rather the system itself (a politic as well as generally accurate line of argument, considering that many of the senators present were doubtless responsible for the appointment of incumbent consuls). By the time the consular service did achieve some degree of efficiency, four years had passed, a new administration came into office, and the experienced men were replaced. "As a business proposition," Garfield contended, "that did not appeal to anybody."[25]

Consular reform understandably appealed most to the small and medium-sized businessmen who belonged to chambers of commerce and boards of trade, and Garfield's remarks to the committee reflected this appeal. "The first question," he told the senators, "asked by your manufacturer or exporter who has not been in the field long enough to have agents of his own, is, What can I learn about my particular branch in this, that, or the other country? And his first point of inquiry is the United States consul." Senator Lodge also emphasized that the large corporations had their agents abroad to gather and transmit commercial information, while the smaller firms, "unable to go to this expense, are put at a disadvantage because the consular service fails to give them what they have a right to expect." But some larger manufacturers were also interested in consular improvement. A businessman from Auburn, New York, told the committee that the largest manufacturer in town had his own agents abroad and also received reports from an agency in Philadelphia. Twenty percent of his business was export business, and he was hoping to increase that figure. Thinking that the better the reports made by consuls, the better the reports he would receive, the manufacturer was "most emphatically in favor of this bill."[26]

These were not entirely new arguments to the committee. Yet some of the senators remained skeptical of a system that would select men on the basis of an examination and remove them only for cause. No doubt they were reluctant to part with political power and patronage, but some of them were also genuinely uneasy about the quality of the system they were being asked to approve. Senator Edward O. Wolcott of Colorado expressed doubts that the bill should require the president to select from among the five men who had scored highest on a written examination. He thought that no examination could test a man's personality, which was more important than certain mental qualifications. Wolcott suggested that the president, assisted by the senators, designate who was to take the examination. Wolcott then went on to describe a system of selection based on personal acquaintance rather than the more rigid test scores and other standards of the emerging bureaucratic society: "A man comes from Massachusetts as an applicant, and I should say that Senator Lodge, knowing this man and his friends, would be the fittest person to designate who should take the examination. If you open the doors to the whole world to be consuls, as you do here, you eliminate from the appointment of consul that element of personal fitness. That is the only thing to my mind." Senator Joseph B. Foraker of Ohio, like Wolcott a Republican, also displayed some qualms about the proposed system. He hinted that in its haste to imitate other consular systems the American service might become a "life business" in which once-ambitious consuls might no longer feel compelled to work.[27] Although in 1900 there was no system for promotion anyway, so that American consuls were rarely rewarded for exerting themselves, the misgivings expressed by Foraker and Wolcott would be understandable to Americans of a later generation, frequently frustrated in their confrontations with impersonal and unresponsive bureaucracies.

But the reformers too were aware of the dangers posed by a tenure so secure that it would lead to what Garfield termed a "dry rot" bureaucracy. Provisions in Hunt's bill for a one-year probation period (still a feature of today's federal civil service) and promotion for meritorious work were designed to combat the problem. As Garfield argued, the new procedure would not anchor a man to a particular post without promotion. Easier mobility from one post to another in the same grade, as well as duty at the department, would help prevent a consul from stagnating in one place.[28]

The hearing before the Foreign Relations Committee produced few tangible results. Both the Foreign Relations Committee in the Senate and the Foreign Affairs Committee in the House reported out bills favorably (the Adams bill in the House and a committee substitute for Lodge's bill in the Senate), but in neither case did the measure come up for further consideration.

Conspicuously absent from the hearing in March were representatives of the civil service organizations. Their absence was part of Hunt's and Garfield's strategy of keeping them far in the background, so that nothing could obscure the public and congressional view of the commercial groups clamoring for consular improvement. In January 1899, Garfield wrote George McAneny, secretary of the National Civil Service Reform League, suggesting that the league supply only "inspiration" for the movement. "I am satisfied," Garfield assured him, that the league's previous efforts had made the movement possible, "but fortunately, in the present instance, the business interests of the country have taken the lead." Hunt was less gentle with the "so-called professional reformers"; he publicly noted their lack of influence with either party and privately termed the league "a nuisance." Garfield discouraged even McAneny's suggestion that the local civil service associations pass resolutions favoring the Lodge and Burton bills, telling him that he had found in Washington "the greatest jealousy of anything smacking of civil service reform." Hunt and Garfield had no desire to make their already difficult task impossible by openly associating with elements that were unsavory to the congressmen. It was not until 1902, when former Civil Service Commissioner Roosevelt was in the White House and Congress had seen the considerable support of businessmen for reform in the service, that Garfield welcomed the open support of the "professional reformers"—so long as they remained in a subordinate capacity.[29]

Shortly after the March hearing, former Secretary of State John Foster warned Garfield not to be optimistic about immediate success. "I do not have much faith in the present Congress on this subject," he wrote the Cleveland business leader. "Its members are absorbed in other matters, and few of them realize that the commercial interests of the country are demanding the legislation. Until by some vigorous demonstration they are awakened to a realizing sense of this fact, nothing I fear will be done." Garfield shared that opinion; during the following months he and Schwab worked to improve their organization and to secure the active involvement of the commercial associations, which were supposed to be already "demanding the legislation."[30]

For some months, the reformers had contemplated establishing a small executive committee of businessmen from the leading chambers of commerce. Garfield initially had expected the group to carry weight with Congress while mobilizing additional business organizations across the country to descend upon Washington at a signal from the executive committee. One enthusiastic convert was the young National Business League of America. Based in Chicago, this organization considered itself an important shaper of public opinion. William E. Cushing, a member of the Cleveland chamber's committee on consular reform, met John W. Ela, the league's counsel, at a meeting of civil service reformers and suggested to Garfield late in 1899 that Ela's organization be added to the contemplated committee. Garfield agreed and optimistically passed on to Schwab the opinion of Cushing that the league "would be a very valuable assistant to us."[31]

By late autumn of 1900, the plan had evolved toward establishing a representative in the nation's capital. Garfield wanted a person who would write businessmen explaining the bills before Congress, visit commercial groups to secure their active support, help them arrange interviews with congressmen, and generally coordinate matters in Washington. He envisioned the proposed central committee chiefly as a means to finance that project, and as another link connecting businessmen with Congress and with each other. Here too the going was slow, for congressional recalcitrance was not the only obstacle to consular reform. Apart from the National Business League's support, the Cleveland and New York chambers had received little tangible help from other businessmen. At the end of 1900, Garfield had not received a single favorable response from additional commercial groups to his requests for assistance in maintaining a Washington representative.[32]

During 1901, Garfield's central committee gradually took shape. In June, the reformers held a preliminary meeting in Buffalo, where the representatives of the Cleveland, New York, and Chicago organizations welcomed delegates from the Buffalo Merchants Exchange. Garfield urged the establishment of a bureau in Washington, but most of the men wanted to wait. There was unanimous agreement, however, that they should enlist other organizations and push for the formation of a central committee before the next session of Congress.[33]

Garfield's attempts to recruit other principal trade associations continued to meet with an unexpected apathy. In November, less than a month before Congress was to reconvene, he reported that the organization was not yet complete because "the replies have been aggravatingly slow in coming in." Schwab sympathized and told his Cleveland colleague that he was not surprised. He himself had recently written more than one hundred commercial groups to obtain their support for ratification of the French reciprocity treaty; he had received twenty favorable answers and another twenty indecisive ones. "The balance of sixty odd organizations," he complained, "have not even favored me with a reply to my communications repeatedly addressed to them."[34]

Finally, in December, delegates from eleven commercial organizations gathered in Washington to found the National Committee on Consular Reorganization. In addition to the four groups attending the June meeting, another seven associations had signed on: the Washington Board of Trade, the Philadelphia Commercial Museum, and the Pittsburgh, Baltimore, Cincinnati, San Francisco, and Boston chambers of commerce. The delegates acknowledged most of the principal architects of the new organization when they elected Garfield as the committee's president, Schwab first vice-president, and F. A. Scott (secretary of the Cleveland Chamber of Commerce) secretary-treasurer.[35]

Garfield then wasted no time in establishing a representative in Washington. Relying as usual on his friend in the State Department, he secured the services of Corcoran Thom, a young Washington lawyer and friend of Hunt, as the National Committee's agent. Hunt had promised that Thom would "travel anywhere and drum up . . . influence splendidly." Garfield sent Thom to visit commercial groups and educate businessmen about exerting pressure. He was sure that Thom's efforts would finally give some direction to business groups that wanted to help, "but do not know how

to go to work except through the primitive fashion of resolutions."
The improved organization and the growing interest in the movement among commercial bodies was heartening to Garfield, and he
felt he should reassure his new agent, who might not appreciate the
progress that had already been made. "I trust you will not be discouraged with the somewhat scattered fashion of our work," he
wrote Thom in February 1902. "For the last three years I have experienced the difficulty of dealing with people at arm's length in this
matter, and while it doubtless seems to you quite hazy and without
sufficient head, I cannot but feel that we are much further along
than ever heretofore."[36]

Thom's appointment did not please all members of the National Committee, particularly those on the fringe of the reform effort. Although Garfield and Schwab strongly favored bringing
pressure on reluctant congressmen by mobilizing their influential
constituents, other businessmen were less comfortable with this tactic. Garfield experienced continued difficulty in persuading the
trade bodies to contribute toward Thom's expenses. "They shout
loudly enough so long as no money is called for," he grumbled to
Hunt. Its early interest in consular reform notwithstanding, the
Boston Chamber of Commerce deplored the use of "lobbyists," as
placing the issue on "the plane of special and selfish legislation." At
the same time, the Boston group did not offer to handle the chore of
marshaling and focusing the support of the businessmen. Garfield
knew that without such work the movement would continue to be
ineffective. Even if the commercial organizations happened to see
the need on their own, at most they would only pass resolutions.[37]

Not only were the reformers at odds about how they should
exert pressure on Congress, but they disagreed also about the provisions of bills to be fought for. When the National Committee was
formed, Adams was still introducing his bill calling for a congressional commission, and Burton's bill had progressed no farther than
Adams's subcommittee. Moreover, changes had been made in the
so-called chambers-of-commerce bill drafted by Hunt in 1899 and
subsequently introduced by Lodge and Burton. Albert H.
Washburn, formerly a consul and then Lodge's private secretary for
several years, pressed his favorite theme of consular inspection; in
November 1901, Hunt included such a provision in his bill. John

Foster dropped by Hunt's desk at the department to suggest a provision by which a person who served in the department for two years could be transferred to a consular post paying a higher salary. Hunt put it in. Such changes did not generally arouse serious disagreement among the reformers.[38]

The real stickler was the same point that had confounded the sometime reformer Grover Cleveland, and it would continue to hamper foreign service reorganization for many more years. According to the Constitution (article 2, section 2), the president is authorized to "nominate, and by and with the advice and consent of the Senate, shall appoint Ambassadors, other public Ministers, and Consuls." There was little question that Congress could reclassify the service or replace the fee system with salaries. It had already partly classified the service on two different occasions and at appropriations time regularly juggled individual classifications and salaries on a piecemeal basis. Such measures had nothing to do with actual appointments to reclassified or newly salaried positions. But even many proponents of civil service reform believed that it was unconstitutional for Congress to pass laws detailing how the president was to appoint those public officials whom the Constitution gave him the right to appoint, subject only to the Senate's approval.[39] Moreover, it was generally believed that by executive order the president could establish policies of appointment, promotion, and removal that could bring greater stability and efficiency to the service. Cleveland's 1895 order had been a step in this direction. Then why the immense expenditure of time and energy on attempts to secure *legislative* action, particularly after the sympathetic Roosevelt became president in 1901?[40] There were several reasons.

The establishment of the new system upon firm ground required cooperation between the president and Congress. If the president issued new rules for the consular service and was still besieged with pleas from senators and representatives to appoint their friends to consulates, he would either give in and thus wreck the reorganization or refuse and thereby make enemies for his other programs and proposals. He needed to have an example of congressional willingness, however grudgingly given, to acquiesce if not participate in the process of establishing a consular service based on merit. Ansley Wilcox, a leading Buffalo lawyer and civil service reformer who was also a good friend of Roosevelt, observed that "the legislation is only permissive at the most," and would merely "outline a sound general principle and give the moral support of Congress to the President in doing what he can do without any legislation."[41] A second important consideration was that the Senate had veto power over presidential appointments. If the chief executive neglected the role of the legislature by too strict an interpretation of his constitutional mandate, the Senate might begin exercising its own mandate by scrutinizing more closely the real or imagined shortcomings of the president's nominees.[42] Finally, while seemingly simpler, in the long run an executive order without some evidence of legislative support would be unstable and liable to reversal when the next president came into office. The problems in the consular service were often created early in new administrations, when a predecessor's policies were no longer legally binding.

In the spring of 1902, with bills favorably reported in each branch of Congress and the newly formed National Committee actively pushing for action on the measures, the Speaker of the House changed his tactics. David B. Henderson of Iowa was an opponent of consular reform and had consistently failed to bring the bills to the floor of the House for consideration and a vote. He was by no means arbitrarily thwarting an outraged majority of his colleagues, since most of them were either apathetic or opposed to the measure. Yet Henderson was apparently concerned about the strength of the National Committee and its allies. Perhaps seeking to forestall any growing support in the House, on May 22 he sent the Adams bill to George W. Ray, chairman of the House Judiciary Committee, to secure an opinion on the bill's constitutionality.

Ray strongly criticized the measure. He attacked the proposed congressional commission, viewed by many of the reformers as a detriment but included by Adams in an effort to make the measure more palatable in the House. Ray considered the commission unconstitutional for a number of reasons and then speculated about whether the bill as a whole was unconstitutional, either because it delegated too much power to the president or because it limited the president's power. Adding for good measure his thoughts on the larger issue, he told the Speaker that "the attempt to carry the consular service under Civil Service rules is, in my judgment, most pernicious. It would be just as wise to provide Civil Service for Representatives in Congress and Senators of the United States and restrict their selection from the Civil Service list." Garfield's reaction was that the pressure had become strong enough to force the Speaker to find an excuse for refusing to consider the bill.[43]

In the months following Ray's decision, the National Committee and other reformers knew that the situation was not promising. That staunch advocate of an efficient foreign service, Congressman Robert R. Hitt, told Thom that the temper in the House among members of both parties was opposed to such efforts, and he contended that even many congressmen usually in favor of civil service were opposed to including the consular corps under the system. Thom's year-end report to the National Committee included equally gloomy evaluations from Adams and Lodge. But the reformers did not ease up, as they prepared for what Garfield called "the fall campaign." Senator Lodge was exhausted by the fight over the Philippine Government Bill when he left Washington in July, but he renewed his efforts upon his return in December. Garfield clearly revealed his own perseverance in December 1902, more than four years after he had become actively involved in the movement. "In reply to an inquiry as to when we expected to get our bill passed," he wrote his mother, "I explained that our hairs were hardly beginning to turn gray yet, & that presumably we had many years of fight in us."[44]

Although their determination remained strong, the reformers were aware that they would have to make some modifications in the measures they were submitting to Congress. In December 1902, stung by Ray's attack, Adams finally dropped his proposal for a congressional commission and introduced the old Burton bill with Burton's blessing. Lodge reintroduced his bill and also demonstrated his interest in combining legislation with an executive order. The Massachusetts senator reported from committee an amendment to the annual diplomatic and consular appropriation bill, providing for a salaried classification of the consular service and for the transfer of consuls from one post to another without the necessity of a new appointment. The rest of the desired provisions, such as appointment, promotion, and retention on the basis of merit and efficiency, he was willing to leave to presidential order.[45]

The Senate threw out the amendment on the familiar point of order that substantive legislation could not be passed as part of an appropriation bill. But Lodge's action indicated the direction in which the reformers were beginning to move, and during 1903 this trend gained momentum. Adams told Corcoran Thom that nothing more could be expected from the new Speaker, Joseph G. Cannon of Illinois, than from his predecessor, and he suggested obtaining an executive order to accomplish the goal. Further persuasion came from George McAneny, former secretary of the National Civil Service Reform League and a member of Gustav Schwab's Committee on Foreign Commerce and the Revenue Laws of the New York State Chamber of Commerce. McAneny had remained in close touch with the consular reform movement. As he wrote William Cushing of the Cleveland chamber in October 1903, he felt "very strongly that unless we divide the subject in some way as this, that is, ask of Congress the things that Congress only can give and throw the responsibility for all that remains upon the Executive, we shall get nothing or next to nothing for a long time to come." Cushing passed the advice along to a receptive Garfield, who agreed that both legislation and an executive order ought to be used. Garfield dryly observed to McAneny that it was interesting to watch "the zeal of members of Congress to protect the President from encroachment by the Legislative branch."[46]

During the 1903–1904 congressional session both Lodge and Adams introduced a so-called short-form bill. Drafted by McAneny, Garfield, and Ansley Wilcox, it resembled Lodge's abortive amendment of the previous session. Its principal features were the division of the service into classes, compensation by salaries, and the transferability proposal. The principal change from previous bills was in the provision governing appointments, promotions, and removals, which read simply: "That the President is authorized to prescribe such regulations for the admission of persons into the classified consular service, and for promotions therein and for removals therefrom as will best promote the efficiency thereof." The presi-. dent, of course, already had this power, but the reformers were seeking to co-opt Congress into the spirit of reorganization on the efficiency principle.[47]

The new tactic did not bring the desired results, however. Its failure was at least partly due to the determined and vociferous opposition of the National Business League. Since January 1900, the Chicago organization had been among the most active groups in the movement. While perhaps overly endowed with what Schwab once termed "breezy energy," it nevertheless did its part by mailing thousands of copies of bills and requests for support all over the country. It was also one of the very few associations to contribute money for Thom's services. But the league did not share the moderate philosophy of Garfield and the others, and by mid-1903 it was calling for a no-compromise, hard-line stance. "This League will never support, nor will commercial interests be satisfied with, any half measure," league secretary A. A. Burnham warned Garfield. "If we persist, and all pull together, as we will, there will be no question as to a successful conclusion." The following spring, while the short-form bills were pending in Congress, the league circulated a resolution (fittingly adopted on April Fool's Day) which opposed them on the grounds that they were inadequate. Garfield appealed for compromise, but Burnham replied that consular reorganization was "so immediately necessary to our foreign trade" that "we persist for the whole loaf, and in so doing are only asking that which, as every opposing Congressman well knows, is but the natural birthright of commercial interests." Adams had thought that his bill would finally be brought to the floor for consideration, and he was consequently embittered by the league's action. "I enclose a 'body blow' from alleged friends of Consular Reform," he wrote Garfield. "Unless your friends can counteract it, it will end the matter this session. I am disgusted." The reformers remained divided, and the bill remained moribund.[48]

The split in the ranks of the reformers during the spring of 1904 marked the beginning of a decline in the National Committee's efforts. The committee would probably have exerted itself again the following year, but by then the initiative had passed to Elihu Root, the new secretary of state, who was interested in consular reorganization and willing to push for it.

Meanwhile an important change was occurring in Harry Garfield's life. In June 1903, the president of Princeton University asked him to accept the school's new chair of politics. Woodrow Wilson was looking for a man who had learned something about politics firsthand, and he thought Garfield fit the requirements. In some ways it was a hard decision for the Cleveland businessman, involved as he was in the business and political life of his city. He had to decide where he could do the most constructive work while at the same time satisfying his personal ambitions. "The great question is," he wrote his brother, "where can the best work be done? Work that will produce the largest results." He finally concluded that it could be done at Princeton and accepted Wilson's offer.[49]

For years Harry had fervently preached, through such organizations as the Municipal Association and the National Committee, the obligation of citizens to work for the improvement of the political and social fabric. "Public life in some form is in the blood," he wrote James, "& we must not sacrifice the inheritance." He thought that much could be accomplished "through one of our great universities, now awakening to the new conception of education, having citizenship for its object—a citizenship no longer supine, but trained, vitalized, earnest." Moreover, he saw a potential political career blocked in Cleveland. He could not, he wrote his mother, enter the national political arena "through the elective channel flowing from wards of a great city, until those polluted dumping grounds have been cleaned out." Princeton would offer a better chance for a political career, and he believed it would also give him a chance for personal development. Gaillard Hunt was delighted with the offer and urged his friend to accept. It was only in the church or the college, the part-time historian wrote with more than a trace of envy, "that we get the association and the work that we care for most. They are not perfect, but they are less imperfect than Cleveland or Washington. . . . Ah, Jupiter, what a vision of congenial work, dignity and usefulness such a place offers to my eyes!"[50]

Even after Garfield joined the Princeton faculty a few months later, he remained active in the consular movement, and in the fall of 1905 both he and Hunt advised Secretary of State Root about legislation. In 1908 Garfield left Princeton to assume the presidency of his alma mater, Williams College, where he remained almost continuously until his retirement in 1934. During World War I he went back to work for Woodrow Wilson, this time as Fuel Administrator, and in 1920 he founded the Institute of Politics at Williams. The Institute held annual meetings to bring together noted scholars and statesmen, and it was yet another reflection of Garfield's continued interest in public affairs. His personal philosophy and public activity were well described in his inaugural at Williams in 1908 when, summarizing the purpose of his address, he quoted from Mark Hopkins: "The highest earthly conception is that of a vast Christian commonwealth, instinct with order and with such triumphs and dominion over Nature as modern science is achieving and promises to achieve."[51]

The year after Garfield assumed the Williams presidency, Gaillard Hunt left the State Department to become chief of the Division of Manuscripts at the Library of Congress, the job he had turned down in 1897. He returned to the department in 1917 in an editorial capacity and in 1921 became chief of its Division of Publications.[52]

Hunt and Garfield had played a crucial role in the effort to place the consular branch on a more efficient level. The bureaucrat in Washington, thwarted in his efforts to secure more satisfying work in the public service and angered by the number of incompetent political appointees, enlisted the Cleveland businessman and municipal reformer in an attempt to make the consular corps a vocation for ambitious and trained young men. Both were aware of the needs of America's growing foreign trade, and they felt a corollary need for trained consular officers to promote it. It was certainly commercial interest that drew men like Gustav Schwab into collaboration with them. But interwoven with this factor, for Hunt and Garfield, was the need to battle forces that made for inefficiency and national shame and thus worked against the national interest. They wished to establish an orderly society in which selfish interests and political pull had no place, a society composed of citizens who were, as Garfield put it, "trained, vitalized, earnest."

The two reformers complemented each other well. Hunt, with his vantage point in Washington, was principally the idea-man, especially during the early years, drawing up bills and outlining the steps his friend should follow. Garfield brought impressive credentials and good connections to the cause, as well as an apparently inexhaustible energy. Together the two succeeded in mobilizing the important chambers of commerce in active support of consular reform, a difficult and often frustrating task. By the spring of 1904, the National Committee on Consular Reorganization included a dozen of the most important commercial bodies in the country, and it provided a sounding board for the exchange of ideas among businessmen, civil service reformers, congressmen, and others interested in the cause. Learning from repeated failures, it modified its original proposals to conform to what it might realistically hope to obtain from an unsympathetic Congress and a sympathetic but cautious president. Hunt and Garfield, and the movement generated by their activities on behalf of consular reform, bridged the gap between the sporadic and uncoordinated efforts during the depression of the 1890s and the final phase in 1905–1906.

4 FREDERIC EMORY'S COMMERCIAL OFFICES

The consular corps was not the only part of the foreign service that was the object of reorganizing efforts during the 1890s and early 1900s. At the same time, and without the publicity and notice accompanying the fight for consular reform, far-reaching changes were already taking place within the State Department itself.

On Maryland's Eastern Shore, across Chesapeake Bay from Annapolis, lies Queen Annes County. In the mid-1880s a young newspaperman chronicled its history for the local *Centreville Observer* in a series of sketches, which the Maryland Historical Society compiled and reissued in book form some sixty-five years later. The author was Frederic Emory.[1]

Emory took pride in his native soil, pointing to the harmonious balance in the local economy between manufacturing and agriculture. He was just as proud of the county's political tradition, which since the Civil War had not only maintained a strong spirit of independence from boss rule, but had also been "one of the most reliably democratic counties in the state." By "democratic" Emory meant its continuing allegiance to the banner and principles of the Democratic party. He himself was a particularly ardent member of the "Democracy."[2]

Frederic Emory was born in 1853 at Centreville, the county seat. His family owned slaves, and his father was a member of the local vestry. After receiving his education at Centreville Academy and at Saint John's College in Annapolis, he entered newspaper work when he was about nineteen. By the time he was twenty-six he was editor of the *Baltimore Evening Bulletin*.[3]

At some time during the next three years, Emory left the *Evening Bulletin* and by 1882 had become one of three regular editorial writers for the *Baltimore Sun*. He remained there more than ten years. The *Sun* must have provided a congenial atmosphere for him, because it was not only a Democratic newspaper but also a strong defender of the gold standard and low tariffs. Such sentiments prompted Emory and his fellow editorialists to flay both the Republican disciples of high protection and the elements within their own party that advocated a currency based on the silver standard. Emory and the *Sun* were strongly entrenched in the metropolitan wing of the Democratic party and were leading spokesmen for Grover Cleveland's Democracy.[4]

It was probably through his political editorializing that Emory became acquainted with Senator Thomas Francis Bayard of Delaware. Bayard was a prominent metropolitan Democrat, who served during Cleveland's first administration as secretary of state. By 1879, while still editor of the *Evening Bulletin*, Emory was writing Bayard to congratulate him on his stand in the Senate against the bimetallists. The relationship remained distant until about 1890, when Emory increasingly elicited Bayard's views in order to quote them in the *Sun*'s columns lambasting the Republicans.[5]

Emory was a frail and nervous man, and his newspaper work frequently wore him down. In the summer of 1892 he was forced to leave the *Sun* and take a long rest at his country home. He was in no financial position to retire, and he asked Bayard to let him know of any possibilities for employment. Emory later told Bayard that while he might secure a job with another newspaper, he was not looking forward to "the confinement and late hours of a newspaper office which, in the past, have proved so detrimental to my health." Nor was the compensation sufficient for him to risk another breakdown. At the same time, he was unwilling to try his luck in New York with letters of introduction that Bayard offered to supply, partly because he feared that his strength might "not be equal to the rough and tumble of such an effort."[6]

Another reason for Emory's reluctance to resume newspaper work or go to New York was his hope of receiving a government appointment in the new Cleveland administration. In March 1893 he asked Bayard about the possibilities of a job in one of the executive departments or a consulate, preferably in Great Britain.[7] Bayard delivered, and later that month Emory was appointed secretary of the International Bureau of American Republics, the forerunner of the Pan American Union.[8]

Emory was intensely grateful to his sponsor, who did not return to Cleveland's cabinet but became instead the first United States ambassador to Great Britain. Not only had Bayard gotten him a sorely needed government appointment, but he had also lent him money. "As time wears on," Emory wrote him after two months on the job, "I feel an increasing sense of obligation for the opportunities that are opening to me here, not only in a material sense, but as changing the whole perspective of life for me, and as affording me a most valuable experience." He was anxious to do well in his new position, in order to show that Bayard's confidence in him had not been misplaced. Blessed by the Cleveland administration's generosity, he also was more eager than ever to use his experience and contacts in journalism to explain (anonymously) the administration's policies, particularly in foreign affairs. He was proud of his work and sent letter after letter, with clippings enclosed, across the Atlantic to Bayard. Occasionally he received help in his publicity work from Henry L. Bryan, Bayard's close friend and former private secretary, who was attached to the State Department while editing and distributing the laws enacted by Congress.[9]

In April 1894, a year after he had entered government work, Emory was appointed chief of the Bureau of Statistics in the State Department. For some months he had held mixed feelings about his job in the Bureau of American Republics. The work had enabled him to care for his mother and sisters, who evidently depended on him financially. He was also gaining valuable experience and had seen his "sphere of . . . possible usefulness constantly widening." Nevertheless there was tension between him and the bureau's director, and the organization's future was by no means assured. Although the new position did not pay as well, it did offer the ever-important "wider field of usefulness," and Emory also thought that employment in the State Department proper would enhance his chances for future promotion. The Bureau of Statistics post had become vacant when Edward I. Renick, another Marylander, became the department's chief clerk. He recommended Emory as his successor, and Secretary of State Walter Gresham quickly agreed.[10]

The bureau that Emory took over had been functioning almost continuously since 1854, and its antecedents stretched back to George Washington's first administration. As early as 1791, Congress requested reports from the consuls about the nation's foreign trade, and two years later Secretary of State Jefferson submitted them. In 1842 Congress required the secretary of state to lay before it each year a list of changes in foreign commercial regulations, and an 1856 law ordered the annual transmittal of all commercial information sent to the State Department by consuls and diplomats. A statistical office to edit the consular reports, extract material, and arrange it for publication was established at the State Department in 1854 and more formally organized in 1856.[11]

The first report, four volumes long, was issued in 1856. Only one of the four volumes was devoted to the text of the consular reports; most of the remainder contained statistics. Over the years the reports themselves occupied more and more space in the series, (which became known as *Commercial Relations of the United States*), until by 1869 they accounted for the whole edition. Yet they continued to be published by the State Department's "Statistics Office," whose name was changed in 1874 to the "Bureau of Statistics."[12]

Because of the State Department's growing interest in promoting exports, the reports were published monthly as well as annually after 1880, and soon afterward the bureau began issuing special consular reports at irregular intervals. Even before these developments, the Bureau of Statistics had occasionally furnished abstracts of consular reports and other items of commercial interest to newspapers and businessmen.[13]

Thus by the time Emory took charge of the Bureau of Statistics in 1894, it had been operating for decades as a source of commercial information. At the same time, there was plenty of room for improvement, and for the next eleven years Emory worked to correct deficiencies and to extend the information service for American manufacturers and exporters. Those efforts owed much to Emory's attitudes and assumptions, which merit a closer view.

When Frederic Emory reflected upon American society—and he did so frequently—he was particularly engrossed by the transformations accompanying industrialization. He believed that industrialization was homogenizing the United States, muting discordant differences between the sections, and welding the American people into a more cohesive economic, social, cultural, and political unit. The process was inevitable and irresistible; in describing it he used such phrases as "destined to spread like a wave" and "purely mechanical"; he predicted that "like a huge steam roller" it would "pass and repass over the face of society, reducing it practically to a uniform level." Emory stood in awe of this steamroller and usually viewed it favorably. He agreed with de Tocqueville that although democracy did not produce the most skilled government, it did release "a superabundant force, and an energy which is inseparable from it," which in turn worked "wonders." Indeed, it was due as much to industrial technology as to democratic institutions that the United States did not have a peasantry, lines of social demarcation, or even a "privileged class." He confidently asserted that the inheritance laws would break up the industrial plutocracy that had temporarily developed. He might have been a ghostwriter for Andrew Carnegie as he painted a rosy picture of social mobility: "The moment a boy enters a factory he is on the road of progress which may lead to any height, and at any rate is sure, if he be sober and industrious, to bring him to the goal of good citizenship and intelligent participation in affairs." What was true for the individual was also true for the mass, since industrialization was raising the general cultural and political level. Like the good metropolitan Democrat that he was, Emory was fond of pointing to the role of the southern cotton manufacturing industry in giving "employment to the mountaineer and 'cracker' element which, for generations, had drawn a precarious existence from the soil and lived in habits of shiftlessness and comparative indolence." Their political habits were also showing improvement, which Emory defined as resistance to Populism's siren song. [14]

In Emory's opinion, industrialization had also prompted the United States to look abroad to find markets for its domestic surplus. Just as greater homogeneity and centralization of American society within its borders were inevitable results of the relentless wave of industrialization, changes in American foreign policy were equally certain. Emory believed that "the present attitude of the United

States toward the rest of the world is the result of economic changes which were beyond the control of any party or any clique of politicians." Without foreign markets to siphon off surpluses of manufactures, factories would be forced to close down for several months of the year, or else operate fewer hours and with reduced wages. Such overproduction in the 1890s was "the actual cause of the 'hard times' which have prevailed in recent years."

Idle factories and workers had no place in Emory's ideal of a stable, prosperous, democratic society with a rising level of popular culture and political participation. Foreign trade was necessary to keep the factories running, to serve as "the balance wheel of our industrial mechanism, even in times of great domestic prosperity." The balance wheel was important not only for industrial harmony, but for sectional accord as well. Without the China market as an outlet for its cheaper cotton cloth, Emory wrote in 1903, the South would be forced to manufacture lines of goods that competed with those of New England factories. Thus both sections had an important stake in a policy of foreign trade expansion, what Emory termed "a reciprocity of interests which is likely to continue and to be woven more and more inextricably into the web of our industrial activity."[15]

Emory's emphasis on foreign trade dovetailed neatly with his antipathy toward a protective tariff, which hindered the flow of international commerce. "Barter is the first law of trade," he argued. "We can not hope to sell without buying." Both he and Bayard found the tariff "an insidious form of state socialism" and a menace to individual freedom. After returning from the 1893 World's Fair in Chicago, Emory wrote Bayard that an exhibition of foreign merchandise was "a splendid object lesson to the people of the burdensome nature of a protective tariff. The cost of the smallest articles on exhibition *duty paid*, is so great as to be prohibitory to everybody of limited means." A protective tariff was not only unjust; by limiting trade it was dangerous to the social order. Lower trade barriers and the resulting increase in foreign commerce, on the other hand, would give all classes a stake in the "industrial fabric" in case "any serious shock should come."[16]

If industrialization and a foreign policy increasingly devoted to securing foreign markets were both inevitable, according to Emory's outlook, America's success in obtaining those markets was not. Unlike agricultural and other raw products, manufactured articles were not going to sell themselves, at least not for very long. The United States faced rigorous competition in the world's markets from European nations whose manufacturers had long outgrown the domestic market and were accustomed to producing and selling according to foreign tastes. Those nations were awakening to the threat of American commercial competition, and they were exerting efforts to combat it. Consequently, Emory warned, American manufacturers and exporters had to seek out, cultivate, and hold foreign markets even in times of domestic prosperity, so that they "will not have to win them back again in the hour of need, but will always have them as a safety-valve in times of repletion." While past success of American manufactured goods in foreign markets had been due to a brilliant economy of production, Americans would now have to pay greater attention to selling their products. In Emory's words, "we must have the best machinery, not merely for manufacturing goods, but for selling them when made." And it was the responsibility of the federal government, specifically the State Department, to provide this machinery to help American manufacturers sell their products overseas. The machinery should consist of the best possible commercial intelligence service to gather information about needs and opportunities in foreign markets and to get it into the hands of American manufacturers and exporters. To this mission Emory devoted his next eleven years.[17]

When Bayard's protégé entered the State Department in the spring of 1894, he threw himself into the work of molding the Bureau of Statistics into a more useful agency. One of his predecessors in the post, historian Worthington Chauncey Ford, considered the job a thankless one and encouraged the new incumbent to think of it "merely as a steppingstone to something better." Ford was well aware of the disadvantages under which Emory was working. "Your Bureau depends on its chief," Ford told him, "as it has never had proper equipment to do what is expected of it. . . . I wonder at your industry."[18]

Among the first objects of that industry was *Commercial Relations*, the compilation of the consuls' annual reports describing commercial opportunities in their districts. Emory set about to make it a more complete survey of foreign trade than it had ever been. Early in 1896 the bureau published a two-volume set for 1894 and 1895 with Emory's 220-page introductory review of the world's commerce—the first such review to appear for fifteen years. Such work, he confided to Bayard, "is a real joy to me because I feel that I am contributing something to the sum of progress in the government service." Secretary of State Olney attributed the useful review to Emory's improved system in the bureau, and he pleaded with manufacturers and exporters to exert greater energy in seeking foreign markets.[19]

Commercial Relations was just one of the bureau's publications that contained consular reports edited by Emory. There was also the regular issue of *Consular Reports*, published monthly since 1880; *Advance Sheets, Consular Reports*, containing selected notices of immediate interest and issued three or four times a month for the covenience of the press as well as commercial and manufacturing concerns; and *Special Consular Reports*, issued at irregular intervals on particular subjects in accordance with the department's instructions to the consuls. The bureau also prepared the circular instructions that directed the consuls' commercial reporting, and it received, edited, and published their replies. In 1894 the bureau's mailing list for its publications included 1,200 newspapers and journals, all members of Congress, 600 libraries, 150 boards of trade, and 3,000 individuals and firms. It was also Emory's responsibility to prepare special memoranda on commercial subjects that might be ordered by the secretary of state or requested by congressmen. In addition, he spent a great deal of time answering inquiries, sometimes totaling fifty to one hundred a day, from individual businessmen and commercial organizations.[20]

Emory enjoyed his new job, and his superiors rewarded him with greater responsibility. For six weeks in the autumn of 1896 he took on the duties of chief clerk in addition to his regular work. He continued to be moved by a desire to please his sponsor and wrote Bayard early in 1895 that "nothing could give me greater satisfaction than to feel that my official work is realizing, to some degree, your estimate of its capabilities, and my cherished aspirations to be of some real use."[21]

Emory's desire for useful activity was one reason he churned out articles and editorials praising administration policies and occasionally attacking the Republicans. He also clipped the results for Henry Bryan to send Bayard in the diplomatic pouch. Still another purpose behind his continued writing was to keep open his newspaper connections. In the event that administrations again changed hands after the next election, he might be a victim of the political axe—particularly if the Republicans knew who was producing some of the Democratic propaganda.[22]

In the summer of 1896 such a turnover appeared likely. The agrarian wing of the Democratic party, under William Jennings Bryan, wrested control away from the Cleveland-Olney-Bayard forces, and it seemed to many observers that Republican William McKinley would enter the White House in 1897. Like many "gold Democrats," Emory renounced his party's standard-bearer and supported McKinley, despite McKinley's image in the early 1890s as the high priest of protectionism. By 1896 the candidate had toned down his protectionist stance and adopted a more balanced program, including the pursuit of foreign markets through a reciprocal trade program.[23] Furthermore, to Bayard and Emory only one thing was as important as a low tariff: maintenance of the gold standard.[24] Bayard described Cleveland as guiding "the Ship of State clear of that reef of financial death—a Silver Standard," and both he and Emory considered even the Sherman Silver Purchase Act a radical extreme. Hence it was not difficult for them to decide which candidate to support. Emory neatly dichotomized the issue: "Never before, I imagine, has the line been so sharply drawn between the forces of order, morality, and reason and those of anarchy, greed, and blind unrest." He wrote for the *Sun* a series of articles entitled "Silver in Other Lands," which hammered home the thesis that around the world poverty and backwardness characterized those countries foolish enough to maintain a silver standard. Emory and Bayard were doubtless gratified by the election of the man whose policies they had once fought so fiercely.[25]

Only a few days after the election, Emory moved to improve his bureau's facilities. Complaining to Third Assistant Secretary Rockhill that he was "thoroughly tired of trying to make bricks without straw," he requested help in seeking additional funds from Congress. "The Bureau of Statistics offers us the germ of a most valuable Bureau of Foreign Commerce," he told Rockhill, "but this germ can not develop without the fructifying aid of legislation." Rockhill lent his assistance, and the next appropriations act gave Emory's office a 25 percent increase in funds (from $20,000 to $25,000). It also authorized the secretary of state to change the bureau's name to the "Bureau of Foreign Commerce" beginning with the next fiscal year.[26]

While Congress was still considering the State Department's request, Emory was working along another front. In January 1897, he journeyed to Philadelphia for the second annual meeting of the Republican-oriented National Association of Manufacturers, where he lost no chance to explain his bureau's needs and opportunities for service. On the day the convention opened, greeting the delegates in the *Philadelphia Public Ledger* was a lengthy article entitled "Our Foreign Trade," anonymously penned by Emory. It emphasized the need of manufacturers for foreign markets and also discussed the State Department's administrative machinery for collecting and disseminating foreign trade information. Emory urged the establishment of a corps of commercial attachés to be stationed at embassies and legations. He also advocated improved facilities at the State Department itself, specifically a force of skilled translators, accountants, and editors, to direct the trade promotion work of diplomats and consuls. And he suggested that in light of the department's difficulties in obtaining funds from Congress for the bureau's work, the NAM might want to appoint a committee of inquiry to secure legislative action.[27]

Having prepared the ground, Emory appeared at the convention the next day to participate in a symposium on trade extension. He may have been uneasy about entering what he considered a den of protectionists, and he wisely refrained from sharing his tariff views with the delegates. Rather, Emory exhorted the manufacturers to "concerted action, concerted effort" in pursuit of foreign markets and invited them to make their needs known to the State Department. "The sphere of the Department's operations," he explained to any delegates who might not have read his article, "should be so broadened as to enable it not merely to keep step with, but to lead the growth of foreign commerce. . . . The Government cannot make trade, but it may be able to help you make it. It is for you to put into its hands the proper tools." The manufacturers listened with interest, and the next day many of them approached him to obtain more information.[28]

Whether because of his anti-Bryan articles, the impression he made at the NAM convention, the quality of his work in the department, or other reasons, Emory kept his job after the McKinley administration took office in March. Ironically, the Cleveland Democrat's most significant and lasting contributions to the State Department were made during the next eight years, under Republican administrations.

In mid-1897 Emory took the final step in changing the name of his office to the Bureau of Foreign Commerce. He wrote Secretary of State John Sherman in June that soon after he had entered the Bureau of Statistics, he had become aware of the public's inability to distinguish among the Bureaus of Statistics in the State, Agriculture, and Treasury departments. The problem as it affected State would be removed by changing his bureau's name. Of more importance to Emory, who was ever intent on securing business support for his agency, was that the new designation was likely "to impress upon the public mind the importance of the commercial functions of this Department." Sherman exercised the authority granted in the appropriations act, and the new name took effect on July 1.[29]

That autumn, Emory initiated a significant improvement in the bureau's service. In October he sent a memorandum to Assistant Secretary of State William R. Day outlining a plan for publishing the consular reports on a daily basis as well as in the monthly and annual collections. Day approved, and in December, after recovering from one of his frequent illnesses, Emory presented the plan to Secretary Sherman. The bureau was already issuing as "advance sheets" a few consular reports as soon as it received them. Emory's proposal was that every day, Sundays and holidays excepted, the department publish advance sheets of commercial information for the benefit of newspapers, trade organizations, and individual merchants and manufacturers. The interest in the export trade shown by businessmen during the depression years of the 1890s, Emory told Sherman, had stimulated the consuls to greater activity. As a result, the consular reports were improving and thus were more useful. If this measure was initiated, he argued, and if the cable could be used to supply commercial information in cases where speed was crucial, "nothing, it seems to me, would be left to be desired in this branch of the work." But Emory had not forgotten the more elaborate apparatus he had outlined to the NAM earlier in the year, and he referred to "additional facilities which are sorely needed for the development of other features of the work."[30]

The proposal for daily advance sheets went through, and the Bureau of Foreign Commerce began issuing them in January 1898. It is impossible to determine whether the new procedure significantly increased American foreign trade, but in subsequent years State Department officers praised Emory's innovation in fulsome terms. John Ball Osborne, Emory's successor in the bureau, had no doubts about the concrete results; in 1907 he called it "the most valuable improvement that has ever been introduced in the governmental system of aiding the export trade." According to Assistant Secretary of State Francis B. Loomis, the frequent publication added to the consuls' growing interest in commercial reporting by giving them a greater chance to see their names in print. In mid-1898 Emory's bureau also began receiving the necessary appropriations for cable fees.[31]

Emory's work in the Bureau of Foreign Commerce earned him the trust and confidence of his new superiors, a development, he told Bayard, that was "naturally flattering in view of my political opinions and antecedents." Almost apologetically he explained to his old sponsor and mentor that both McKinley and Day (the de facto secretary) "have placed me under the strongest sense of obligation by their treatment of me." By May 1898 Henry Bryan could report to Bayard that their friend was "now in a strong position and has made a very important office out of his Bureau of Statistics."[32]

Although it is difficult to gauge the extent of Emory's influence on foreign policy apart from the stimulus given by his efforts in the Bureau of Foreign Commerce, both Day and Secretary John Hay seem to have respected him, and Emory occasionally offered his opinions on diplomatic policy.[33] Early in 1898, he suggested to Day that the United States assist Great Britain in the Far East to help maintain the commercial open door since, as he explained to Bayard, "the thing seemed at the time to be going by default." Shortly afterward, he reported, the department's policy appeared to shift in that direction, but he was careful not to claim sole credit for the policy change.[34]

In June, while the possibility of Philippine annexation was exciting widespread business interest in the China market, Secretary of State Day requested congressional funds for a commercial mission to China. Although he was unsuccessful, the attempt helped convince a number of businessmen, notably members of the New York State Chamber of Commerce and the newly formed American Asiatic Association, that if necessary the administration would take diplomatic action to preserve the open door in China from encroachment by the European powers. Those businessmen were even more gratified the following month, with the publication of Emory's introduction to *Commercial Relations*, the annual edition of consular reports. The essay had been composed the previous April, just as war was breaking out with Spain but before Dewey's annihilation of the Spanish naval force at Manila Bay. Emory observed that because of the domestic overproduction of manufactured goods, the "enlargement of foreign consumption of the products of our mills and workshops has . . . become a serious problem of statesmanship as well as of commerce." He made clear what he considered the principal object of that statesmanship, at a moment when the United States had just gone to war with Spain:

> The more important incidents of the past year in foreign diplomacy have, therefore, a significance for us which might not have attached to them in the absence of concerted efforts to extend the sale of our goods. . . . The world has watched the progress of the diplomatic drama in China with an interest which has been heightened by the knowledge that the practical outcome might be either the opening of new channels of trade to the commerce of the globe, or the appropriation of them by particular nations for their own special benefit. China has, for some years, been one of the most promising fields for American enterprise, industry, and capital, and the entrance of that vast Empire upon the path of western development under conditions which would secure equality of opportunity to the United States, would doubtless result in immense gains to our manufacturers in

the demand, sure to follow, for lines of supplies and goods of various descriptions that we are preeminently fitted to provide.[35]

At an early date, therefore, Emory both contributed to and reflected the State Department's concern for the maintenance of the open door in China. By appearing to commit the department to a certain direction, his essay and Day's request for a commercial mission might also have narrowed the administration's future options. Emory himself was convinced that by the time John Hay returned from London in the autumn of 1898 to become secretary of state, the department was "already committed to a policy which foreshadowed opposition to exclusive privileges." A year afterward, Hay dispatched the famed open door notes to the European powers and Japan, designed to preserve equal access for American products to the China market.[36]

With the Republican ascension in 1897, a sharp change had occurred in Emory's extramural writing. There is no indication that he continued to write unsigned articles praising Democratic policies. It would have been foolish for him to do so, and he hinted as much to Bayard. Instead, when not busy with his heavy government workload, he devoted his time to building a house, producing a novel, and writing signed magazine and newspaper articles on his pet themes of industrialization and foreign commerce.[37]

A year after taking office, the McKinley administration temporarily increased Emory's duties. Demonstrating confidence in the Maryland Democrat and in his capacity for work, the president appointed him provisional director of the Bureau of American Republics, in addition to his regular assignment. Emory received the higher salary of director and served as chief of the Bureau of Foreign Commerce without pay. The previous director had died after a long illness, leaving the organization in need of financial and administrative rejuvenation. Emory soon supplied it. He ended the policy of hiring solicitors on commission to drum up advertising from commercial houses for bureau publications, because the commissions were eating up much of the revenue derived from the advertising. He also succeeded in making the Latin American nations feel that they had a significant voice in the organization, thereby arresting their growing dissatisfaction. Chile ended its status as the sole hold-out and joined the association early in 1899. Working closely with the NAM and the Philadelphia Commercial Museum, Emory finished the job begun by his predecessor of compiling a commercial directory of the American republics. The two organizations helped by furnishing him with lists of manufacturers and exporters interested in trade with Latin America. Although he had originally been appointed for only a few months, the reorganization and improvements took so much time that he received an open-ended appointment as director.[38]

In the spring of 1899, after he had finished his reorganizing work, Emory gladly turned the directorship over to William W. Rockhill, his former State Department colleague. While not interested in remaining as permanent director, he still was pleased that members of the Republican administration, as well as all the Latin American representatives, wanted him to stay. He was especially gratified, he wrote Day, that he had proved his usefulness to those who had "the political success of the administration close at heart."[39]

For several years after resigning the directorship, Emory did not find the time to enlarge the work of his commercial office in the manner he had once envisioned. Whether the lack of additional improvements was due to his frequent illnesses, work on his house or his novel, heavy day-to-day responsibilities, or other causes is not certain. In any event, the next important development came when Congress was in the process of creating the Department of Commerce and Labor.

Businessmen for many years had petitioned Congress to create a Department of "Commerce and Industries" or "Commerce and Manufactures" to foster and promote those branches of the economy. Such bills had been introduced during the late nineteenth century, and many of them called for the transfer of the consular corps from State to the new department. Congress eventually left the consuls under State's control, but Senator Knute Nelson's bill creating the Department of Commerce and Labor early in 1903 did provide for the transfer of Emory's Bureau of Foreign Commerce. At C & L it would be merged with another bureau, but would continue publishing the consular reports. Nelson's bill also stipulated that the new department would request commercial reports of, and receive them from, the consuls. Yet the State Department managed to retain a role in collecting and disseminating commercial information, thanks to Emory and Senator Lodge.[40]

In January 1902, after conferring with State Department officials (including Emory, no doubt, since he was always in the foreground in matters affecting his bureau), Lodge introduced an amendment to Nelson's bill. The amendment provided that in light of the proposed transfer of the Bureau of Foreign Commerce, a new bureau would be created in the State Department. Its function would be to examine the incoming consular reports and to edit out political or diplomatic information before sending them to C & L for commercial editing and publication. The new bureau would also transmit to the consuls requests from C & L for special reports and other commercial information. The crux of the State Department's argument, which it would use repeatedly in future years, was that the consular reports coming in from the field often contained a good deal of diplomatic and political data, some of which was confidential and none of which was the business of any other department.[41]

Early in 1903, for the first time since the Republicans had come into power six years before, Emory's future was in doubt. When the Bureau of Foreign Commerce moved to C & L in July, there was no chance he would become head of the consolidated office; the chief of the other bureau involved in the pending merger had solid Republican credentials and was much closer to administration leaders than Emory could hope to be. Emory might go to C & L with his bureau and continue to publish the consular reports, but his office would be only a subdivision of a larger bureau. Or he could stay at the State Department and head the new entity to be created there. But compared with the scope of his work over the past nine years, to say nothing of his plans for its enlargement, shuffling papers between C & L and the consuls was not very appealing. In either case he would have a narrower range of activity.[42]

By the spring of 1903 Emory had decided to improve his situation within the State Department. He wrote his friend John Bassett Moore in May that he was "making decent provision for my approaching decapitation as Chief of the Bureau of Foreign Commerce and devising the safest means of fitting my head on again as

Chief of the new bureau." At one time, he confided to Moore, he had been inclined simply to resign, but finally decided it would be "an ignominious surrender to 'abhorrent influences' that were seeking to loot the Department. . . . Confidentially, I may say that they might have won, had I not made a stand, as no one else seemed willing to cast himself into the breach." The pending merger actually had some advantages. Emory would no longer have to publish the consular reports, and perhaps now he would have the time "to develop a kind of commercial intelligence Service for the State Department itself—a service properly systematized and kept up to date—which, it has long seemed to me, was badly needed."[43]

The day after writing Moore, Emory moved to resurrect his commercial office. He asked Secretary Hay to provide a name for the new bureau and to extend its duties and scope of operation beyond the narrow confines stipulated in the bill creating Commerce and Labor. There were still, he told Hay, certain functions of the Bureau of Foreign Commerce that the State Department should continue to perform after July 1. These included sending occasional consular reports to government departments besides C & L, answering inquiries by businessmen about foreign tariffs and other commercial matters, and compiling commercial information for the department's own use. He suggested adopting the title "Bureau of Commercial Relations," which would permit the secretary of state to continue transmitting to Congress the annual reports on changes in foreign commercial systems. That practice had been neither repealed nor impaired by the recent act. Ever alert for an opportunity to secure public or congressional attention, Emory observed that the continuance of the practice "might be availed of, with great advantage to bring important facts to the attention of Congress."[44]

Hay sent Emory's letter to C & L for its reaction. The proposal caused concern, since officials there were envisioning much responsibility for their own organization in foreign trade promotion and little for the State Department. But the only point they could concretely object to, for the time being, was Emory's proposed title for the new bureau. They insisted that it would be confusing for any government agency outside their department to have the word *commerce* in its title. As a result, Hay approved all of Emory's recommendations except the title, for which he substituted "Bureau of Trade Relations." That office continued the functions of the Bureau of Foreign Commerce, except for the publication and distribution of consular reports.[45]

With considerable assistance from Assistant Secretary of State Francis Loomis, Emory now found time to work out part of his plan for creating a more comprehensive commercial intelligence service. In January 1905 President Roosevelt submitted for congressional action a lengthy State Department request for six commercial attachés, who would be stationed at embassies and legations to coordinate the commercial reporting of the diplomatic and consular branches. The proposal was signed by Loomis as acting secretary of state, and it was the result of ideas and convictions both he and Emory had held for many years. Several times Emory had advocated a system of commercial attachés, while Loomis had recommended their appointment as early as the Harrison administration. In 1897 he had suggested that they double as consular inspectors in the countries to which they were assigned.[46]

The Emory-Loomis proposal touched repeatedly on the familiar theme of domestic surplus of manufactures and the "grave importance," in Roosevelt's words, of providing the export trade in manufactures "with all the official apparatus necessary to its full and free development." It emphasized that this would be a trial arrangement, and that changes would no doubt be made in the future. "It would seem to be but the part of ordinary prudence not to wait for the emergency," Loomis concluded, "but to work at once to perfect such machinery while there is still time for experiment and trial." To answer possible objections, Emory supplied a memorandum for the congressmen. He too stressed that enactment of the plan would not be a final solution, but rather that it would enable the State Department to put together a working model that Congress could later modify.[47]

Even on the original limited basis, the proposal sought to improve the entire foreign service, and particularly the consular corps, as a source of commercial information. Reflecting Loomis's 1897 plan, it stipulated that the attachés would also be consular inspectors. They would be assigned to embassies and legations, with diplomatic accreditation to the host government, and could thus serve as a coordinating link between the diplomatic and consular services for trade promotion. Selected from among capable members of the consular service, they would help instill some enthusiasm in the consuls. Loomis believed that the attaché would be "a living example and object of emulation for every aspiring man in the service."[48]

By this proposal Emory sought to enhance the State Department's stature as the branch of government most directly concerned with foreign trade promotion. He explained privately that it was an attempt to secure "for the Department itself the position before Congress and before the country which it ought to occupy." In the summer of 1904, when Loomis and Emory formulated the plan, C & L was effectively between secretaries and still disorganized.[49] The two men probably thought it was the best possible time to attempt a flanking movement and reassert State's role as the primary trade promoter. The previous winter, C & L's officials had requested appropriations for "special agents" to travel overseas and collect trade information. Although they had failed, they might succeed the next time and thus further circumscribe State Department activity vital both to the country's prosperity and State's annual appropriations.

Before sending their request to Congress, Emory and Loomis attempted to head off opposition from C & L by keeping it informed of the proposal. That strategy failed. C & L's new secretary, Victor H. Metcalf, reminded Loomis in December that the act creating his department had given it responsibility for developing foreign and domestic commerce. He added that since only his own organization had this duty, any office doing purely commercial work should be under C & L's "complete control and subject to its exclusive direction." Emory secured a hearing with Metcalf to attempt to change his mind, but without result. Not only did C & L oppose the plan, but that old friend of consular reform, Chairman Robert R. Hitt of the Foreign Affairs Committee, declared that it was unnecessary. Even Loomis failed to sustain his support sufficiently to suit Emory, and the proposal failed to get out of committee. Emory wrote John Bassett Moore that he had "accomplished substantially all I had hoped for—which was to get it before Congress and the country. I think we shall hear from it again."[50]

But Emory would not be on hand to push for his proposal in an official capacity. Even before Roosevelt submitted the project to Congress, Emory had decided to resign from the State Department. Never in very good health, by the end of 1904 he was exhausted and nearing another breakdown. He had stayed on, he told Moore, because he believed that he "had work not only to do, but to *save*, and that it would be deserting my post until it was carried (as well as I *can* carry it) beyond the danger-line." He then summed up his feelings about his government career and what it had meant to him: "I don't wish to exaggerate the importance of my efforts—they are, indeed, comparatively insignificant—but the objects I sought were for me, in my own small sphere, of vital gravity. I don't think the little work I have done can be destroyed. It may be hidden, or even disfigured for a time, but it will remain. Is not that enough for one who really has no ambition for mere place or for empty applause?"[51]

In January 1905 Emory submitted his resignation to Secretary Hay and at the end of March retired to his country home on the bank of the Chester River in his beloved native county. Hay accepted the resignation regretfully. "You leave an enviable record on the files of this department," he wrote Emory, "and still more in the knowledge of our foreign commerce which you have in all these years diffused through the country at large." Emory devoted some of his newfound leisure to blasting Congress and its neglect of the foreign service with such salvos as "Congress as a Nursery of Graft" and "Our Fettered Foreign Service." He occasionally wrote a more temperate and thoughtful article about what he considered the wellsprings of American foreign policy—the fact and the promise of United States commercial expansion.[52]

Three and a half years after retiring, Frederic Emory died. He had slowly recovered his health, only to contract pneumonia on a visit to Washington in the winter of 1907–1908. He developed tuberculosis, and after a summer of suffering died on September 20, 1908, two days after his fifty-fifth birthday.[53]

During his eleven years in the State Department, Emory contributed significantly to his branch of the public service. His labors were motivated by a craving to perform useful work that would please those who had placed their confidence in him and given him opportunities, and also by a conviction that America's industrial growth depended on a greater development of foreign trade.[54] A political appointee himself, Emory left to others the task of working for consular reform legislation, preferring to increase the consuls' zeal and efficiency by ensuring that their commercial reports were published promptly. Like his colleague Gaillard Hunt, he was aware of the value of public relations and particularly of the need to enlist businessmen's support for appropriations. Often frustrated by what he considered insufficient interest in foreign trade among the nation's businessmen, he strove to acquaint them with State Department efforts to help them sell in the world's markets. Thanks to his work between 1894 and 1905, the State Department retained important responsibilities in the field of foreign commerce. The later commercial offices at the department owed their existence largely to Frederic Emory.

5 WILBUR CARR, ELIHU ROOT, AND CONSULAR REORGANIZATION

For Wilbur John Carr, a young farmer from Taylorsville, Ohio, the journey from his home to Washington, D.C., was both spatially and conceptually farther than Frederic Emory's trip from across Chesapeake Bay. Carr had to uproot himself at an early age from a farming community; Emory merely had to move from one form of publicity work to another. Beginning his public service as a junior clerk in the State Department, Carr remained in Washington for forty-five years—until he left the city in 1937 to serve as minister to Czechoslovakia. Along the way, his contributions to the foreign service earned him such accolades as "the father of the foreign service" and its "master architect." In its broad outlines his life story was in the Horatio Alger tradition.[1]

When Wilbur Carr left the family farm near Taylorsville (population fifty-two), he joined the flood of young Americans moving to towns and cities. He possessed a "burning desire to make my mark" and chose shorthand as the means to accomplish his goal. Graduating from the Commercial College of what is now the University of Kentucky in 1889, eighteen-year-old Wilbur Carr enrolled in a shorthand course in Oswego, New York. The next year he became secretary to the principal of a boys' military academy at Peekskill, New York. There he continued his education, obtaining experience in disbursing, managing supplies, and keeping accounts. He even helped the principal write a commercial geography.[2]

Carr was anxious to pursue a law career and, prompted by friends' suggestions that he do so at night while working for the federal government by day, he took the civil service examination in stenography and typing in the spring of 1892. He was offered and accepted a position as clerk, class one, in the State Department.

Chief Clerk Sevellon Brown telegraphed him to come right away: "You are needed as soon as you can get here."[3]

Carr entered the State Department in June 1892. His responsibilities soon extended beyond typing and shorthand, as his hard work and intelligence brought him to the attention of his colleagues and superiors. Early in 1894 he helped Francois Jones draft the detailed foreign service legislation that Senator John Morgan introduced in April. Shortly thereafter he was transferred to the Consular Bureau and immediately made a favorable impression on his new chief. Like all of Carr's superiors then and later, Walter Faison found the young clerk "extremely useful to me" and expressed confidence that soon Carr would be "familiar with consular matters and able to take a great deal off of my hands."[4]

Carr's initial assignment to the Consular Bureau was brief; he served a tour of duty in each office of the department and for a while even edited the *Foreign Relations* series. For more than a year he was private secretary to Third Assistant Secretary of State W. W. Baldwin, who had high praise for him and warned Secretary of State John Sherman that "the larger part of his talent is being quite wasted to the Department, where it is employed in merely mechanical details." In March 1897 Carr returned to the Consular Bureau and proceeded to carve out a career.[5]

Meanwhile, Carr was actively pursuing his law studies at night. He earned the LL.B. degree from Georgetown University in 1894 and the LL.M. from Columbian (now George Washington) University five years later. When he was admitted to the Washington Bar, he confided to his diary that he felt "quite a man now."[6]

This excitement was in marked contrast to his feelings about his employment. Although he was then second-in-command of the Consular Bureau, the job was not rewarding. Often bored by his work at the State Department, Carr looked forward to practicing law. "At the office everything is lifeless as usual," he complained early in 1901. "How very tiresome Government employment is." He also was unhappy that much of his work was "unused and unappreciated." In April, almost nine years after entering the department, he continued to complain. "Usual work at the office," he wrote. "Am of opinion that I shall have to attempt something greater than mere consular work such as is given me. It is dwarfing to the mind." Desperately seeking stimulating work which would be both useful and recognized as useful, Carr expected the Law to offer it.[7]

What did provide such work was not the Law, but rather Carr's elevation to the top position in the Consular Bureau. His chief, Robert Chilton, Jr., became exhausted from overwork, and Carr ran the bureau from June 1899 to May 1900 while Chilton recuperated from a nervous breakdown. Although the bureau chief gamely returned to the department, his health would not permit him to remain. Early in 1902 Chilton resigned, suggesting that Carr take his place. Gaillard Hunt also applied for the post, but Carr secured it. The new position gave him the stimulation he required and the opportunity to perform useful work that received recognition. It also enabled him to work toward what became his most cherished goal—forging an institution that would reward ambitious and competent young men, like himself, who sought their self-actualization in service to their country.[8]

When Carr took over the Consular Bureau, the State Department's contributions to the consular reform movement were principally Gaillard Hunt's. Unlike Hunt, Carr was no publicist and did not have well-connected friends who could exert pressure on Congress or business groups. His contributions were of a different kind. In December 1902, he assisted Third Assistant Secretary Herbert Peirce in reworking Hunt's bill, submitting the draft to Senator Henry Cabot Lodge. Certain that Congress would continue to reject the measure if changes were not made, Lodge struck out all material relating to examinations and promotions, and submitted it as his "short-form" bill.[9] At the request of the Senate Foreign Relations Committee, Carr drew up a classification schedule to accompany the bill. But he was not optimistic, and even before the measure failed, he complained about the absence of State Department leadership in the reform effort. Carr was unaware of Gaillard Hunt's extensive contributions, but correct about the department's top officers when he asserted that the department "has done scarcely anything to bring about a reorganization or to suggest how it should be brought about."[10]

More effective leadership required a different secretary of state. John Hay, who held the post from 1898 until 1905, had dismal relations with Congress and, according to Assistant Secretary Hill, "detested" the Senate. Department Solicitor James B. Scott believed that under Hay "relations between the Department of State and the Senate were, in no humorous sense of the word, foreign relations." Hay also was frequently ill and absent from the department, and this hampered a strenuous undertaking like securing foreign service legislation. Even when he was healthy and at work, he was a poor administrator. One spring evening Carr walked home with Charles Ray Dean, the assistant secretary's confidential clerk, and later recorded Dean's comments in his diary: "Hay dislikes trouble. Lacks 'backbone' sufficient to make a strong administrative officer. Says [Third Assistant Secretary] Cridler would 'raise hell' if certain things were done and therefore he will not do them."[11]

The chief difficulty was not Hay's lack of interest in foreign service reform; like his immediate predecessors he bemoaned the number of political hacks in both branches of the field service. Shortly after he became secretary he even sent Senator Lodge a proposal for a corps of mobile diplomatic secretaries, who could be stationed either in the department or at posts abroad as needed. The problem was rather Hay's disinclination and inability to work for reform. Although secretary of state, he neither asked Roosevelt that certain appointments be made, nor did he object to any; as Charles Dean observed, he did not want to make trouble. And given his poor relations with the legislators, he was not one to trudge up "the Hill" to make requests. The result was continued delay in foreign service reform.[12]

John Hay died July 1, 1905. On the way back to Washington from the funeral in Ohio, Roosevelt asked Elihu Root, a corporation lawyer, to take charge of the State Department. Root accepted, and with his appointment the department had a chief not only with an interest in reorganization but also with strong administrative ability and good relations with Congress. Roosevelt once called Root "the ablest man that has appeared in the public life of any country, in any position, in my time." Even considering Roosevelt's fondness for expansive statements, it was quite a compliment, and the president's regard for Root was widely shared. Root had recently reorganized a War Department whose shortcomings had been brutally laid bare by the Spanish-American War. In the process, he had forged solid relations with Congress by appearing at committee hearings to press his case. His personality also differed from Hay's; it is difficult to imagine Root being cowed by anyone, much less by a third assistant secretary of state. Thus in temperament, experience, and his ability to work with Congress, Root was an ideal secretary for bringing to a successful conclusion the movement for consular legislation.[13]

Root's world view was also important to foreign service reform. He was one of a small group of turn-of-the-century cosmopolitans who have best been described as "neo-Hamiltonians." In addition to Root, the group included Theodore Roosevelt, Henry Cabot Lodge, Alfred Thayer Mahan, Senator Albert J. Beveridge of Indiana, Brooks Adams, and other men who idealized their country as a centralizing nation-state that would have to play an active part in the world's affairs. As Root told the New York state legislature in 1909, he was "a convinced and uncompromising nationalist of the school of Alexander Hamilton." Like Hamilton, he thought in structural terms and sought to initiate or foster lasting institutions that would serve as a framework for American society. In many respects Root was a conservative, and he placed his faith in the gradual development of such institutions to ensure no sharp break with tradition. "The only things which are new that will stand," he once told Philip Jessup, "are those which are an outgrowth of the old." Placing such emphasis on the nation, he naturally felt deeply about a citizen's responsibility to serve the nation in a public capacity. This conviction, coupled with the opportunities offered by the growing power and scope of the national government, helped take him to Washington in 1899 as secretary of war and administrator of America's new overseas empire. Root's views of public service, corporate nationalism, and gradualism came together in a speech he delivered while secretary of war to a National Guard Association meeting in Columbus, Ohio: "One of the saving things about doing work in the public service is that it is work for all time. You and I come and go; what we do for ourselves dies with us; but the great country, the institution, lives; the power of civilization, the great bulwarks of liberty, of justice, of human happiness, remain, generation after generation, century after century; and what these men, my friends, citizens of Columbus, what these men are doing is laying stones in the structure of national strength that will endure century by century." The foreign service was the second major American institution for which Root helped build a secure foundation.[14]

Like a number of his contemporaries, though less shrill than many, Root was actively interested in United States commercial expansion. Here too he was a gradualist. His tenure as secretary was not marked by the heavy-handedness and lack of subtlety that were to typify the acknowledged "dollar diplomacy" during the Taft-Knox years of 1909–1913. Another mark of his conservatism was his aversion to what he considered too much government presence in the marketplace. He informed National Business League secretary A. A. Burnham that although the State Department was "actively engaged in many ways and many directions in striving to pry open and hold open the doors for the entrance of American commerce and to make its progress and extension easy, I do not believe in too much Government." He believed rather that most of the effort should come from "the association of individual private enterprise"— prodded, guided, and otherwise served, if necessary, by the State Department.[15]

The new secretary of state took the oath of office in July 1905 and immediately departed Washington's summer heat, leaving the department in the hands of subordinates. During the summer he attended only to those matters requiring his immediate attention, but when he returned in September, consular improvement was one of the first items on his agenda.[16] As a centralizer and cosmopolitan he shared the determination of other foreign service reformers to remove this valuable national instrument from the control of locals, from what he termed "local political conditions."[17]

In September, Root began compiling data on the consular corps, and Wilbur Carr regularly worked all day and into the night to help supply information. Gaillard Hunt gave the secretary a complete history of the consular reform movement, and Ansley Wilcox sent him a copy of Adams's "short-form" bill, drafted by himself, Harry Garfield, and George McAneny. In November, James Garfield took his older brother to the department to confer with Root. Harry supplied Root with a list of the members of the National Committee on Consular Reorganization and others he knew were interested in the cause. He was confident that with an able secretary of state pushing for reform the movement would finally succeed.[18]

Root moved to accomplish certain goals without legislation. In October he established an efficiency record for consuls, based on his similar action for army officers at the War Department. While the new report would cover the "ability, promptness, and diligence displayed by each officer in the performance of all his official duties," the emphasis was clearly to be on the consul's trade reports, "judged according to the degree of ability, painstaking, discrimination, knowledge, and interest in the subject exhibited by him." Root asked the Commerce and Labor Department and the Bureau of Trade Relations to supply the necessary information to the Consular Bureau on the basis of trade reports. Unlike his predecessor, Root evidently had a good deal to say about consular appointments, and in the following months he and Roosevelt made a number of promotions after examining the officers' efficiency records. Root also drafted, and Roosevelt issued on November 10, an executive order extending Cleveland's ten-year-old order to cover consulates whose annual compensation exceeded $2,500.[19]

Root was well aware that his initial administrative measures were adequate only to a point. As he wrote Senator Lodge late in October, consular reorganization "is going to take money, and it is going to take affirmative legislation. I am trying to work out some definite ideas as to the best method, and I hope to be able to discuss the subject intelligently with you when you come to Washington." In November, Root and Lodge revised Gaillard Hunt's old bill, and Carr drew up a classification scheme. Lodge introduced the measure early in December. Borrowing another tactic from the Hunt-Garfield consular campaigns, Root sent a copy of the bill and a memorandum to commercial groups across the country. He also sent the package to newspaper and magazine editors, as he had done when pushing for army legislation.[20]

The bill's goals and provisions resembled those of previous efforts. Appointments as consul or consul-general were to be made, after examination, only to the lowest grades, and promotions granted only on the basis of demonstrated efficiency. Salaries ranged from $2,000 for a grade nine consul to $12,000 for a grade one consul-general (compared with the established scale of $1,500 to $5,000), and all fees were to be turned in to the Treasury; consuls would be compensated by salaries alone. Consuls, and consular agents receiving a salary over $1,000, were forbidden to engage in business or practice law for compensation. No foreigners could be appointed to clerical positions with annual salaries of $1,000 or more. The suggestion for consular inspectors to bring the field offices under the department's scrutiny received a positive reception from Root. "I had experience with that in the army," he remarked years later, "and knew you couldn't expect a man to do the work if he was never inspected. Many consulates hadn't been seen for twelve years or more." If necessary, in the more hopeless cases, the inspectors were to take charge of consulates until another consul could be sent to administer the office properly. Lodge likened the method to a bank examiner's taking over and administering a bank that was being mismanaged.[21]

Also crucial for effective consular reorganization was a new classification system. It was essential to the reformers' philosophy of creating a structure that would appeal to the career ambitions of able young men. A modern classification of the consulates would furnish the necessary career ladder. The new promotion system, Root believed, would provide "some incentive to do good work; so that a fellow will know that if he works hard and accomplishes results he will get some credit for it and some attention paid to him." As an additional advantage, the classification was based on the principle of appointment and promotion to classes rather than to specific posts. As one senator accurately described the change, it was to "rather make the consul the officer of a system than an officer of a particular station."[22]

Shortly after Lodge introduced the measure, the Senate Foreign Relations Committee held formal hearings. Root broke sharply with tradition when he himself appeared before the committee. His very presence and his patient, conservative arguments greatly enhanced the bill's chances. The senators must have appreciated being courted, particularly when they compared Root's attitude with his predecessor's.[23]

At the hearings, Root added his voice to arguments the reformers had been using for years. Emphasizing the need to create an efficient service free from politics, Root drew a parallel with army appointments: "I do not think it is too much to say that we have taken the army out of politics. . . . I give you my word that in the four years and a half I was in the War Department there was never such a question asked—whether the young man was a Democrat or Republican." Even the frequently skeptical senior senator from Georgia, Augustus Octavius Bacon, had to agree that it was indeed "true in the military service." "Well," Root rejoined, "it ought to be true of the consular service."[24]

Root and the other reformers probably did not expect to secure passage of the entire bill. If they did, they were quickly disappointed. The Foreign Relations Committee amended the measure, striking the sections relating to examinations and promotion on the basis of merit. There still existed a widespread sentiment that such provisions were unconstitutional, and reform-minded senators like Lodge wanted to eliminate the most objectionable portions before the bill went before the entire Senate. With these features removed, the bill obtained a unanimous committee endorsement and received Senate approval on January 30, 1906.[25]

The committee's action discouraged some reformers, including even Gaillard Hunt and Gustav Schwab. Both thought that the Senate had removed the most important features, rendering the measure worthless. Schwab told Harry Garfield that he doubted his chamber of commerce would "take further interest in it. I for one, do not intend to take any further steps to urge the passage of the measure." But Garfield was more optimistic, and more willing to compromise. He was also alarmed at the prospect of many years' effort wasted through businessmen's apathy, just as success was in sight. He quickly persuaded Schwab to change his mind, and the New York chamber threw its support behind the amended Lodge bill.[26]

When the House Foreign Affairs Committee held hearings on Lodge's measure, Root again journeyed up to Capitol Hill. He had no desire to lecture the legislators or to place blame for the political nature of the consular system's operation. Explaining the dilemma confronting a president who wished to take the system out of politics, he stressed the need for harmony and gradualism:

This classification will be a little help toward the establishment of . . . a method that should be established by common consent of both the President and Congress. . . . To make the change without an understanding means a row. It means a fight. It means hard feeling. And any improvement in such a system ought to come by general consent, and this classification is going a little way on the part of Congress toward indicating the acceptance of a little different system—

MR. GARNER: To helping the President to get away from the Senate? (Laughter).

SECRETARY ROOT: To helping him to get away from a bad practice in which both Houses have concurred. (Laughter).[27]

Root sent Carr to work with the Foreign Affairs Committee during its deliberations. Carr impressed the legislators with his grasp of the detailed classification proposal and his persuasive arguments for reorganization. Like his chief, he was a good politician. Representative Edwin Denby of Michigan, brother of the State Department's chief clerk and member of the three-man subcommittee considering the bill, desired an increase in the proposed salary of the consulate at Windsor, Ontario. Carr made the change because, he insisted, the increase was "desirable from a tactical point of view and quite justifiable on other grounds." Yet Carr was pessimistic about the bill's chances in the House. The committee would probably render a favorable verdict, but similar actions had not brought success in the past. Denby reported that Speaker Cannon was working against the measure and that most congressmen had no interest in it. "I should not regret to see the bill fail," Carr observed, "because I believe the sentiment will be stronger next year, and there may be a chance for a better bill then."[28]

As the Lodge bill was slowly winding its way through Congress, the reformers were mobilizing outside assistance. Congressman Robert Adams, by now acting chairman of the Foreign Affairs Committee, advised the National Board of Trade in January that it could help by sending delegates to talk with congressmen, personally obtaining their support. "Passing resolutions, gentlemen," Adams told them bluntly, "does not secure legislation." Shortly afterward, the New York Board of Trade and Transportation, a member of Harry Garfield's National Committee, called for a businessmen's convention to meet in Washington in March. Well over a hundred businessmen, representing some seventy commercial organizations, met in the capital at the New Willard Hotel on March 13. Among the delegates was the ubiquitous former Assistant Secretary of State Francis B. Loomis. The businessmen received advice and encouragement from Congressman Adams, Senator Lodge, Secretary Root, and even the president. Adams and the others implored them not to expect ideal legislation; the important thing, as Loomis later reported, was to secure "some sort of legislation which should recognize the necessity of reorganizing the consular service and making at least a definite, if small, step in the desired direction." As a body, the delegates called upon Speaker Cannon at the Capitol and persuaded him to bring the bill to the floor of the House for consideration.[29]

Adams had been awaiting this moment for a long time, and the next day he delivered the measure from the Foreign Affairs Committee, with a unanimous committee endorsement written by Carr and Denby. The Pennsylvania congressman asked his colleagues that he "be pardoned for expressing a little personal pleasure and satisfaction that after sixteen years of labor in and out of this honorable House, I have this morning the first opportunity to submit for its consideration on the floor, the consular reorganization bill."[30]

During its deliberations Adams's subcommittee had eliminated the provision allowing the transfer of consuls from one post to another in a given class without Senate approval of each new assignment. The Foreign Affairs Committee was certain, Adams explained to the House, "that the stricken portion would not meet the approbation of the country." More likely, it did not meet the approbation of the entire committee. With the objectionable section removed, the bill received the full committee's valuable unanimous support. The measure still retained the most important features, upon which future reforms could be based: a more up-to-date classification, compensation by salaries alone, and an inspection system. The House passed the bill five days after the committee's report, and Roosevelt signed it April 5. Denby considered Carr largely responsible for the bill's success, because of his patient and diligent work with the committee. Root agreed.[31]

Adams then concluded his legislative work for the session. He secured passage of the annual diplomatic and consular appropriations bill, which provided necessary funding for the reorganized service, principally in salaries. An important new provision gave consuls and diplomats travel expenses at the rate of five cents per mile for trips to and from their posts, and for other travel under orders of the secretary of state. This step eased the financial burdens for consuls and made the service even more attractive. The day after he had shepherded the vital provisions through the House, Adams killed himself with a revolver shot in the mouth. Heavy losses at stocks and bridge-whist probably prompted his suicide.[32]

After obtaining what he could by legislation, Root used an executive order to accomplish the remainder. To assist him, he summoned to Washington the five consular officers he considered the best in the service. He appointed these men and Carr to an advisory Consular Reorganization Board under instructions to make recommendations concerning the new inspection system, appointment and promotion in the consular corps, and related matters. Frank H. Mason, consul-general at Paris, presided over the group, which began its work on June 4.[33]

The board made a number of important recommendations. It divided the world into five consular inspection districts, each to be covered by an inspector who would investigate each office every two years. Other suggestions included appointment by examination and promotion by demonstrated efficiency, better use of the thirty-day instruction period, and the Americanization of the consular service. The board also emphasized export trade promotion as the consuls' primary function. "There still exists a widespread belief," the officers lamented, "that the principal if not the only duty of a consul is to certify invoices." While this task was, of course, still important, it "should be a secondary rather than a principal duty." The board's report suggested overhauling the service with an eye to closing many consulates, especially in Germany and Canada, where a large number of them existed primarily to certify invoices and perform other routine tasks. New consulates should be established to promote American trade and otherwise protect American interests. Illustrating its complaint, the board observed that some two-thirds of the United States' official representatives in South America received salaries of less than $1,000 annually.[34] It recommended that the United States should have there "a well-trained, well-paid corps of consuls working together systematically for the purpose of winning new markets." Times had indeed changed since another group of principal American consular officers, likewise meeting with the chief of the Consular Bureau, had convened in Paris in 1890 to spend days discussing invoice certification while ignoring export trade promotion.[35]

Armed with the board's recommendations, department officials prepared an executive order for Roosevelt's signature. Carr drafted two-thirds of the final product and Root the remainder. Root sent the final draft to Roosevelt on June 25, and two days later the president issued the order. It contained the two major provisions that the Foreign Relations Committee had struck from Lodge's bill almost six months earlier—appointment to the lower grades only after examination, and promotion on the basis of demonstrated efficiency.[36] The examination would be open only to individuals between the ages of 21 and 50. The order also created a Board of Examiners (consisting of the third assistant secretary of state, Consular Bureau Chief Carr, and the Civil Service Commission's chief examiner) to determine the scope and method of consular examinations. The order itself specified that the examinations should include a modern foreign language, "the natural, industrial and commercial resources and the commerce of the United States, especially with reference to the possibilities of increasing and extending the trade of the United States with foreign countries; political economy; elements of international, commercial, and maritime law." Before applicants could be eligible for appointment to a lower-grade consulate in countries where the United States exercised extraterritorial jurisdiction, they had to pass an additional examination dealing with the fundamental principles of law.[37]

Although the reformers had no intention of applying a strictly competitive system to the consular service, the order was heavily couched in civil service language. Root wanted to mobilize public sentiment behind the new system and believed that the civil service rhetoric was essential if he was to succeed in removing the consular corps from politics. The order explicitly disavowed political considerations in the selection process.[38]

Once the initial steps were taken, additional improvements in the consular service could come from within the State Department. Although theoretically the consuls were under the overall administrative direction of the third assistant secretary of state, Wilbur Carr had played a growing role in the reform effort since his 1902 promotion as chief of the Consular Bureau. Relatively free from routine and tedious work, he could use his abilities in helping design and build a new consular corps. Indeed, while attempting to direct Lodge's bill through the Foreign Affairs Committee in 1906, he wondered whether he should secure "some more lucrative employment which will also be less exacting and involve less expenditure of nervous energy." At least he could no longer complain that his work was "dwarfing to the mind."[39]

Carr continued to receive both the recognition he wanted and important duties in the department. In 1907 Root appointed him the department's chief clerk, a more remunerative and prestigious position than his bureau post. But Carr and the consular corps were not separated; Root merely shifted the Consular Bureau from the third assistant secretary's direction to the chief clerk's. Carr had thought that a major problem in achieving consular reform was the Consular Bureau's subordinate position. Now, for all practical purposes, it was subordinate only to him, and he could direct the future course of the service. Second Assistant Secretary Alvey Adee, Root, and Assistant Secretary Robert Bacon all wanted him to consider himself a fourth assistant secretary and be prepared to direct the department when the titled officers were absent. Carr was no doubt gratified by his new status but soon found it did not always extend outside the department. "Secretary Root's daughter was married at 4 o'clock," he disappointedly jotted into his diary late in 1907. "I was not invited although the Assistant Secretaries were, but it was only proper. I have no social relationships with the Roots while they have. Besides I have more than enough to do without social obligations."[40]

Having secured responsible duties and the respect of his

superiors, Carr continued his quest for a stimulating and useful vocation. His biographer contends that Carr's "ultimate desire was to have a career that would leave some record of service behind him," and her point has merit. During his adult life Carr was self-conscious about what he thought was an inferior education, and felt he had to compensate by unremitting work. Certainly he sought recognition and a "record of service." But more precisely, he wanted his record of service embodied in an institution that would not only reflect his own success while rendering a public service and stimulating him, but that would also provide opportunities for other competent and ambitious young men like himself. Only rarely was he consciously concerned with questions of broad policy unrelated to administration. He believed it more important, both for himself and his consuls, to be a loyal, nonpartisan, and useful subordinate and thereby make a successful career. Carr anticipated that a modern consular service, by rewarding hard work, ability, and loyalty to superiors, would systematize his own success formula and chart a course for others to follow.[41]

Carr was also intently bent on self-improvement. He filled notebooks with short, quotable maxims about work or success, many of them clipped from newspapers and magazines. Among them were: "Succeeded in Business but Failed as a Man"; "We Must Grow or Die"; "My System: Get the Thing Done"; "Be Ready"; and, so typical of Carr, "Duty Done, and Happiness are Inseparable." Occasionally, he would write out in longhand the Gettysburg Address, assorted proverbs, and other favorite quotations. His studying ranged far beyond his law-school courses, as one diary entry for 1897 demonstrates: "Wrote out a story of Christian charity inspired by Hoods Bridge of Sighs. Retired 3:00 a.m." Even in 1914, when he had been among the department's top officers for years, Carr drew up a plan for self-improvement that included exercise, concentration, systematic reading, and memory training.[42]

In building the new consular service, Carr was aware that changes would have to occur slowly. Like Elihu Root, he was a gradualist by temperament and did not feel obliged to accomplish everything at once. Among the many maxims he jotted down was: "If you gain only one inch a day, in a year you'll have gained three hundred and sixty-five inches. And if you gain an inch a day for awhile and hold it, you soon begin to gain a foot a day." Both Carr and Root knew that past efforts to correct defects in the consular corps had failed because they lacked public support, and both men took pains to avoid alienating public or congressional opinion by hasty action. The course of consular reorganization reflected their belief in the efficacy of gradual reform.[43]

ADMINISTERING THE NEW SYSTEM

By mid-1906 the crucial elements for a modern consular corps existed, thanks to both legislative and executive action. Congress had classified the service (generally according to the State Department's format), placed it on a salaried basis, provided for greater Americanization of the personnel, and created a corps of inspectors. Executive action had instituted the new efficiency records, appointment by examination, and an avowed intention to promote on the basis of demonstrated efficiency. Together these contributions gave the State Department the tools necessary to forge a modern consular service.

Roosevelt's executive order stipulated that applicants for consular appointments be tested on certain specific subjects, and it created a board of examiners to prepare a fuller list of appropriate regulations. The board issued its conclusions in December. Borrowing liberally from the report of a similar board that Root had convened a year earlier, it decided that in addition to the subjects specified in the executive order, the written examination would include: "American history, government, and institutions; political and commercial geography; arithmetic (as used in commercial statistics, tariff calculations, exchange, accounts, etc.); the modern history, since 1850, of Europe, Latin America, and the Far East, with particular attention to political, commercial, and economic tendencies." Counting equally with the written test would be an oral examination, designed to determine the applicant's business ability and personality. The candidates would be graded separately on the two tests and would have to attain a combined average of 80 percent to be considered eligible for appointment. The examining board would forward to the secretary of state a list of the successful candidates, who would remain on a list of eligibles for a maximum of two years, until they either withdrew their names or received appointments.[44]

The first examination under the new arrangement took place March 14 and 15, 1907. The board tested eighteen candidates and passed ten, and its handling of the examination greatly pleased even the frequently truculent National Business League. The department gave the event extensive publicity, both to attract good applicants in the future, and to dissuade poor ones. Another reason, Root told Albert Shaw, editor of the influential *Review of Reviews*, was that if the new system was strongly established by the end of the Roosevelt administration, no succeeding president could overturn it. "The more fully the change of method is understood by the people of the country," the secretary predicted, "the more certain it is to receive that kind of approval which will prevent anybody in the future from trying to backslide." Root sent to Shaw and other editors copies of the recent examination, the new regulations, a list of those applicants who had passed, and a list of the states that were below their share of representation in the consular service, as determined by their proportion of the nation's population. Before Root's publicity campaign, the department had regarded the test questions as confidential and had never published them.[45]

Later examinations did not always yield such a high percentage of eligibles, and Root was occasionally concerned that the testing procedure was being applied too rigorously. "You know," he once remarked to Carr after going through a pile of rejections, "these are supposed to be examinations for admission to the consular service, not for exclusion from the consular service." He cautioned Assistant Secretary Robert Bacon about appearing, in Bacon's own words, "too radical," and Bacon directed the board of examiners to follow a lenient policy in permitting reexaminations. "In this way," he reassured Root, "I hope to soothe the feelings of unsuccessful candidates without any real danger to the service." By the end of Root's secretaryship, the department had examined 171 applicants for the consular corps and passed 75.[46]

As demonstrated by one of Root's enclosures to the editors, the State Department was overseeing the appointment of men to the consular service on the basis of a quota system. When Roosevelt signed the consular bill in the spring of 1906, few southerners were in the service. Of the 274 principal consular officers in May 1906, only 9 came from the South, excluding the border states of Maryland, Kentucky, and Missouri. Virginia had a single representative—a $1,500 position at Guadeloupe, while Alabama, Arkansas, Mississippi, and South Carolina were all unrepresented. Senator Lodge's Massachusetts, on the other hand, had 16, with an average salary of $2,275.[47] Consequently, the executive order in June stipulated that when candidates of equal merit applied, appointments would be made to the service so as to obtain proportional representation among the states and territories.

The department's officers knew that such a sectional imbalance could not continue if the reform was to last. Unless the situation changed, the Democrats would overturn the new system as soon as they came to power. While supporting the Lodge bill early in 1906, Congressman Henry D. Flood of Virginia, a Democratic member of the Foreign Affairs Committee, spoke for many of his colleagues when he served notice that the South wanted adjustments made in the field foreign service. Carr drew up a list of the consuls according to the states from which they were appointed. He then established each state's "share" of the service, based on its percentage of the national population.[48]

The department made special efforts to recruit applicants from the southern states by means of what one officer called "a constant propaganda," directed particularly at southern colleges and southern senators, drawing attention to the new career opportunity. Root recalled years later: "I used constantly to send round 'Dear Senator, we want a man from Georgia, or Alabama, or Mississippi, for Consul. Cannot you find a good man who can pass the examination?' Very slowly we succeeded in getting them." By early 1911, sixty-three consuls had been appointed under the new system, thirty-one from the South and thirty-two from the North, and consular reform was gaining considerable bipartisan support.[49]

A potential obstacle to redressing the sectional imbalance lay in the availability of many more interested and qualified applicants from states already over-represented in the service. But the president's constitutional prerogatives in appointing diplomats and consuls, long an impediment to consular legislation, could now serve the department's interests. Because of the constitutional provision, the examination was not fully competitive; not everyone was allowed to take it. It was open only to those "designated" by the president. Since he naturally lacked the necessary information to decide whether or not an applicant should be designated, the State Department handled the matter. Qualified applicants from southern states were often given preference over persons with approximately the same qualifications from the North.[50]

Applicants sent the department information about themselves and recommendations from acquaintances and employers. They also were strongly urged to have their senators anoint their candidacy with an endorsement. The department was not playing old-style politics; the Senate had to confirm consular appointments and under senatorial courtesy would reject any that was unsavory to a colleague from the candidate's state. The new system faced enough difficulties without alienating the Senate. Also, by securing such endorsements, the department served notice that it respected senatorial prerogatives, while simultaneously co-opting the senators into working with the new procedure. Although it may have favored a more competitive system, the National Civil Service Reform League was satisfied by 1912 that after six years the new examination format had produced "marked improvement" in the quality of consular appointees.[51]

An integral part of reorganization was a new "Consular School." As the Consular Reorganization Board recognized, even if good men were appointed they still required training. Shortly after the second consular examination in 1907, the department began to make use of the previously farcical thirty-day instruction period. After receiving appointments, new consuls came to Washington for thirty days. They studied the consular regulations, became acquainted with the various documents they would use on the job, attended lectures by government officials—particularly from the Departments of State and C & L—and absorbed information about the country to which they were assigned. The new appointees were detailed for brief periods to the Bureau of Trade Relations and to C & L's Bureau of Manufactures. They served a similar detail in customshouses to learn about the proper handling of invoices. Inspector Alfred Gottschalk believed that the new school would be "the real foundation-stone of a Newer Service."[52]

There was considerable public discussion about training consuls and diplomats in the special courses cropping up at many universities around the country. George Washington University was busily boosting itself as a national institution, located in the nation's capital, whose graduates could stock the government service in Washington and overseas with a new breed of trained personnel. Perhaps for public relations purposes, Root gave verbal backing to national support for education, along the lines of the Morrill Plan, to train students in foreign commerce. He also supported the idea of government assistance for a single school to train candidates for the foreign service.[53]

But many universities were opposed to any government support or encouragement for a single institution, since they had their own projects. The initial planning for what later became the Harvard Business School, for instance, envisioned an institution to train persons for public service, including the foreign service. In 1909 the National Business League issued a pamphlet containing statements from eighteen college presidents, inveighing against any government school. The presidents maintained that their own institutions could supply the need, and the National Business League agreed.[54]

Although pleased at the growing interest in foreign relations that the furor both reflected and excited, and always willing to welcome new allies, the State Department did not intend to accept such education in lieu of its own examination and in-house training. Alvey Adee observed to Carr that given the limited number of vacancies in the foreign service, a foreign service college or even such a specialty as a college major "would in most cases ensure disappointment, instead of appointment," and he supported training at the department as "the only feasible plan." This was the procedure the department followed, notwithstanding Root's public encouragement to ambitious college presidents and commercial organizations.[55]

Although not so controversial as the examination system, other parts of the reform package were just as important. The tests could screen only candidates who came forward to take them. Competent and ambitious men in search of careers were not going to apply, or remain very long in the service should they apply and be selected, unless they believed that good work would result in promotion. Carr, Root, and others knew that promotions as well as initial appointments had to be taken out of politics. By providing improved salaries and a classification more in line with the consulates' real value to the department, Lodge's bill helped achieve a structure conducive to systematic promotion. Both the biennial inspections and evaluation of the consuls' commercial reports provided data for the efficiency records Root had established in 1905. [56]

But the department did not want young officers to be so jittery about negative comments on their records that they were afraid to exert themselves. Consular Bureau Chief Herbert Hengstler told one group of new consuls, "Every consular officer in the service must sooner or later, if he is any account at all, have some complaints against him." The State Department also instructed the principal officers to have their subordinates at the consulates prepare and submit reports to Washington, both to "stimulate the gathering of useful information of commercial, industrial, or political importance," and more especially to give junior officers "the opportunity to do independent work and so to make their abilities known to the Department."[57]

Carr and his assistants tried to promote or at least transfer a consul every two years. They would have liked to obtain legislation providing for appointment to grades or classes rather than to specific posts; consuls could then have been more easily transferred from one post to a similar or slightly better one within the same grade. Yet the new system could function without this provision.[58]

The primary consideration for promoting or transferring consuls was usually their language proficiency, except in the case of appointment to the oriental countries, for which the State Department was slowly developing a pool of student interpreters. Both in initial appointments and in reassignments, the department tried to consider a man's qualifications and aptitudes. As Root was fond of saying, "Not only do you ruin the peg, but you spoil the hole when you attempt to drive a square peg in a round hole." The flexible character of the selection process aided the efforts to place the right peg in the right hole. Because language and other requirements of the posts varied considerably, appointments did not have to be made in score order from the certified list.[59]

Essential to the successful operation of the classification and promotion systems was the inspector corps. Root believed that from an administrative point of view it was "the one thing indispensable for all other consular improvements." The permanent establishment of inspectors provided the department with crucial information about the consulates and their personnel, making possible for the first time a single consular system directed from Washington. Root had initially contemplated using the consuls-general to conduct more thorough investigations. But he decided that they had enough work at their own posts to keep them busy.[60] Also there was no guarantee that the consuls-general would be any more capable than the officers they were inspecting.

Shortly after the House passed the Lodge bill in March 1906, Carr visited the Post Office, War, and Navy departments to study their inspection forms and regulations. He drew up the inspection procedures and then helped Root select the men. The original list included Carr's former chief, Robert Chilton, Jr., but he preferred to remain at the Toronto consulate. In June the Consular Reorganization Board created five inspection districts: North America, South America, the Far East, Africa and the Middle East, and Europe. The board designated for each region a "Consul-General-at-Large," who received $5,000 plus travel and subsistence expenses. The first year, expenses for the five totaled $11,154.[61]

The inspectors' titles caused much discomfort for Alfred Gottschalk, who investigated consulates in the Africa and Middle East region. He complained in 1909 that "the title itself is incomprehensible to English people, whose only application of the term seems to be to criminals set free after a term of imprisonment," such as " 'he is now at large after being discharged from Durban jail.' " Unfortunately for Gottschalk, he had to carry the burdensome title for several more years, until his appointment as consul-general at Rio de Janeiro. The formal designation was not changed from "Consul-General-at-Large" to "Inspector" until 1924.[62]

Carr insisted on frank reports from his consuls-general-at-large about the consuls and their offices. He knew that some earlier "inspections" had given the department little useful data, and so he gave the inspectors detailed and lengthy forms on which to make their report for each consulate. The forms contained these and similar questions:

> Does the principal officer show familiarity with all the business of his office, or does he rely unduly upon the clerical force? Does he read and speak the language of the country? What other languages does he read and speak? Does he invariably report absences from his post in excess of forty-eight hours? What is his social and official standing in the community? Is he regularly at his office and attentive to his duties? Are his habits good? State the results of your inquiries fully and frankly. Is he suited to the work he has to do, or do you think he might be more efficient at another post, and, if so, what kind of post would you suggest? Is he married? Do the members of his family contribute to his standing and reputation in the community? Does he, in your opinion, utilize satisfactorily the opportunities which are offered in his district for writing useful and interesting consular reports and for promoting the development of American trade? If not, specify wherein he has failed and the instructions you have given him upon the subject.

As the last point indicates, information flowed both ways. As well as reporting on the consulates, the inspectors brought suggestions to the officers and attempted to instruct them in their duties. Evaluations assessed not only current performance but indicated too whether a particular officer had potential for a service career. The inspectors also brought to the consulates more than practical suggestions alone. Nelson Johnson, an inspector in the early 1920s, later recalled that he and his colleagues were to "carry from office to office something of the spirit of service that radiated from Carr," thus improving "the service for which we had dedicated our lives as Carr had dedicated his."[63]

As time passed, Carr supplemented the forms and initial orders with additional detailed instructions. When at all possible, the inspectors should talk with each member of the consulate's staff, "since this is the only way in which the Inspector can give a correct rating of the abilities of the various employees and of their personal qualifications, as well as their personal appearance." Inspectors were to report on such matters as the terms of the consulate's lease, when it expired, and when notice was required to terminate it; the amount of money necessary for clerk hire; the items of furniture needed, and whether these should be obtained locally or from the United States. Although each post was different, the department worked to obtain standardized office equipment so that when a consul was transferred he would automatically be well acquainted with his new workshop. Like the officers themselves, the consulates were also beginning to resemble interchangeable parts in a large mechanism.[64]

The inspection procedure made possible a gradual reformation of the service without raising the sticky question of recalling consuls to take an examination. Inefficient officers were retired and their places taken by more competent men. The process took time, principally because of the abundance of inefficient consuls. After inspecting for more than a year, Charles Dickinson sadly described the plethora of political hacks he had encountered. "You cannot know the real situation in Washington," he wrote Carr. "A man may be utterly inefficient and yet make correct and regular quarterly returns. Many of these men have never done any systematic work, have had no business training or success, or are broken in health, and ought to be pensioned and make way for live, ambitious, resourceful and energetic men." To ease the pain for the less efficient, particularly those with politically powerful friends, the inspectors recommended their transfer to quieter posts that were less vital to America's export trade. Alfred Gottschalk suggested that the consul at Algiers be shifted to some English-speaking post where there was little work to do. The French were promoting agricultural development in Algeria, and Gottschalk believed that "an active American Consul could have done much in the way of helping our trade in irrigating machinery, windmills, agricultural implements, etc.—but all this has escaped him. He is still a New Jersey sheriff, and has never learnt to be a Consul." Dickinson gently recommended to the consul at Jerusalem that his archaeological scholarship did not offset his lack of ability for promoting trade and urged him to accept a less important post elsewhere—a suggestion that met Carr's strong approval. The system served to bring both good and poor consuls to the department's attention, with healthy results. It was, as Dickinson wrote fellow inspector Horace L. Washington, "A splendid thing for the good man in the service, but it is hot irons for the other fellows."[65]

The inspectors also gave the department insights into the perspective of the men in the field. "Incomprehensible as it may seem to you," Dickinson informed Carr, "I have found no office where there is not a grievance of some sort against the Department." Included among the consuls' complaints as relayed by Dickinson were "the unsympathetic tone of the Department's dispatches, the lack of appreciation of the Consul's numerous troubles, the refusal to grant further allowances for clerk hire when all that Congress has appropriated had already been allowed . . . the feeling that promotions are dictated by personal likes and dislikes, or political influence, etc., etc., etc." Both Carr and Consular Bureau Chief Herbert Hengstler welcomed suggestions from the field, and the inspectors formed an important channel of two-way communication. "I wish every officer would write me as frankly as you have," Carr thanked Dickinson, "because it would enable us in the Department to get the point of view of the Consuls and thus be able to eliminate most of the dissatisfaction from the service." One immediate result was the adoption in the department's correspondence of what Carr termed "a little more sympathetic" tone.[66]

The inspectors also suggested that certain offices could be relocated or closed and new ones established elsewhere. In 1907, armed with data from the inspectors, Carr prepared a bill making adjustments in the classification "to meet existing commercial conditions." Root assured Congress that the adjustments would not result in any appropriations increases. The department recommended that twenty-eight offices be closed (thirteen in Europe, nine in Canada, one in Mexico, three in the Caribbean area, and the offices at the Falkland Islands and St. Helena) and that seventeen new ones be opened (four in the Middle East and North Africa, three in the Far East, five in Mexico and Central America, two in India, and one each in British Columbia, Chile, and Hungary). The adjustments were part of the continuing emphasis on export promotion and were a response to criticism, including that from the Consular Reorganization Board, that the structure of the service had to be altered to help capture markets in the non-European world. Congress complied, and the adjustments were made. The State Department required legislative approval only to create a new office or to provide new salaries. The president could and did decline to appoint consuls where the department recommended terminating the office.[67]

The department's greater ability to reshape the service by creating, closing, or shifting consulates had an additional benefit. By closing consulates, it could sometimes get rid of inefficient officers who had strong political backing. When Nicholas Murray Butler, president of Columbia University, sent Root a list of complaints about the service, the secretary acknowledged continuing defects and revealed some of his strategy. "What the memorandum says about the Consul at Dusseldorf is true," Root told Butler. "I could have had the finest fight imaginable on hand by reason of removing him, and probably have imperiled my whole consular reorganization. I shall get rid of him very soon without any fight at all, for I am about recommending that the consulate at that place be abandoned."[68]

The growing standardization of the service included a gradual Americanization of its personnel. The department for many years had been anxious to replace foreigners with United States citizens. At the 1890 conclave in Paris, the consular officers had also advocated this policy. They expected that when Americans returned home from serving in Europe, they would bring back to the United States valuable industrial secrets. As time passed and trade promotion became the consuls' primary responsibility, the problem became one of securing men who would push American products and whose loyalty was unquestioned. Elihu Root assured one correspondent that this view was not based "on any spread-eagle or sentimental ground, but upon practical business considerations" relating to "the extension of American trade." By staffing the consulates and even the consular agencies with such subordinates, the government would free the principal officers from time-consuming routine tasks and also train younger men in consular work. Accordingly, the 1906 reorganization act contained a provision requiring that clerkships with annual salaries of $1,000 or more be filled by American citizens.[69]

Money was, of course, one of the major problems in Americanizing the service. It was generally much cheaper to obtain the services of foreign assistants than to pay Americans. The principal officer could frequently supplement his subordinates' small salaries with unofficial fees that came his way, but the department wanted all fees turned in to the Treasury and finally secured the necessary legislation in the 1906 Lodge bill. To make up for this lost source of income, Congress appropriated an additional $105,000 for clerk hire and increased the amount in subsequent years. By early 1909, about 85 percent of the minor officials receiving more than $800 annually were American citizens. In 1908 Congress granted the State Department more flexibility when it began providing the total amount of money for clerk hire as a lump-sum appropriation, rather than designating an amount for each post. The department could now employ American clerks where it considered them most essential.[70]

Another major obstacle to Americanization of the service was also disappearing, as a result of the improved job security for new consuls. For more than forty years, the department had regularly received appropriations for thirteen "consular clerks," who were appointed by examination, were salaried and tenured, and could be sent anywhere the needs of the service required. Not only was this number insufficient, but the clerks usually declined promotion to the highly uncertain position of consul. This handful of men with the most qualifications and experience in the service thus remained at the lowest level. But with the extension of greater security to the whole service after 1906, more of the consular clerks were willing to accept promotion, and the State Department worked to increase their number. By 1912 there were thirty of them, then known as "consular assistants," who could be assigned to consulates or to the department as needed, and simultaneously receive valuable training for their future service careers. Their examinations covered the same subjects as the regular consular tests, but they were graded more leniently. The consular assistants did not have to take a second examination before promotion as consul. Early in 1913 the department secured appropriations for a total of forty such officers. [71]

Another group that came to fill subordinate positions was the student interpreter corps. It was particularly difficult to Americanize the posts in the Far East and Middle East because of the need for employees who spoke the difficult oriental languages. Secretary John Hay had requested student interpreters in 1900, and Third Assistant Secretary Cridler informed Senator A. G. Foster about the advantages of replacing foreign interpreters with "our own citizens who would have a personal interest and pride no foreigner could be expected to feel in the performance of this important duty." In 1902 Congress provided for ten such officers in China. Although Hay established a board to recommend the appropriate selection process, it was apparently not until 1906 that the department finally formulated rules for the student interpreters. The corps was expanded to Japan in 1906 and to Turkey in 1909. Applicants had to be unmarried, between the ages of nineteen and twenty-six, and pass a rigorous entrance examination. To prevent the students from seeking employment elsewhere as soon as they received their language training, they were obliged to sign an agreement to continue in the service as long as they might be needed, up to ten years. [72]

Americanization, whether by consular clerks, student interpreters, or other means, was not going to occur overnight. In 1908 Third Assistant Secretary Huntington Wilson explained to Consul-General Willard Straight at Mukden that the "question of supplying American assistants is difficult just now because we do not wish to stock the service with men not ultimately to be of it and we do not wish to turn the students loose before they get a decent start in the language. It is a hopeless problem but it will soon work itself out as our present crop of students matures." More progress was nevertheless taking place in the nonoriental world. In 1909 Consul James Dunning painted a rosy picture of his consulate at Milan for the National Board of Trade. Only a few years before, his office had been staffed by one American and one foreigner. But by early 1909, four of the six employees were Americans, three of the six had college training, all spoke at least three languages, one four, and another five.[73]

   The improved mobility and flexibility of the reorganized service was by no means confined to overseas operations. Reformers had long suggested greater movement of personnel between the State Department and the consulates, and Gaillard Hunt's bill had even provided that department clerks could be transferred to the consular corps without examination. Although Root and Carr were unwilling to allow clerks to bypass the test, they did believe that efficient bureau chiefs should be able to look forward to promotion into the consular service. According to the executive order they drafted for Roosevelt, department officials receiving a salary of $2,000 or more could be transferred without examination to the consular corps in any grade above the two lowest classes. "For the good of the service as well as the efficiency of the Department," Carr explained to a skeptical A. A. Burnham, "there should be as much interchange as practicable between the [field] foreign service and the Department of State and vice versa." In this fashion, Chief Clerk Charles Denby and Assistant Solicitor Henry Van Dyne both entered the consular branch in 1907. The department's geographic divisions, initiated the same year, also promoted the interchange, as consuls and diplomats came from the field to staff these offices.[74]

   A related innovation provided yet another linkage—this one between the consuls and American businessmen. In January 1907, the capable American consul at Birmingham, Albert Halstead, informed the Consular Bureau about a British plan to bring their own officials home to visit businessmen and become acquainted firsthand with their needs. Seven months later, Halstead recommended adoption of the British plan, explaining it would enable American consuls to discuss foreign commerce with exporting manufacturers and acquire a better knowledge of industrial development in the United States. They could also give manufacturers advice more effectively than through the published reports. Carr evidently liked the suggestion, for he soon proposed a version of it to Secretary Root. Several consuls were already in the habit of using some of their home leave to visit manufacturers, with appreciable results.

Above: Gaillard Hunt, 1910
Below: Harry Garfield
Courtesy of the
Library of Congress

Frederic Emory, 1902
From World's Work

Wilbur Carr, 1906
*Courtesy of the
Library of Congress*

Carr obtained Root's permission to make such visits mandatory and even to pay the consuls' traveling expenses in certain cases. [75]

In October 1907, less than a month after Carr secured Root's approval for the program, a financial panic struck the country. Although not nearly so severe as the 1893 panic and deep depression during the 1890s, the panic of 1907 and subsequent depression dealt the economy a sharp blow. [76]

The prevailing economic climate, which prompted some Americans to wonder if they were in for more of the economic and social upheavals of the previous decade, may have added impetus to Carr's new program. One anxious official was Consul-General Edward Ozmun in Constantinople, who had served on Root's Consular Reorganization Board the year before. In a lengthy dispatch, Ozmun expressed the frustration common to foreign affairs officials, who were trying to impress upon American manufacturers the need to cultivate foreign markets and thereby avoid economic and social disaster. "Having no great markets all over the world," Ozmun complained bitterly,

> except in the case of a comparatively few articles, we have either a feast or a famine. A feast during good times, when disregarding the plain teachings of the fundamental principles of economics, we loudly proclaim our greatness and the altitude of our commercial superiority. We rivet our eyes to the exclusion of all else on our internal affairs and, with our eggs all in one basket, fall down and worship the fickle idol of a home market. . . . We have a famine, the like of which has no parallel in any other commercial country, when our home markets fail. Our mills close, thousands are unemployed, Coxey's armies march through the country and only the free soup kitchens show great activity.

Ozmun suggested that the department bring consuls home to confer with American manufacturers as a means of increasing exports—a proposal similar to the program recently launched by Carr and Root. "I have no doubt," Ozmun assured his superiors in Washington, "that by a carefully conducted propaganda of this sort, directed by the Department, under the auspices of our Chambers of Commerce, our export trade could be enormously increased. . . . It would be in other ways a splendid work for the future, for by a great trade extension we avoid the gravest perils of panics and hard times." Root was impressed with what he called Ozmun's "valuable suggestions" and sent a copy of the communication to the Secretary of Commerce and Labor.[77]

Within the week, Root expressed his conviction to Congress that diplomats and consuls should keep in close touch not only with political and commercial subjects abroad, but also with "commercial and industrial development at home." Word of the new policy traveled quickly among businessmen, and the president of the Chattanooga Manufacturers Association was soon praising the "movement" for sending consular officers to visit the principal manufacturing centers. Sounding a recurring theme, he informed Root that "ignorance is one of the chief obstacles to the extension of Foreign trade, especially among our smaller manufacturers." That same month, the governor of Hawaii and the secretary of the Honolulu Chamber of Commerce dropped by the department, asking that consular officers on their way to and from the Far East be instructed to disembark at Honolulu and visit the chamber of commerce. Carr urged consuls stationed in the Far East to comply, judiciously adding that of course the department could not pay for expenses incurred in the process. Longer itineraries became more feasible in May 1908, when Carr secured from the comptroller of the Treasury an opinion permitting payment of salaries to consuls temporarily on duty in the United States while visiting manufacturers.[78] Together with the beginnings of a regular transportation allowance two years before, the comptroller's ruling would be a great help to the department in its efforts to bring the consuls into regular contact with American businessmen.

The first beneficiary of the decision was Julius Lay, consul-general at Capetown, who wished to spend two weeks after the expiration of his leave visiting agricultural implement manufacturing centers to discuss trade opportunities in South Africa. Consular Bureau Chief Hengstler labeled it "an excellent opportunity for these exporters to get in touch with conditions in South Africa," and Carr agreed. Lay's tour, extended from two weeks to six, was a great success. The consul-general demonstrated to American manufacturers the differences between the kind of plow sold by Americans in

South Africa and the German model, and how the differences affected the market for American plows. He even found certain implements manufactured in the United States that he thought would find a good market in South Africa but were unknown there. [79]

Lay received a warm welcome from the American manufacturers he visited, which he attributed to the depression's "highly desirable result of compelling our exporting interests to weigh seriously the advantages of the foreign market." Like some of his colleagues, Lay had been frustrated by the slight chance "of permanently interesting American business men in the export trade while domestic business continued so prosperous as to tax their entire productive capacities." But after the depression had shown the dangers of overreliance on the domestic market, Lay could gladly report that American manufacturers "see as never before how vital it is to command regular outlets for their products abroad."[80]

With growing frequency, the department sent consuls to confer with their natural constituency—members of small or medium-sized firms that often lacked large international sales forces. Consuls usually tried to avoid the banquet circuit in favor of more personal contacts, and the emphasis was on question-and-answer working sessions with a company's administrative officers or with a manageable number of representatives from different firms. In time, publication of the itineraries and home addresses of the consuls in the daily consular reports enabled interested businessmen to get in touch with them. Although the benefits were reciprocal, the department and consuls considered the arrangement chiefly a means to dispense important commercial information and arouse greater interest in foreign markets. An officer of the Pittsburgh Chamber of Commerce praised the new procedure as "one of the best things ever started for business men. . . . We have been somewhat asleep regarding manufactured articles, and we could do a great deal more." Another advantage, of course, was that Carr's consular corps could increase its utility in the eyes of businessmen as a service that merited their support. [81]

After many years of effort, reformers finally secured enabling legislation and a supplementary executive order, and the long-awaited improvement of the consular service began. The result was

an organization that would, as Wilbur Carr hoped, "be of real benefit to American commercial interests." The consular corps was now
truly a system, dependent upon the effective functioning of several
integrally related parts. It was no longer simply a collection of individual offices with few links to other offices or to the State Department. When consuls began conferring systematically with American
manufacturers, they formed yet another linkage—between what
Carr once called "purchasing centers abroad and producing centers
at home." By 1911 he could joyfully point to a development that he
considered perhaps the most important of all: the gradual emergence of a greater "spirit of loyalty and energy in behalf of the
country's interests and the good name of the service than has ever
been known before, [which] will compare favorably with any similar
organization in the world. Advancement upon merit is not a theory,
but a fact, and the results show the wisdom of it."[82] Loyalty, energy,
the nation's interests, advancement by merit—Carr was realizing
his ultimate desire for a consular service that embodied his own
most cherished values.

6 DIPLOMATIC AND DEPARTMENTAL REFORMS, 1905–1908

As Elihu Root was mapping out strategy for consular reorganization in the fall of 1905, other portions of the foreign service also received his attention. James Garfield observed happily that Root was "shaking the old State Department from stem to stern," and it was a treatment that applied to all three branches of the service.[1]

DIPLOMATIC REORGANIZATION

If consular reform was difficult, reshaping the diplomatic service was almost impossible. The combination of low salaries and heavy social and financial obligations restricted diplomatic appointments to men of independent means. Many of the secretaries of embassy and legation serving in mid-1905 possessed little more than ample funds, social polish, and good political connections. William M. Collier, the American minister to Madrid, could have been talking about any number of subordinate diplomatic officers when he described his secretary of legation for Root: "He is good-looking, thoroughly gentlemanly, affable, likes Madrid and Madrilenas, is popular and lives handsomely. His faults, which are not the worst in the world, are the result of his having too much money to make hard work a necessity for him." He also did not read Spanish.[2]

The pace of work in many missions was not very heavy. Collier's affable secretary regularly began his day's work at 11:00 or 11:15 A.M. and often took afternoons off. Future Undersecretary of State Henry Fletcher, then a secretary of legation, complained from Lisbon that "the *work* of the Legation is scarcely worthy of the name"—at a time when he was temporarily in charge. Even when

Fletcher was at Peking, which he called a "busy" post, "in the midst of things diplomatically," he could handle the work of both first and second secretary of legation and play bridge almost every day.[3]

As many foreign affairs officials knew, the principal impediment to diplomatic reform was the relatively abstract nature of diplomatic duties. Henry White had warned Senator John Morgan in 1894 that the public knew and cared little about the diplomatic corps, and the situation remained the same even after World War I. While the consuls had highly visible and easily understandable tasks, diplomacy's special responsibility was rather vague. In 1910 Congressman Champ Clark of Missouri, who was almost to win the Democratic presidential nomination two years later, proposed "to abolish this diplomatic corps and take the money they squander and give it to these consuls, and then there would be some sense in it."[4] For several more decades there would linger the stereotype of a diplomatic service staffed by rich young men in striped pants languidly drinking tea.

Reform in the diplomatic corps trailed consular and departmental reorganization for other reasons also. As improved communication and transportation facilities conquered space and time, diplomatic policy emanated increasingly from the world's foreign offices and less from the missions. This trend made improvement of the State Department more imperative and that of the diplomatic branch less so. Moreover, some officials of the foreign service shared the disdain with which others viewed diplomats and their duties. Although Gaillard Hunt had played a small part in framing the Jones bill of 1894, which had covered all three branches, he considered diplomatic officers "an inferior set" in all nations. "Diplomacy to them is 'the art of tying one's cravat,' " he wrote Harry Garfield, "and their duties hardly rise above that." Even some younger diplomats themselves were wary of reforms that might bring a different class of men into the service. Henry Fletcher preferred to see the service "poorly paid than have a lot of cheap sports of the country prize speller type get in."[5] Such emotions would hamper diplomatic reform for many years and would almost wreck the eventual amalgamation of the diplomatic and consular services in the 1920s.

Still another obstacle was the practice, buttressed by tradition, of rewarding political or personal friends of the president with top diplomatic appointments. A number of United States ambassadors are still political appointees today, but beneath them and beneath the chief departmental officials is a professional substructure of career officers to supply essential expertise and continuity. Root's tenure as secretary of state witnessed a significant beginning of this substructure.

On November 10, 1905, Roosevelt issued two executive orders given him by Root. One, as noted above, extended the provisions of Cleveland's 1895 consular order. The other established, for the first time, an examination for prospective secretaries of embassy or legation. The order served the same function for the diplomatic branch as Cleveland's had served for the consular, and many of the provisions were similar. The top positions—ministers and ambassadors—were not covered. The format was a "pass" examination; the president would appoint a man to a specific rank and post, and send him to the department for testing. It was entirely a departmental project, with no participation by the Civil Service Commission. Root's simultaneous departmental order established an examining board, consisting of Second Assistant Secretary Alvey Adee, State Department Solicitor James B. Scott, and Diplomatic Bureau Chief Sydney Smith. Unlike the old consular test, however, the examination would contain both oral and written portions, and would cover international law and diplomatic usage, as well as modern languages. Candidates had to be between twenty-one and fifty years old and obtain an average score of 80 percent on the oral and written portions.[6]

Root saw the rudimentary examination as a necessary first step in the gradual development of an efficient diplomatic service, and he expected that it would be strengthened in the future. Like Cleveland's consular examination, the first diplomatic testing procedure was an advance in itself and paved the way for further improvements. John V. A. MacMurray, who began a distinguished diplomatic career in 1907, squeaked through what he termed "a very fair but searching examination" administered by Scott. When a Republican administration that was also sympathetic to foreign service reform succeeded Roosevelt's in 1909, Root's examination procedure provided a base for it to build upon.[7]

Although the crucial consular service reclassification was part of a package that required years to push through Congress, Root accomplished an improved alignment in the diplomatic corps almost without notice. Shortly after taking charge of the department, he became convinced that the diplomatic salary list was "devoid of method" and had no relation to the relative importance of the various missions. Root submitted and Congress approved a salary table that graded both secretarial and the top positions at embassies and legations according to the mission's importance. As with his classification of the consulates, Root expected to develop a system of promotion and easy transferability between the missions.[8]

On the same day he instituted an efficiency record for the consuls, Root established one for subordinate diplomatic officials. In a circular instruction to the principal officers, he requested an immediate report on the "ability, fidelity to duty, and efficiency of each subordinate officer in the mission," and asked that additional reports be sent at the end of every calendar year. Without inspectors or commercial reports as sources of information, the department had to rely heavily on the evaluations of ambassadors and ministers. Root was consequently annoyed when the chiefs of mission failed to take the 1905 circular seriously, submitting perfunctory reports of little or no value. Prodding them with a second circular, he reminded them that the efficiency records were essential for the department to determine a secretary's "qualifications for promotion, adaptability for particular transfers, fitness for special responsibilities or kinds of work; or in discovering those who are not useful members of the service." Since the country's ranking diplomats had proved themselves unable to cope with the general language of the first order, the secretary enclosed a form for their guidance. The department desired information about the diplomats' health, family affairs, social position, "Americanism," habits (specifically), manner of spending leisure time, personality (subdivided into twelve parts), "particular forte," church, foreign language skills, future promotions (why or why not), chancery work, and capability of discharging duties as chief of mission.[9] As consuls the department wanted men who were hard workers and capable businessmen, with good standing in their assigned communities. But for diplomats, the requisite traits included more ascriptive qualities that would enable them to mix well with the upper classes in the host country and with the diplomatic representatives of other nations.

The annual diplomatic and consular appropriations bill passed in 1906 contained new provisions that became regular fixtures in the diplomatic corps. Diplomats as well as consuls were given funds for transportation to and from their posts, and for additional travel under the orders of the secretary of state, at the rate of five cents per mile. Also for the first time, the bill appropriated a separate amount ($65,000) for clerk hire at the embassies and legations, stipulating that all clerks hired in the future be American citizens. Until that time it had been necessary to pay clerical salaries from the general fund for diplomatic contingent expenses, which also had to cover stationery, books, seals, flags, postage, telegrams, messenger service, furniture, and rent. Two years later, Congress increased the appropriation for contingent expenses by $100,000, to $325,000. The department used the money to obtain better quarters to house some of the missions.[10]

Since the 1890s, the number of diplomatic secretaries had grown steadily, from twenty-four in 1898 to forty-eight in 1905. Root succeeded in obtaining a dozen more in 1908, bringing the number to sixty. But more important, after 1905 the service began to evolve more systematically. The new examination procedure, the classification, and the efficiency reports were all more rudimentary than their counterparts in the consular service. Just as the diplomatic examination was given individually, so too were the few words of advice that passed for instruction; new diplomatic secretaries did not enjoy the equivalent of the thirty-day consular school. Nor did the diplomats during Root's tenure have the benefit of a Wilbur Carr to supervise the administration of the service.[11] Root's reforms were nevertheless an essential and typically gradual first step, providing a basis for additional changes in the future. The diplomatic corps also benefited greatly from improvements in the State Department.

DEPARTMENTAL REFORMS

Shortly after Root took over the department in 1905, he found the organization inadequate for America's growing activity in the world. "You can not have three billions of foreign trade without having business for your State Department," Root informed Congress. The department's work was burgeoning because more Americans were traveling and living abroad, because foreign trade and investment were increasing, and because political questions connected chiefly with these matters were growing.[12]

Like many other changes in the foreign service, reforms in the State Department resulted from a conjunction between conditions that seemed to call for change and a strategically placed, ambitious person to propose or administer a new system. Gaillard Hunt proposed consular reorganization and engineered much of the business support that eventually helped bring essential legislation in 1906. Frederic Emory effected significant changes in his department offices. Wilbur Carr contributed by working with Congress and administering the reorganizing consular service. The fourth major reformer-bureaucrat, whose principal legacy was the modernization of the State Department's basic structure, arrived at the department as third assistant secretary of state in July 1906.

Francis Mairs Huntington Wilson (known then simply as Huntington Wilson) was from a well-to-do Chicago family. He left Yale in 1896 at the age of twenty-one, with a private income of approximately $10,000 per year, to join the diplomatic service. His father had at one time been an active Republican politician in Illinois, and through his influence and the aid of the Illinois senators, Wilson received an appointment in 1897 as second secretary of the legation at Tokyo.[13]

In time Wilson became restive, as he remained in Tokyo year after year. He was made first secretary in 1900, and his work was competent and thorough; Minister Lloyd Griscom later recalled how Wilson "had every detail of Legation business at his finger tips." But he was also enormously ambitious for promotion, either to another diplomatic post or to Washington. Continued service in Japan would not help him realize his goals, and Wilson repeatedly attempted to secure a transfer. He finally dispatched his beautiful and charming wife to Washington for a personal appeal to her friend, Secretary of War William Howard Taft. When Lucy Wilson called at the State, War, and Navy Building, the portly Taft took her arm and escorted her down the hall to see the new secretary of state. Elihu Root preferred not to receive her, but Taft pulled her in anyway. Root had an eye for feminine beauty and, according to Taft's aide, when he saw "the Juno-like face of Mrs. Wilson and watched her sweep across the room like a long-limbed Atalanta, his eyes began to waver." Root shooed everyone else from the office and closed the door.[14] Soon afterward, early in 1906, Root appointed Lucy Wilson's husband as third assistant secretary of state. After nine years, Huntington Wilson was finally out of Tokyo.

The new third assistant secretary was an interesting and complex personality. John Bassett Moore, certainly one of the most competent and sensible officials ever to grace the State Department, once commented that he had "always felt an attachment for Wilson and appreciated his good qualities, among which were fidelity and a strong sense of duty." Conscientious, a hard worker, and an innovator, Wilson made invaluable contributions to the foreign service. In his own words, he was a "nervously constituted person" with a delicate digestion. He was also peevish, egotistical, extremely sensitive, suspicious, and intensely preoccupied with control and self-control. "I really try to exercise self-control," Wilson wrote in 1904. "I *dispise* [sic] the lack of it. I admire it in these Orientals. I *will* have it, nerves or no nerves,—disposition or no disposition." He was fascinated with order and system, chiefly as a reflection of his preoccupation with controlling his immediate environment. In his memoirs, Wilson related how every morning a servant would awaken him, bringing coffee on a tray with a single cigarette and a box of matches, with a match extended half-way "to spare me unnecessary exertion." (Wilson was in his mid-thirties at the time.) "To compensate," he explained, "I did gentle calesthenics." Unfortunately, perhaps, these are left to the reader's imagination.[15]

As third assistant secretary, Wilson technically had charge of the consular service and was therefore chairman of the Consular Board of Examiners established by the June executive order. But Wilson found in charge of the consular branch an energetic young man who resented the intrusion of a secretary of legation five years his junior. Wilbur Carr considered his new colleague effeminate, undignified, unfamiliar with many of the questions on the consular

examination, and "too much of a clerk." After reviewing a number
of matters with Wilson one evening, Carr complained to his diary of
having "to coach him on practically everything." Principally to escape this intolerable situation, Carr accepted the chief clerkship in
the spring of 1907, succeeding Charles Denby. He considered his
current work more agreeable and more significant, and he wanted to
complete the consular reorganization, but the chief clerkship did
carry higher pay and prestige. More important, he would no longer
have to feel he was doing Wilson's work for him while watching the
third assistant secretary receive the credit. Yet Carr retained administrative supervision over his consular service after he became
chief clerk. Root informed him that he was to "boss the consular
service instead of bossing Mr. Wilson." Wilson himself had
suggested the switch, since he was to take charge of a fledgling Far
Eastern division within the department—part of his own contribution to foreign service reorganization.[16]

Wilson brought to the department a strong desire for foreign
service reform and had already thought about revamping the
Washington headquarters. In August 1905, while fortified with a
few beers, he had penned an article on reorganization, which a
magazine published a few months later. The essay stressed the importance of mobility and transferability in the service and advocated
that new diplomats and consuls serve at least a year in the department before being sent to their posts. Once in the field, suggested
the officer who was beginning a ninth year at his first station, they
should be transferred frequently, and some should be brought back
to the State Department for a tour of duty there. This arrangement
would require the department and the branches of the field service
to have corresponding classifications.[17] Wilson did not advocate the
still-radical step of merging the diplomatic and consular services;
enabling legislation for that action would not appear for many more
years. He was proposing instead that the department be staffed
partly by men from each of the field branches, who would return to
their own branch after their Washington assignments.[18]

The article was only a preliminary sketch of Wilson's comprehensive reorganization scheme for the entire State Department.
He worked on the proposal during the summer of 1906 and in Oc-

tober submitted it for Secretary Root's approval. While it made a number of innovative recommendations, its most important and valuable suggestion was for the apportionment of the department's work into geographic divisions, to be staffed by officers from the field.[19]

As the department's business had grown, the lack of specialization had increasingly hampered its operations. The only officers having regular input into nonadministrative policy decisions were the secretary and the three assistant secretaries. In a single day, any one of them might have to deal unassisted with separate issues involving America's relations with Europe, the Far East, and Latin America. A layer of geographic divisions beneath the assistant secretaries would create a system of specialization like that found in other foreign offices. It would also enable men from the field to bring their knowledge about different parts of the world, and their energy, into the department. As Wilson later told a congressional committee, the advantage of such a system lay in having enough experts in the department "so that nothing can be overlooked in any part of the world that can help America." The geographic divisions would thus make for a more mobile interchange between the department and the field service, with advantages to both.[20]

Wilson's plan divided the world into four geographic units and eliminated the Diplomatic and Consular bureaus. He placed Diplomatic Bureau Chief Sydney Smith in charge of one of the geographic divisions, while he elevated Carr to fourth assistant secretary, in charge of administration. Each geographic bureau had a consular subdivision and a diplomatic subdivision, reflecting a farsighted attempt to bridge the gap between the diplomatic and consular services.[21] "In these days of commercial diplomacy," Wilson argued, "the importance of the political-geographic division overtops that of the technical division between the consular and diplomatic branches of the service." Even the diplomatic and consular correspondence relating to administration was to be filed in the appropriate geographic division. The four diplomatic subdivisions were to be the responsibility of the second assistant secretary of state, while the third assistant secretary would have charge of the four consular subdivisions. With his fetish for symmetry and detail, Wilson wanted the four consular subdivisions in separate rooms, along one side of a corridor, with the supervising assistant secretary's room "precisely" in the middle. The other side of the corridor would be a mirror-image formed by the diplomatic subdivisions.[22]

In its attempt to correct an unsatisfactory situation, however, Wilson's plan was too specialized. Much important correspondence, particularly in the Consular Bureau, was administrative and often did not fall into a particular geographic niche. Although Wilson expected some offices to keep their own correspondence, he overlooked the necessity for the Diplomatic and Consular bureaus to remain independent. Carr initially opposed the scheme because of "the loss of concentrated control of the consular service by dividing the administrative jurisdiction between several men." Wilson made modifications, and Carr threw his support behind the plan, thinking that it would now distribute the workload more equally and "insure proper treatment of the larger questions."[23]

Elihu Root was skeptical. Even more than Carr, he was a firm believer in concentrated control, and he was often reluctant to delegate authority. (Wilson once dryly remarked that Root's idea of Heaven was to stand atop a hill, surrounded by stenographers.) Root was also unhappy with his new third assistant secretary; he was soon regretting the appointment and wishing he had named Carr instead.[24] But the department's business was increasing rapidly, and even the energetic secretary and his top assistants could not continue in the old manner. Five months after receiving Wilson's proposal, in March 1907, Root reluctantly agreed to establish a single small geographic division as an experiment.

America's relations with the Far East lent themselves particularly well to the establishment of a specialized bureau in the State Department. The 1890s depression had prompted some Americans to envision the China market as an answer to their country's economic and social dilemmas. When China faced potential dismemberment at the hands of the European powers and Japan late in the nineteenth century, United States concern resulted in the open door notes of 1899 and 1900. As early as 1894, John Russell Young, former minister to China, had contended that a Far Eastern division in the State Department would be "of inestimable value" to America's "El Dorado empire on the Pacific." Actual or potential encroachments on Chinese territory by the powers continued to make specialized attention necessary, particularly in light of deteriorating American-Japanese relations after 1905. Moreover, not all the threats to the open door were coming from outside the Middle Kingdom; a new menace arose with China's growing resistance to the West. Drawing great strength from that resistance, the Chinese revolution was the first of many in the twentieth century to preoccupy policy makers in Washington and compel their close attention to internal developments. For these reasons, America's Far Eastern relations had a combined importance and complexity unmatched elsewhere. Perhaps because Huntington Wilson was the most ardent advocate of the new system and also had spent nine years in Tokyo, in the spring of 1907 Root placed him in charge of an informal Far Eastern bureau. Wilson was so pleased that he even recommended that supervision of the consular service be given to Chief Clerk Carr.[25]

The new office was strictly a departmental creation, and the State Department had to find the means of staffing and funding it. In reply to Wilson's inquiry, the comptroller of the Treasury ruled that the statutes prohibited detailing diplomats or consuls to Washington for other than temporary duty, and that officers from the field could not be assigned to general duty in the department. But the State Department was becoming increasingly resourceful and persistent in the face of adversity. William Phillips, second secretary of legation at Peking, had been seeking a transfer to the department to prepare himself for a diplomatic career. Although no vacancy existed there at the higher levels, an opening occurred in the ranks of the messenger service, the lowest-paying job in the department. Offered "interesting work" in Wilson's new Far Eastern bureau while theoretically serving as a messenger and earning $900 a year, Phillips jumped at the chance and began his duties in June 1907. Joining him in the new office was Percival Heintzleman, formerly student interpreter and vice consul-general at Canton. Since consuls lacked the independent means of diplomats, particularly of young Boston Brahmins like Phillips, Heintzleman received $1,600 as a clerk of the third class. The two young men set up shop behind a screen in Huntington Wilson's office, and what Phillips termed the "systematic decentralization" of the department had begun.[26]

During the following months, the new office took shape gradually and uncertainly. In July, Root permitted Wilson to route all the Far Eastern correspondence prepared in the department through the new creation, for its information and approval, before sending it directly for signature. Root's directive gave the Far Eastern office the last word, below the secretary and assistant secretaries, about such correspondence. Wilson wanted the room across the hall for his operation, and clerks detailed from the Diplomatic, Consular, and Index bureaus. But it took time to work out the logistics; both space and funds for additional manpower were severely limited. "It certainly seems to me," Assistant Secretary of State Robert Bacon told Root in August, "that we must all pull together with the tools we have until we can get money to buy new tools." Certain other offices, however—particularly Sydney Smith's Diplomatic Bureau—were jealous of the new entity and resented rerouting the Far Eastern correspondence to a new layer between them and the assistant secretaries. For months Smith would only grunt disgustedly at Phillips when the new arrival regularly wished him a cheery "good morning."[27]

For a time, Root remained opposed to creating a permanent bureau; he preferred to leave the nascent structure as a part of the third assistant secretary's office, which he thought provided it "greater dignity." But Wilson still wanted a separate office under his authority, partly because without it he felt more like a bureau chief than a third assistant secretary of state. With Carr's assistance, he achieved a breakthrough in October. Wilson sent Root a proposal from Carr suggesting a means of accomplishing the transition to a geographical division "along the lines of least resistance." The plan struck a compromise between the need for geographically specialized attention to certain matters, and the administrative needs and jealousies of the Diplomatic and Consular bureaus. Phillips and Heintzleman were to assume charge of "exactly coextensive sections" within the Diplomatic and Consular bureaus. As chief of the two sections, Phillips would work under Wilson's direction on Far Eastern matters, while reporting to the two bureau chiefs on administrative questions. Wilson provided a newspaper clipping showing that both the French and Russian foreign offices had recently adopted a completely geographical arrangement. Indicating there were limits to his desires, he promised Root that if Phillips's and Heintzleman's sections "could occupy the room across the hall from mine, I should consider the pioneer political geographical bureau to have become a reality." Enclosed was another memorandum by the helpful Carr, outlining how the desired room, hitherto considered essential for the Index Bureau, could be used for Wilson's purpose.[28]

On March 20, 1908, Root formally established the "Division of Far Eastern Affairs" under the direction of Phillips, "a clerk of the $900 class." The new division, with Heintzleman as assistant chief and two clerks transferred from the Diplomatic and Consular bureaus, would have charge of diplomatic and consular correspondence, "on matters other than those of an administrative character, in relation to China, Japan, Korea, Siam, Straits Settlements, Borneo, East Indies, India and in general the Far East." Wilson had finally achieved his goal, and three days later he shared his glee with the consul-general at Mukden. "I am happy to tell you," he wrote Willard Straight, "that one of my pet hobbies, the politico-geographical division, has at last received formal recognition with . . . an excellent room just across the hall from mine, so I now have much better machinery for my direction of the Far Eastern business."[29]

The new office quickly secured a lasting place in the department's structure. American diplomats and consuls in the Far East could now be directed by a headquarters with greater knowledge about conditions and problems in the region. Another improvement was the department's enhanced ability to encourage and counsel American businessmen. Many years later, Phillips recalled that his division "had a good deal to do with exporters who were in trouble and who didn't know how to carry on their export business in the Far East. We had an educational role to play and a great deal to learn, too." Furthermore, young and ambitious officers from the field, like Wilson and Phillips, would now have a hand in important drafting work, helping to chart policy. Ambassador Thomas J. O'Brien in Tokyo, formerly president of an iron company, was aware of his own lack of expertise and, recognizing the advantages that would accrue, expressed "great satisfaction" over the division's creation. "It will surely be of great advantage," he wrote Root in

June 1908, "if particular officials, having personal knowledge of the people and affairs of the East, shall be always at hand in the Department, to aid in the prompt and wise disposition of the manifold matters that may be expected to constantly arise." Root agreed and by year's end was advocating the extension of the principle to cover America's relations with the rest of the world.[30]

The geographic divisions were expected not only to provide a more specialized and experienced direction of the field foreign service, but also to add to the mobility of foreign service officers. A recurring anxiety was that diplomats and consuls would stagnate if left in one country too long. Patrick Egan, former minister to Chile, complained to Assistant Secretary Hill in 1902 that "in at least nine cases out of ten" the representative stationed for too long a time in one country became "the sycophant of the government to which he is accredited instead of the faithful, independent, manly guardian of the rights of his own people." The officers' healthy Americanism needed to be refreshed by contact with American soil and "American conditions" as a protection from foreign influences, and the geographic divisions in future years would provide an opportunity for at least a limited number of domestic assignments. "The idea is," Wilson told a congressional committee, "to standardize the ability and unify the ideas and tone of the whole foreign service and not allow secretaries to stay in foreign countries and become un-American and forget about conditions at home."[31]

Amalgamation between the diplomatic and consular services was far in the future, but Wilson's geographic divisions were an important step toward transcending the gap between "diplomatic" and "consular" work. Officers from both branches staffed the divisions. As Wilson observed in his proposal to Root, in an age of "commercial diplomacy," the organizational lines had to be redrawn.[32] The principle of geographic specialization has continued as the basis of State Department organization.

During Root's term as secretary, the State Department began to standardize also the methods of disseminating information. European governments systematically advised their diplomatic missions about negotiations and other issues pending either at the foreign office or in the various capitals. The British Foreign Office, for example, forwarded a series of confidential printed sheets to its heads of mission to keep them apprised of developments. Noting the absence of any such system in the State Department, former Minister to Turkey Oscar Straus advocated its establishment as early as 1902. George von L. Meyer, ambassador to Russia, suggested such a scheme to Root in October 1905, and Chief Clerk Charles Denby, who had spent many years in China, recommended a similar plan in a detailed memorandum to Root in January 1906.[33]

Denby, eagerly seeking the vacant third assistant secretaryship, might have felt himself as removed from inner policy circles as if he were still in China. His proposal stressed the potential benefits to department officers and diplomats alike. An information service, he wrote Root, was essential to "meet the urgent need for some method of keeping the diplomatic officers of the United States posted as to progress of our diplomatic matters . . . as well as to put correspondence in form convenient for reference by officers of the Department." Denby suggested that the chief clerk print daily the more important diplomatic papers, distributing them to the departmental and diplomatic officers. (Since consuls were normally not involved in negotiations with foreign governments, it was not necessary that they receive copies.) From time to time, as various incidents were closed, the individual papers could be assembled into sets like the British Parliamentary Papers.[34]

The following month, Root repeated Meyer's and Denby's suggestions before the House Appropriations Committee. He observed that in the past, diplomatic negotiations had been conducted in Washington and in the field with relatively little exchange of information. "There never has been the practice of keeping the two ends informed of what the other end was doing," he explained, "except casually as time passed along by the slow process of the mails." Root wanted to have information cabled from Washington to a distribution point in Europe and disseminated to the missions by mail. He asked initially for two clerks to begin the system and served notice that in the future he would be requesting appropriations for cable tolls and additional clerical help. He wanted an arrangement, he told the committee, under which the American ambassador to France "will be informed as a matter of system, without my having to think every time that information is to be sent to him, and he will be informed systematically of everything that is done here which bears upon what he is doing in Paris."[35]

The formal establishment of the Far Eastern division two years later provided the occasion for initiating a fledgling information service. Just as the Far Eastern division was an experiment to test the feasibility of adopting additional geographic bureaus, a new procedure for disseminating information in connection with Far Eastern business was the prototype for a more complete information service. Less than a month before he officially took command of the Far Eastern division in March 1908, Phillips proposed that the department circulate among United States missions in London, Paris, Berlin, Saint Petersburg, Peking, and Tokyo important correspondence pertaining to Far Eastern matters. Both the State Department and the missions would then have a much more comprehensive picture of other nations' policy and activity in that arena. Second Assistant Secretary Alvey Adee added his endorsement to the favorable response among the department's top officers. "I favor planting the acorn and letting it grow," he told Robert Bacon about Phillips's plan, "rather than trying to set out a full grown Secular oak. I think this is good." Root embodied the proposal in a departmental order on February 27, 1908, instructing the heads of mission in the four major European capitals to send the department duplicates of any dispatches bearing on the host government's relations with the Far East. Peking and Tokyo were naturally to be less selective, sending copies of all dispatches except simple acknowledgements. The duplicates, along with the pertinent departmental instructions, were then copied and distributed as a confidential information series.[36]

Like the Far Eastern division of which it was a part, the new procedure met with an enthusiastic response from diplomats in the field. Ambassador O'Brien in Tokyo thought it "of the highest value . . . to be informed of what others are doing." Montgomery Schuyler, first secretary of legation at Saint Petersburg, found the development "most interesting, illuminating, and valuable." The first item Schuyler received in the series, outlining current policy toward the Chinese Eastern Railway's proposed municipal administration at Harbin, had stood him in good stead during a recent interview with the Russian foreign minister. The communication,

Schuyler gratefully wrote Root, "supplied the precise information necessary to understand and answer Mr. Iswolsky when he unexpectedly opened this subject."[37]

In addition to the information service and geographic specialization, Root also presided over smaller but still important advances. One well-known accomplishment was the improvement of the department's filing system. In 1905 the bulk of correspondence was still filed in chronological order by country (or sometimes simply in chronological order) within sweeping categories such as diplomatic instructions and dispatches, consular instructions and dispatches, notes to and from foreign legations and consuls, and incoming and outgoing miscellaneous. It lacked any subject breakdown. As the volume of correspondence grew and foreign political and economic questions became more complex, it became ever more difficult to use an arrangement that depended so much upon individual memories to track down all the material on a specific subject. Important papers were sometimes misplaced. Several years earlier, Root had reorganized the War Department's filing system according to the "numerical" or "case" method, and soon after entering the State Department he introduced the same procedure. The new system, Root assured Congress, "is going to take more men, but we will have things so they will not be lost."[38]

The problem with the case system was that its growth was inherently limited—an irony in light of Root's penchant for building secure foundations for lasting institutions. Questions soon arose about whether to place a particular document in an existing case or file, or whether to begin a new one. Although Root's system had the advantage of grouping together into a single case the papers on a specific subject, and thus was a great improvement over the previous method, there was no arrangement for grouping together closely related cases. Another problem was that some of the cases became quite large, and without any subdivisions they were difficult to search. As time passed, and correspondence and case numbers multiplied, the system threatened to become unmanageable.[39]

After it had established 25,892 separate cases, the department in 1910 would adopt a much more flexible filing scheme, based on a decimal classification. The new system could accommodate subdivisions to any topic and also facilitate the grouping together of related divisions and subdivisions. Administrative records, for example, were filed under the major class number "1." Number 122 referred to administration of the consular branch, and some finer distinctions included:

122.1	Organization (of the consular branch)
122.11	Examination
122.31	Appointment
122.312	Instruction Period
122.313	Consular School
122.37	Special Detail
122.371	Special Detail to Other Posts
122.372	Special Detail to the Department

Within their numerical designations, the documents were filed in chronological order.[40]

While administering the consular service, Chief Clerk Wilbur Carr also found time to effect a number of minor improvements in the department. Carr became chief clerk in May 1907 and by the end of November could observe, "Without being at all egotistical, I think my record in the chief clerk's office up to the present has been productive of much good." Since taking office, Carr had assumed control of departmental appropriations and made improvements in the bookkeeping and appropriations procedures; the department had a new system of promotions and a combined cipher and telegraph office; and the laws relating to the department and the field foreign service had been compiled. Perhaps most important to the former Ohio farm boy, the chief clerk's office had become "an office that does things, achieves results, looks like a secretary's office and receives the respect of one."[41]

Root and his subordinates failed in their efforts to make certain additional changes. Before congressional committees Root repeatedly emphasized two particular needs of departmental reorganization. One was a new information service similar to the prototype finally established early in 1908. The other was improved machinery for export trade promotion and protection. When Root sent a three-man mission to Berlin in 1906 to discuss tariff revision with representatives of the German foreign office, he was obliged to scout around the government service to find his negotiators. The Departments of the Treasury and of Commerce and Labor each lent him an expert as a special favor, and he added Consul-General Frank Mason as the third member. In Berlin the Americans confronted a nine-man team, whose full-time duty was to provide the German government with expert assistance on foreign commercial questions. The United States government had no such force, and Root wished to remedy the situation. He initially wanted specialists in Commerce and Labor, Treasury, and Agriculture upon whom he could call when necessary.[42]

Perhaps some of Root's interest resulted from his correspondence with Frederic Emory in the fall of 1905. The newly retired Emory had hoped that the "development of the State Department's facilities for the enlargement of our foreign trade" would engage Root's "earnest consideration." He even enclosed a copy of the proposal he and Loomis had unsuccessfully backed the previous winter. A year later, shortly after Root had made his case to Congress for improved commercial facilities, Emory wrote to express his pleasure. When persuading Hay to expand the duties of the Bureau of Trade Relations in 1903, Emory had expected that the bureau would develop into the kind of service that Root was now advocating. Like other foreign service reformers, he saw in the new secretary of state a masterful field general who would fulfill cherished aspirations and press lagging campaigns to a successful conclusion. "How gratifying it is to me," Emory wrote Root, "to feel that you perceive the true relation of the State Department to our industrial growth which must depend, in the end, upon the largest development of our foreign trade!"[43]

When Root became secretary of state in 1905, the Bureau of Trade Relations had not increased its size since its establishment two years earlier, when Emory had obtained two clerks and a messenger. Root increased the clerical force of the bureau from two to six, but he thought that expanding trade and investments, and especially tariff negotiations, required a still larger and more expert force.[44] Just as there was need for greater geographic specialization in handling foreign policy, to which the inauguration of the Far Eastern division was a response, so too was there need for specialization and expertise to deal with the closely related and increasingly complex foreign economic questions. "Unless we are to have the most serious disturbance of our trade," Root warned, "the making of these agreements requires extensive and accurate knowledge regarding the tariff systems and tariff procedures of foreign countries as well as of our own country. Secretaries of State and Assistant Secretaries are not tariff experts. They are not expected to be. There must be somebody who knows and keeps track of the subject." By early 1908, Root's attempts to coordinate and share experts with other executive agencies had failed to produce results, and he was pressing for a buildup in his own department.[45]

The matter was becoming more urgent as time passed. It appeared that the major European powers were turning increasingly to tariffs as a weapon for commercial warfare. Since a growing percentage of American exports consisted of manufactured products, which in many cases European nations could supply for themselves if necessary, policy makers in Washington considered the export trade vulnerable to foreign tariffs. At the same time, domestic critics of United States tariff policy were gaining in power and influence, demanding downward revision of the rates on many items. A reluctant Roosevelt knew that he could no longer dodge the issue, and in a special message to Congress in March 1908, he declared that the time had come to prepare for tariff revision.[46]

A new and most important feature of proposed tariff legislation would be a "maximum-minimum" rate schedule. Foreign nations presumably would wish to escape the onerous maximum rates and would thus arrange their own tariffs and administrative regulations to conform to what the United States considered fair treatment for its products, thus enlarging foreign markets for American goods. Root warned the House Appropriations Committee that when tariff revision occurred, the maximum-minimum provision would throw much additional work upon the State Department and especially the Bureau of Trade Relations. Although the new tariff measure was not passed until the following year, after Roosevelt and Root had both left office, it was apparent in 1908 that a significant increase in the department's commercial staff was imperative.[47]

The State Department was likewise unsuccessful during the Root years in its attempts to secure a force of commercial attachés.

Carr was impressed with the use of such officers by other foreign services, particularly the British, and in 1907 he strongly recommended their adoption by the United States. He suggested to Root that the department request appropriations for attachés to be stationed in the Far East, Europe, and South America. They would have diplomatic status by virtue of their theoretical attachment to a particular legation or embassy, but like the officers in the Emory-Loomis proposal, they would travel widely to obtain commercial data. Their diplomatic position would enable them to obtain information more easily, since doors would be opened for them that would remain closed to the consuls or to the special commercial agents already operating under the direction of the Commerce and Labor Department. Root approved Carr's suggestion and requested the attachés during the 1907–1908 congressional session. But Congress turned him down. The legislators probably believed the attachés would only duplicate the work of C & L's special agents.[48]

When Carr repeated his recommendation the next year, he received support from Far Eastern division chief William Phillips and from John Ball Osborne, Emory's successor as head of the Bureau of Trade Relations. Phillips and Osborne believed that American trade with the Far East would "increase much more rapidly if it was more energetically pushed," and they advocated a system of commercial attachés to help with the pushing. Phillips optimistically argued that American businessmen lacked information, not desire, and that the "immense advantages to American exporters of skilled Commercial Agents . . . cannot, I think, be overestimated." Root shared his subordinates' interest in commercial attachés but now believed they should be supplied by the Department of Commerce and Labor. Consequently, he did not renew his request of the previous year.[49]

Root was secretary of state for only three and a half years, yet his tenure was probably more important than any other secretary's to the cause of foreign service reform. Between mid-1905 and early 1909, the service made significant advances in all three branches. Root's contribution was not primarily the furnishing of ideas; there were others who could do that, mostly subordinates in the service. What Root did was to translate their ideas into reality.

In this manner, he stimulated those who might otherwise have seen their efforts as futile; Carr believed that "the most wonderful characteristic of the man is his ability to stimulate others."[50] Both Carr and (especially) Wilson, two ambitious men, thought that Root delegated too little authority. Perhaps they were right. A centralizer by nature, Root had recently fought hard in the War Department to wrest power from the bureau chiefs and give it to a new general staff. His initial lack of enthusiasm for the "systematic decentralization" advocated by Wilson, Phillips, and Carr is understandable—especially since the scheme's originator was Wilson. Yet it is to Root's considerable credit that he gave the geographic division a trial and by the end of his term in office was attempting to extend the principle to cover America's relations with other parts of the world. By the time he left the State Department in January 1909, the department's expansion was well under way.

Between 1905 and 1909, the foreign service began to become a unified system. No longer was it a collection of relatively discrete field offices having only loose ties to the headquarters in Washington. The inspectors, the efficiency reports, and the geographic division principle began to link members of the field foreign service with the department, while the inspectors, classification, and more frequent promotions and transfers worked to connect the offices abroad. The geographic division effected greater mobility both laterally from the field and vertically into policy-making circles, while the methods of disseminating diplomatic information, like the officers themselves, became more standardized.

7 CONTINUATION UNDER KNOX

In November 1908, the American electorate accepted Roosevelt's designated successor and sent William Howard Taft to the White House. Taft's election assured the foreign service that the new system would not be overturned just as it was taking hold. The next four years saw extension and elaboration of the gains made during the Root years.

Soon after the election, Taft asked Root to continue as secretary of state. Root wanted to stay on, but reluctantly declined. His wife was exhausted from the Washington social whirl and was anxious to rest and spend time with her family. Root became instead United States senator from New York (appointed by the state legislature) and in this position had to be in Washington only about a third of the time. He resigned from the department in January 1909, and Assistant Secretary Robert Bacon became secretary for the six-week interregnum. Root was not easily reconciled to his senatorial status, and he looked back longingly to his position as the ranking cabinet officer and head of a busy, exciting, and important department. "I am still feeling like a cat in a strange garret," he wrote a friend in March, "and am trying to readjust myself to the new conditions, with many regrets."[1]

When Root refused the secretaryship, Taft asked him to recommend a successor. Meanwhile, probably as a matter both of friendship and courtesy, he offered the position to Senator Lodge— after learning from Roosevelt that Lodge was not interested. Root suggested Senator Philander Chase Knox of Pennsylvania, another corporation lawyer, who had once served as attorney-general in Roosevelt's cabinet. Root extended the offer at Taft's request, and

Knox consented on the condition that he would not have to work very hard at the new job. "He said he did not want to keep his nose to the grindstone," Root later recalled, "and wanted to take things a little easily."[2]

Chiefly to allow Knox his desired leisure, during Root's last days as secretary the department initiated a scheme to create the position of "under secretary of state," for an officer who would assume responsibility for much of the day-to-day operation. It was Root's understanding that Bacon would step down in March from his temporary post as secretary and accept the new office, as Bacon agreed to do. The same provision sought to create the position of fourth assistant secretary of state, which would go to Carr. Knox himself introduced the proposal in the Senate as an amendment to an appropriations bill, and Huntington Wilson kept him supplied with supporting memoranda. The senators speedily obliged their colleague, but the House considered the title "Under Secretary" too British and rejected the entire provision.[3]

The position of undersecretary was only one of the requests made by the department between Taft's election and his inauguration. Root had become convinced of the need to extend the geographic divisions, and beginning in December the department pressed Congress for the necessary funds. The request was made more urgent by certain personnel changes. William Phillips, head of the Far Eastern division, was a favorite of Roosevelt's, and by late 1908 the president wanted to give him Huntington Wilson's job. Wilson was ready for a foreign assignment, and Root gladly arranged to get rid of him by having him appointed minister to Argentina. With Wilson's appointment, Phillips left his $900 clerkship and moved into Wilson's vacated slot as third assistant secretary. This shift helped prompt immediate attention to the Far Eastern division, formally established less than a year before. Independently wealthy or not, other diplomatic secretaries might not share Phillips's eagerness to come into the department as a $900 clerk; consuls certainly would not. Thus in January 1909, the department sought additional funds for continuing the regular salaries of three secretaries of embassy or legation and three consuls while they served in the geographic divisions. At least one diplomat and one consul would be assigned to the Far Eastern division. The others would staff two new geographic offices, one devoted to the Near East and the other to Central America. The latter would be a Caribbean division whose projected scope included Venezuela and Colombia on the South American continent. [4]

Carr, Phillips, Wilson, and Senator Knox outlined for Congress the advantages of using specialists from the field to staff geographic divisions. The new officers were to serve as "an informal medium of communication between the Secretary of State and the actual conditions in foreign countries," by supplying memoranda and conferring personally with the top department officials. Their foreign experience would enable them to supplement the dispatches from the field and ensure that the secretary of state received a complete picture of the situation. They would divert from the secretary and assistant secretaries an "enormous mass of matter," by summarizing the political dispatches for them. The interchange with the field would familiarize men assigned to the department with headquarters routine and also enable them to remain in touch with conditions in the United States. Finally, new consuls and diplomats, or those recently reassigned, could be coached about the conditions they would find at their posts. [5]

Congress turned down the State Department's request despite Knox's support, but it was only a temporary setback. Later that year the department secured funds to extend the geographic divisions, and much more. The result was due partly to coincidence and partly to the ascension of Huntington Wilson, who had become assistant secretary of state and Knox's right-hand man in the new regime.

Elihu Root never understood how Wilson managed to secure the important assistant secretaryship. As Wilson was preparing to leave for Argentina, it was widely reported in the press that Knox's assistant secretary would be Beekman Winthrop, once Taft's secretary in the Philippines and currently assistant secretary of the Treasury. Winthrop was Taft's choice for the post, and the president-elect anticipated no trouble from Knox about the appointment. [6]

Knox might not have objected had he not received some shrewd advice from a friend whose suggestions he was soliciting. When the newspapers announced Winthrop's pending appointment, W. A. Day, vice-president of the Equitable Life Assurance Company, wrote Knox to register a strong protest. Not only was Day unimpressed with Winthrop's abilities, but he predicted that Knox's success as secretary would depend "upon the loyalty and singleness of purpose of your chief assistants, quite as much as in their ability." With Winthrop as assistant secretary, Day wrote, and "one of Lodge's men [Phillips] as Third Assistant Secretary of State, you will be surrounded, I fear, by men who will feel that they owe little to you and much to others outside the Department."[7]

There was also the crucial matter of Knox's desire for leisure; he was doubtless aware that Winthrop was not at all familiar with the State Department's work. Bacon was experienced, but even if the undersecretary provision had gone through, Knox was determined not to appoint Bacon, probably because he was much too close to Root and would feel under no obligation to Root's successor. Knox needed a chief officer whose loyalty rested with him rather than with the previous regime or even with Taft, but one who was also experienced enough to direct the department and thus allow him the leisurely tour of duty he desired.[8]

Into this situation stepped Huntington Wilson. It is not clear whether Wilson had his eye on a top job in the department when he first began sharing with Knox his views about the proposed undersecretaryship, a position he had initially suggested in the 1906 reorganization plan. Wilson never lacked ideas about reorganization or words with which to express them, and in January and early February he was probably engaged in some last-minute proselytizing and apple-polishing before leaving for his new post. As Wilson elaborated his pitch about the undersecretary and other aspects of departmental organization, the possibilities must have begun to dawn on Knox. Here was someone who would be both a loyal assistant and an experienced one, who believed that an undersecretary "should be the alter ego and understudy of the Secretary of State and should know and reflect his ideas." Thus the secretary's time would be "free for broader questions." Here too was the originator of the geographic divisions and the prime mover for continued departmental reorganization, a development which, when completed, promised to facilitate the diffusion of policy making and remove even more burdens from the secretary's shoulders. Root's warnings to Knox about Wilson doubtless only added to his attraction; the Taft administration was still very much in Roosevelt's shadow early in 1909, and advice about appointments could not have been very welcome. By February 9, well before Congress rejected the undersecretary provision, Knox had asked Wilson to remain as his chief assistant.[9]

During the first months of Taft's administration, a special session of the new Congress was already meeting. Taft had convened it to deal with the long-anticipated tariff revision, and the new Payne-Aldrich Tariff Act furnished the department with the rationale necessary to secure its reorganization. It created the first "double tariff" in United States history, containing both a maximum and minimum set of schedules. In March 1910, the maximum rate was to be applied to all countries exporting goods to the United States. For a nation to avoid this levy, 25 percent higher than the minimum, the United States government would have to satisfy itself that the applicant did not "unduly discriminate" against American products in favor of goods from other nations. The procedure would entail an extensive examination of the country's tariff rates, administrative practices, and sanitary regulations. Once everything was declared in order, the president would extend the minimum rates to the country's products by executive proclamation. The dual schedule was a new tool to help achieve equal opportunity for access to foreign consumers—the time-honored American principle of the open door.[10]

Early in 1908, Secretary Root was already urging additional reorganization in the department because of pending tariff revision. Seeing its golden opportunity in 1909, the State Department pressed its reorganization scheme on the same Congress that was enacting the Payne-Aldrich tariff. Late in July, only two weeks before the session ended, Knox requested a lump-sum appropriation of $100,000. The secretary explained, in deliberately vague terms, that the money was needed both to carry out responsibilities that the new tariff would place upon the department and to handle the ever-growing business of fostering America's foreign commerce, particularly in the Far East and Latin America.[11]

In a lengthy follow-up letter a week later to the chairman of each Appropriations Committee, Knox elaborated on his request. Although American exports to Latin America and the Far East comprised a relatively small portion of total United States exports, policy makers repeatedly interpreted the trade figures as showing the magnitude of the trade potential. Knox expressed certainty that the small percentage of South America's imports supplied by the United States demonstrated "at a glance the immense possibilities presented to American commerce." He also contended that the small American share of the China market "reveals clearly the great possibilities, when it is remembered that the actual total importation is but a fraction of what China will ultimately import when the consuming ability of that nation of 400,000,000 people has been developed proportionately with that of other populous nations." Consequently, whether the United States increased its exports by taking trade away from its commercial rivals or by keeping constant its share of inevitably growing markets, it could expect a rosy future in the non-European world.[12]

While devoting most of his space to generalities about America's economic expansion, Knox paused briefly to mention the new tariff law, which "alone necessitates considerable expansion of the work of the Department of State, particularly in the Bureau of Trade Relations." The secretary then quickly shifted back again, pointing to a more general value for an enlarged and more active Bureau of Trade Relations. "Its personnel should be such also," he explained, "as to make possible special study of the foreign field for financial investment, including the means by which government encouragement of such enterprise may, through resultant trade, help to open up the new markets, promote closer business relations, and thus redound to the general national benefit." As usual, a comparison was made with other countries' foreign services. Both the British and the German foreign offices, Knox informed Congress, were equipped with talented specialists, many of them from the diplomatic and consular services.[13]

The department's proposal was stalled until Senator Eugene Hale, the powerful chairman of the Appropriations Committee, stepped into the picture. Hale visited the department to announce that if Knox really wanted the appropriation to pass, he need only appoint Hale's son, a former secretary of legation and currently secretary of the American delegation at the Hague Peace Conference, as third assistant secretary of state. The bargain was struck, and the department consoled the evicted William Phillips by appointing him secretary of embassy at London.[14]

As Hale was fulfilling his part of the bargain in the Senate, the State Department received valuable assistance from his counterpart in the House. James A. Tawney of Minnesota, chairman of the Appropriations Committee, was sympathetic to the department's request. In debate on the House floor he masterfully parried pointed questions about the apparent duplication between the State Department's $100,000 and an allotment to the president of $75,000 for tariff investigation and negotiation. Temporarily quieting the protest, Tawney explained that the president's money was for investigation of presumed tariff inequities, and the State Department's for negotiations once the discriminations were uncovered. None of Tawney's colleagues questioned whether $100,000 was necessary for negotiating away obstacles that had yet to be found and assessed.[15]

Congress has traditionally been more consistently interested in the tariff than in any other foreign relations issue, because this is also clearly a domestic issue. The legislators have been vitally aware of their constituents' interests as producers or consumers. Hence the State Department did not have to spell out at any great length the necessity for extra funds; Knox needed only to explain his request partly in terms of new responsibilities brought by the impending Payne-Aldrich tariff. Actually, the department's principal tariff duties involved neither protection nor revenue, but rather negotiations to lower foreign barriers and thus increase United States exports. Yet governmental reorganization to foster American exports was going forward only slowly. It was the department's apparent connection with the touchy issue of protection that prompted Congress to drop $100,000 into Knox's lap with scarcely a murmur.[16]

The State Department used the money to effect the long-sought reorganization. Blocked in its efforts earlier that year to make Carr fourth assistant secretary, it accomplished the same goal by appointing him "Director of the Consular Service" at the same salary as the second and third assistant secretaries. It also created the positions of resident diplomatic officer and counselor (the only offices that had not been in Root's proposal) at $7,500 each, eight officers "to aid in important drafting work" (four at $4,500 and four at $3,000), an assistant solicitor, a law clerk, and a number of clerkships. The department kept the remainder of the $100,000, about one-fourth, as a lump sum for emergency use within the District of Columbia.[17]

Although some considered the counselor to be the contemplated undersecretary with a different title, he was not involved with the department's administration (which Huntington Wilson handled during the Knox years). He was instead a specialized legal officer primarily concerned with negotiating commercial and other treaties.[18] By creating this position the State Department expected to save money. Congress in the past had repeatedly granted special appropriations for negotiation of such matters as fisheries and boundary disputes, since competent international lawyers had to be engaged to represent the United States. The cost for outside legal assistance had risen steadily from $23,000 in 1906 to $49,000 in 1909. The counselor would now handle many of these issues, and despite the high salary required to attract a first-rate lawyer, the new arrangement cost less. As an additional benefit, the government retained the experience of this official by virtue of his continuous employment. The first counselor, Henry Hoyt, was a close friend of President Taft. Both he and his successor, Chandler P. Anderson, enjoyed a large degree of independence within their own sphere, much to Huntington Wilson's discomfort. In 1912 Knox persuaded Congress to elevate the counselor's prestige by making him subject to a presidential instead of a secretarial appointment, placing him in the same category as the assistant secretaries.[19]

The resident diplomatic officer, according to a State Department publication, was supposed to use his "actual experience of important diplomatic questions" in helping the secretary of state with policy formulation and execution. But since Huntington Wilson could perform that function himself, the resident diplomatic officer was placed in charge of the new Latin American division. Thomas Dawson, the first incumbent, was perhaps the foremost expert on Latin America in the foreign service. He had worked out the details by which the United States undertook its customs receivership in Santo Domingo in 1905 and was the author of *The*

South American Republics. Dawson remained in the department until June 1910, when he was succeeded as resident diplomatic officer by H. Percival Dodge, formerly minister to several Latin American countries. Dodge likewise took charge of the Latin American division.[20]

At the heart of reorganization was the establishment of positions for eight officers to aid in important drafting work. With these men Knox and Wilson established the geographic divisions on a firm foundation and also expanded the Bureau of Trade Relations. In November and December three new geographic offices were created, for Latin America (no longer just the Caribbean region), the Near East, and Western Europe. Each was to "have charge of correspondence, diplomatic and consular, on matters other than those of an administrative character" relating to its specific area. All nonadministrative and nonroutine correspondence was to be sent directly from its initial reception in the Index Bureau to the appropriate geographic division. Correspondence bypassing the geographic offices related to exceedingly routine matters that raised no new questions and had no political bearing—deaths, marriages, citizenship, passports, weekly sanitary reports, and invoices, for example.[21]

Two of the $4,500 drafting positions went to staff the existing Far Eastern division, and Percival Heintzleman moved into one of the $3,000 slots in the same office. Transferred to Washington were Ransford Miller, the new division head, who had been serving as Japanese secretary and interpreter of the embassy in Tokyo, and his new assistant Edward T. Williams, consul-general at Tientsin. Although Latin America contained many more separate political entities than the Far East, that division initially received only a single $3,000 appointee to work with Dawson. The last of the eight drafting officers assigned to a geographic division was Evan Young, consul at Saloniki, who became chief of the Near Eastern division at $3,000. By November 1910, a year after the establishment of the three additional geographic bureaus, their relative strengths were: Latin America—chief (the resident diplomatic officer at $7,500) and two assistants (at $3,000 each), eight clerks, and a messenger; Far East—chief and one assistant (both at $4,500), two clerks, and a messenger; Near East—chief (at $3,000), two clerks, and a messenger; Western Europe—supervised by Third Assistant Secretary Chandler Hale, and including three clerks and a messenger.[22]

The other two $4,500 drafting positions went to the Bureau of Trade Relations. Since Frederic Emory's retirement in 1905, the bureau's chief had been John Ball Osborne, a former consul who had served as assistant secretary of the Reciprocity Commission from 1897 to 1905. Osborne shared Emory's concern that foreign markets would be essential for America's growing industrial surpluses, and he wrote about tariffs and consular reform for several popular journals.[23] He remained chief of the bureau until mid-1912. In August 1909, under the new appropriation, his office acquired the services of two "commercial advisers," who were to help with the department's tariff work and with its more general promotion of foreign trade.

At the time they were appointed commercial advisers, Charles Pepper and Mack Davis were both special agents with the Commerce and Labor Department. Pepper was a former newsman, widely traveled and particularly knowledgeable about American trade and trade potential in Latin America. Roosevelt had once sent him south to examine the possibilities for an inter-American railroad. Davis was a former president of the Millers' National Federation and had recently been abroad investigating possibilities for enlarging flour exports. Senator Charles Dick of Ohio recommended him to Taft, explaining that Davis had enjoyed "extended opportunities as a flour manufacturer and exporter for taking up the various phases of foreign trade, and . . . has also been identified with large industries in the steel and iron trade and in the manufacture of electrical apparatus." The secretary of Commerce and Labor was under the impression that because his agents' reassignments resulted from the new tariff law, their absence would be only temporary. But in thanking Taft for recommending his "transfer" to the State Department, Charles Pepper demonstrated an awareness of the appointment's more permanent character. His new position promised "congenial labor in the field which has interested me greatly for several years past," Pepper told the president, "and I trust that my experience abroad may be of benefit in helping to make our people realize what the opportunities are for extending our trade and what the Administration is doing to open foreign markets to them."[24]

The remaining appointment among the eight drafting positions supplied a chief for the department's Information division. That office was not only contemplated but already functioning before the August appropriation. As early as December 1905, Elihu Root had recommended such a system to Congress, and in 1908 he initiated it in the Far Eastern division. Since Root's first request, Congress had appropriated for two clerks at the London embassy to handle information dissemination, but the department used the funds for other purposes. Early in 1909 both Carr and Phillips recommended making the distribution from the department. Echoing earlier suggestions by Chief Clerk Charles Denby and by Huntington Wilson, Carr added that the arrangement could furnish material for the *Foreign Relations* series as well as supply information to the missions. The State Department accordingly changed the wording of the appropriation, and Congress cooperated. In June, Wilson instructed the diplomats to send duplicates of all dispatches relating "to political subjects and to matters which in your judgment would be of interest and guidance to diplomatic officers in other Embassies and Legations." The extra copy went to the new Division of Information, formally established the following month. Although the $100,000 appropriation followed the creation of the new entity, it did allow the appointment of the well-known journalist Philip Patchin as its chief. Patchin had been the Washington correspondent for the *New York Sun* and had also worked in several Latin American countries.[25]

The Division of Information received copies of diplomatic dispatches, instructions, all incoming and outgoing telegrams, and other items that the bureau chiefs thought would keep American diplomats around the world abreast of current negotiations and other developments. The division's clerks separated the material by subject, sent the papers to the appropriate geographic division for clearance, and had the documents printed in pamphlet form for distribution abroad. Secretary Knox described the advantage of the new system when he observed that only in this manner could "the various embassies and legations, dealing at different angles with the same matters, be kept uniformly well informed of the attitude and interests of the Government." The pamphlets also benefited department officers, recently transferred diplomats undergoing instruction in the department before leaving for their new posts, and neophytes entering the service. The Information division subscribed to a number of newspapers, including sixteen foreign papers, and received hundreds of clippings from diplomatic officers. From them it prepared a daily synopsis of the news, and by ten in the morning each of the assistant secretaries and bureau or division heads had a succinct summary that took five or ten minutes to read. The division also published the *Foreign Relations* series. By November 1910, Patchin had five clerks and a messenger on his staff.[26]

As a result of the 1909 developments, the office of third assistant secretary, which had once supervised the consular service and then the Far Eastern division, now had less responsibility and a wide variety of minor chores. Its new incumbent was Chandler Hale, the senator's son. Young Hale, described by historian Graham Stuart as "not a man of outstanding attainments," took charge of the least important of the four new geographic divisions—Western Europe. He also was responsible for internal conferences, ceremonial questions, and expenditures in the department and field foreign service, until the last duty was reassigned to Carr in 1911. Hale was only nominally responsible for the administration of the diplomatic corps, which remained under Huntington Wilson's close scrutiny.[27]

The diplomatic service benefited considerably from departmental innovations such as the systematic dissemination of information and the greater mobility of personnel provided through the geographic divisions. During 1909 Wilson and Knox effected additional improvements.

In the spring the department began conducting a school, along the lines of the two-year-old consular school, for men who had passed the diplomatic entrance examinations and were awaiting appointment as secretaries of embassy or legation. The prospective diplomats heard lectures by officials from within the department and from other government agencies, learned to write dispatches, and became acquainted with diplomatic procedure. They also were warned to write the department instead of their senators if they had a grievance. Later that year, after the geographic offices and Information division extended their operations to the world, new officers could receive thorough briefings once their assignments were known. By the time they left Washington, they were much better prepared for their work than their predecessors had been.[28]

In June, Wilson and Wallace J. Young, secretary of the board of examiners for both the diplomatic and the consular services, began drafting regulations for the appointment of secretaries of embassy and legation. Knox sent Taft the resultant executive order on November 26, and the president signed it the same day. Just as Carr, Root, and Roosevelt had built upon the Cleveland-Olney executive order for the consular service, so too did Wilson, Knox, and Taft combine to perform the same feat for the other branch of the field foreign service, building on Root's and Roosevelt's executive order of November 1905.[29]

The order provided that initial appointments to secretaryships were to be made to the lower grades only after examination, and that vacancies in the higher secretarial grades were to be filled solely by promotion on the basis of demonstrated efficiency. Only persons between the ages of 21 and 50 who had been "designated" by the president were eligible to take the examination. Added to the existing board of examiners for the diplomatic service were the chief of the Appointments Bureau and the chief examiner for the Civil Service Commission, and the assistant secretary of state was substituted for the second assistant secretary. Subjects prescribed for the examination included the usual international law, diplomatic usage, and a knowledge of French, Spanish, or German, along with three new subjects: American history, government, and institutions; modern history (since 1850) of Europe, Latin America, and the Far East; and the "natural, industrial and commercial" resources of the United States, "especially with reference to the possibility of increasing and extending the foreign trade of the United States." Other sections of the order included provisions aiding greater mobility between the field and the department, a reiteration of the desirability for sectional balance in the service, and the establishment of an efficiency record for clerks in the department. Knox sent advance copies of the order to 116 newspaper editors, asking them to give it publicity.[30]

The young diplomat Joseph Grew was one of many who greeted the development with enthusiasm. He predicted that Taft's order would "make it just so much harder for a new administration to overturn things and reclothe the Service in its former character of a Congressional plum orchard. This is very gratifying." Ansley Wilcox of the National Civil Service Reform League's committee on consular reform seemed surprised that the order had been issued without pressure on the executive branch. Displaying either unawareness or a poor memory about the dynamics of foreign service reform for more than a decade, Wilcox informed his colleagues that the "step was taken by the President and the Department of State under Mr. Secretary Knox of their own motion; that is, without any considerable fresh agitation from outside."[31]

Like the consular examinations, the diplomatic tests were noncompetitive, but still weeded out more than they passed. Here too the department required senatorial endorsements and used a state quota system to designate candidates. By June 1912, the board had examined 104 persons and passed 42. Knox could report to Ansley Wilcox in December 1911 that over 50 percent of the diplomatic secretaries had entered the service after an examination.[32]

The geographic divisions employed more of the diplomatic secretaries than were detailed there as drafting officers. Had Congress permitted the appointment of diplomats and consuls to grades instead of posts, the State Department could have assigned as many officers as it wished to the geographic divisions. But until 1915 appointments were made to specific posts, and consequently the department detailed officers from the field as clerks in the geographic divisions and paid them a clerk's salary, as it had done with Phillips and Heintzleman. Two little-noted sections of the November executive order exempted the procedure from normal civil service restrictions. The secretary of state was allowed to request the Civil Service Commission to conduct special examinations for clerical positions of class two or higher. At the secretary's discretion, the special tests were to follow "the lines of the present foreign service examination." Such officers were described to outsiders as engaged in "special research work," and after their tour of duty in the department they returned to the diplomatic service without taking another examination.[33]

Other improvements related to the housing of American ambassadors or ministers. The department was able to ease the problem by providing generous allowances for office rent and even personal housing from the contingent expenses fund. That fund rose from $190,000 in 1905 to $325,000 in 1909 to $375,000 in 1911. In 1911 Congress passed the Lowden Bill, providing for the gradual purchase of buildings for American missions and consulates. Although some of the bill's provisions severely limited its effectiveness, and it produced few immediately tangible results, the measure did commit the government to a positive program. The department could spend up to $500,000 per year (no more than $150,000 in any one location) and it had to receive a specific appropriation for each purchase. Congress had rejected a more generous bill the previous year, and even the more modest measure met with opposition from legislators who saw it as a scheme "for exploiting the Public Treasury" and preferred to spend the money for domestic buildings, such as post offices. Oscar W. Underwood, the influential congressman from Alabama, even used the House debate to recommend abolishing diplomatic representation. Not until 1926 was a different and somewhat faster-moving buildings program instituted.[34]

THE SYSTEM IN OPERATION

By the end of 1909, Knox, Wilson, and Carr all possessed much of the machinery they had sought, each for his own reasons. Knox had acquired a substructure that allowed him to set his own working pace. As secretary of state, Root had habitually labored all day and into the evening; he wrote Whitelaw Reid in 1907 that the "pot is kept boiling here so constantly that I have to neglect everything that possibly can be neglected." Knox had quite a different approach. He normally took afternoons off to play golf, which Root must have found incredible. Taft considered him lazy, and some historians have echoed the charge. But other contemporaries disagreed. Hugh Wilson, a future assistant secretary of state, found Knox a man who often made a "deceptive impression" because he "seemed lazy." Yet the secretary of state would arise each day at four-thirty or five and get a great deal of work out of the way before breakfast, so that, Hugh Wilson recalled, "when he took his hat and stick and strolled out it was as a man of leisure, stopping to chat with acquaintances on the way, his funny little round face creased in smiles." Knox kept in touch with developments by receiving, from the various bureau and division chiefs, daily lists of incoming telegrams or papers about matters of particular interest. His mental acuity was partly responsible for his apparently leisurely schedule. "He excels in quick vision and quick working mind," Carr noted in his diary. "Sees through a question quickly and seizes the weak point. This remarkable quality of mind enables him to do in a short time tasks that would occupy an ordinary man hours or days."[35]

Knox was also more willing than Root to delegate responsibility to his subordinates. Henry White, then ambassador in Paris, complained that Knox had "handed over his functions, in so far as the foreign service is concerned, to Wilson." White was astounded that all the telegrams he had received from the department on business, and more than four-fifths of the written instructions, were signed by Wilson. Knox frequently lunched with his assistant secretary at the Shoreham or the Metropolitan Club, and over a meal of good wine and good food they discussed policy matters. Then Knox departed for the golf course, and Wilson returned to the department. But the secretary kept his lines open to other department officials too. He sometimes would phone his director of the consular service around six o'clock in the morning, giving a sleepy Wilbur Carr fifteen minutes to get ready before Knox's automobile arrived. During the drive the men would decide pending issues, though at a higher level than Carr had known under Root. When Carr had sought Root's approval for promotions in the consular service, the secretary had gone over each case with him. But Knox simply accepted Carr's recommendations, informing Carr that he would hold him responsible for the promotions.[36] Although some of the differences in the administrative techniques of the two secretaries can be ascribed to temperament, Knox also had a larger and more seasoned crew of officials to whom he could delegate responsibility.

Elihu Root
*Courtesy of the
Library of Congress*

Huntington Wilson, 1909
*From Pan-American
Union Bulletin*

Philander Knox
Courtesy of the
Library of Congress

Charles Nagel
Courtesy of the
Library of Congress

The reorganizing foreign service, particularly the departmental and diplomatic branches, also had benefits for Huntington Wilson. He was gratified both by the recent reorganization measures and by his new position of responsibility. While once his principal hobby had been a two-man Far Eastern division, now it was the entire foreign service. He equated his station with a first secretaryship of legation (a position he knew well), whose incumbent was supposed "to make all necessary suggestions of initiative and submit drafts upon everything, and hold himself responsible that nothing shall be forgotten." Wilson expected heads of bureaus or divisions, for their part, "to take similar responsibility toward the office of Assistant Secretary. In this way there is built up a logical pyramid of successive responsibilities which ought to leave no loopholes for the neglect or slighting of any bit of business."[37] More than any of his colleagues, many of whom were also interested in greater efficiency through better organization, Wilson was infatuated with the power and efficiency of structure—especially a symmetrical structure like a pyramid—to accomplish results. Perhaps it was his intense concern with organization and structure that made him relatively tactless with many people.

Wilson had his own diplomatic secretary to help him manage the pyramid. Early in 1910, he brought the witty and personable Hugh Gibson, second secretary of embassy at London, to Washington as his private secretary. Gibson initially was supposed to improve the State Department's rocky public relations, but almost immediately he acquired additional responsibilities. Gibson regularly arrived at his desk before nine and went through what he described as "all the interesting stuff that comes to the Department," including the cables. He also digested the Information division's synopsis of daily news, and other matters brought to him by the bureau chiefs for the attention of Knox and the assistant secretaries. When Wilson arrived around ten, Gibson briefed him, and Wilson in turn briefed Knox. At ten-thirty Wilson and Gibson met with the press and dispensed the news, repeating the performance at three-thirty. Gibson also took it upon himself to see that matters were brought to Wilson's attention in as final a form as possible. He remained at the department until mid-1911, when his place was taken by another diplomatic secretary.[38]

Particularly after 1909, Wilson's interest in continued reorganization was often bound up with his own status. Several times he pleaded with Knox to change the title and raise the salary of his office to increase its standing. Since the House had vigorously objected to the designation "Under Secretary," Wilson suggested that the title be changed to "Principal Assistant Secretary of State," to distinguish the office more clearly from the other assistant secretaryships. Repeating a recommendation he had made in 1906, he proposed abolition of the chief clerk's position and the addition of that salary to the principal assistant secretary's. Although Wilson sincerely believed that organizational efficiency demanded there clearly be only one chief assistant to the secretary, more personal considerations were also important. He was interested in the higher salary for the greater prestige it would supply for his running battles with Counselor Chandler Anderson, who received a much larger salary. A raise in status and salary would help dispel any lingering uncertainty that Wilson was indeed second-in-command in the department and acting chief during the secretary's frequent absences.[39]

Just as important to Wilson were his unrealistic political ambitions. He expected to leave the foreign service at the end of the Taft administration in order to tour Latin America and write a book, becoming an authority on that region as well as the Far East. He expected then to enter politics, he recalled years later, "in the hope that I might in time be elected to Congress, perhaps to the Senate, and ultimately become a logical candidate to be Secretary of State. It was quite a good blue print." But Wilson intended his political career as more than simply an ordeal necessary to become secretary of state. His love for order and organization extended to the society at large, and he probably imagined that as a powerful person he could help reshape his individualistic country into the more unified, interventionist state he desired. He was convinced that if in "the public esteem" the assistant secretaryship conformed to his own notions of its importance, he could later use it advantageously in his political career.[40]

Wilson's contributions to the foreign service went beyond specific organizational improvements. Knowing that the consuls were in Carr's able hands, he turned his attention to the younger diplomats and department officers. Sometimes tactless and heavy-handed in his dealings with peers and superiors, Wilson related better to subordinates. An enormously ambitious man himself, and only thirty-three years old when he became Knox's chief assistant, he was sympathetic with the ambitions of young men who were frustrated at working in the shadows of their superiors. While still third assistant secretary, he befriended Assistant Solicitors William C. Dennis and J. Reuben Clark, bringing their work to Root's attention; he and Clark became close friends. When Hugh Wilson (no relation) was first considering the diplomatic service as a career, he dropped by the department to discuss the matter with the busy assistant secretary of state. "His reputation was that of a bloodless machine, and his appearance accorded with his reputation," the younger Wilson recalled, "but no one could have been kinder." Hugh Gibson and other young diplomats considered Wilson both the department "workhorse" and the person contributing most to building a career service, viewing him much as the consuls did Carr. In 1942, during the last years of his life, Wilson received glowing praise from John V. A. MacMurray, special assistant to the secretary of state, who had entered the diplomatic corps in 1907. In a warm letter, MacMurray spoke of

> an age almost of innocence—of youthful wonder and the feeling of companionship in a thrilling adventure—days in which the thinking of all of us youngsters in the Department was largely formed upon your ideas and your hopes for the Service. . . . I (like most of the others) felt an enthusiastic loyalty to you in what you were doing to build up the Department and the Service, and took pride in the forcefulness and the courage with which you fought for your ideas. And that at least remains in the memories of those of us who survive, even though there be all too little general appreciation of what the Service owes to you.[41]

It probably required ambitious men like Wilson and Carr to help create and to administer an organization that was based so much upon the ambitions of its members.

During the Knox years, Wilson and other departmental officials worked hard to kill the stereotype of diplomats as unnecessary ornaments, hoping to bestow upon that branch some of the public esteem enjoyed by the consuls. Looking to both future and current needs, the State Department continued to use diplomacy for enlarging foreign markets, while accelerating the use of diplomats individually as trade promoters. A 1909 department memorandum predicted, in language reminiscent of the late Frederic Emory's, that the "time is coming when the foreign market will be more important to our prosperity than at present," and that while the home market remained unequaled, "we need foreign markets as a balance wheel." Wilson repeated to Taft the oft-mentioned belief that "the home market will ultimately be entirely inadequate for the American manufacturer and producer, and for that reason it would be suicidal not to be provident enough to make the effort to build for the future and now to gain a foot hold in what must be our future markets. This task falls to our diplomacy."[42]

As a form of information service, Wilson instructed the consuls to send a copy of all their commercial reports to the American embassy or legation to keep it abreast of commercial "needs and possibilities." Department officers and even President Taft took pains to highlight the economic promotion work of diplomats, from helping Americans place foreign loans to obtaining orders for battleships. "The day is past," Knox told the Foreign Affairs Committee, "when a man representing this country shall simply wear a silk hat and ride around in an automobile. Our representatives now must be men who can help this country in a practical way." Diplomats occasionally imitated consular practice by traveling to address commercial bodies about overseas opportunities.[43] Although neither commercial diplomacy nor the use of diplomats specifically for trade promotion work began during Knox's tenure as secretary, the period from 1909 to 1913 saw an intensification of earlier trends, as the department sought to enlarge foreign markets and simultaneously justify the increased expenditures for this little-understood branch of the public service.

The 1909 reforms probably meant less to Carr's ambitions than to Wilson's. Carr was not looking to a future political career and had already begun reforming and administering the consular corps. His appointment as director of the consular service in November

1909, however, did allow him to relinquish the chief clerk's duties and devote more of his attention to the consuls. As one of his charges put it, "Mr. Carr has come into his kingdom at last. Long may you direct the Consular Service!"[44]

Whether or not the United States now possessed what bureau chief Herbert Hengstler described in 1909 as "the greatest and best consular service now existing in the world," there was little question but that considerable progress had been made, and the progress continued during the Knox years. Consular representation in China had long been one of the biggest headaches for the department, but in 1909 William Phillips could report great improvement both in the quality of the personnel there and in the system. Special grants of travel allowances enabled consuls to become acquainted with local Chinese officials and conditions (a significant development given the nature of the Chinese polity); much better commercial reports resulted. Secretary Charles Nagel, whose Commerce and Labor Department frequently clashed with the State Department over trade promotion, nevertheless admitted in 1911 that the consular service had "so greatly improved that appreciation of this work is general." By mid-1912, the department was receiving 22,000 consular reports annually—almost five times as many as in 1905. Forty percent of each consul's efficiency rating was based on his commercial reporting (promptness in replying as well as the character and quality of the information), 30 percent on personality and general ability, and the remaining 30 percent on general attentiveness to other consular duties and success in his official capacity.[45]

The inspection system produced valuable information about officers, offices, and equipment. Inspection reports helped the department to close many offices that were no longer essential. A significant decline occurred in the number of consular agencies, those offices considered necessary for one reason or another but not important enough for a consul. Between 1900 and 1910, their number dropped from 395 to 262, and to 232 by 1913. With growing frequency, subordinates in the consulates were likely to be American citizens, a trend that was aided by the greater appropriations for clerk hire. When Root took over the department in 1905, its allotment for those clerks was $153,000. When he left office in 1909, it was $243,000, and four years later it amounted to $375,000.[46]

By the last month of the Taft administration, almost 500 applicants had been examined for the consular service under the new system, and only 211 found eligible. Because the number of successful candidates exceeded the number of vacancies, the department could, in Huntington Wilson's words, "take the cream off the eligible list, and also apply the quota rule in an effort to distribute the appointments over the country." Sectional distribution among the 89 appointees as consuls improved markedly between 1907 and 1913: half the men came from the southern states. (But northerners outnumbered southerners as appointees to consular assistant positions by 20 to 8, and by 38 to 8 for the student interpreter appointments.) The surplus of eligibles and the general increase of efficiency were both testimony to the growing belief among young men that the consular service under Wilbur Carr was providing career opportunities. Trained initially in the department, keenly supervised by Carr, and induced to make careers for themselves by promoting their country's export trade, the consuls were forming a more homogeneous body, made up of what one contemporary astutely termed "standardized units."[47]

The Bureau of Trade Relations and its antecedents had been the State Department's de facto commercial office for several decades before 1909, and its contributions increased markedly after Frederic Emory became its chief in 1894. In 1906 limitations of space had forced it out of the State, War, and Navy Building and into other quarters. After the 1909 appropriation more than doubled its size, the bureau moved into the Union Trust Building, located to the east across the White House grounds, a block from the Treasury Department. That appropriation enlarged its work force from eight to eighteen persons and its funding from $9,320 to $28,740, but did not significantly change the character of its duties.[48] After 1909, a larger proportion of the bureau's attention was devoted to enlarging American exports through consideration of commercial treaties and foreign tariffs. Matters relating to American capital investment in foreign countries were handled principally in the geographic divisions rather than in the Bureau of Trade Relations.

By early 1912 the bureau contained twenty employees in five

subdivisions. Osborne and the commercial advisers, together with one clerk and two messengers, comprised the office of the chief of bureau. The correspondence and files section was the largest, with seven clerks. Although editing and censoring commercial reports from the field had long been the bureau's chief public rationale, only two clerks performed this task in the consular division; the other clerk in the division watched over the publishing of the reports by the Department of Commerce and Labor. Three clerks were assigned to the tariff and statistical division, while a single clerk had charge of the 16,000-volume library. Consular Assistant DeWitt Poole was one of several young men who did research and prepared memoranda on a variety of specific assignments for Osborne and the commercial advisers. "We worked over there at my level," he recalled forty years later, "mostly unconscious of the State Department as the ministry of foreign affairs."[49]

After 1909 the bureau increasingly initiated its own consular investigations on certain subjects, without consulting the Department of Commerce and Labor. The resulting reports, like other information from consuls, diplomats, and the bureau's own research, were sent on to individuals and firms. The bureau occasionally issued its own publications, such as the twelve-page "Compilation of Prices of Agricultural Implements in Canada and the United States," while other commercial data found their way into presidential messages or congressional documents. Multigraphed press releases gave publicity to trade and industrial information, simultaneously highlighting the State Department's commercial contributions. Osborne, Pepper, and Davis even took the stump, urging businessmen's participation in foreign trade. They also cordially welcomed manufacturers and exporters to the department to discuss foreign business.[50]

The State Department was proud of the bureau's achievements. Knox said in 1912 that the enlarged Bureau of Trade Relations had obtained for the United States more than $200,000,000 worth of new business. Although the secretary was hardly a disinterested party and may have exaggerated, American businessmen as well as department officials credited the State Department and its field foreign service with substantially increasing the country's exports. "The 'dollar diplomacy' is a sure winner," wrote James R.

Morse, president of the American Trading Company, "and every patriotic citizen should be proud of the present policy of our government." Between 1909 and 1913, total exports from the United States increased by 48 percent. Exports of finished and semi-finished manufactures rose by 76 and 77 percent respectively.[51]

Perhaps most important among the 1909 developments was the extension of the geographic division principle, which firmly established the basis for future department organization. Although the Diplomatic Bureau survived for many more years, the important diplomatic drafting work shifted to the divisions, and additional voices were added to the policy-making process.[52] This change resulted from Wilson's twin desires to bring the department into closer touch with the field and to give capable subordinates a share of the responsibility and interesting work. Here the department had a flexibility it did not enjoy with the field foreign service as a whole, because the carefully worded appropriation stipulated only the number of drafting officers and their salaries, not where they were to be stationed. When the department decided in 1910 that it needed another Latin American specialist, it sent Heintzleman from the Far Eastern division to the field and brought a diplomatic secretary into the Latin American division to take his place. It was, in microcosm, the same authorization the department continued to seek for management of the field foreign service and did not obtain until 1915.[53]

Through the geographic divisions the foreign service took significant strides toward becoming a cohesive body. New consuls or diplomats about to embark for their posts talked over problems and possibilities with men who knew the area firsthand. Not only new officers, but also those with new assignments or on home leave, spent time with their colleagues in the geographic divisions, swapping information and the latest gossip.[54]

The divisions furnished department officials like Carr and Wilson, as well as visiting businessmen, with more specialized information about the political situation in China or Nicaragua, or the commercial possibilities in Argentina. Wilson once described the arrangement as "universal specialization." Explaining it to a House committee, he observed that if someone were to move to Nebraska and begin ranching, he would naturally like to talk with somebody who had been in Nebraska and understood the ranching business there. Soon after he arrived to head the Far Eastern division, Ransford Miller sent Carr a memorandum that demonstrates the kind of specialized knowledge the geographic offices provided.

> I was informed by the local agent at Yokohama, just before my departure, that the Standard Oil Company was considering the question of establishing refineries in Japan, and he requested me to confer with their New York office on the subject. The question at the bottom of the proposition is the relative duty upon crude and refined oil, and as the establishment of refineries would represent an investment of several millions [of] dollars of American capital, I think it would be well for Mr. Sammons [the new American consul-general to Yokohama] to look into the matter at this end as well as in Japan, where, as you know, the tariff schedule is now being revised by the Diet.[55]

By supplying such expertise, the divisions allowed the department to give intense and sustained attention to important matters, which resulted in the sale of battleships to Argentina and Turkey, United States participation in the Hukuang loan to China, construction by American firms of grain elevators in Russia, the dispatch of five Americans to serve as financial advisors to the Persian government, and other vaunted accomplishments of the Taft-Knox years.[56]

"DOLLAR DIPLOMACY"

Between 1909 and 1913 the Taft administration gave wide publicity to a campaign for promoting exports, particularly to the non-European world. It also aggressively pushed the investment of private American capital in the Caribbean (to increase the physical security of the continental United States and the Panama Canal and to develop more extensive markets for American producers) and in China (to help that country retain its territorial integrity and thereby preserve the commercial open door). The administration pursued these policies with a heavy-handed activism, prompting first contemporaries and then historians to call these the years of "dollar diplomacy" and contrast them with what had gone before.[57]

There were, to be sure, differences between the Roosevelt and Taft regimes in their conduct of foreign policy. The American government's use of private capital as a foreign policy tool was much greater under Taft than ever before. Moreover, the personalities of the principals helped set a different tone for the Taft years. The president himself had none of Roosevelt's appreciation of the European balance of power. He appears to have taken little active part in framing foreign policy, preferring to leave that responsibility to his secretary of state and the State Department. Philander Knox also differed markedly from his predecessor. Although Root had privately referred to the Latin Americans as "dagos," he assiduously cultivated their respect and friendship. Knox, on the other hand, made no effort to hide his contempt for them. In State Department matters, he dealt principally with the broader questions, delegating responsibility for much of the policy implementation. This practice brought to center stage Huntington Wilson, who ran the department much of the time and drafted many foreign policy speeches for Taft and Knox. Wilson's temper was short, and he often expressed contempt of the "rotten little countries" in the Caribbean who refused to keep their houses in order. He was fond of stressing American "rights," including the "right" of the United States to determine its own immigration policy while insisting on its "right" to participate in commercial and financial ventures in Manchuria, and he labeled as "absurd" Roosevelt's careful handling of Japanese sensitivities on these related issues.[58]

Finally, one cannot escape the impression that the very existence of the new foreign affairs machinery gave a double impetus toward greater activism during the Taft years. For one thing, the geographic divisions were staffed principally with younger men who sometimes shared Wilson's lack of judgment. Hugh Gibson, Wilson's deputy and occasionally acting chief of the Latin American division, likened the nations of that region to children who refused to remain in bed where they belonged, or to obstinate marbles in a Chinese checkers game, which refused to stay in their proper holes. Even Wilson once expressed his opinion to Alvey Adee that the geographic divisions were sometimes too brisk in the conduct of their business. The older man smiled blandly and replied: "You remember that line in the poem, 'The thoroughbreds set the pace'? Well, if we bring back the thoroughbreds to do the Department work, we may expect them to set the pace." The greater activism derived not only from individual temperaments, but also from factors inherent in the enlarged organization itself. There was an understandable desire to put to good use new or expanded offices. Experts now could and did give more sustained and more specialized attention to commercial questions and to the various geographic regions, facilitating the department's ability to intervene on behalf of the perceived national interest. "I am getting worried about the battleships," a nervous Huntington Wilson told Dawson in the Latin American division early in 1910. "Can't you think up some further pressure upon the Argentine?"[59]

But underlying these differences between the two administrations, differences often of tone and style, were important continuities in foreign policy goals. Roosevelt, Root, and their predecessors had also sought a world conducive to America's physical, economic, and social well-being, in which economic expansion played a key role. In 1908 Root and other State Department officers were beginning, very cautiously, to assist American capital investment in Manchuria. In the Caribbean, the attempts of the Knox regime to create stable protectorates were modeled on Roosevelt's customs receivership in Santo Domingo. Considerable continuity also existed in matters of foreign affairs organization, as Knox added little to what Root had recommended or attempted to obtain.[60]

Officials in the Taft administration had important reasons for stressing the novelty of their efforts. They demonstrated the common tendency to minimize contributions of predecessors. Also, as the administration's political fortunes darkened, the assistant secretary of state and other spokesmen increasingly sought support because of, not in spite of, "dollar diplomacy." Wilson especially gloried in the term, and it became much more a distinguishing label for the Taft-Knox years than it would have if only critics had used it. Finally, the vulnerability of the reorganized State Department compelled the administration to stress how much more than ever before it was fostering commercial expansion. If the State Department had been engaged in this activity for many years, a curious Congress would want to know, why were all these new and expen-

sive offices required? Only so much mileage could be derived from
the Payne-Aldrich tariff argument—particularly when Congress
could observe after early 1910 that every nation had complied with
the requirements and was enjoying the tariff's minimum schedule.
Thus the heightened rhetoric of "dollar diplomacy" was used partly
to maintain a rationale for the reorganized foreign service.[61]

8 A RIVAL: THE DEPARTMENT OF COMMERCE AND LABOR

Early in George Washington's first administration, Congress created the United States government's first executive departments—State, War, and Treasury. Over the years it added Navy, Interior, Post Office, and Justice. Although their individual concerns usually differed, the departments had a common function: to administer the public business. Each had responsibilities long associated with sovereign governments in the Western world. But in 1862 Congress created a new kind of executive department, the Department of Agriculture, which attained cabinet rank in 1889. Unlike waging war, conducting foreign relations, or administering justice, "agriculture" was not a government activity in nineteenth-century America. The new department was instead an educational agency, established to supply information to farmers and other agricultural businessmen, and thus promote the practice of agriculture.[1]

During the 1880s and 1890s considerable interest arose among merchants and manufacturers for a cabinet-level department, comparable to the Department of Agriculture, to represent and promote their own interests. During the depression in the 1890s, at least eight bills were introduced providing for such entities as a "Department of Commerce" or a "Department of Commerce and Manufactures." The return of prosperity near the end of the decade failed to end the clamor, and legislators introduced more bills during the next few years. Responding to the widespread interest, the Republican party's platform in 1900 supported the creation of such a department.[2]

As in the consular reform movement, the smaller or medium-sized manufacturing and mercantile firms were the most active proponents of a commerce department, making their voices heard through the National Business League, the New York State Chamber of Commerce, the National Board of Trade, the National Association of Manufacturers, the Cleveland Chamber of Commerce, and other groups. They insisted that commerce and manufacturing deserved no less a voice than agriculture in the national government, as they proudly pointed to statistics showing their stronger and growing position in the nation's economy.[3]

Apart from their desire to have representation equal to that of the agricultural interests, there were more concrete reasons for businessmen's concern. The Treasury Department was unwieldy and contained many bureaus more closely connected with commercial matters than with fiscal policy or revenue collection. Among these were the Lighthouse Board, the Bureau of Steamboat Inspection, the Bureau of Navigation, and the Bureau of Statistics. If these offices could be taken from the Treasury Department, businessmen reasoned, and put into a new department, Treasury would be more efficient. More important, the transferred offices could then aid commerce more efficiently. Furthermore, the middle-sized and smaller businesses expected the new organization to serve their interests while checking the growing power of the trusts.[4]

The most important function that supporters anticipated was the extension of foreign commerce. A new Department of Commerce, absorbing Treasury's Bureau of Statistics and State's consular service and Bureau of Foreign Commerce, would provide an information agency that would be essential to American success in world markets. Several European countries had such organizations, and if the United States was going to stay in the commercial race, it would need one too. In an age that associated power and effectiveness with consolidation, many businessmen anticipated significant results if the various commercial offices could be grouped together in a single department. National Business League Secretary A. A. Burnham was confident that with the new commerce department and a reorganized consular service, "this country will be well equipped to meet all competition in the markets of the world." Congressional debate over the new entity brought out the same emphasis. One bill's sponsor, Senator Knute Nelson of Minnesota, considered his measure largely an effort to avoid the social and economic crises attending industrial overproduction.[5]

In February 1903, President Roosevelt signed into law Senator Nelson's bill to create the Department of Commerce and Labor.[6] The law required the new department to "foster, promote, and develop the foreign and domestic commerce, the mining, manufacturing, shipping, and fishery industries, the labor interests, and the transportation facilities of the United States." It created only two new bureaus—Manufactures and Corporations—and transferred to the new department a number of offices, chiefly from the Treasury Department. Among these was the Bureau of Statistics, which incorporated Frederic Emory's much smaller Bureau of Foreign Commerce as a division that would continue to publish the consular reports. Nelson's bill left the consuls with the State Department, where the Bureau of Trade Relations was created to serve as liaison between C & L and the consuls. The new department was authorized to initiate its own requests for commercial information; the Bureau of Trade Relations would relay these to the consuls, sending the resulting reports back to C & L.[7]

OSCAR PHELPS AUSTIN AND THE BUREAU OF STATISTICS

Like Emory's Bureau of Foreign Commerce, the office that absorbed it in mid-1903 had antecedents stretching back many decades. In 1820 Congress for the first time formally recognized a need to collect foreign trade statistics. It required the secretary of the Treasury to provide annual statistical accounts of all goods exported from and imported into the United States. In 1866 Congress provided for a Bureau of Statistics in the Treasury Department to prepare these statistics of navigation and commerce, requiring their publication monthly as well as annually.[8] By the turn of the century, both the *Monthly Summary of Commerce and Finance* and the annual *Foreign Commerce and Navigation of the United States* were hefty publications devoted to statistics on imports and exports of raw, semifinished, and finished goods; internal commerce; prices; warehouse transactions; the number and tonnage of vessels entered and cleared; and similar subjects.

The Bureau of Statistics obtained its export and import

figures from the customs collectors. Regulations directed importers at each United States port to file with the collector a statement of quantity and, if possible, value; exporters were required to file a manifest. Each port compiled figures by product and by countries of importation and exportation. The products were classified in six broad categories, according to sources of production: agriculture, mining, forest, fisheries, miscellaneous, and manufactures. In 1906 a more precise classification was adopted, basically the same as the one used today: crude foodstuffs (such as coffee and wheat), foodstuffs partly or wholly prepared (sugar, flour), crude materials for use in manufacturing (raw cotton, raw silk), manufactures for use in manufacturing (lumber, pig-copper), and manufactures ready for consumption (shoes, sewing machines).[9]

Treasury's Bureau of Statistics had increasingly sought to foster the export trade by getting information into the hands of commercial interests. Bureau chief Oscar P. Austin referred to foreign commerce as "the especial province" of his office. He saw his task as analyzing and summarizing statistics, he told Congress, so that if a shoe manufacturer wished to know the number of pairs and value of shoes that had been sent to each country for ten years, he could determine where there might be customers for his product. Like Emory's Bureau of Foreign Commerce, Statistics built up a sizable correspondence with businessmen seeking data about foreign markets.[10]

Regrettably, the zeal to promote foreign commerce by churning out statistical information remained far ahead of the statistics' reliability, even after the 1906 reclassification of products. Export statistics were less accurate than import figures, partly because the latter were related to revenue collection and thus received more official concern. Vast quantities of American exports were transshipped at Liverpool and other European ports, perhaps winding up as far away as China. Yet United States trade statistics often showed only the declared values exported to the first point of transfer without regard to the final destination. One informed official observed that although the Bureau of Statistics reported exports to Switzerland in 1907 amounting to $618,017, the more accurate official Swiss figures showed that American merchandise entering Switzerland totaled $13,537,821.[11]

General Organizational Development of
Commercial Offices before 1912

Before July 1, 1903

TREASURY DEPARTMENT

| Bureau of Statistics |
| O. P. Austin, chief |

STATE DEPARTMENT

| Bureau of Foreign Commerce |
| Frederic Emory, chief |

After July 1, 1903

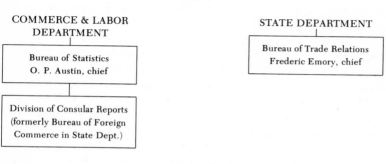

COMMERCE & LABOR
DEPARTMENT

| Bureau of Statistics |
| O. P. Austin, chief |

| Division of Consular Reports |
| (formerly Bureau of Foreign |
| Commerce in State Dept.) |

STATE DEPARTMENT

| Bureau of Trade Relations |
| Frederic Emory, chief |

After July 1, 1905

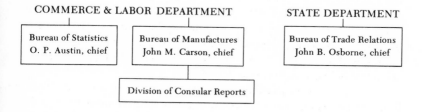

COMMERCE & LABOR DEPARTMENT

| Bureau of Statistics |
| O. P. Austin, chief |

| Bureau of Manufactures |
| John M. Carson, chief |

| Division of Consular Reports |

STATE DEPARTMENT

| Bureau of Trade Relations |
| John B. Osborne, chief |

John M. Carson, a key official at C & L, pointed out a major flaw in the statistical categories the government continued to use after 1906. His observation is important because historians have naturally relied on these categories in assessing the nature and extent of America's foreign commerce. According to Bureau of Statistics figures, as Carson told a congressional committee, manufactured goods amounted to 40 percent of America's export trade in fiscal 1909. But Carson pointed out that the picture was skewed because, among other things, "manufactures ready for consumption" did not include any prepared foodstuffs, although the latter were also manufactured and often just as ready for consumption. Carson asserted that manufactured products actually totaled some 70 percent of United States exports and included bread, flour, canned fish, canned fruits, chemicals, yarns, "and various other commodities which are the result of mechanical manipulation, requiring large industrial plants and the employment of skilled labor."[12] Despite such drawbacks in statistical methods, the Bureau of Statistics spewed forth its figures, particularly with an eye toward promoting exports.

From 1898 until 1912, the bureau was under the direction of Oscar Phelps Austin. Born in 1847 and raised in Nebraska, he was six years older than Frederic Emory, but his background was similar in several respects. He too was a newspaperman; in 1881 he settled in Washington as a correspondent for newspapers of New York, Chicago, and other cities. During the 1888 presidential campaign he traveled with Benjamin Harrison as the Associated Press representative. He was as ardent a Republican as Emory was a Democrat and handled publicity work for the Republican National Committee in 1892 and 1896. From 1900 through 1912 he compiled the quadrennial Republican "text book," which the party faithful used on the political hustings. In 1898 President McKinley and Senator Mark Hanna rewarded Austin by appointing him to head Treasury's Bureau of Statistics. Hanna wanted someone who could use the strategic office to publicize the advantages resulting from the administration's protection policies.[13]

Austin was an ardent publicist. He built up a system in the bureau that dispensed semiweekly statements to thousands of newspapers, providing commercial data to underscore Republican prosperity. It is highly unlikely that his office falsified statistics in order to paint the rosy picture that Hanna wanted. But the bureau chief did tend to interpret commercial statistics optimistically, and he was quick to recognize their political value. In 1908, for example, the Bureau of Statistics distributed statements designed to show that the depression following the 1907 panic was not confined to the

United States. Austin explained that if only a small percentage of the announcements were reproduced in the newspapers, "it means the distribution (at somebody else's expense too) of millions of copies of the statement and thus . . . minimizes dissatisfaction with conditions at home and conduces to content and confidence for the future."[14]

Like Emory, Austin had broad horizons. For many years he served as an officer of the National Geographic Society. He too saw the changes wrought by industrialization and urbanization and noted the drop in agricultural products as a proportion of total exports. He too advocated programs to increase exports of manufactured products, predicting that if the United States was to keep its commercial standing, it would have to export more manufactured goods and compete with European rivals. The competition would be especially fierce "in the higher grades of manufacture, of which labor forms the most important part." Austin considered that the prime necessity was to employ the large numbers of potentially troublesome workers flooding into factories from American farms and from overseas. "We must give to our labor as large a share as possible in the value of our exports," he warned the National Board of Trade. He advised one group of new consuls not to spend time promoting agricultural goods, or even prepared foodstuffs, because they would increasingly be consumed at home.[15]

As in Emory's case, Austin's views on foreign commerce were closely related to his attitudes about domestic politics; for this reason he differed in certain respects from his State Department counterpart. Fundamental to Emory's outlook was the need for tariff reduction, part of the nineteenth-century Liberal program advocated by the Cleveland Democracy. Austin was a protectionist and a neomercantilist, and like Henry Clay more than half a century earlier, he advocated a relatively closed "American system." He thought that the United States should serve a metropolitan function, importing primarily those products unobtainable within its borders—such as coffee, rubber, and other kinds of tropical raw materials—and turning many into finished goods in American factories. Important to the success of such a mercantilist arrangement would be the ability of the United States to sell its burgeoning surpluses of manufactures in the non-European countries, particularly in the tropics: these were the areas with a high proportion of finished manufactures among their imports, and no bothersome tariff barriers against them, from which the United States should be obtaining its own imports. Austin apparently believed that if the United States sought to increase its European markets, it might have to make tariff concessions. Such a course could harm American prosperity and would certainly be bitterly fought by American manufacturing interests, the backbone of Republican party strength.[16]

But most American manufacturers seemed reluctant to meet the competition of Europeans who had long since outgrown their domestic markets and were accustomed to producing specifically for foreign tastes. The frequent indifference of the Americans angered bureaucrats like Austin and Emory, who saw trouble ahead if shortsighted businessmen did not cooperate with the government in a more systematic cultivation of overseas customers. Austin castigated manufacturers for failing to imitate the Europeans and accused them of sending overseas the same kinds of products they fashioned for the domestic market. He complained that American cotton textiles, an important export item, found a large market in northern China and Manchuria only because the climate there was similar to that of the United States. Virtually no American textiles were shipped to southern China or the tropics, because they could not compete with European goods designed for tropical climates. No doubt the unwillingness to produce specifically for foreign markets was one reason for the unfavorable balance of trade with Asia and Latin America.[17]

THE BUREAU OF MANUFACTURES AND ITS EQUIPMENT

When Congress created the Commerce and Labor Department in 1903, two sections of the act were especially important to the department's organization in general and to Austin's bureau in particular. Section 5 provided for a Bureau of Manufactures, whose duties were to "foster, promote, and develop the various manufacturing industries of the United States, and markets for the same at home and abroad, domestic and foreign, by gathering, compiling, publishing, and supplying all available and useful information concerning such industries and such markets. . . ." Congress expected that the secretary would arrange details of structure and personnel in such a way as to accomplish the ambitious task of developing American industries by distributing information. In section 4, the secretary received specific power to reorganize the statistical work and even to consolidate statistical bureaus and offices transferred to the new department. Senator Nelson's committee anticipated, but did not require, that the secretary would in time consolidate the Census Office and Austin's Bureau of Statistics (which by then would contain State's Bureau of Foreign Commerce) into a single statistical office. The lack of specific directives opened the door to bureaucratic skirmishing within the department, delaying some of the intended reorganization for almost a decade.[18]

The heart of the problem was that the anticipated consolidation of several statistics agencies—the Census Office, the Bureau of Statistics, and the Bureau of Labor—would relegate one or more powerful bureau chiefs to a subordinate position. Most frequently discussed was an arrangement to place all statistical work under the control of the Census Office, already the largest statistical division. For obvious reasons of status, Austin opposed this plan. He argued that such a consolidation would rob employees in the three offices of the all-important pride in their work that had thus far resulted in enthusiasm and efficiency.[19]

A few weeks before the department began operations, S. N. D. North, then chief statistician in the Division of Manufactures of the Census and soon to become Director of the Census, hammered out a compromise with Austin and Carroll D. Wright, commissioner of labor.[20] The deal was made at the expense of the yet unhatched Bureau of Manufactures, which lacked a spokesman and established interests. Under the plan that North urged upon Secretary George B. Cortelyou, the Census Office would handle all statistics directly related to domestic manufactures, except for the inquiries carried on by Wright's labor office. Both agencies were already equipped for this work. Austin's Bureau of Statistics would be consolidated with the proposed Bureau of Manufactures under a single chief to form a "Bureau of Foreign Commerce." The proposed entity would have three subdivisions: the Division of Trade Statistics to compile the export and import returns (Austin's current task), the Division of Foreign Commerce to publish the consular reports (Emory's

Bureau of Foreign Commerce), and a new Division of Publicity and Information to handle the work contemplated by Congress when it created the Bureau of Manufactures. Three influential bureau chiefs could thus be kept content, and the reorganization could still go forward. Cortelyou might well have adopted the proposal, but he was simultaneously getting other advice from James Garfield.[21]

Now head of the new Bureau of Corporations in C & L, Garfield had his own organizational scheme to push. He wished to combine the proposed Bureau of Manufactures with the Bureau of Labor into a "Bureau of Industries." Garfield expected that the new entity would deal with current and future problems of industrial growth by bringing capital and labor into what he vaguely described as a "close relationship." The Bureau of Statistics and the Census Office could then be consolidated into a single large statistical agency under the director of the census.[22]

Cortelyou was cautious and saw no reason to act with careless haste, considering his most important task "to lay well and substantially the foundations for the work of the future." He failed in the end to line up behind either recommendation and resigned in mid-1904 to run Roosevelt's election campaign. Later that year his successor, Victor Metcalf, organized a small Bureau of Manufactures that was not consolidated with Statistics or Labor or any other office. Austin argued in vain that the new bureau's work should not be separated from his Bureau of Statistics.[23]

The embryonic Bureau of Manufactures managed to survive attempts by rival factions to divide it among other agencies. Yet by the time Cortelyou left the department for the relative peace and quiet of a presidential campaign, Manufactures was still nothing more than a section in the organic act that had created C & L. The first significant move toward organizing the bureau came in December 1904, when Roosevelt appointed J. Hampton Moore of Philadelphia as its chief. Moore had been active in the president's campaign, and the appointment was probably his reward.[24]

Like everyone else concerned, the new chief was puzzled about the bureau's duties and considered them vague. Secretary Metcalf passed along Moore's questions to the department's legal officer, who informed Metcalf that the law's language was "extremely broad and general" and urged him to organize the bureau as he wished. Moore began sounding out some associations of manufacturers, asking them what his bureau could do to promote their interests.[25]

By April, Moore was oriented to the point that he considered the Bureau of Manufactures part of a comprehensive "forward trade movement," which included commercial education, encouragement of manufacturing and trade opportunities within the United States, operation of a string of commercial museums, foreign trade promotion, and other functions. During that same month, the bureau began more systematically to establish connections with its constituency. It sent a large number of form letters to commercial and industrial associations across the country, informing them of its existence and requesting information about firms and products involved in the export trade. The replies were indexed and filed for future reference.[26]

Moore resigned in June to accept a higher paying position in private business, but the work continued under his successor, John M. Carson. The 67-year-old Carson was manager of the consolidated Washington bureaus of the *New York Times* and *Philadelphia Public Ledger* and had long been the acknowledged dean of the capital's press corps. Years before, he had helped found the famed Gridiron Club and had served as its first president. He also possessed good Republican credentials and occasionally did field work for the party. Joining Carson in the Bureau of Manufactures as its new assistant chief was the elderly Edgar J. Gibson, editorial writer and Washington bureau manager for the *Philadelphia Press*, who likewise had good political connections.[27]

Despite Moore's inclusion of domestic commerce on his list of agency responsibilities, the Bureau of Manufactures from the beginning concentrated solely on increasing the export trade. John Carson exaggerated the novelty of his office, but did not misstate its purpose, when before a House committee he called it "the first organized effort of the Government to promote the sale of our manufactures in foreign markets." The bureau sought to help the smaller and medium-sized firms by providing information to compensate for their lack of knowledge about the foreign field.[28]

Bureau employees contributed to the familiar chorus about

industrial overproduction. Charles Donaldson, head of the bureau's Division of Consular Reports, referred to "the need for new foreign outlets for our wares" because of the "intense activity in industrial life, and . . . the skillful automatic mechanisms being brought into use." Donaldson emphasized that these outlets would "become a necessity when the first dull period occurs in business." By providing information and urging businessmen to use it, the Bureau of Manufactures was expected to produce large results. As Secretary Oscar Straus told Carson, Manufactures was "supposed to lift this country on the Pisgah of prosperity."[29] It was from the Pisgah mountain range that Moses had first looked down upon the promised land, and Straus's biblical allusion suggested the sort of benefits many expected from the new entity. But the bureau was only slowly acquiring tools to accomplish its task.

Between 1903 and 1905, Commerce and Labor repeatedly asked Congress to supply funds for a corps of special agents to supplement the consuls' work. The agents would not be confined to a single district, and they could travel widely to study foreign market opportunities. Secretary Cortelyou told the House Appropriations Committee that they would be "broad-gauged" men who were "big enough" to travel and report on trade conditions throughout entire regions. A year later Secretary Metcalf made the same request, reminding the committee that the large corporations could "send their own agents abroad; but the small manufacturer, the small producer, and the man with limited capital can not stand the expense."[30]

Metcalf was successful, and in 1905 Congress provided $30,000 for the special agents. The adoption of the proposal was due principally to the support of legislators from the cotton-producing states. Since successful consular legislation and the State Department quota system were still in the future, those Democratic strongholds were virtually without representation in the consular service; their representatives in Congress thought the cotton interests suffered accordingly. Congressman Leonidas Felix Livingston of Georgia observed that Congress supplied the funds "for the purpose of getting our cotton goods into China and Japan." C & L repaid the southern states with numerous reports on foreign commercial opportunities for cotton products.[31]

The department secured the services of four agents, dispatching two to the Far East, one to South America, and one to Canada and Mexico. Bureau of Manufactures chief Carson explained that the agents would "inquire into the business conditions there, what merchandise is imported, from what countries it is imported, whether any similar merchandise is imported from the United States, and if not, why not; the tastes and habits of the people, their preferences for imported merchandise, their purchasing power, and generally into everything connected with foreign trade." Secretary Metcalf instructed the first group that their investigations would concentrate on "industrial and commercial, and incidentally agricultural conditions." Many products, Metcalf told them, were classified as agricultural, yet were "the result of manual manipulation and therefore may properly be included in the scope of your investigations. This applies to all products of farm, notably wheat flour and other meals." Mindful of his congressional friends, Metcalf told his new employees to make "manufactures of cotton . . . a subject of careful inquiry." Although the appropriations placed them under the secretary's office, the agents operated out of the Bureau of Manufactures.[32]

The special agents took to the field and soon began sending back lengthy reports on trade conditions in Brazil, Canada, China, Japan, and other areas. From China, the agents sent samples of imported cotton goods. The Bureau of Manufactures distributed some eight thousand of these, together with information about prices and the popularity of various patterns, to cotton manufacturing centers and commercial organizations throughout the southern and eastern United States. The agents gradually became more specialized, conducting investigations in particular lines of goods. By early 1908 their number included two experts in cotton fabrics, one in cottonseed products (cottonseed oil was a major export item), one in leather goods, one in agricultural machinery, and one in large machinery and machine tools.[33]

Most of the special agents were recommended to the department by national industrial organizations, sometimes after solicitation by C & L. Congressman Livingston gave a good description of the snowballing process that resulted in the greater attention to specific commodity lines. After the original appropriation was

granted, Livingston recalled in 1910, "the cotton seed men came in
and insisted . . . that the by-products of the cotton, which was [sic]
chiefly cotton seed, ought to be advertised and pushed ahead, and
that was granted. Then the . . . agricultural implement men came
along, and said they ought to have a show, too. Then the shoe men
came along and said they ought to have a show." By early 1912, the
number of agents had grown to thirteen.[34]

    Some congressmen questioned the practice of such
specialized promotion for the benefit of particular industries. At a
committee hearing in 1908, Albert Sidney Burleson of Texas and
James Tawney of Minnesota grilled Secretary Oscar Straus about his
advocacy of a special agent to investigate foreign markets for flour.
Straus replied that he had been receiving letters from the flour millers, that "it is a very large interest, and it appears to me that if we
can help this large interest in any way, the Department should do
it." Carson chimed in with the overproduction argument that milling capacity had far outgrown domestic demand and that to keep the
mills going for more than six months—thus keeping both mill labor
and farmers satisfied—the millers would have to sell more of their
product abroad. A few months later, the Millers' National Federation was understandably "deeply grateful" to Straus when he appointed a special agent to report on foreign commercial opportunities for American millers.[35]

    The Bureau of Manufactures began another important ser-
vice in 1905. In June 1903, Cortelyou had received an inquiry from
South Africa about the possibility of enlarging that market for
American products, and the secretary asked Austin for suggestions.
Austin saw the chief problem as bringing American businessmen
into closer touch with foreign importers. He proposed that the department compile lists of American manufacturers and exporters,
using the most recent census, and of foreign merchants willing to
handle American goods, using consuls to supply the information.
Austin repeated the suggestion to Metcalf in November 1904. During the next year, the new Bureau of Manufactures began sending
out questionnaires and compiling lists of American manufacturers.
By early 1907, it was eliciting such information about individual
firms as location of branch establishments, product descriptions,

capital assets, capacity per day, per month, or per year, where products were sold and, if abroad, the countries and ports to which they were shipped. In 1908 bureau chief Carson asked that the State Department send him any requests by foreign merchants for names of reliable American manufacturers or exporters. He explained that his office was in a position "to help the consul put the prospective purchaser in communication with those firms who can supply and are especially desirous of such orders." The Bureau of Manufactures also had begun to receive names of foreign importers from the consuls.[36]

Before the creation of Commerce and Labor, responsibility for furnishing businessmen with the names of foreign importers had rested with the State Department. It was a troublesome issue and remained so for years after the Bureau of Manufactures was organized. Manufacturers in the United States who were interested in selling their products abroad were understandably anxious that they contract to send their goods only to honest and reliable merchants. They frequently wrote United States consuls, inquiring about the local reputation and commercial rating of various firms. The State Department was eager to help, but it was hindered by two considerations. First, there were commercial agencies such as Dun and Company, whose business was to furnish commercial ratings for a fee. Second, and more important, some department officials were reluctant to have the government take the responsibility of assuring prospective sellers that a foreign importer was financially responsible. In 1894 Frederic Emory and his predecessor in the State Department's Bureau of Statistics, Edward Renick, wished to change the department's policy and allow consuls to transmit commercial ratings, but they were overruled. Third Assistant Secretary William Rockhill argued that by giving a rating the consul was making an official statement that might be unjustly biased by his sources. Renick fumed that trade could "not be fostered if our consuls are *forbidden* to assist in cases of this kind." In a memorandum almost a year later, Emory called attention to the conflict between official policy as outlined by Rockhill and the current instructions to consuls to "do everything they consistently can to aid American business enterprises and to widen the markets for our surplus products." He tried to find a middle ground, publishing in the *Consular Reports* details about how to ascertain the reliability of foreign importers.[37]

The problem remained for many years, but the State Department gradually moved toward supplying the information. One method was to give a pointed reminder to inquirers, who were often dissatisfied with merely the names of foreign merchants and insisted on a commercial rating, that consuls would not supply the names of any firms they did not consider reputable. Later, consuls were even permitted to comment on the general reputation of individual firms, although they could not give specific commercial ratings. (Consular replies to businessmen's inquiries were increasingly channeled through the State Department, where they could be carefully monitored.) The department strongly advised businessmen to corroborate such comments with agencies like Dun's, and to obtain from them a specific commercial rating.[38]

After Carr took charge of the consular service, his position resembled Emory's and Renick's. He believed that if "the consular service is to be made of real value to the business interests of the country, . . . one of its functions must be to put the foreign purchaser in touch with the American manufacturer and exporter." As he told officials of Dun and Company, such information was "recognized as essential to the upbuilding of our foreign trade."[39]

Carr and his colleagues retained maneuvering room, however, and they applied the policy on an ad hoc basis. Carr wrote some companies that consuls could not supply information about a merchant's general standing; he wrote others that they could. Perhaps the difference depended on how much discretion he was willing to grant a particular consul, or what amount of assistance he wished to render a particular company, or whether the firm was complaining about a consul's response. From time to time the department even supplied foreigners with assurances about the good repute of American firms seeking foreign business, in instances where, according to John Osborne, the bureaucrats considered it "amply justified by the large interests at stake in the trade expansion of the United States." As with other trade promotion issues, the guidelines were not always clear, but the goal was the same—to expand the export trade. As Osborne noted in 1911, "the bars of the old time conservatism of the Department of State have been thrown down to some extent in recent years."[40]

By compiling lists of reliable foreign merchants, the Bureau of Manufactures could make this important service more complete and systematic. In 1906 the Department of Commerce and Labor requested that the consuls supply the names of all business houses within their districts which imported, or might be interested in importing, American goods. Two years later, C & L asked that consuls classify these firms according to the lines of goods handled and then rank them in order of general reputation. The National Business League worked with the Bureau of Trade Relations and certain consuls to publish American export trade directories for eleven countries. The league was experimenting with the plan and hoped to persuade the government to publish a single directory covering the whole world.[41]

By 1910 C & L was pressing Congress for funds to publish such a world directory. To drum up additional interest among merchants and manufacturers, Carson sent out a form letter outlining the project and enclosing an order blank. "The names have been carefully gone over," he assured the businessmen, "and only those of individuals and firms have been selected for publication who are known to be actively engaged in foreign trade or who are equipped for such trade, and who are regarded in their respective localities as financially sound and trustworthy." The initial response was heartening, and Carson passed along extracts from the more enthusiastic letters to Congressman James Tawney for his use on the House floor.[42]

Congress complied and appropriated $6,500. At C & L's request, in June 1910 Carr ordered the consuls to submit names of those importers generally regarded as financially responsible and to arrange the names in the order of their commercial standing in the community. The Bureau of Manufactures used the facilities of export-oriented groups like the Boston Chamber of Commerce to help bring the directory to the attention of individual firms likely to be interested. Published early in 1911 and selling for five dollars, the *World Trade Directory* within a year had repaid the government twice the amount appropriated by Congress.[43]

By assuming publication of the consular reports, the Bureau of Manufactures established another important link with the nation's business community. Austin's Bureau of Statistics had absorbed Emory's old Bureau of Foreign Commerce in July 1903 and published the consular reports until Manufactures was organized. In mid-1905, the Division of Consular Reports was shifted to Manufactures, where it continued to turn out daily, monthly, and annual editions. During one six-month period in 1907, the bureau received 5,500 consular reports and another 500 pieces of commercial information from other sources, including the special agents and English-language newspapers. The United States was the only major power that published trade information daily. Germany published data only three times a week, and Great Britain weekly, but both of those countries had additional channels to their businessmen.[44]

Between 1905 and 1907, a number of officials began to perceive the necessity of a more confidential means of disseminating commercial intelligence. There was evidence that merchants and manufacturers of other nations were availing themselves of the information that C & L broadcast so widely. Consuls-General Frank Mason and Alexander Thackara at Berlin and Consuls Albert Halstead at Birmingham and Thomas Sammons at Newchwang alerted the State Department to this problem. Halstead described how the British Board of Trade funneled its news through the chambers of commerce, while Mason and Thackara praised the German policy of confidentiality. Huntington Wilson found Halstead's report "very interesting" and became "enthusiastic" over the proposed establishment of a confidential network. Wilbur Carr and Secretary Root also encouraged C & L to develop such a system.[45]

C & L was already moving in that direction. Oscar Austin had expressed his own misgivings in 1905. He considered that the "use of our consular reports for the benefit of our business rivals is so frequent and the benefit thus given to our trade rivals so great" that he recommended curtailing "the miscellaneous and wide distribution which has prevailed in the past." In February 1906, a subordinate official in Manufactures' consular reports division, Charles S. Donaldson, initiated Foreign Trade Opportunities. The new service called attention, through the widely disseminated published reports, to specific opportunities for the sale of American goods.

Short announcements stated that in a certain country a party desired to communicate with Americans who manufactured or handled a particular product, and that additional information could be obtained by writing the Bureau of Manufactures. A typical statement read: "*Condensers*—A brewer and malter in Bohemia is in the market for condensers with the latest improvements." Inquirers were furnished with the details, including the name of the consul who had initially supplied the information. Donaldson informed Secretary Straus in 1907 that the Foreign Trade Opportunities had already led "not only to sales of small and large lots of American goods, but to new connections, enabling exporters to build up a larger trade in the opening wedge thus driven in." He also thought the new system stimulated the consuls by recognizing their efforts, and he was probably correct. Another benefit was that growing numbers of businessmen were brought into direct contact with Manufactures, and the lists of manufacturers and merchants active or interested in the export trade lengthened considerably.[46]

Although the system was retained in its original form for many years, it had drawbacks. One was the matter of time; a few days spent exchanging letters might be crucial. Another was that by giving the geographical location, the published message was likely to alert foreign industrial rivals. The bureau thus began to supplement Foreign Trade Opportunities with other means of communicating items of interest. It sent "confidential circulars" and "confidential bulletins" to American firms it believed might be in a position to act on them. The circulars (very often only a single page) and the bulletins (more extensive and infrequent monographic studies) notified American businessmen about such topics as a proposed American bank in Russia, a drainage project near Rio de Janeiro, the Greek army's need for shoes, a street railway and lighting project in Harbin, and the market for cast-iron pipe in Canada. American diplomats as well as consuls supplied tips.[47]

The form in which the bureau prepared the circulars depended on the type of information, the urgency of its transmission, and the number of firms to be notified. Individual letters, carbon copies, multigraph copies, or printed copies (if the number exceeded 100) might be used for different pieces of information. The most important items went out quickly in the mail via confidential circular, while the bureau published the great majority of confidential pieces in Foreign Trade Opportunities. Responses to the latter doubtless helped enlarge the mailing list for confidential circulars and bulletins. In fiscal 1910 the bureau printed 119 confidential circulars and 1,567 Foreign Trade Opportunities, and two years later the annual figures had grown to 136 and over 2,000 respectively. By March 1911, one-third of the bureau's outgoing correspondence (altogether 55,000 pieces annually) consisted of confidential circulars. As a result, the able consul-general Alexander Thackara in Berlin could write in 1912 that "there is no longer as much particular information in the [published] Reports of value to foreign competitors."[48]

CHARLES NAGEL'S DEPARTMENT

Since the establishment of the department in 1903, officials at Commerce and Labor had often been preoccupied with questions of departmental organization. The growth and achievements of the Bureau of Manufactures did not quiet criticisms that the department had one too many statistical bureaus and that the Bureau of Statistics should be merged with either Census or Manufactures. Oscar Straus had formed a special departmental committee, composed of academicians as well as bureaucrats, which recommended the consolidation of Statistics and Manufactures into a "Bureau of Foreign and Domestic Commerce." But the Roosevelt administration had come to an end before Straus could act.[49]

Charles Nagel, Saint Louis lawyer and businessman, succeeded Straus as secretary of Commerce and Labor in March 1909. Although he was not President Taft's first choice for the post, his ideas fit in with the administration's general tenor and direction, which one newspaper described as "a great correlated, unifying national policy." Nagel was an articulate spokesman for the inevitability of greater centralization of power in the federal government. An important official in an administration under attack by Republican insurgents as well as Democrats, he sought a cohesive national policy that would benefit both the country and the Taft regime. Nagel found such an approach in a broad commercial program stressing foreign commerce and including such elements as a subsidized merchant marine, a national chamber of commerce, and an antitrust policy that would not undercut firms that the federal government was urging to expand overseas.[50] As secretary of Commerce and Labor, Nagel was in a strategic position to advance such a program. The first head to last a full four years, he had that advantage over his predecessors in the post.

Soon after taking charge of the department, Nagel was briefed on the past attempts to consolidate Manufactures and Statistics. In July he sought to apply the appropriations for the two bureaus to a consolidated Bureau of Foreign and Domestic Commerce, but the comptroller of the Treasury turned him down. The acting attorney-general rebuffed Nagel's appeal a few days later. Both officers told him that the provision in the 1903 organic act giving him consolidation powers should be taken literally; it applied only to those bureaus transferred to C & L, not to bureaus created by the act itself.[51]

Nagel attempted to secure such legislation at the next congressional session. He wrote Congressman David J. Foster of Vermont, pleading that C & L had thus far made only a beginning, "and that we shall have to collect information and more especially distribute it among the people upon a very much larger scale than has so far been true." For the most part, he argued, "large interests may be trusted to get large orders by their own efforts. The information which is calculated to arouse general interest in international trade can be provided by the Government alone." Nagel was anxious to mobilize business support and cooperation, and he informed Foster that consolidation of the two bureaus would make it "very much easier to establish satisfactory relations with the commercial forces of this country." As usual, Congress was slow to respond and did not grant Nagel's request.[52]

Rebuffed in his attempts to secure consolidation, Nagel did the next best thing. In 1910 he set about reorganizing the Bureau of Manufactures, making it a more effective instrument for export promotion. During the summer and fall, he eased both Carson and Assistant Chief Edgar Gibson out of the bureau, assigning Carson as a special agent and sending Gibson to the Tariff Board. Nagel brought in the much younger and more vigorous chief clerk of the department, Albertus H. Baldwin, to head Manufactures. Baldwin was not a newsman or publicist or well-connected politically; he was appointed from the classified civil service, as Wilbur Carr and Gaillard Hunt had been. Nagel was proud that his four most important departmental appointments, including Baldwin, came from the classified service.[53]

Under Baldwin, the volume of work in the Bureau of Manufactures grew considerably. In 1911 the bureau received 20,043 inquiries about items in Foreign Trade Opportunities, compared with 12,937 the previous year. By the fall of 1912, its correspondence from businessmen had grown to 75,000 pieces, up from 35,000 only two years earlier. Certain improvements were made to place American businessmen into closer contact with foreign buyers. Late in 1911 Baldwin began obtaining from the consuls the names of representatives in the United States of foreign importing firms, so that the bureau could put American manufacturers in touch with them. Also in 1911, Manufactures made the barest of beginnings in promoting domestic commerce. Under the caption "Home Trade Opportunities," the *Daily Consular and Trade Reports* carried information about contracts to be awarded by executive departments. Baldwin hoped that the domestic side of the work could gradually be expanded.[54]

Among the significant changes before 1912 were those involving the department's special agents. In 1910 their designation was changed to "commercial agents," because many of them had felt they were looked down upon as secret agents and recommended the revision. The next year, Congress provided funds for the department to dispatch the commercial agents on a regular basis to confer with American businessmen. Like the State Department, C & L believed that such a development would make the agents more efficient in collecting information and in disseminating it. Nagel was impressed with this aspect of British and German policy and had told Congress, "We ought to go further by way of communicating with commercial organizations in this country." By early 1912, the department had thirteen commercial agents on a payroll of $60,000, traveling abroad and meeting with business groups at home.[55]

The Bureau of Manufactures thus became increasingly active in promoting foreign commerce and in several ways was linked to the commercial public. Although Nagel believed that much remained to be done, he could proudly inform one correspondent in December 1911 that the "interest in the commercial branch of my department has greatly increased." At that time, the bureau's mailing list contained nearly 18,000 names of manufacturers, classified according to some 400 different kinds of products.[56] Such a situation did not sit well with the State Department, which considered itself the government's primary trade promoter. Indeed, from the earliest days of C & L's development, there had been a fierce struggle between the two departments.

RIVALRY

State Department officials had entertained uncomplimentary thoughts about the new department since before its inception. Middle-echelon bureaucrats, anxious to enlist businessmen's support, were particularly disturbed. Gaillard Hunt scoffed to Harry Garfield that a Department of Commerce and Industry could not "increase commerce or industry any more than the Department of Agriculture can increase the litters of pigs." And Frederic Emory was upset in the spring of 1903 by what he considered attempts to "loot" the State Department of its proper functions.[57]

With the emergence of C & L's special agents corps in 1905, consuls and department officials found additional reasons to be annoyed. They complained that some of the agents made superficial investigations and lifted many of their "on-the-scene" reports from data collected by the local American consul. When the Bureau of Manufactures published the results, the abused consuls fumed. Consul-General Edward O. Ozmun pointed out that it was "particularly discouraging to a consular officer to have his work purloined." Other consular and departmental officers believed that while the agents sometimes supplied valuable information, the same amount of money could be more profitably spent on a system of commercial attachés—under the State Department's control.[58]

The State Department's irritation was compounded when the consuls and special agents began running into one another at businessmen's conventions, competing in the domestic dissemination of commercial information as well as in its collection. Consul-General Lewis Iddings at Cairo appeared at one gathering to find

Charles Pepper, then working as a special agent, already present to dispense data about trade opportunities in Egypt. C & L was dispatching its returning agents to selected commercial centers years before it received an appropriation from Congress for that purpose. It sent one agent, recently returned with textile samples from a visit to the Lancashire district in Great Britain, on a tour of the manufacturing centers of the South, and it detailed a leather expert to New England. In 1907 Wilbur Carr wanted the special agents withdrawn from overseas investigations and confined to the United States. The State Department's failure to secure this arrangement may have prompted Carr's suggestion only a few months later that consuls should systematically be dispatched to confer with businessmen. In 1911 the State Department ignored Baldwin's pointed request that since the Bureau of Manufactures was "in close relations with practically all the important organizations of manufacturers and exporters in the United States," returning consuls should be funneled to meetings with businessmen through that bureau's facilities.[59]

Another source of tension between the two departments was C & L's publication of the consular reports. State Department officials believed that the Bureau of Manufactures gave editorial preference to reports from its own special agents, publishing them at length, while often condensing or even omitting consular reports. This practice discouraged both the consuls, who were trying to build careers chiefly as commercial reporters, and the department officials cheering them on. Inspector Alfred Gottschalk found this discouragement an "unfortunately general" feeling in the service. Some consuls, distressed that their reports were not getting into print, began notifying various trade papers in the United States that upon application to the Bureau of Manufactures they could obtain a report on a particular subject. If Manufactures received enough requests, it would publish the report.[60]

Although some friction over publication was inevitable because of the division of labor, it was considerably intensified by poor performance in the Bureau of Manufactures during its early years. In 1906 Consul-General Eugene Seeger at Rio de Janeiro was outraged by a piece of editing that made him and his reporting look ridiculous. Included in the published version of his report on Brazil were references to millions of horses roaming the grassy plains and

large quantities of corn and wheat growing in the Amazon basin. He
wrote Assistant Secretary of State Bacon:

> If, for instance, the French government would publish the
> following: "Consul X in New York reporting on the commer-
> cial record of the United States says: . . . On the extreme
> eastern part of the country are the deserts or sandy plains, on
> which roam millions of camels, many being caught and sold
> in the different markets of the world. . . . Quite large quan-
> tities of tea and coffee are grown in the Mississippi Basin, but
> none for export;" you would have a counterpart of the above
> mentioned official statement which unfortunately is attrib-
> uted to me.

Seeger reminded Bacon of the discouraging effect such editing had
on consular reporting efforts and suggested that American commerce would "be better served, if the Official Consular Reports
are published without the addition of fantastic embellishments
which recall the most vivid scenes of Robinson Crusoe or the Ara-
bian Nights." C & L Assistant Secretary Lawrence Murray admitted that the published report was unjustified. On another occasion,
President Roosevelt sent a blistering letter to Secretary Oscar
Straus demanding an explanation from Carson "for the gross
carelessness (to use no harsher term)" that had allowed the publication of a special agent's report containing "an insult to England."[61]

Despite Straus's warnings to the Bureau of Manufactures, he
was kept busy apologizing to the State Department for such errors.
Assistant bureau chief Gibson was responsible for examining the
copy after it was edited, but he made the remarkable statement to
Straus that he did not always have time to do it. To Straus's question
about the publication of a confidential passage which the Bureau of
Trade Relations had clearly marked for deletion, Gibson replied that
the section "seemed to the gentleman who edited the copy helpful
to the sense of the article."[62]

The classic blunder occurred late in the summer of 1907.
Gibson saw an item printed in the *Washington Post*, credited to the
State Department, about Chinese tariff rates. He clipped it and
published it in the consular reports. Officials at State were dismayed
because the subject involved diplomatic negotiations, and they

wanted to know where the Bureau of Manufactures had obtained the information and why it had placed it in an official government publication. In a letter signed by Assistant Secretary Murray, C & L defensively explained the item's origin and scolded State for not forwarding the dispatch for publication. With admirable restraint, Alvey Adee pointed out to Murray that since "the subject matter is contained in despatches relating to pending diplomatic negotiations," his department could hardly have forwarded them. Murray promptly apologized to Adee, explaining that his previous letter had been drafted in the Bureau of Manufactures (almost certainly by Gibson) and that he had signed it when he was extremely busy with other matters. "It is an absolutely stupid letter from start to finish," Murray generously admitted. "The Bureau of Manufactures of this Department has during its existence kept the Secretary constantly apologizing for its stupid and humiliating blunders. This is simply one more added to the already long list."[63]

Although he sent threatening letters to his Bureau of Manufactures, Straus retained Carson and Gibson in their positions. Unlike Charles Nagel, Straus was a former gold Democrat and may have believed that he lacked the political clout to remove men with Republican friends in high places. After 1907 the frequency and magnitude of the publishing errors did diminish, flaring up only occasionally thereafter. The bureau's proven capacity for such carelessness helped spur the State Department's desire for expanding the confidential information network, both through confidential circulars and by sending consuls to confer personally with businessmen.[64]

Officers at C & L, on the other hand, had their complaints against the State Department. In their opinion, the 1903 act had given them the primary responsibility for promoting foreign commerce. Yet they were forced to give instructions to the consuls and receive reports from them through a State Department bureau that had grown to rival their own Bureau of Manufactures. Austin and Carson, with the support of the National Business League, wanted the consuls and the Consular Bureau shifted to the new department. They argued that since the consuls' work was commercial, it should be under C & L's jurisdiction. Both Straus and Nagel, however, were more interested in having their department communicate directly with the consuls than in absorbing either the consular corps or the Consular Bureau. They insisted that direct communication would significantly shorten the time between the writing of the reports and their dissemination.[65]

State Department officers saw both proposals as threats. The same bureaucrats who usually stressed the consuls' utility to commerce often took pains to point out their many additional duties relating to other aspects of foreign relations. Obliged to sell the consular service on the basis of its utility to the export trade, these officials had to beware of going too far. If Congress or the public believed that consular functions involved only trade promotion, the State Department might lose the consuls to the rival department. A lengthy memorandum by Carr in 1908 spelled out the variety of consular tasks for Secretary Root, arguing that by placing the consuls under C & L for commercial reporting the government would be creating "a dual administrative jurisdiction which is fatal to efficient and economical administration." Carr and his colleagues were also quick to protest any attempt by C & L to bypass State and communicate directly with consuls and diplomats. They were anxious to avoid establishing any precedent for dual control, and they made it clear that any instructions or even suggestions that C & L wished to send to State's field foreign service would travel through the State Department.[66]

Officials at State were also certain that unless their department edited the consular reports, all sorts of embarrassing material would find its way into print. Gaillard Hunt once protested the provision in an early Commerce Department bill which would have given the new department substantial control over the consuls. "The consuls would be in a pretty mess if they were under the contemplated department and ourselves at the same time," he wrote Harry Garfield. "If all the commercial reports were printed we would spend our lifetime apologizing to other nations."[67] Similar arguments had prompted congressional provision for the Bureau of Trade Relations in 1903.

There was ample cause for their concern. Like the special agent who, in an official published report, described a Latin American merchant as a "hustling native," consuls and even diplomats were likely to make imprudent and potentially embarrassing remarks. A consul in Japan sent in a Foreign Trade Opportunity regarding the market for American moving pictures, which he reported receptive to "love affairs, with hugging and kissing, or pictures calculated to stir the passions." In a magazine article, former consul Albert Washburn recounted an even more vivid example. While traveling into the interior of the country to which he was assigned, a consul had made special note of "the swarms of naked savages" along the riverbank. "He confided to the Department," Washburn told his readers, "in the course of his formal 'report,' that if he had had a rifle handy he would have taken a 'crack' at the game; and he hinted that there were 'lots of our boys' who would enjoy the same absorbing sport if they were fully informed of the attractions offered. The ruthless blue pencil of a department clerk deprived the country at large of this rare gem of humor, with all its possibilities." Although the consular service improved vastly over the years, it was John Osborne's opinion in 1912 that there were still "few consuls indeed" whose trade reports did not "require *close* scrutiny" for potentially embarrassing statements.[68]

To counter complaints from C & L about delays in publication arising from the current practice, Osborne prepared elaborate studies. They showed an average delay of only three days in the State Department, compared with an additional thirty days at Commerce and Labor before publication. In their stress on the "average" delay, however, the figures were deceptive. Particularly after the geographic divisions began functioning in 1907, the most valuable reports often circulated among officials at State. Osborne's bureau was careful to leave the date of receipt off any document forwarded to C & L, to avoid "adverse criticism." At the same time, the Bureau of Manufactures was putting the most significant commercial reports into confidential circulars and getting them out to businessmen on the same day it received them. Thus C & L could charge with some justification that delays at the State Department were preventing American businessmen from receiving important commercial information as quickly as possible. On the other hand, the reports that circulated among State Department officers were important to the conduct of foreign policy. If State had possessed confidence in the discretion of either its field foreign service or the

Bureau of Manufactures, perhaps it could have followed Baldwin's suggestion that the consuls send directly to his bureau copies of their "strictly trade and commercial" reports (assuming there was such a thing).[69] But if that had been done, State would probably have found it much harder to justify the continued existence of the Bureau of Trade Relations.

Much of the tension and hostility between the two departments, while exacerbated by specific instances and even issues, was due to a fundamental and essentially irreconcilable difference of opinion about their respective roles. The State Department's position, which officials there stated frequently and forcefully to congressional committees, to businessmen, and to each other, was that State was the collector of commercial information abroad for Commerce and Labor to disseminate at home. Osborne insisted in 1912 that "the conduct of the foreign relations of the United States belongs, logically and as a matter of right, *exclusively* to the Department of State. No part of this function can be surrendered or delegated to another executive department."[70]

Osborne's demarcation was fictional on two counts. C & L had its own field foreign service gathering information (a practice State wished to see terminated), and State not only sent its consuls to confer with commercial groups at home but also encouraged American businessmen to visit the Bureau of Trade Relations and geographic divisions (practices which the senior department had no desire to abandon). Nevertheless, State Department officers stuck to this line of argument. Carr even traveled to Nagel's home town in 1910 to inform the Saint Louis Businessmen's League that although Nagel and his department were doing good work, "the real responsibility for the preservation of markets rests upon the Department of State."[71]

To some degree, of course, officials at State were confusing the actual division with what they desired. They were convinced that only their organization had the machinery and the outlook necessary to deal with commercial matters all over the world. One official summed up their attitude when he contended that the many errors in the first *World Trade Directory* would not have been committed if experienced consuls had been in charge of the Bureau of Manufactures, and he asked rhetorically: "How can people whose horizon is bounded by F Street prepare a 'World Trade Directory'?"[72]

Commerce and Labor naturally had a different perspective. As State drew the line between foreign affairs and domestic affairs, C & L drew it between commercial and noncommercial work. Baldwin and his colleagues considered the other department only an "accessory" in foreign trade promotion, while their department, and the Bureau of Manufactures in particular, was "primarily the commercial promotive branch of the government." Supported by the 1903 organic act, they thought that State had no business taking the initiative in foreign trade promotion. Baldwin emphasized "the fundamental fact that the *initiative and essential control* of commercial development must rest with the Department of Commerce and Labor." Carson asked that State's diplomatic instructions dealing with commercial overtures to foreign governments be submitted to his bureau for its opinions. Nagel himself made the sweeping statement to a Senate committee that regarding "commercial matters" the State Department should act "upon the advice and counsel of the Department of Commerce."[73] Since officials at C & L insisted on their primacy in trade promotion, they took strong exception when the State Department rhetorically divided the responsibility at the boundaries of the United States.

By 1912 the Department of Commerce and Labor had developed into a full-fledged rival in a field that once had belonged solely to the State Department. Each agency was equipped with its own field foreign service and continuously sought to improve its contacts with American businessmen. Rather than accepting the situation, bureaucrats in each organization considered the other a continuing and ever-growing threat to the operations of their own department, and by mid-1911 they were on a collision course.

9   SHOWDOWN

Accompanying the expansion of the federal bureaucracy around the turn of the century was a growing concern for efficiency and "business methods" in its operations. By the early months of the Taft administration, the rising chorus of criticism over alleged waste and duplication had become sufficiently general to spur bipartisan action. In 1909 Congressman James Tawney of Minnesota, the powerful Republican chairman of the House Appropriations Committee, voiced strong disapproval of a rapidly rising federal budget, which amounted that year to one billion dollars.[1]

During the special congressional session convened by Taft in 1909 to enact a tariff law, the Senate established a Public Expenditures Committee to investigate the "expenditures and business methods" of the government departments. From this committee emerged a bill, introduced at the following session by the influential Nelson A. Aldrich of Rhode Island, providing for a Business Methods Committee to comprise three members of the House, three of the Senate, and three presidential appointees. Aldrich claimed that $100,000,000 could be saved by improved business methods. After amending the measure to remove any participation by the executive, the senators approved it in February 1910. But the bill died in the House of Representatives. The House already had a number of investigatory committees, one for each executive department, and it was unwilling to adopt the Senate's format.[2]

In the wake of these uncoordinated efforts, Taft managed to establish his own unit. In June 1910, Congress supplied $100,000 for a presidential commission to investigate governmental efficiency —the first executive probe explicitly funded by Congress. The appropriation provided that the commission would employ "accountants and experts from private life."[3]

During the next few months, presidential secretary Charles Norton headed a preliminary investigation. Frederick A. Cleveland, director of New York City's Bureau of Municipal Research, joined the group at Norton's request in September. And on March 8, 1911, the "President's Commission on Economy and Efficiency" was formally organized, with Cleveland as chairman; it began its inquiry two months later. The Cleveland Commission's work would remain unequaled in scope until the Hoover commissions of the 1940s and 1950s.[4]

Congress found the president a sympathetic listener to its complaints about inefficiency in the executive branch. Taft was not simply buckling to congressional pressure, but had come to the White House convinced of the desirability of reorganization in some departments. His own experience as a cabinet officer had attuned him to the problems accompanying a growing bureaucracy; he once remarked that as secretary of war he had never really known what was going on in that department.[5] A presidential commission, particularly one funded by Congress, presumably could effect some needed changes under White House guidance while simultaneously muting criticism from the legislators.

The 1910 elections must have given even greater impetus to the Commission on Economy and Efficiency. For the first time since 1892, the Democrats obtained control of the House of Representatives. The eager Democrats were ready to pounce on evidence of waste in the executive branch, and they revived some of the moribund House committees for investigating expenditures in the executive departments. The Cleveland Commission began its work only a month after the new Congress convened for a special session in April 1911. Among the topics on its agenda was the alleged duplication in foreign trade promotion between the State Department and C & L, especially the Bureaus of Trade Relations and Manufactures.[6]

As the Cleveland Commission began its inquiries, the conflict between the State Department and C & L was coming to a head. Each side felt itself vulnerable to the aggrandizement of the other; each feared it would be cut off from the nation's organized businessmen. In this climate, Bureau of Manufactures chief Baldwin made the first move. In June 1911, he shared with Nagel his concern over the State Department rhetoric that divided trade promotion responsibilities at the water's edge. Hewing to State's line, Huntington Wilson had recently told a congressional committee that the Bureau of Manufactures was a "domestic affair," and commercial adviser Mack Davis carried the same message to his former colleagues at a convention of the Millers' National Federation. Baldwin's principal worry was that such reiteration might soon be construed as fact, leading the commercial organizations to think that C & L had "no clearly marked field of activity." He warned Nagel that if the State Department was "allowed to assume direct relations with the commercial interests of the country," it would "gradually build up a service in commercial matters which must duplicate to a great extent our own work."[7]

Yet Baldwin had no desire to accept Wilson's foreign/domestic demarcation and ask the State Department to adhere to it, thus eliminating State's activities at home. Such a course would have forced Commerce and Labor to surrender its commercial agents and the anticipated commercial attachés. It would then be easier at some future time for State again to extend its activities in the United States than for C & L to resume an overseas role. If C & L was going to have any significant and lasting connection with the foreign field, it would have to be more than merely the domestic disseminator of information collected abroad by the State Department.

Acting on Baldwin's appeal, Nagel attempted during the summer of 1911 to meet with Knox and reconcile the irreconcilable. Nagel was anxious to accommodate the two departments' differences over trade promotion as part of his national commercial policy, but he was no more willing than before to alter C & L's traditional demands. Officials at State were in much less hurry and not at all anxious to sit down with Nagel or his subordinates to hammer out a solution. Perhaps they understood the futility of any such parley. Answering Nagel's letters after delays so long they bordered on rudeness, Philander Knox reiterated the State Department line and suggested that the Cleveland Commission be solicited for its views on the issue. Nagel's patience with the elusive State Department officials finally wore thin. In October 1911, in a frosty letter to Knox, he renewed C & L's request that copies of the consular reports be sent to it directly, bypassing the Bureau of Trade Relations.[8] Officials in both departments were undoubtedly well aware that this would weaken the legal justification for the existence of the Bureau of Trade Relations, and the State Department might soon be without the services of its commercial office.

Nagel's request brought matters to a head. In the setting of the recent Knox-Nagel correspondence about the departments' relative spheres of operation, State Department officers considered Nagel's request a major threat. Led by Wilbur Carr, they proceeded to move against their rival. Carr had concluded that the best defense was a swift offensive strike. Presenting his case to a receptive Huntington Wilson in November, he argued that the Bureau of Manufactures and the commercial agents should be transferred to the State Department. He sounded the same theme Baldwin had used in his appeal to Nagel only a few months earlier. "It is my conviction that unless the Department takes a strong stand upon what it conceives to be not only for the best interests of the Government service but particularly for the advancement of our foreign trade, and seeks the support of the business men themselves, it will be found sooner or later that sentiment has crystallized in favor of extending the functions of the Department of Commerce and Labor, and the Department of State will have upon its hands a fight for the retention even of many of the agencies now under its control."[9]

Carr suggested that the State Department enlist the support of Taft and his commission to obtain the necessary legislation from Congress. If State was to obtain control of the trade promotion machinery, he concluded, "on the ground of eliminating so-called red tape and making the foreign service more directly responsible to commercial interests, as well as on the ground of economy and efficiency, it would evoke considerable enthusiasm, and if the State Department then seized and made the most of its opportunity it would have no difficulty in [the] future in retaining the support of the business public." Wilson heartily agreed with his colleague and anticipated that "the big fight is yet to come." Carr asked Osborne to draft a comprehensive letter for Knox to send the president. "The idea," he explained, "is to lay before the President the whole plan from the point of view of combining in one place the machinery for the promotion of foreign trade." Although the department did not line up either Taft or the Cleveland Commission behind its program, Congress began to move in that direction.[10]

Within a few weeks of Carr's memorandum, C & L's fortunes appeared to dim. It had been widely rumored in Washington that the House Appropriations Committee was preparing to shift the Bureau of Manufactures to the State Department. The proposed transfer was to be accompanied by consolidating, within C & L, the Bureau of Statistics and the Census Bureau.[11]

State Department officials confidently anticipated a favorable report both from the Cleveland Commission and the Democrat-dominated Appropriations Committee. They were not disappointed when the congressional committee delivered its report on May 1, duly consolidating the Manufactures and Trade Relations bureaus within the State Department and terminating appropriations for C & L's commercial agents. The report also provided for the merger of the Statistics and Census bureaus.[12]

The situation then changed with dramatic swiftness. On May 9, the committee's leadership amended the bill on the floor of the House, over Republican objections. As finally enacted by the House the measure consolidated Manufactures with Statistics to create the "Bureau of Foreign and Domestic Commerce." It failed to appropriate for the Bureau of Trade Relations, or for the State Department offices first established by the $100,000 appropriation in 1909. These included the geographic divisions, the commercial advisers, the counselor, the resident diplomatic officer, and Director of the Consular Service Wilbur Carr himself.[13] Only six months earlier, Carr had predicted that his department might soon be fighting to retain many of its offices. With the passage of the House version of the appropriations bill, his fears were realized.

Largely responsible for the turnabout was the Cleveland Commission, which turned out to be an enormous stroke of luck for Charles Nagel and his department. In 1911, Cleveland had called for a report on the supposed waste caused by duplication of work among the Bureaus of Manufactures, Statistics, and Trade Relations. To draw up the report he selected commissioner William F. Willoughby, formerly of the Department of Labor, president of the Executive Council of Puerto Rico, and most recently assistant director of the Census in C & L. At the time of Willoughby's appointment to the commission, Nagel had regretted losing his services.[14] But Willoughby turned out to be much more valuable to him on the commission than he ever would have been in the department.

Predictably, Willoughby's report favored his old department. Its language was harsh, free of the subtleties that characterized the correspondence of cabinet officers like Knox and Nagel, and lacking even the lesser degree of politeness department officials displayed when arguing their cases before congressional committees.[15] He castigated the State Department for causing the most "glaring example of duplication of organization, plant, personnel, and work" in the government service, because it had "entered upon the policy of developing the foreign trade of the United States" without any congressional directive to do so. Willoughby believed that the "greatest evil" of the current arrangement was that manufacturers and merchants were confused about just where to turn for commercial information. He consequently recommended that the Bureau of Trade Relations be abolished and that the Bureaus of Manufactures and Statistics be consolidated into a "Bureau of Manufactures and Commerce." Consular reports would then go directly from the field to C & L, with galley proofs sent to State before publication to meet objections about improper material getting into print.[16]

Willoughby's view of the two departments' proper roles matched the opinions of his former colleagues. C & L was to be "purely . . . a promotive bureau for the advancement of the interests of American manufacturers and merchants." The State Department, on the other hand, would serve as "an agency for conducting diplomatic negotiations and representing before foreign governments particular individuals who . . . have been subjected to conditions which it is desirable if possible to have modified." According to Willoughby's format, State would have to abandon its policy of promoting foreign trade.[17]

Although Willoughby did not submit his report to the Cleveland Commission until May 1912, both C & L and the House Appropriations Committee knew about its conclusions well in advance. The commission's secretary had supplied a summary to the Appropriations Committee as early as February 1. C & L was likewise kept apprised of developments through its pipeline into the Cleveland Commission; Nagel received the same summary memorandum later in February, informally through his department's chief clerk. Early in March, Nagel heard also from John J. Fitzgerald, Democratic chairman of the committee and a vociferous assailant of government waste. Fitzgerald asked Nagel to send him a copy of the 1908 recommendation by Secretary Straus's departmental committee, which had urged the consolidation of Statistics and Manufactures. Nagel complied and enclosed one of his own annual reports echoing the suggestion. Thus the Appropriations Committee's May 1 report transferring the Bureau of Manufactures to the State Department was apparently only a sham. The committee's reversal between May 1 and May 9 did not reflect any sudden change of heart; it was instead a tactical maneuver that the Democratic majority hid from the Republican committee members. Democratic congressmen justified the change on the basis of the Cleveland Commission's report and the 1908 recommendation of Straus's committee, both of which they had studied for months.[18]

Willoughby's report was a hard blow against the State Department, particularly in the context of the genuine and widespread desire (most loudly voiced by Democrats) for greater economy in the executive branch. Congressman Joseph Johnson of South Carolina, who engineered the reversal on the House floor on May 9, had spoken for many of the legislators several months earlier when he bluntly warned Knox at a committee hearing: "I hope the next time you get your assistants all around you, you will canvass very carefully this question of practicing economy and, if possible, make suggestions where reductions can be made." Senator Lee Overman of North Carolina recounted how both the Bureau of Manufactures and the State Department had demonstrated cotton-baling techniques to southerners. Overman considered such assistance necessary, but he could not understand why two government agencies had to be engaged in the same work. As he emphasized to Knox, "the question in my mind is, can this duplication be stopped and money saved? That is the point." Even Taft had once wondered if the State Department's appropriations were not excessive.[19]

Most of the legislators who were upset by the apparent duplication held the State Department responsible. Like Willoughby, many of them accused the Bureau of Trade Relations of exceeding the authority provided by the 1903 act and by the initial $100,000 appropriation. The State Department's dissembling at the time of that 1909 appropriation, however necessary, was eventually costly. Couching its argument in terms it thought most likely to receive a sympathetic response from Congress, it had given the impression that the funds were essential mainly for negotiating commercial treaties resulting from the Payne-Aldrich tariff provisions. As early as the following congressional session, some legislators questioned the wisdom and legality of State's "trade and treaty relations" provision, especially when they saw the money going partly for the director of the consular service, the geographic divisions, and a resident diplomatic officer. It was obvious that these offices had little to do with the tariff. In March 1910, Congressman Champ Clark of Missouri, Speaker of the House a year later, accurately accused State of using the tariff argument to effect substantially the same reorganization that Congress had rejected early in 1909. "This section is a deliberate attempt to whip the devil around the stump," he charged. "You call these new officers by another name, and you undertake to get them that way. . . . It seems, when this deficiency bill came in [the previous August] it slipped in here when nobody was paying any particular attention to what was going on." Only the day before, Congressman Fitzgerald had charged a wasteful and "unnecessary" duplication between Taft's tariff commission and the State Department's tariff work. By 1912, congressmen were arguing that because the minimum tariff applied to all countries, there was no longer any need for State's appropriation.[20]

Other factors added to State's vulnerability. First, Taft was dealing with a Congress that contained a growing number of Progressives and Democrats. This situation worked to the department's disadvantage when coupled with the political target offered by "dollar diplomacy." In addition, Knox's apparent aversion to work helped make him considerably less popular with Congress than his predecessor had been.[21]

Officials at the State Department were stunned by the sudden reversal in the House. Huntington Wilson thought it "ridiculous" that congressmen should consider the Bureau of Trade Relations' role solely in light of the tariff's maximum-minimum provision. Actually, a department memorandum echoed, "that work was an incident, the main work being the general promotion of American trade." More than simply alarmed at the turn of events, Wilson was highly indignant. "As for initiative by the Department of Commerce and Labor," he petulantly sniffed to Knox, "if we had been waiting for that Department we should have accomplished practically nothing during the last three years. . . . Apparently because we have made something out of this work another bureau comparatively moribund wishes to take it over since we have proved it to be worth having."[22]

Hoping to reverse the action of the House, the State Department worked frantically to secure business and congressional support. Wilson drafted a form letter to businessmen, enclosing a memorandum predicting dire consequences for America's foreign commerce if the department's recent reorganization was destroyed. He reminded them that they expected support from the diplomatic and consular services for their foreign commerce, an "expectation the activities of this Department have encouraged on the part of the business men of the country." R. G. A. Phillips of the American Multigraph Company was among the many who replied to Wilson's appeal and offered assistance; he agreed that the House action would have "a very depressing effect on our trade with foreign countries." Wilson also pressed State's case on senators and representatives, while advising Knox on enlisting Taft's support. For his part, Knox repeated to the Senate Appropriations Committee the long-familiar litany about the imperatives of commercial competition with other great powers. Those countries possessed modern foreign offices, he argued, and if the United States wished to keep up in the race, the newly reorganized State Department could not be dismantled.[23]

Whether because of the business pressure mobilized by State, a traditionally friendlier disposition toward that department, or other circumstances, the Republican-controlled Senate opposed the House bill in mid-June. The measure then went to a conference committee. After some nudging by Knox, a reluctant Taft informed the Senate Appropriations Committee that he shared the State Department's views about the necessity for the Bureau of Trade Relations and continuance of the 1909 reorganization scheme. Knox almost secured adoption in the conference committee of the Senate's version, which restored all the offices eliminated by the House. But Congressman Fitzgerald loosed a tirade against the State Department that forced wavering House members back to their version and necessitated a compromise. State was allowed to retain the facilities and positions provided by the 1909 reorganization, except for the resident diplomatic officer; but it lost the appropriation for the Bureau of Trade Relations.[24]

The discontinuance of that appropriation did not mean that Nagel's department could at last communicate directly with the consuls. When amending the appropriations bill on the floor of the House, congressmen neglected to repeal the section in C & L's 1903 organic act providing for State Department control over the consuls' commercial correspondence. Although Nagel had no desire to see State lose its geographic divisions or other offices, he was anxious that C & L communicate directly with the consuls on commercial matters. Yet shortly after the reversal in the House, he was informed by his department's legal officer that under the bill's current provisions, the proposed Bureau of Foreign and Domestic Commerce would still have to correspond with the consuls through State. Nagel's appeals to the Senate went unheeded as the senators sought to assist the State Department. Knox was evidently confident that he could obtain restoration of all the funds and offices, and he was not about to accede to Nagel's request. Nagel's best chance would have been in the House, but after May 10 it was too late. C & L had missed a golden opportunity.[25]

In August 1912, after Congress had legislated the Bureau of Trade Relations out of existence, State Department bureaucrats held a post mortem to decide how best to continue their commercial activities. They vehemently disagreed with the view that their sole field of operations was a pure "diplomacy" divorced from commercial issues. Huntington Wilson belligerently told Knox that "without legislation *prohibiting* the Department of State from using the foreign service for commercial expansion it would be ridiculous to say that this Department's Bureau of Trade Relations was to sit with folded hands and the foreign service be allowed to drift along doing the country a minimum of good."[26] The problem in August was how to continue fostering foreign trade without a Bureau of Trade Relations and without flying too blatantly in the face of congressional intent as expressed in the appropriations bill. If the department failed to exercise caution, the House might correct its oversight of the previous session and specifically enjoin State from engaging in certain activities.

Wilson collected opinions from Osborne, Carr, Charles Pepper, and Chief Clerk William McNeir. Aware of the need to avoid offending the rival organization and its congressional supporters, they agreed that the Bureau of Trade Relations ought to be continued under a different name and should not be concerned with editing the consular reports, its original raison d'être. Since the 1903 arrangement was still in effect, the Consular Bureau should assume the duties of funneling the consular reports to C & L, leaving the reorganized and renamed commercial office free for studying tariff provisions, negotiating commercial treaties, and assisting businessmen in obtaining foreign contracts and markets. Charles Pepper emphasized the importance of not confining the duties of the office "to current matters of this kind, which develop of themselves, but . . . there should be a free field for initiative and constructive work such as may suggest itself from time to time."[27]

Carr conferred with Baldwin, who was sometimes less sweeping than Carson, Austin, or Nagel in asserting his department's prerogatives, and he agreed that State had the right to initiate its own consular investigations. For his part, Carr recommended that in such cases State should attempt to consult with C & L beforehand. He even suggested that all commercial reports not of a confidential or diplomatic character be forwarded without editing, if the secretary of C & L would agree in writing to submit the copy for proofreading before publication. This had long been one of C & L's proposals and thus constituted a major capitulation by the State Department. But the climate was conducive to such concessions; as Carr told Wilson, State did not want "a recurrence of our recent experience with Congress."[28]

On September 12, a departmental order created the "Office of Foreign Trade Advisers" to continue the work of the Bureau of Trade Relations. Like Frederic Emory fifteen years earlier, Charles Pepper was aware that his department needed an office with a catchy title to attract the attention of the business public. Pepper had predicted that such a new designation would help offset the temporary loss, "if not of influence yet of prestige, among commercial organizations and the business community generally"; because of recent congressional action against the Bureau of Trade Relations, the assumption would be that State was no longer involved in trade promotion. With the office's new name and an open-ended list of duties, Pepper was confident that "the larger aspect of the commercial functions of the Department can be kept well to the front and can be impressed both on the general public and on the business interests of the country." Pepper and Evan Young, former chief of the Near Eastern division, became the first foreign trade advisers. The two men were paid, as before, under the provision for eight officers engaged in drafting work.[29]

The functions of the new Office of Foreign Trade Advisers during its earliest years are not completely clear. The departmental order establishing the office on September 12 gave it the same responsibilities as those exercised by the old Bureau of Trade Relations. But another order by Wilson less than three weeks later transferred to the Consular Bureau the task of forwarding consular reports to C & L. For a time, Hengstler's Consular Bureau exercised this function; in the aftermath of the agreement reached by Baldwin and Carr, it did virtually no editing of the reports. Eventually, however, officials at the State Department recovered from their shell-shock. Even though prudence might dictate that the Consular Bureau and not the commercial office handle the consular reports, if the Office of Foreign Trade Advisers did not exercise this function its legal justification would be greatly weakened. Consequently, by mid-1913 the commercial office had resumed routing the consular reports to C & L; by 1916 it was censoring them.[30]

Although the appropriations bill failed to place the consuls directly in touch with C & L, it did achieve another of Nagel's goals by consolidating Statistics with Manufactures. Nagel was pleased, and he told a Senate committee that the new Bureau of Foreign and Domestic Commerce would serve as "the corner stone of the whole department. . . . It will not be for me, but somebody some day will preside over a great department." Senator Murphy Foster of

Louisiana agreed that "the possibilities of that are very great in the way of solving the great economic problems of the day." In 1912, as in earlier years, officials anticipated that some of the nation's economic difficulties would be remedied by selling America's surplus products overseas. The rosy expectations aroused by the creation of the Bureau of Foreign and Domestic Commerce bore a striking resemblance to those accompanying the birth of C & L and the Bureau of Manufactures only a few years earlier. Once again the United States was, in Charles Nagel's words, "at the very inception, the threshold of the whole policy."[31]

Meanwhile, O. P. Austin was scrambling to retain his position. Disturbed by the original version of the appropriations bill for relegating his Statistics bureau and himself to a subordinate place in the Census Bureau, he remained agitated after the House changed course and provided for the Bureau of Foreign and Domestic Commerce. The bill's language transformed the Bureau of Manufactures into the Bureau of Foreign and Domestic Commerce, and then merged Statistics with it. Austin complained to Nagel that this form of consolidation "would be an injustice to the Bureau of Statistics and to its people." After all, he pointed out, for forty-six years Statistics had served as "*the* Bureau of Foreign and Domestic Commerce of the United States." If the bill's language could only be changed to confer the new title upon Statistics and allow that office to absorb the Bureau of Manufactures, it would somehow "minimize the confusion in the public mind."[32]

Working along other fronts, Austin mounted a campaign for the top position in the Bureau of Foreign and Domestic Commerce. Drawing upon his many years of newspaper, political, and government work, he solicited endorsements from individuals and commercial organizations. The favorable letters poured in to Taft. Numerous commercial bodies endorsed Austin, as did an occasional congressman. Charles Needham at George Washington University told the president about Austin's work on his political science faculty. Gilbert Grosvenor, director of the National Geographic Society and for many years Austin's associate in that organization, even appealed to Mrs. Taft. Austin himself made similar overtures to Taft and to Republican party chairman Charles D. Hilles, playing on chords of long-term party loyalty and service. He reminded the president of his relationship with Taft's "honored father," while observing to Hilles less than three months before the presidential election that *"this is not a good time to 'swap horses,'* while we are crossing an unusually muddy stream." He even asked Theodore Roosevelt, by then Taft's bitter rival for the presidency, to put in a good word for him with the administration. Not surprisingly, Roosevelt declined.[33]

Austin's efforts failed. Despite the many letters of endorsement, he had little influential support. Charles A. Conant, the respected international financial authority, urged Taft to retain Austin's services, but conspicuously avoided endorsing him for the top spot. John Fahey of Boston, a Democrat and a leading organizer of the United States Chamber of Commerce only two months earlier, was more direct and advocated Baldwin's appointment instead.[34] Fahey was careful to label his opinion personal, noting that the more important commercial bodies, such as his own Boston Chamber of Commerce and the United States Chamber, did not make endorsements for public office. He observed that Austin was sixty-five years old, while Baldwin was young and had done a commendable job with the Bureau of Manufactures. The new bureau was largely the old Bureau of Manufactures with a new name, and there was no reason why anyone other than Baldwin should be appointed to head it. Arguing that Austin's appointment would be "a serious mistake," Fahey warned that it would be "considered as purely political by most of the businessmen who are familiar with conditions and will be a great disappointment to them."[35] In that election year, the Taft administration needed no additional headaches.

Fahey's articulate statement of an important business viewpoint no doubt coincided with Nagel's own opinion. The secretary earlier had taken pains to appoint his most important bureau chiefs from the classified service rather than from the ranks of Republican newspapermen. He too was pleased with Baldwin's work in the Bureau of Manufactures and saw the new Bureau of Foreign and Domestic Commerce as an enlarged Bureau of Manufactures. He must have been reluctant to hand over what he considered the department's cornerstone to another newsman for faithful past services to the party. On August 23, Nagel recommended Baldwin as chief of the bureau and Austin as one of two assistant chiefs. Taft concurred, and the appointments were approved. To add injury to insult, Austin suffered a 25 percent salary cut ($1,000) with his demotion.[36]

By the end of 1912, Commerce and Labor's position in relation to the State Department was a strong one. After nine years, the long-awaited Bureau of Foreign and Domestic Commerce was at last a reality. Its emergence had been delayed by bureaucratic infighting, a high turnover of department heads, and probably also by State's active and well-publicized trade promotion work. Meanwhile, the State Department was lying low. It was determined not to endanger the enormous gains it had made during Republican administrations by antagonizing C & L, Congress, or the new Democratic president elected in November—Woodrow Wilson. It had survived the congressional axe, retaining virtually all the 1909 reorganization and even the Bureau of Trade Relations with a different name. In time, as Charles Pepper expected, it would once again seek businessmen's support on the basis of its trade promotion activities. When it did, the brief period of forced amity would have ended and the battle with the rival department resumed.[37]

10 A MULTIFACETED SALESMANSHIP

Between the 1890s and World War I, the United States government greatly improved its facilities for conducting official relations with other nations and for assisting economic (principally commercial) expansion abroad. Concern about foreign markets did not, however, prevent foreign affairs officials from recognizing two additional sets of advantages offered by the new machinery.

Officials at both State and C & L believed that the appearance of greater usefulness in trade promotion would help their agencies obtain additional appropriations and legislation for reorganization. Such legislation would extend their facilities for promoting exports and, in the State Department's case, would also improve other aspects of the foreign affairs apparatus. After 1903, each department was seeking to sell itself as the nation's chief foreign trade promoter. The sense of rivalry added to the State Department's efforts a note of urgency more immediate than that of some ominous date in the future when the United States might be unsuccessful in competing for foreign markets. The State Department realized that its rival threatened to usurp the rationale that was easily State's best hope of awakening business and congressional interest in its own development.

At a third and more personal level than either marketplace expansion or interdepartmental rivalry, a reorganized foreign service offered work that was stimulating to the reorganizers—work that promised recognition, greater access to decision-making, and more security to individual members of the bureaucracy. The new generation entering the foreign service was being offered a career and a chance to make its mark, as Wilbur Carr had made his.

The crucial point is that there was no apparent contradiction in this three-sided arrangement; each element helped reinforce the others. By assisting, and often pushing, American manufacturers and exporters through the "open door," officials believed they were helping their country, their department, and themselves.

THE PERCEIVED ECONOMIC IMPERATIVE
AND THE NATURE OF THE RESPONSE

The foreign service concentrated on expanding foreign markets for producers and exporters of manufactured goods, particularly finished manufactures. Government officials thought that the United States would have to continue exporting not only its current surpluses of manufactures in the face of vigorous European competition, but that it would have to send abroad a larger share of its production, in order to provide what Emory and others called a "balance wheel" for domestic prosperity. S. N. D. North once described this international issue as "the industrial situation" and characterized it as "a pretty large question,—the largest question there is,—the world question, in fact."[1]

Much of the government's promotional machinery took the form of an information service, supplying data to those businessmen already attuned to export markets while arousing the interest of others. Consuls and special agents visited manufacturers, beseeching them to move into foreign markets. One prominent consul-general described the task as his "missionary labors," and the analogy was apt. Like missionaries winning new converts while ministering to the faithful, government agents concerned themselves with more than merely serving the anointed. Truxtun Beale, former minister to Persia and to Greece, displayed this same concern when he suggested in 1897 that the new Reciprocity Commission send an agent to confer with manufacturers, thereby "arousing their interest, and in many instances . . . overcoming their inertia, of which there is always a great deal to overcome in striking out in new channels of trade."[2]

Many of the smaller and medium-sized firms, with little or no export experience and without extensive foreign sales forces, would welcome the foreign markets information supplied by the two departments. Consequently, they formed an inviting field for gov-

ernmental missionary work. Moreover, their greater participation in
the export trade would mean a more broadly based and more stable
balance wheel for the United States economy. As Charles Nagel
warned Taft in 1911, although American exports were increasing,
they were heavily concentrated "in the hands of a very few industries, and those are precisely the ones against which the government
is now proceeding in anti-trust actions."[3] The government thus had
to ensure the general distribution of commercial intelligence to encourage more widespread participation.[4]

Although the large corporations continued to account for the
bulk of manufactured exports, government assistance to smaller
companies was responsible for some of the increase in America's
foreign trade. "We took advantage of the facilities granted by the
Consular Service when we inaugurated our Export Dpt. in April
1910," the Duryea Manufacturing Company (belting and petro-
leum) wrote Knox only seven months afterward. "By following up
each likely Trade Opportunity . . . we came into contact with 14
different firms, all· of high standing . . . from all corners of the
globe. With 8 of these firms we entered in firm agency agreements
regarding our different products, 4 of which have developed since a
very substantial and promising business." Likewise, C. W. Kelsey,
president of the Kelsey Motor Company, wrote that his company
had "started out as a very small concern a year or two ago, and
largely due to the help of the Consular Service and the Department
of State, its export business became one of its largest factors." During the first four months of 1912, an observer reported, 109 manufacturing concerns began to solicit foreign orders actively.[5]

Whether government officials were correct about the needs
of the political economy is a difficult question, requiring intensive
study by economic historians before it can be answered satisfactor-
ily. But that is not to rule out every kind of tentative and less ambitious evaluation based upon hindsight.[6] Considering the evidence
available to the men who staffed the middle and upper echelons at
State and C & L, their attitudes and assumptions are hardly surprising, particularly in the aftermath of the 1890s depression.

Those bureaucrats shared with political and business leaders
a common belief that economic depressions often were caused by
overproduction, by supply exceeding effective demand. They ex-

pected a greater extension of United States exports into foreign countries to help bring demand into better balance with production and productive capacity, at least for a time. And between the late 1890s and World War I, exports of finished and semifinished manufactures did grow at a faster rate than their domestic production, particularly between 1909 and 1914. In other words, a larger proportion of these goods was being exported in 1914 than in 1900.[7]

Another way to narrow the gap between production and consumption was, of course, to limit production while maintaining profits and employment by arrangements among competing firms. Searching for various ways to control production and fix prices, businessmen had for many years turned to pools, trusts, holding companies, or mergers. Even when successful, these methods often flew in the face of the nation's expressed competitive ideals and thus provoked a strong public outcry, which in turn sometimes spurred government attempts to broaden businessmen's participation in the export trade. There was no contradiction between these two methods of balancing production and consumption, and some firms doubtless directed their attention both toward foreign markets and toward domestic agreements or consolidation. Not until after 1914 did additional alternatives begin to gain widespread attention. The "regularization" movement sought to stabilize production at the firm level, while trade associations constituted another attempt at cooperation among firms in the same industry. Improved statistical data helped the development of both programs.[8]

Although government officials did underestimate the future ability of the home market to absorb manufactured goods, their oversight is understandable.[9] Even economists and statisticians did not know what was happening to real wages amid the current price inflation. But if the bureaucrats somehow had known, they still would have had no reason to change their notions about the absorptive capacity of the home market. Although real wages did in fact increase overall between the 1890s and World War I, they did not keep pace with the rise in production; American wage earners' share of United States production thus declined.[10] Attempts by the federal government to create domestic demand were still many years in the future.

The attention that officials paid to the relationship between increased exports of manufactures and the maintenance of a favorable trade balance also is not surprising. They could not have predicted the agricultural surpluses that would come with World War I and remain an important part of the American social and political landscape for over half a century. Moreover, the census of 1910 confirmed their perceptions about dwindling agricultural surpluses and continued population movements. Between 1900 and 1910, the population increased 21 percent (urban by 38 percent, rural by 9 percent); during the same period, rural population fell from 60 to 54 percent of the United States total. Despite their highly inflated prices, exports of crude foodstuffs for the same decade declined in value by over 50 percent, and prepared foodstuffs by 19 percent. Thus if the United States was to maintain a favorable trade balance while gradually paying off its foreign debt, it would apparently have to rely increasingly on exports of finished and semifinished manufactures.[11]

Government attention to markets outside western Europe is likewise understandable. Here American manufacturers and exporters could compete in more neutral markets, whose imports included a large proportion of manufactured products. Not only did Europeans manufacture similar lines of goods for their own and the other European markets nearby, but they were moving toward higher tariffs to protect their industries. Noting this trend toward protectionism, the United States ambassador to Turkey observed in 1906 that together with South America and the Far East, the Levant offered "one of the few remaining neutral fields where such trade can be both indefinitely and profitably extended."[12]

Historians have sometimes minimized the importance of non-European markets for American producers by pointing to the relatively small quantities of United States exports sent to them (often neglecting to mention the impressive percentage increases in exports to the Far East during the 1890s and to Latin America in the following decade).[13] But export figures, particularly those before World War I, must be read with two points in mind. First, as officials were aware, the statistics did not reflect the fact that goods were frequently transshipped after reaching their initial destination. Particularly before the opening of the Panama Canal in 1914, many goods bound for Asia and South America were doubtless shipped via Europe, with the trade statistics recording Europe as their final destination.[14]

Notwithstanding this built-in distortion, the decades preceding World War I witnessed an increase in the proportion of American exports to the non-European world.[15] Like the growing percentage of manufactures among exports, this trend seemed likely to continue. And that is the other important consideration: government officials were not nearly so concerned with current trade as they were with the trends that they saw in the export figures. Like officials in more recent years, they tended to rely on the current statistics when the figures buttressed their expectations and policies, paying them less attention when they occasionally did not.

TRADE ASSISTANCE POLICIES

As trade promotion became the major consular function during the 1890s, some of the more conservative restraints on consular assistance to exporters began to give way. One reflection of this trend was the department's growing willingness to furnish (at its own discretion) to American businessmen the names of reputable foreign importers.[16] There were other signs of a willingness to break with traditional practices. In 1901, the Consular Bureau reminded Frederic Emory that, according to regulations, consuls were not permitted to "act as agents in the sale of goods." Yet as the years passed, many consuls began doing just that, with the hearty approbation of the State Department. During a training session in 1909, one neophyte asked John Osborne whether consuls were permitted to interview foreign importers and demonstrate the superior qualities of American goods. "Oh, yes," the bureau chief assured him; "consular officers are doing that constantly. There are many instances where they report that they have induced foreign dealers to make a trial importation or to give an order in the United States which they had been contemplating giving abroad."[17]

The line between proper and improper activity was frequently razor-thin. If consuls erred on the side of pushing American products with too much zeal, they received only a gentle admonition from Washington. Carr and Hengstler were reluctant to crack down on overactive consuls; they did not want their charges playing it safe and seeking to avoid criticism. When one consul actually transmitted an order to an American businessman from a foreign dealer, Carr suggested only that he "should, in a kindly way, be put right."[18] On the other hand, when a consul exhibited excess caution or attempted to hide behind regulations prohibiting certain forms of activity, he felt Carr's stern reprimand. Carr informed one recalcitrant subordinate that his refusals to supply certain information were "calculated to create an unfavorable impression of the interest taken by you in promoting trade in American products." Another, the consul in Trieste, who refused the request of an American company to insert an advertisement in a local publication, received an even sharper rebuke. "The Department notes with surprise and regret your action in this matter," Carr wrote the unfortunate officer. "Not only is the general tone of your reply subject to criticism, but the fundamental statement made by you that 'American consuls are not advertising agents for American firms' is most incorrect. It is expected that American consular officers will cheerfully do everything in their power to extend American trade, and if need be and if possible attend to any preliminary details in connection with such work." Carr was determined to forge an institution that would be useful to American businessmen, and he expected a similar attitude from his consuls. He also expected that institution to reflect his own values, and because he was an extraordinarily hard worker himself, he resented any sign of laziness.[19]

Just as the department maintained a flexible position on furnishing names of foreign importers, it also sought to keep its options open on the general question of consular assistance to businessmen. One consideration was the reputation for responsibility, or lack of it, of the American firm making the request. For the benefit of the export trade in general, the State Department was leery about assisting companies that might be unable to meet their obligations and thus reflect upon all American enterprises. In 1911, on the basis of suggestions from commercial adviser Mack Davis, the department systematized its ad hoc approach. "I think the Department should be as liberal as practicable in the character of service its consular officers may render," Davis told Carr. One problem was that at the more important European posts, consuls were too busy with their regular duties to give much time to special requests, while at other posts there was less to do. Moreover the department was particularly interested in rendering assistance that would open new markets for American manufacturers. There were many large cities, Davis wrote,

> such as Alexandria, Egypt, Smyrna, Turkey, Constantinople, Salonika, and other cities of large population in Europe where Americans have comparatively little direct trade and almost no representation. Consuls at such points might properly undertake detailed work of a general character that could not be attempted by consuls at London, Liverpool, Paris, Hamburg, or Berlin, where Americans are well-intrenched and where competition is keen as between the Americans themselves. So that it seems to me that the Director of the Consular Service would necessarily have to pass on each inquiry where special work was requested of our consuls.

Although Davis was anxious that businessmen not expect to use the service as they would their own salesmen, he too walked and crossed the increasingly faint line between what a consul should and should not do. "Consuls ought not to distribute samples and literature as a part of their regular duties," he suggested, adding, "but I can conceive of a good many cases where even such service on the part of consuls would not overburden them and might prove highly beneficial." Carr agreed. Such flexibility would allow the department to gauge its response to requests for assistance according to a number of factors, including the nature of the overture, the reputation of the company making it, the burden it would impose on the consuls, and whether it was compatible with the interests of America's export trade as defined by Davis, Carr, and their colleagues.[20]

Some of the top diplomatic officers were also becoming more active in promoting trade. Diplomats had traditionally considered themselves aloof from the commercial world, leaving matters of "trade," with all its menial connotations, in the hands of lowly consuls, while they themselves dealt with political "affairs of state." This common stereotype was in fact simplistic; not only did a diplomat try to secure equal treatment for his nation's commerce, but among the principal reasons for political overtures and policies was the desire to maintain conditions suitable for commercial intercourse. Nevertheless, many top diplomats insisted on viewing their role as separate from commercial affairs.[21]

The State Department increasingly prodded chiefs of mission to greater activity on behalf of American commercial interests, urging them to do more than simply assure equal treatment for American products. "Broadly speaking," Alvey Adee, Robert Bacon, and Elihu Root informed United States Minister to Chile John Hicks in 1906, "you should employ all proper methods for the extension of American commercial interests in Chile, while refraining from advocating the projects of any one [American] firm to the exclusion of others." The foregoing was almost word-for-word the instruction Secretary of State Richard Olney had sent the minister to China in 1896—an instruction which itself had been a sharp turn toward greater diplomatic intervention on behalf of business enterprises. But by 1906, the increasing international commercial competition prompted the department to make its pleasure even clearer. "At a time when the diplomatic representatives of some Powers appear to be expected to solicit custom for their country's productions," Hicks was told, "and to insist on their compatriots getting a share of foreign contracts, incidentally attempting to thwart bidders of other nationalities, the Department is not likely to disapprove of your showing considerable energy in behalf of American trade." As with other aspects of trade promotion, the department was careful to retain flexibility. The same instruction noted, "It is not practicable to define your duties exactly, in this connection, nor is it desirable that any instructions which may have been given shall be too literally followed." One of the prime considerations, as always, was the "standing" of the company involved.[22]

In 1912 a mission chief played a key role in an incident involving the State Department's trade promotion machinery. Nicolay Grevstad, United States minister at Montevideo, secured an agreement from the Uruguayan government to place a trial order for 5,000 tons of the best American navy coal. A strike in Great Britain had choked off Uruguay's principal source of supply, and Grevstad saw an opportunity for the United States to pierce the market and overcome the widespread assumption that American coal was inferior to the British product. Grevstad telegraphed the good news on April 8, promising that if "quality and price give satisfaction this market is won." Upon its reception at the State Department the message was routinely sent to the appropriate geographic division. Early the next morning, the Latin American division notified the Bureau of Trade Relations. Osborne was ready to rush the matter to the Commerce and Labor Department for distribution to responsible companies through its confidential circular system, but Charles Pepper persuaded him to keep it in the State Department. Thus on that same day, the Bureau of Trade Relations notified five or six reputable coal companies and subsequently used its cable facilities to relay bids and other information from the companies to Grevstad for communication to the Uruguayan government. At one point the work became so hectic that the beleaguered Osborne facetiously requested "a special coal clerk designated to act as middleman."[23]

The work paid off, for on April 20 Grevstad informed the department that the Uruguayan consul-general in New York would buy the 5,000 tons from the best offer among the bids relayed by Washington. Meanwhile, the Germans were pressing Montevideo for a 20,000-ton order, and Grevstad emphasized that the first American shipment had to be of high quality to secure future orders. By early May the necessary arrangements were made, and the American consul in Montevideo gave credit to "the prompt and clever work of the American Minister to Uruguay."[24]

Not all the mission chiefs were as energetic as Grevstad, however. Even by the end of the Taft administration, despite the department's efforts some were still reluctant to soil their hands with commercial work. The vice-president of the Pocahontas Coal Company wrote Carr early in 1913 that certain ambassadors had provided extremely valuable assistance—when they were "willing to become interested in the commercial side of the export question."[25]

Other questions of commercial policy were more complex, and some of them are still bedeviling United States policy makers. Despite all the attention given to exports, virtually no heed was paid to the import trade to foster a sound commercial exchange. Frederic Emory was intensely interested in tariff reduction, but after 1897 he was in no position to castigate Republican tariff policy publicly or to develop instruments for promoting imports. As Wilbur Carr succinctly described official policy, the spirit both of the consular regulations and of the department's instructions was to develop the export trade, while allowing "the import trade in competitive articles to take care of itself and be fostered by the consular activities of the foreign countries interested." Like the 1906 Consular Reorganization Board, of which he was a member, Carr even recognized occasionally what he called "the broad proposition that we cannot expect to sell everything and buy little or nothing in return." But in Carr's case, at any rate, it was only a surface recognition. He and foreign trade advisers Pepper and Young concluded only with considerable reluctance that they could not deny consular assistance to American citizens who were importers.[26]

In failing to distinguish between different kinds of imports, the department's policy was unsophisticated; as one consul pointed out, some imports, whether raw, semimanufactured, or even finished goods, were essential and did not compete with American products. Yet the foreign service was caught up in promoting only exports and gloried in the favorable trade balance. DeWitt C. Poole, a consular assistant in the Bureau of Trade Relations and later chief of the Division of Eastern European Affairs, many years afterward provided some valuable insights into what he and his colleagues were about. Looking back from the perspective of 1935, Poole was amazed at the policy of supporting a high tariff while seeking to "pump" American goods into foreign lands. But Poole observed that back in 1911, "we did not hurt our heads about these inconsistencies —we accepted the policy as obviously wise—was it not known that a favorable balance of trade was desirable? The word *favorable* settled the question. Obviously it was desirable that exports should be increased by every possible means." Emphasizing the neomercantilistic nature of the department's outlook, Poole reported that policy makers considered greater exports necessary to pay off the national debt to foreign creditors and end the debtor status of the United States.[27] Another important consideration, of course, was that by fostering the import trade the State Department would lose many more influential friends in the United States than it would gain.

Although the State Department remained generally untroubled by its lack of assistance to importers, another issue began to require its more discerning attention. During the nineteenth century, American companies had established manufacturing plants abroad. In many cases these facilities began as sales outlets and evolved into factories employing indigenous labor and often foreign capital. The principal advantages of the arrangement lay in the competitive edge gained by cheaper labor, reduced transportation costs, and the opportunity to escape high import tariffs levied by the host country or to benefit from lower tariff rates levied by third countries against exports originating with the host country.[28]

American companies had extended their manufacturing operations to foreign countries on their own initiative during the nineteenth century, unassisted by their government. On his 1896 inspection tour, Robert Chilton provided a good summary of the kinds of foreign expansion the State Department smiled upon. He was "greatly impressed with the importance of our interests in Mexico and especially the number and character of American citizens who have gone there in connection with rail-roads, mining, smelting, selling and operating electric and milling machinery, representing and selling different American manufactures, installation and operation of telephones &c., &c." Such operations, supplying the ingredients of a developing nation's economic infrastructure, used American manufactured products and promised to provide outlets for many more as the country developed. They did not include large-scale productive enterprises employing substantial amounts of indigenous labor in competition with American workers. This was the nub of the issue and helps place into historical perspective the present-day opposition of American labor to "branch factories," or "extraterritorial factories" as the State Department came to call them. Shortly after the Civil War, American employees of the Singer sewing machine company voiced concern about losing their jobs because of the company's far-flung and growing network of foreign production facilities. This was an attitude that the State Department shared at the beginning of the twentieth century, and one that for a time informed the department's responses to the increasingly frequent appeals for diplomatic or consular assistance on behalf of branch factories.[29]

Overseas firms owned by American citizens were theoretically entitled to the protection and assistance of the United States government. But in practice, citizenship was a legal nicety that mattered less than the perceived needs of America's export trade. In a 1906 circular instruction to diplomats and consuls, the State Department ruled that branch factories were foreign firms and therefore deserved no official assistance for their operations. C & L voiced its agreement the following year. (Branch factories were entitled, however, to official protection and redress of grievances.) More important than the nationality of their ownership or capital was the fact that such operations employed foreign labor. Their new location often gave their products advantages over similar goods manufactured in the United States for the same markets—to the presumed detriment of American production and of American labor's continued employment. As Carr summed up department policy in 1909, when companies moved "all or part of their plants from the United States to a foreign country they are no longer entitled to the assistance of the Government of the United States so far as their foreign factories are concerned, for they then become competitors with their compatriots in the United States." But he drew an important distinction between branch factories employing foreign labor and competing with American products, and "the matter of securing concessions where public utilities are to be supplied by American capital and equipped with the fruits of American industry, or where mines are to be opened up by American enterprise, all of which may properly call for such aid as the American consular officers can give."[30]

The State Department again demonstrated its attachment to export promotion and its indifference to legal questions in 1911 when it took up a closely related issue. The question was whether official assistance should be made available to a foreign firm located in the United States and engaged in exporting American goods. Osborne and Davis both believed that such a firm was entitled to official services, "by reason of its participation in the export trade in American products," and they bucked the question to the State Department's legal branch. Assistant Solicitor Frederick Van Dyne, a former consul, while feeling keenly "the desire to extend our export trade," nevertheless concluded reluctantly that there was no legal basis for such assistance. Solicitor J. Reuben Clark agreed with Van Dyne's legal opinion, but thought it need not affect actual policy. "Herewith proposed expression of opinion on *legal* phase of this question," he told Counselor Chandler Anderson. "As a matter of *policy* we might I think exercise our good offices if we so desired." Anderson and Carr both agreed with Clark. The consular service director promised official efforts "to protect the good name of *bona fide* American goods," but warned the company that claims for damages or redress would naturally have to be made by its own government.[31]

Despite the department's determination to gear its policies to the promotion of American exports, no matter whose citizenship was involved, such questions became more complex in time. Officials began to realize that the issue required more than simply coming out squarely in favor of promoting exports and breaking with legalistic or conservative practices.

The circular of 1906 did not settle the matter, as questions continued to arise. United States consuls in Canada, faced with requests for aid from Americans moving some of their production operations across the border, asked Washington for clarification.[32] And in February 1910, the International Harvester Company requested the department's backing in the company's efforts to build a factory in Russia.

According to one expert, Russia provided "the greatest field for the export of American agricultural machinery in the world"; with sales of $6.5 million in 1909, International Harvester enjoyed the lion's share of that market. But influential members of the Russian government were pressing for high tariffs on agricultural machinery to encourage its domestic manufacture. In July 1909, Cyrus McCormick, president of International Harvester, visited Russia and discussed with various officials the establishment of a factory in their country. He was warmly received and encouraged. Other Harvester officials traveled to Russia during the following winter to advance the scheme. They wanted the State Department's assistance in dissuading the Russians from levying on imported equipment parts the heavy tariffs believed to be imminent.[33]

Amid these pleas for assistance, and with the Harvester request specifically in mind, Huntington Wilson drafted a circular instruction for consuls and diplomats on March 10, 1910. Sent two weeks later, the circular was no sharp about-face; instead, new qualifications were added to familiar warnings. But the direction was toward greater flexibility. Undertakings that might receive government assistance, the circular outlined, were those designed to thwart foreign competition by slipping under the tariff wall of another country and establishing a branch there. Such a step might justifiably be considered as "preserving and fostering the main export business for the benefit of which the branch has thus been established." This circumstance, the circular warned, had to be "clearly distinguished from a case where a foreign branch is a serious undertaking maintained to build up a trade which would compete with the genuine American export trade, and might even result in making the branch in the foreign country a base for distributing foreign-made goods to third countries in competition with American exports." If this was the situation, diplomats and consuls were to fulfill their legal obligations by supplying only those services demanded by courtesy. In conclusion, the officers were instructed to keep the State Department fully informed of the particular project, including "its probable effect upon genuine American business interests." Later that year C & L reiterated its agreement with the State Department's position.[34]

The new policy received its first workout with International Harvester's request. Ambassador to Russia W. W. Rockhill strongly opposed any assistance and was certain that Harvester would do what Singer had already done in Russia—set up a plant, use indigenous labor and foreign capital, and successfully shut out competition from competing American companies. Rockhill's opinions were later echoed by Consul-General John Snodgrass in Moscow, who likewise drew the parallel with Singer. The sewing machine company had successfully lobbied with the Russians to raise their tariffs, thereby excluding other American firms from the Russian market, and Snodgrass expected Harvester to follow suit.[35]

Osborne and, initially, Wilson agreed that Harvester's case did not merit much official assistance, but Wilson changed his mind a week later, early in May. Perhaps he was persuaded by the company's arguments, which contained points very similar to some of his own in the circular he had prepared less than two months previously. He told Osborne to reconsider the question, reminding him that if Harvester did not build the factory perhaps the Germans would. Once again, the omnipresent issue of international economic competition had intruded. A decision of the Russian government to postpone the levy of tariffs removed the need for any State Department assistance. But an important effect of the Harvester request was to leave the department with a modified policy toward branch factories.[36]

That policy after the spring of 1910 showed elements of the caution expressed in the March circular and of earlier negative attitudes, as well as reflecting the circular's new provisions and Wilson's switch on the Harvester case. As in its other trade assistance policies, the department had adopted an ad hoc approach to the issue. If the company could in the long run help further American exports and the employment of American labor, then it was entitled to assistance—regardless of the owners' citizenship. The problem was determining whether the export trade was helped or harmed. It was an issue for which United States policy makers were still seeking a solution in the 1970s.[37]

TRADE PROMOTION, SELF-PROMOTION, AND THE REFORM PROCESS

As the foreign service reformers built a structure oriented chiefly toward trade promotion, the dynamics of the process reflected certain aspects of political and social structure in the United States. The reformers' main obstacle, and yet their only hope, was Congress. Many organizations and associations have required only a public climate that was not sufficiently hostile to prevent their development. But agencies of the United States government have required affirmative action in the form of annual appropriations or other legislation from a frequently indifferent and occasionally unfriendly Congress. Since the State Department was more removed from the public view than other government agencies and was considered by some persons to be superfluous, its task was especially difficult. Not only did Congress have a stake in maintaining the spoils system and its own control, but it also lacked sustained interest in foreign affairs.

Such indifference can be attributed largely to the very structure of congressional representation in the United States. Direct representation as a political institution was a product of America's colonial experience, confirmed during the Revolution in the face of London's claims of "virtual" representation, and was a hallmark of both the Articles of Confederation and the Constitution. But this arrangement, designed to protect local interests, would eventually prove an obstacle to officials of the national government and others with national horizons who wished to mobilize public sentiment on behalf of what they considered pressing national issues. The horizons of most legislators in Congress have naturally remained generally bound by the local preoccupations of their constituents and thus have often extended no farther than the boundaries of the state or congressional district. Congressman Robert R. Hitt once referred to "the inexorable rule of duty, first of all, to a constituent." Agreement from a different normative perspective came when Assistant Secretary of State David J. Hill complained: "Every mother's son in the House expects to make capital for his re-election by cutting down the appropriation bills." In 1910, the chairman of the Foreign Affairs Committee, who had served on the committee more than eight years, inquired about the location of Guayaquil, Ecuador. "Which side of South America is that on?" he asked John Barrett, head of the Bureau of American Republics. Three years later, Wilbur Carr returned from a House appropriations hearing particularly disgusted with the congressmen's narrow outlook and convinced more than ever that estimates had to be couched in the simplest and most popular terms. Nor was the situation appreciably better in the Senate. The expansionist Senator John Morgan, once chairman of the Foreign Relations Committee, confessed in 1906: "Senators know less about foreign affairs than about anything else, because they are not compelled to study them."[38]

Despite their eventual success in securing larger appropriations and improved organization, foreign service officers from the late nineteenth century to the present have bemoaned public indifference to and ignorance of foreign affairs, and the resulting congressional parsimony toward the foreign service. In 1919 Maurice F. Egan, formerly minister to Denmark, furnished a good example of · their bitterness:

> Whatever improvement exists at the present moment in our
> consular service is due to the constant pressure of the best
> men in the State Department against the old abuses, to
> which the people, on whom the responsibility for any of our
> governmental evils entirely rests, were culpably indifferent.
> Local politics had guided them; local politicians dominated
> them; local political issues filled their minds; and the only
> thing they required in the matter of our foreign service was
> that a "good Republican" or a "good Democrat" should be
> rewarded.[39]

Similarly, the geographic horizons and daily concerns of most
businessmen were more local than those of officials in the foreign
service. These officials thus felt frustrated by businessmen's shortsighted indifference to foreign markets, and some of them even
seemed to derive pleasure from downturns in domestic prosperity,
anticipating that manufacturers would be shaken from their lethargy
and cultivate foreign markets. On one occasion, Consul-General
Thomas Sammons agreed with Ambassador Rockhill that American
businessmen "have been too prosperous at home." Francis B.
Loomis, the experienced foreign service officer, commented in 1909
that the "work and achievements of our foreign service have been
far in advance of the actual desires and wants of the manufacturing
community."[40]

The men who reshaped the United States foreign service
probably had a more difficult assignment than their counterparts in
Europe. Governmental bureaucracies in the European nations were
already playing a major role before the emergence of democratic
political institutions. Because those democratic institutions had to
accommodate themselves to established bureaucracies, the latter
have not found it necessary to engage in the sort of political activity
that government agencies in the United States have considered essential. The men staffing the British Foreign Office, for example,
thought the public was simply to be led, not taught.[41] State Department officers never had that luxury in the pre–World War I era;
they believed, with good reason, that they had to educate and pros-
elytize in order to create a modern foreign service. Success came
only after they succeeded in convincing others that a reorganized
foreign service had important benefits.

Historians of American foreign policy have frequently noted the pressures that businessmen and other interests have exerted on the executive branch in general and the State Department in particular.[42] That is certainly a valid approach, for it is useful to know which interests have exerted pressure, on whom, and with what results. But scholars have seldom examined the reverse of this process—the attempts by the foreign affairs bureaucracy itself to mobilize interest groups. This one-sided emphasis is by no means unique; sociologists too have failed to examine the impact of organizations on their environments. One sociologist has termed it "the most significant failure of all organizational theory."[43] Such neglect has the effect of portraying the outside elements as active and aware, and the organization itself as comparatively sluggish and unconcerned. The result in this instance has been to obscure the activity of State Department officials in bringing pressure to bear on their organization's environment, an activity that was crucial to the development of the foreign service before World War I. The constraints the reformers faced were formidable, but by no means insuperable.

As historian Robert Wiebe observes, in the late nineteenth century "foreign affairs had no firm constituency." Yet a few government officials interested in foreign service reform recognized that such a constituency was essential to pressure Congress for action, and they worked to create it. Selling their branch of the government as useful and worth reorganizing, they did not generally preach its utility for protecting missionaries or aiding tourists or upholding the nation's dignity, although they did not entirely ignore the value of the last two functions. They did emphasize the need for foreign markets to accommodate America's growing industrial output and maintain domestic prosperity. When the panic of 1893 and resulting economic chaos, combined with the political changeover guaranteed by the election of 1892, brought an outcry for consular reorganization from various business groups, it must have appeared to would-be reformers that their constituency was shaped and ready to lend vigorous and sustained support. While Francois Jones and Wilbur Carr wrote reform legislation and Gaillard Hunt sought to mobilize additional commercial groups, Frederic Emory encouraged businessmen to enter foreign markets and gave advice on how to go about it. But when prosperity returned in 1897, the initial surge faded, as many businessmen became less interested in foreign service reform. Government officials were therefore obliged to cultivate them. Robert Chilton spoke for the reformers when he recognized that "our only hope is in this direction."[44]

Although the associated businessmen did constitute a segment of American society that was relatively easy to mobilize, there were other reasons for government officials to seek their aid. Businessmen had the political clout lacking in other interested or potentially interested groups, such as the civil service advocates; members of Congress were likely to listen seriously to the desires of manufacturers and merchants from back home, especially those organized into boards of trade or chambers of commerce. Apart from tactical considerations, government officials (especially those at the top levels, who almost always came into public service from the business world) shared the pervasive positive image of the businessman as the bedrock of American society, upon which prosperity depended. Oscar Straus once scoffed at the notion of receiving advice about his department from men who could not even afford a decent pair of shoes, while Elihu Root praised the members of the New York State Chamber of Commerce as the country's "real rulers."[45]

State Department officials used business pressure on Congress to secure consular legislation and appropriations for the foreign service, often mobilizing and directing that pressure themselves. After 1906, Carr, Wilson, and others made repeated attempts to obtain legislation that would give congressional sanction to Roosevelt's and later Taft's executive orders, while also providing for the appointment of diplomats and consuls to grades instead of posts. "It would seem desirable," Carr observed to Root in 1907, "that another effort should be made by the Department to obtain legislation on this subject and that it should endeavor to utilize the influence of the commercial organizations in that direction." In 1912, Huntington Wilson addressed a form letter to more than a thousand chambers of commerce and still more newspapers, soliciting their help for a foreign service bill drafted in the department.[46] The reformers were unsuccessful until 1915, however, as Congress remained reluctant to abandon tradition.

The most significant post–1906 legislation for the State Department was the $100,000 appropriation in 1909 and subsequent years, which effected a major departmental reorganization. To obtain the funds, the department had to slip the reorganization through in the guise of tariff machinery—a matter of vital importance to congressional locals. Once the reorganization was achieved, the department could presumably work more efficiently to promote the export trade, enhance its image, enlarge its constituency, and secure further legislation. Willard Straight caught the spirit of events in the summer of 1909, and two days after Congress had granted the $100,000 appropriation, he happily shared his views with Carr. "If we succeed in getting established in China and South America all at the same time," he wrote optimistically, "we will have to double the Department I should think, and one good result of the publicity which has been given the new movement should be considerable appropriations for and an added sympathy with, the creation of a sufficient and well organized foreign service."[47]

Because of the need to justify its work, particularly after the emergence of C & L in 1903, the State Department's trade promotion rhetoric contained an element of superficiality; appearance and public relations occasionally triumphed over substance. Many of the commercial reports transmitted by the consuls were helpful, but others were not. There was a natural propensity towards quantity, sometimes at the expense of quality. While making his rounds, inspector Alfred Gottschalk was disturbed by the disparity between some consuls' zeal and their efficiency. "The younger men we are getting into the service all seem *too* young," he wrote Hengstler in 1910. "They come out with the idea that they are 'to help trade' and there their knowledge of studying commercial conditions seems to end." Years later, Carr regretted that he had been forced to use simplistic examples of trade promotion when he went before Congress. He had tended to talk in terms of how many thousands of dollars' worth of barbed wire the consul at Dakar had helped American manufacturers to market, rather than what he knew to be consuls' more important and more sophisticated commercial value. But as Carr himself had observed at the time, his own options and those of other reformers were limited. He complained in 1911 to the National Board of Trade that a congressional committee usually wanted "to know the results in dollars and cents." Hard figures could provide skeptical congressmen with proof that at least some of the public was enjoying a return on federal expenditures. The former consul and Bureau of Trade Relations officer DeWitt Poole later recalled that it was the department's "propaganda" demonstrating "concrete results" which obtained support in Congress for the consular service.[48]

The benefits to the foreign service officials as individuals formed the third and final element in this web of reciprocity. Just as the energy and activity of certain officials in the executive branch was the key factor in foreign service reform before World War I, the reason many of them so directed their efforts was the coincidence between perceived national, institutional, and personal interest.[49] Reorganization and larger appropriations provided a common solution for individual needs, as the growing specialization frequently created new slots and new opportunities. Frederic Emory found in the foreign service a chance to perform interesting and useful work. He could help repay his sponsor Bayard for his many kindnesses and at the same time further the Cleveland Democracy's low tariff–foreign markets doctrine whose merits he felt so deeply. Wilbur Carr also found interesting work, and a chance to make his mark by forging an institution that would reward those qualities in others which he valued in himself. Gaillard Hunt found an exhilarating opportunity to fight the spoilsmen he thought were polluting the government service to the detriment of intelligent and competent men like himself. And Huntington Wilson found a means of laying the groundwork for his future ambitions, while indulging his love for systems and symmetry and thus helping to satisfy his need for an ordered environment. Through their efforts, Emory, Carr, Wilson, and to a lesser degree Hunt, all found stimulating, useful work that brought them the recognition they required.

The young men entering the foreign service under the new arrangements were expected to possess that same desire for stimulating and useful work. If they produced, they would be rewarded by the managers of the service, since the reorganized system was structured around the career ambitions of its members. Secretary of State Charles Evans Hughes told a group of new officers in 1921 that each of them should plan and prepare, so that when "his generation rules the world he will be there as one of its chief rulers." These ambitions were used as a goad, particularly among the consuls, motivating them to demonstrate their usefulness by working to increase exports. Pinpointing the relationship, De-Witt Poole recalled in 1935 that "it was our job as Consuls to bring about that result by promoting trade. We were told explicitly that our worth to the Government would be largely judged by our effectiveness in this direction. By *promoting* trade we would be promoting ourselves." As a result, the consuls and diplomats would receive recognition and advancement, Carr and Wilson would receive their appropriations for the department and the field foreign service, and businessmen would receive valuable assistance in their efforts to increase exports and thereby foster American prosperity and well-being.[50] It was so obviously a worthwhile and realistic arrangement.

Near the end of his distinguished diplomatic service, John V. A. MacMurray recalled his early career as a time of "youthful wonder and the feeling of companionship in a thrilling adventure." In his biography of Willard Straight, Herbert Croly captured the same mood of exhilaration when he referred to the happiness Straight derived from "projecting the figures of his imagination on the canvas of the world."[51] Reorganizing the foreign service to help the United States play a more active role in the world supplied an outlet for the energies of all the actors. Whether they were employed in Washington bureaus or overseas, the world was indeed providing the stage for their zeal and imagination.[52]

11 EPILOGUE: 1913 AND AFTER

By 1913, after sixteen years of Republican rule, the foundations and framework of the modern United States foreign service had appeared. Of the State Department's two field forces, the consular corps was easily the more improved. New officers entered the lower ranks after an examination. They no longer departed for their posts unprepared, but underwent both group and individual training in the department. The inspection procedure continued the instruction and, with an assist from the geographic divisions, bound the overseas consular facilities and those of the State Department into an integrated system supervised by the watchful Wilbur Carr. Inspection reports also provided information and suggestions about the status of consulates, better enabling the department to request reclassification of offices according to their current importance. In this manner had emerged a career ladder which, in combination with a policy of promotion on merit, stimulated ambitious young men to exert themselves in promoting America's export trade. The substitution of salaries for fees and the growing Americanization of the service also resulted in more homogeneity and greater control from headquarters in Washington.

Less improvement had occurred in the diplomatic branch by the end of the Taft administration. It was still open only to persons of independent means, since the allotted salaries could just begin to cover a diplomat's expenses. In 1894 Henry White had cautioned Senator Morgan against pushing for diplomatic reform, because of public indifference, and the situation had improved little by 1913. The desire of prominent congressmen such as Oscar Underwood and Champ Clark to abolish the diplomatic corps and use the money

for the consular branch reflected the continuing difficulty faced by
the State Department in convincing the American public, or its representatives in Congress, that a modernized and efficient diplomatic
service was necessary or even particularly useful.[1]

Yet the executive branch managed to initiate a good deal of
diplomatic reorganization. By 1913 more than half the secretaries of
embassy and legation had passed an examination, and since 1909
new secretaries had undergone training at the department. The reclassified diplomatic service, like the consular branch, was administered to stimulate career aspirations; advancement in these two portions of the foreign service now reflected "service" to the nation, not
to any political party. Since the diplomatic corps lacked an inspection system, the geographic divisions were all the more important in
linking the department with the missions. Although the State Department was thwarted in its efforts to have diplomats and consuls
appointed to grades instead of to posts, it succeeded significantly in
bypassing this stipulation. Not only were diplomats assigned to the
geographic divisions as "drafting officers," but they also worked
there while disguised on paper as clerks. And in 1911 the department and Frank Lowden finally succeeded in committing Congress
to a policy of acquiring buildings for diplomatic missions and consulates.

Changes in the State Department itself were also of crucial
importance. They provided closer and more continuous direction
from Washington of America's foreign relations. They also allowed
both of the field branches to be linked to the department—and in a
fashion even to each other—to create a unified foreign service.[2] The
geographic divisions and the Division of Information, initiated during Root's tenure as secretary of state and expanded under Knox,
connected the department with the field. In the geographic offices
younger officials were able to have a voice in the policy-making
process. The growing specialization and increased staff in the department also allowed the United States to keep in closer touch with
developments in various parts of the world. In addition, the decimal
classification was a great improvement over Root's filing system; it
allowed for an expansibility that its predecessor lacked, and it continued to be used by the State Department for more than half a
century.[3] Finally, weathering crises in 1903 and 1912, the depart-

ment's commercial office had increased its utility by supplying information and guidance to businessmen and serving as a key part of the policy-making machinery.

The field foreign service was no longer the congressional toy it had been at the turn of the century. By 1913 it was an executive, more specifically a State Department, operation. The department selected its employees, trained, transferred, and promoted them, closely supervised their work, and, if necessary, fired them.

For its part, after ten years the Department of Commerce and Labor seemed well on its way to fulfilling the expectations that had attended its birth in 1903. During the spring of 1912, C & L finally obtained its consolidated Bureau of Foreign and Domestic Commerce, as well as an institutionalized connection with the nation's businessmen through the United States Chamber of Commerce.[4] It made further advances during the next few years. In March 1913, during the last week of the Taft administration, it became the "Department of Commerce" in name as well as in fact, when Labor received separate cabinet status. President Woodrow Wilson's new secretary of commerce was manufacturer William Redfield, president of the American Manufacturers Export Association, who for years had been involved in the export trade. Soon after taking office he began to enlarge the department on the foundations that Nagel and others had built.[5]

Two lengthy memoranda in March and April from A. H. Baldwin, chief of the Bureau of Foreign and Domestic Commerce, provided much of the substance for Redfield's subsequent reorganization. In the first, Baldwin sought to obtain a corps of commercial attachés, which various State Department officials had unsuccessfully sought for their own organization. But Baldwin, in the flush of his dual victory over the State Department and O. P. Austin, was much more ambitious than other proponents had ever been. He recommended that Commerce's "own field foreign service" should consist of fifty or sixty officers, to be stationed abroad at "strategic points in the world struggle for foreign trade."[6]

A follow-up memorandum in April elaborated Baldwin's views about his bureau's future role, which he believed included "an almost unlimited range of activities." He suggested the establishment of geographic divisions modeled on the State Department's organization and also recommended that the editorial division eventually acquire commodity experts to complement the geographic experts. Baldwin also wanted the department to establish regional offices in commercial centers across the country, to help consuls and commercial agents disseminate trade intelligence. He even envisioned an eventual domestic role for his agency. His wide-ranging plans included sponsoring studies of "the efficient distribution of commercial products, the commercial planning of cities, the scientific location of factories and the scientific local distribution of articles of commerce"; establishing "adequate records of sources of raw materials of all kinds"; examining "overindustrialized" areas; and studying the relationship between labor supply and the establishment of industries. [7] It was an ambitious scheme, but it remained only an ambition; the bureau's attention to the domestic scene continued to be confined chiefly to export trade promotion.

Redfield soon began to carry out Baldwin's suggestions and to secure Woodrow Wilson's support. Reminding the president that America's foreign trade (imports and exports) exceeded $4.2 billion annually and had been expanding at the rate of $500,000 a day during the preceding eleven months, Redfield observed that the "relation of this enormous trade to the prosperity and happiness of our people is so obvious as to need no comment." The president and the United States Chamber of Commerce lined up behind Redfield's expansion program. In July 1913, the first branch office of the Bureau of Foreign and Domestic Commerce began operating in New York, and during the next two years additional branches opened in Chicago, San Francisco, Boston, New Orleans, Atlanta, Saint Louis, and Seattle. Congress granted Redfield's request for commercial attachés, and ten of them began their duties during fiscal 1915. By the early 1920s, the geographic and commodity divisions were also realities. [8]

For the next few years, Democratic Congresses were kind to Redfield and his department, motivated partly by the economic opportunities accompanying the war in Europe. But even before August 1914, Congress was receptive to the secretary's appeals for more funds and personnel. During the hearings on the appropriations bill that established the commercial attachés, one short exchange captured the prevailing spirit:

> SENATOR SMOOT: "Give the Secretary all he asks for, because we certainly need some foreign business."
> SECRETARY REDFIELD: "You are dead right on that."

When Redfield took over the department in 1913, the Bureau of Foreign and Domestic Commerce was receiving appropriations of $225,000. By mid-1914 the figure, including the amount for the new commercial attachés, had jumped to $397,000, and in 1920 it was $910,000.[9] State Department officials no doubt ground their teeth in envy and frustration at the ease with which the Commerce Department could secure appropriations for promoting foreign trade.

Like many other officials before and since, Redfield was convinced that matters in his department had been ignored until he arrived on the scene to take charge. A 1916 document rejoiced that the department had been "given new life" during the secretary's tenure, and Redfield himself smugly compared Bureau of Foreign and Domestic Commerce spending with that of the old Bureau of Manufactures.[10] His spending yardstick was as dubious as it was unnecessary, since the new office was a consolidation of Manufactures and the larger Bureau of Statistics. Furthermore, although the department was now endowed with much larger appropriations and with important new facilities for trade promotion, Redfield built on foundations already in existence. It was Charles Nagel who had secured the consolidation of Manufactures and Statistics, a consolidation based on a 1908 recommendation of C & L officials, taken in turn from a similar 1903 suggestion. Nagel had viewed the consolidation as only a beginning, and he expected future appropriations to build on that foundation. The commercial attachés had been proposed several times by the State Department, and both this feature and the branch offices were urged upon Redfield by Nagel's choice as head of the department's foreign commercial office.

Woodrow Wilson's election in 1912 brought an end to the sixteen years of Republican presidents which had given foreign service reorganization time to take hold. When the presidency had last been lost to the opposition party, in 1896, a massive turnover in the field foreign service accompanied the succession. Consequently, officials both at the State Department and overseas awaited the new administration with anxiety. They knew that many gains would be lost if the spoils system resumed its hold, since appointment and tenure on the basis of qualifications and efficiency were at the heart of the reforms. The modified civil service provisions under which the foreign service operated were not embodied in legislation, and there was no legal impediment to their elimination. Especially anxious was the new generation of career diplomats serving as chiefs of mission, such as Henry Fletcher in Chile and Edwin Morgan in Brazil. Fletcher hoped that since political appointees still held some thirty ambassadorial and ministerial positions, the dozen career men would be allowed to remain.[11]

Wilbur Carr alternated between cautious optimism and despair, both for his own future and for that of his consular service. Four days after the election, anticipating "a probable change of occupation," Carr thought he might return to Ohio. "My father's farm appeals to me after this turmoil of politics," he wrote on November 9; there he might find "a duty to perform, constructive work to be done, a community to build up." At other times Carr was more optimistic, and he sought to quiet the fears of officers like Consul-General-at-Large Alfred Gottschalk, who himself was maintaining "a bold front" before the nervous consuls in his inspection district. Yet Carr kept his options open, and well into the spring of 1913 was writing to Willard Straight and Robert Bacon, both with connections on Wall Street, about possible employment in private business.[12]

The tentative optimism in some quarters was due largely to Woodrow Wilson's reputation as a reformer and to the reaffirmation of civil service principles in the Democratic platform of 1912. The platform proclaimed, "The law pertaining to the civil service should be honestly and rightly enforced, to the end that merit and ability shall be the standard of appointment and promotion, rather than service rendered to a political party." But many wondered if such pious pronouncements would stand in the way of southern Democratic senators and representatives who continued to clamor for an overturn of the merit system in the field foreign service to allow a greater representation of the southern states. The new administration had a strong southern image (Wilson himself, of course, was a native Virginian), and it seemed likely to treat sympathetically the appeals from southern congressmen.[13] The southerners' position was all the stronger due to Democratic control of Congress for the first time in eighteen years.

Also ominous was the lack of sympathy for the foreign service reforms exhibited by the new secretary of state. William Jennings Bryan, titular leader of the Democratic party for many years, had accumulated many political debts in his three attempts for the presidency, and he was most eager to find positions for deserving Democrats. "Now aren't you sorry you did not entertain him when he spent his week in Seoul," Willard Straight twitted Edwin Morgan about Bryan. "Moral—Lay up your treasures even though it be in a political hell, for you never know when the devil may drive the bandwagon." As inauguration day drew near, with the new administration's policies still unclear, the gloom at the State Department intensified. Wilbur Carr sadly observed that an "air of depression creeps thicker and thicker over the Dept. as the end of the administration draws nearer, and the associations that we have formed are about to be broken." The more irreverent Hugh Gibson dryly remarked that "lots of people have begun holding wakes over themselves already."[14]

Luckily for the foreign service, pressure on the administration was coming from other sources besides expectant Democratic job seekers and southern members of Congress. The National Civil Service Reform League naturally kept a close eye on the course of events. More important, various business groups, including the new and rigorously nonpartisan United States Chamber of Commerce, warned Woodrow Wilson that "revocation or suspension" of the executive orders "would retard the commerce of the country, and prove of serious injury to its business interests." In addition, many of the president's friends and associates, some of whom were in touch with worried foreign service officers, urged the strengthening of the career system. Such sentiment found a receptive listener in the new president, and he was able to restrain his secretary of state from effecting a general turnover in the consular and diplomatic services.[15]

By the fall of 1913, it was clear that most of the reforms had

been saved. The new administration left the consular service virtually intact. Yielding to Bryan in only a few instances, Wilson appointed less than half a dozen consuls by executive order, enabling
them to bypass the examination procedure. The secretaries of embassy and legation were similarly sheltered from the spoils system.
By December, the National Civil Service Reform League could report an "admirable" record in these two branches.[16]

Other areas did not fare so well. Several political appointments were made to the geographic divisions, although care was
taken to find posts in the field for the displaced career officers. Fred
Dearing, formerly assistant chief of the Latin American division,
was distressed by the appointment of Boaz Long, an advertising
man from New Mexico, to head his old office. Willard Straight, on
the other hand, was not so troubled. "Advertising . . . is probably
the best thing the State Department is doing nowadays," he wrote
Henry Fletcher. "It is an American trait and one which people understand." Moreover, the geographic divisions retained many diplomats and consuls to provide the necessary expertise and continuity. In another area, foreign trade advisers Pepper and Young
were replaced by William B. Fleming and Robert F. Rose, whose
attitudes on the tariff were more congenial to administration policy.[17]

No departure from previous policy was the displacement of
the career ministers and ambassadors by political appointees.
Woodrow Wilson did not share Bryan's indifference to training and
experience at all levels of the service, but he found those qualities
unimportant and even detrimental for chiefs of mission. "Every
day," he wrote John Bassett Moore in mid-1913, "I feel more and
more keenly the necessity of being represented at foreign courts by
men who easily catch and instinctively themselves occupy our own
point of view with regard to public matters." Wilson replaced all but
three of the mission chiefs, retaining career officers Henry Fletcher
at Santiago, Edwin Morgan at Rio de Janeiro, and Maurice F. Egan
at Copenhagen.[18]

The turnover aroused much criticism from those who had
hoped to retain the principle of career ministers and ambassadors
and was perhaps a blow to many young diplomats who expected to
be rewarded eventually by appointment to these top jobs. Yet it was

probably unrealistic to expect that Wilson would retain the career ministers, who were all Republican appointees. When Taft had succeeded a Republican president, he had made a number of removals and new appointments as mission chiefs.[19] Even today, United States ambassadors to a number of countries are important political contributors or otherwise friends of the president. The problem has been resolved partly by the larger number of ambassadorships that has become available as the number of independent nations has increased. Few political contributors or their spouses are attracted by a life in remote and unglamorous posts.

By the end of 1913, the most important features of the foreign service's reorganization had been preserved. To be sure, the new system was hardly strengthened by appointments of inexperienced men to the geographic divisions, the Office of Foreign Trade Advisers, and most of the top diplomatic positions. But a substructure to help formulate and conduct foreign policy, and carry on foreign relations, had survived. An important precedent now existed for future changes in the national administration. Although Democrats had made threatening noises about what they would do to appropriations when they came to power, the Democratic Congress found it impossible to make cuts in the foreign service. The first appropriations from the new group of legislators decreased the funding for the State Department by less than $2,000 below the previous year and raised it by $500,000 for the field establishment (chiefly for embassy buildings).[20] And in 1914, President Wilson threw his support behind a measure to improve the foreign service further.

For many years, foreign service reformers had unsuccessfully sought legislation permitting the appointment of diplomats and consuls to grades rather than to posts. Since 1907, the State Department had been bringing officers from the field into the geographic divisions and sending consuls to confer with businessmen. During the Taft administration, it also assigned diplomatic officers to the geographic divisions both as drafting officers and as clerks, and early in 1913 the department received appropriations for forty of the highly mobile consular assistants. But appointment to grades would have given the State Department greater flexibility in stationing diplomats and consuls where they were most needed, whether in the field, in the department, or on special assignment in the United States. The reformers thus continued to press for such an improvement. They were equally insistent upon legislation embodying the provisions of Roosevelt's and Taft's executive orders to establish more permanently the merit system in the field foreign service.[21]

In the spring of 1914, the department tried again. Third Assistant Secretary William Phillips, back in his old position after several years in the London embassy, sent the proposed measure to the Foreign Relations and Foreign Affairs Committee chairmen, Senator William Stone of Missouri and Congressman Henry Flood of Virginia. The two congressmen introduced the bill on May 19 and 20, and Carr proceeded to guide it through. With support from Woodrow Wilson and sufficient, if inconstant, backing from Bryan, the bill passed the Democratic Congress and received Wilson's signature early the next year. The outbreak of the World War in August had added to the urgency of the bill's administrative features regarding appointment to grades. Forced to shift its personnel to meet changing needs, the State Department badly needed the more flexible system. Although it is likely that the measure would have passed Congress without the outbreak of the war, no doubt the new crisis helped speed its passage.[22]

The Stone-Flood Act of 1915 finally established the method of appointment to grades, improved the classification system of the diplomatic and the consular branches, and for the first time gave some legislative affirmation to the principle of appointment and promotion on the basis of demonstrated merit. It neatly skirted the constitutional issue, requiring the secretary of state only to report to the president names of qualified applicants for initial appointment or promotion on the basis of examination or the efficiency record. It did not require the president to appoint from the list.[23]

After the passage of the Stone-Flood Act, the consular corps continued its evolution as an organization offering a public service career. In 1918 some of the consuls on detail to the department formed the American Consular Association, to foster an esprit de corps in the service. Consul-General-at-Large Ralph J. Totten believed the new organization might help "the younger man to appreciate the seriousness and dignity of the work and the importance of obeying orders of the Department without question or argument like soldiers are taught to do." Wilbur Carr had always stressed to new consuls the importance of loyalty, obedience, and zeal, and he continued to seek ways to promote these qualities. Anticipating that the *Bulletin* published by the American Consular Association would help "lay the foundations for a Consular literature," he pleaded with distinguished veterans like Frank Mason and Robert Chilton to write their memoirs. "We must have a considerable amount of biographical material," he told Chilton in 1922, "to help stimulate the young officers to build up tradition and add to the attractiveness of the service." After the Rogers Act consolidated the diplomatic and consular branches into a single field foreign service in 1924, Carr headed the new entity as an assistant secretary of state.[24]

Probably the most famous piece of foreign service legislation, the Rogers Act was drafted chiefly by a consul working in the State Department under Carr's supervision. It was particularly a boon to the diplomatic corps, which had always had difficulty convincing the American public of its significance. Not only were the two field branches now merged, but salaries in the nine classes of the unified service were raised to range from $3,000 to $9,000—a considerable boost from the previous $2,500 to $4,000 scale for diplomatic secretaries.[25] The constitutional argument that the president could appoint anyone he wished to the foreign service had finally lost its force. For the first time, Congress required that such appointments could be made only after an examination.[26]

Subsequent years brought additional improvements. The Moses-Linthicum Act of 1931 made several important changes and authorized representation and post allowances for foreign service officers, as well as for chiefs of mission. A reorganization measure in 1946 reclassified the service and provided for assignment of foreign service personnel to other agencies which had proliferated during World War II. And as a result of the Wriston Report in 1954, civil service employees in the State Department whose duties concerned foreign affairs were taken into the foreign service. The United States finally possessed an integrated foreign service, sixty years after Francois Jones and his allies had drafted their bill.[27]

After World War II, the Cold War brought the State Department new arguments for increased funds, and greater public interest in foreign affairs now made it less necessary to rely on commercial organizations and trade promotion rhetoric. Yet the department by no means took public relations for granted. As in other government agencies, its public affairs offices grew considerably after the war. One example was the Office of Community Advisory Services, created in the 1960s as part of the State Department's public relations effort. The pre–World War I department had sent consuls and other officials to confer with business groups; O/CAS dispatched foreign service officers, home on leave from their foreign posts, to discuss their work with the local newspaper, radio or television station, Lions Club, and Rotary.[28]

Even before the important developments that followed two world wars, the basis of the modern foreign service had emerged. Later generations would build on foundations and fill in an outline created between the 1890s and 1913 by an assortment of "master architects." Like their predecessors, they would find in an expanding foreign affairs bureaucracy the means to help their country, their institution, and themselves. During a reorganization meeting in the Bureau of Foreign and Domestic Commerce in 1941, the bureau's new director spoke at length about the potentially dire consequences of postwar economic adjustments and the need to deliver useful information to the nation's businessmen. Turning his attention from national requirements to a rough mixture of institutional and personal needs, he asked rhetorically: "What do *you* get out of this reorganization? *First, you get a job to do.* No organization can exist or make careers for its people unless it has a job to do." Whether he knew it or not, the bureau chief was appealing to a time-honored and powerful web of interests.[29]

APPENDIX A:
ROSTER OF
SELECTED STATE
DEPARTMENT
OFFICIALS

This list shows only the *departmental* service of the more frequently mentioned State Department officials and includes any departmental positions held before 1890, but not all those after 1913. The information is from various issues of the department's *Register*.

Adee, Alvey A.: clerk, 1877–1878; chief, Diplomatic Bureau, 1878–1882; third assistant secretary, 1882–1886; second assistant secretary, 1886–1924

Anderson, Chandler P.: counselor, 1910–1913

Bacon, Robert: assistant secretary, 1905–1909; secretary, January–March 1909

Bryan, William J.: secretary, 1913–1915

Carr, Wilbur J.: clerk, 1892–1902; chief, Consular Bureau, 1902–1907; chief clerk, 1907–1909; director, Consular Service, 1909–1924

Chilton, Robert S., Jr.: clerk, 1877–1889; chief clerk, February–April 1893; confidential clerk to second assistant secretary, 1893–1895; chief, Consular Bureau, 1895–1902

Clark, Joshua R., Jr.: assistant solicitor, 1906–1910; solicitor, 1910–1913

Davis, Mack H.: commercial adviser, 1909–1912

Dawson, Thomas C.: resident diplomatic officer and chief, Division of Latin American Affairs, 1909–1910 and June 1911–1912

Day, William R.: assistant secretary, 1897–1898; secretary, April–September 1898

Denby, Charles: chief clerk, 1905–1907

Emory, Frederic: secretary, Bureau of American Republics, 1893–1894; chief, Bureau of Statistics, 1894–1897; chief, Bureau of Foreign Commerce, 1897–1903; chief, Bureau of Trade Relations, 1903–1905

Foster, John W.: secretary, 1892–1893

Gibson, Hugh S.: confidential clerk to assistant secretary, 1910–1911

Gresham, Walter Q.: secretary, 1893–1895

Hale, Chandler: third assistant secretary, 1909–1913

Hay, John: assistant secretary, 1879–1881; secretary, 1898–1905

Heintzleman, Percival S.: assistant on Far Eastern affairs to third assistant secretary, 1907–1908; assistant chief, Division of Far Eastern Affairs, 1908–1909; drafting officer in same division, 1909–1910; assistant chief in same division, 1911–1914

Hengstler, Herbert C.: clerk, 1898–1907; chief, Consular Bureau, 1907–1918

Hill, David J.: assistant secretary of state, 1898–1903

Hunt, Gaillard: clerk, 1887–1902; chief, Passport Bureau, 1902–1907; chief, Bureau of Citizenship, 1907–1909

Jones, Francois S.: clerk, 1892–1897

Knox, Philander C.: secretary, 1909–1913

Loomis, Francis B.: assistant secretary, 1903–1905

MacMurray, John V. A.: clerk, April–July 1911; assistant chief, Division of Near Eastern Affairs, 1911–1912; chief in same division, 1912–1913

Miller, Ransford S.: chief, Division of Far Eastern Affairs, 1909–1913

Moore, John B.: law clerk, 1885–1886; third assistant secretary, 1886–1891; assistant secretary, April–September 1898; counselor, 1913–1914

Olney, Richard: secretary, 1895–1897

Osborne, John B.: assistant secretary, Reciprocity Commission, 1897–1905; chief, Bureau of Trade Relations, 1905–1912

Pepper, Charles M.: commercial adviser, 1909–1912; foreign trade adviser, 1912–1913

Phillips, William: assistant on Far Eastern affairs to third assistant secretary, 1907–1908; chief, Division of Far Eastern Affairs, 1908–1909; third assistant secretary, January–October 1909

Poole, DeWitt C., Jr.: consular assistant in Bureau of Trade Relations, 1910–1911

Quincy, Josiah: assistant secretary, March–September 1893

Renick, Edward T.: chief, Bureau of Statistics, 1893–1894; chief clerk, 1894–1897

Rockhill, William W.: chief clerk, 1893–1894; third assistant secretary, 1894–1896; assistant secretary, 1896–1897; director, Bureau of American Republics, 1899–1905

Root, Elihu: secretary, 1905–1909

Scott, James B.: solicitor, 1906–1910

Sherman, John: secretary, 1897–1898

Smith, Sidney Y.: clerk, 1881–1897; chief, Diplomatic Bureau, 1897–1919

Van Dyne, Frederick: clerk, 1891–1900; assistant solicitor, 1900–1906, 1907, and 1910–1913

Williams, Edward T.: assistant chief, Division of Far Eastern Affairs, 1909–1911

Wilson, Huntington: third assistant secretary, 1906–1908; assistant secretary, 1909–1913

Young, Evan E.: chief, Division of Near Eastern Affairs, 1909–1912; foreign trade adviser, 1912–1913

APPENDIX B: ABBREVIATIONS AND RECORD GROUPS

ABBREVIATIONS

BAR records: Records of the Bureau of American Republics
C & L: Department of Commerce and Labor
Dip/Cons: Diplomatic and Consular Appropriations Bill
HAG Papers: Harry A. Garfield Papers
JRG Papers: James R. Garfield Papers
LC: Library of Congress, Division of Manuscripts
LEJ: Legislative, Executive, and Judicial Appropriations Bill
NAM: National Association of Manufacturers
NCSL: National Civil Service League
NCSRL: National Civil Service Reform League
PCEE: President's Commission on Economy and Efficiency
RG: Record Group

RECORD GROUPS (NATIONAL ARCHIVES, WASHINGTON, D.C.)

40: Department of Commerce
46: Senate
51: Bureau of the Budget
59: Department of State
84: Foreign Service Posts
151: Bureau of Foreign and Domestic Commerce
233: House of Representatives

NOTES

PREFACE

1. Earlier works on the history of the State Department and field foreign service include Gaillard Hunt, *The Department of State of the United States, Its History and Functions* (New Haven, Conn., 1914), and Tracy H. Lay, *The Foreign Service of the United States* (New York, 1925). Both Hunt and Lay were employed for a time at the State Department. Political scientist Graham H. Stuart produced two valuable books upon which historians have frequently relied: *American Diplomatic and Consular Practice* (New York, 1936), and *The Department of State* (New York, 1949). Warren Ilchman, another political scientist, followed in 1961 with *Professional Diplomacy in the United States, 1779–1939: A Study in Administrative History* (Chicago, 1961). Important publications by historians on aspects of the foreign affairs machinery include Donald M. Dozer, "Secretary of State Elihu Root and Consular Reorganization," *Mississippi Valley Historical Review* 29 (December 1942): 339–50; William Barnes and John H. Morgan, *The Foreign Service of the United States: Origins, Development, and Functions* (Washington, D.C., 1961); Katherine Crane, *Mr. Carr of State: Forty-Seven Years in the Department of State* (New York, 1960); Thomas G. Paterson, "American Businessmen and Consular Service Reform, 1890s to 1906," *Business History Review* 40 (Spring 1966): 77–97; Waldo H. Heinrichs, Jr., "Bureaucracy and Professionalism in the Development of American Career Diplomacy," in John Braeman et al., eds., *Twentieth-Century American Foreign Policy* (Columbus, Ohio, 1971), pp. 119–206; Jerry Israel, "A Diplomatic Machine: Scientific Management in the Department of State, 1906–1924," in Israel, ed., *Building the Organizational Society: Essays on Associational Activities in Modern America* (New York, 1972), pp. 183–96; Burton I. Kaufman, "The Organizational Dimension of United States Foreign Economic Policy, 1900–1920," *Business History Review* 46 (Spring 1972): 17–44; Kaufman, *Efficiency and Expansion: Foreign Trade Organization in the Wilson Administration, 1913–1921* (Westport, Conn., 1974).

2. James R. Childs made the mistake about the Commerce Department in his *American Foreign Service* (New York, 1948), p. 13. Probably relying on Childs's account, Barnes and Morgan repeated the error in their useful history, *Foreign Service*, p. 222. They were followed, in turn, by W. Wendell Blancké, *The Foreign Service of the United States* (New York, 1969), p. 21. See Barnes and Morgan, *Foreign Service*, p. 210, for the error about the training school.

3. I have borrowed the term from separate tributes to two of the principal organizers. In 1922, Director of the Consular Service Wilbur Carr described former Secretary of State Elihu Root as the "master architect" of the modern foreign service. Ambassador Joseph Grew later applied the same accolade to Carr himself, on two separate occasions. "Carr Looks Ever Forward," *American Consular Bulletin* 4 (July 1922): 204; "Speech by Mr. Grew," ibid., 6 (September 1924): 214; Joseph C. Grew, "The Master Architect," *American Foreign Service Journal* 9 (June 1932): 211.

4. Robert K. Merton, *Social Theory and Social Structure* (New York, 1957), pp. 287–420; Samuel P. Hays, "Political Parties and the Community-Society Continuum," in William N. Chambers and Walter D. Burnham, eds., *The American Party Systems: Stages of Political Development* (New York, 1967), pp. 152–81; Thomas J. McCormick, "The State of American Diplomatic History," in Herbert J. Bass, ed., *The State of American History* (Chicago, 1970), pp. 119–41. A good brief introduction to the terminology is McCormick's in Lloyd Gardner, Walter LaFeber, and Thomas McCormick, *Creation of the American Empire: U. S. Diplomatic History* (Chicago, 1973), pp. 192–93.

5. William E. Leuchtenburg, "The New Deal and the Analogue of War," in John Braeman et al., eds., *Change and Continuity in Twentieth-Century America* (New York, 1966), pp. 81–143.

CHAPTER 1

1. Graham Stuart, *American Diplomatic and Consular Practice*, pp. 23, 30–31.

2. Ibid., pp. 35–36.

3. Wilbur J. Carr, "The American Consular Service," *American Journal of International Law* 1 (October 1907): 894–96, 905–7; Barnes and Morgan, *Foreign Service*, p. 58; Stuart, *Diplomatic and Consular Practice*, p. 360; Chester L. Jones, *Consular Service of the United States* (Philadelphia, 1906), pp. 4–5.

4. U.S., Department of State, *Regulations Prescribed for the Consular Service of the United States* (Washington, D.C., 1896), pp. 149–53, 51–55, 142–45, 36–37; Eugene Schuyler, *American Diplomacy and the Furtherance of Commerce* (New York, 1886), p. 53; Jones, *Consular Service*, pp. 46–56, 63–65; Barnes and Morgan, *Foreign Service*, p. 60.

5. Barnes and Morgan, *Foreign Service*, p. 350; Department of State, *Regulations*, pp. 8–9; Department of State, *Register of the Department of State*, 1900.

6. Department of State, *Regulations*, pp. 7–8; John W. Foster, *The Practice of Diplomacy* (Boston, 1906), p. 218; Department of State, *Register*, 1900; Barnes and Morgan, *Foreign Service*, p. 350.

7. Chilton to William W. Rockhill, April 5, 1897, and Assistant Secretary of State to Jesse W. Sparks, June 29, 1896, Miscellaneous Reports and Correspondence on Consular Inspections, State Department records, RG 59, National Archives (see p. 253 for list of abbreviations); Chilton to Richard Olney, June 18, 1896, and same to William Rockhill, September 21, 1896, Inspection Reports on Consulates, RG 59.

8. J. E. Conner, *Uncle Sam Abroad* (Chicago, 1900), p. 57; "Service Honors

Mr. Carr," *American Foreign Service Journal* 9 (July 1932): 256; Seeger to David J. Hill, February 22, 1901, David J. Hill Papers, University of Rochester Library.

9. *Good Government* 12 (June 15, 1893): 156; Chilton to Harry A. Garfield, April 10, 1901, HAG Papers, LC.

10. Department of State, *Regulations*, pp. 20, 229; draft of remarks to the Foreign Service School by Wilbur Carr, April 9, 1937, Wilbur J. Carr Papers, LC; Mason to White, January 19, 1901, Francis B. Loomis Papers, Manuscripts Division, Department of Special Collections, Stanford University Libraries.

11. Unless the context clearly indicates otherwise, "consulates" will be used as a generic term including consulates-general.

12. Joseph O. Kerbey, *An American Consul in Amazonia* (New York, 1911), pp. 59, 182–83; Department of State, *Regulations*, p. 196; Congressman Robert R. Hitt to Ralph G. Root, April 15, 1899, letterbook, Robert R. Hitt Papers, LC; Secretary of State Elihu Root to Senator Redfield Proctor, March 12, 1906, and to Congressman Herbert Parsons, May 29, 1906, Miscellaneous Letters Sent Regarding Consular Affairs, RG 59.

13. James R. Childs, *American Foreign Service* (New York, 1948), p. 8; Henry S. Villard, *Affairs at State* (New York, 1965), p. 46; Perry Belmont, "Defects in Our Consular Service," *Forum* 4 (January 1888): 524.

14. Address by A. E. Ingram, July 1, 1909, Lectures to Consular Officers, RG 59; Jones, *Consular Service*, pp. 21–22; Katherine Crane, *Mr. Carr of State*, p. 50; Wilbur Carr to Herbert Peirce, June 12, 1902, Consular Bureau Decisions and Precedents, RG 59.

15. Chilton to Rockhill, September 21, 1896, Inspection Reports on Consulates, RG 59; Day to the Attorney General, July 12, 1898, Consular Bureau Decisions and Precedents, RG 59. Part of the problem with consular agents and fees may have been ameliorated by President William McKinley's 1898 executive order stipulating that consular agents were to receive one-half of the official fees they collected. But the order left much room for abuse by failing to cover unofficial fees. Department of State, *Register*, 1903, p. 23.

16. U.S., Congress, House, *Diplomatic and Consular*, Rept. 842, 49th Cong., 1st sess., 1886, p. 3; U.S., Congress, *Congressional Record*, 43d Cong., 2d sess., 1874, vol. 2, p. 3964; Carl A. Hansmann to Chilton, April 11, 1899, Robert S. Chilton, Jr., Papers, Duke University Library.

17. U.S., Senate, *Amending Act for Reorganization of Consular Service*, Rept. 256, 60th Cong., 1st sess., 1908, pp. 13–14; Chilton to Richard Olney, n. d., Inspection Reports on Consulates, RG 59. At the time of Chilton's complaint, there were thirty-three consulates and consulates-general in Canada and seventeen in Mexico.

18. Schuyler, *American Diplomacy*, p. 76; William D. Foulke, "The Qualifications of a Consul," *Good Government* 19 (March 1902): 42–43; George H. Murphy to Wilbur Carr, August 30, 1899, Inspection Reports on Consulates, RG 59.

19. Albert H. Washburn, "Some Evils of Our Consular Service," *Atlantic Monthly* 74 (August 1894): 242–43; Root to George W. Wickersham, May 17, 1919, NCSL Collection, Pendleton Room, U.S. Civil Service Commission Library, Washington, D.C.

20. Wilbur Carr, draft of remarks to the Foreign Service School, April 9, 1937, Carr Papers.

21. Senate, *Report of the Select Committee*, Rept. 507, 50th Cong., 1st sess., 1888, p. 123; Crane, *Mr. Carr*, p. 51.

22. Carr, "American Consular Service," pp. 896–97; Washburn, "Some Evils of Our Consular Service," p. 246; address by Skinner, *Proceedings of the American Manufacturers Export Association*, September 1911, p. 79.

23. John Riddle to Francis B. Loomis, June 20, 1904, and Dickinson to David J. Hill, September 4, 1901, letterbook, Charles M. Dickinson Papers, LC; Report of Convention of Consuls-General and Treasury Agents at Paris, August 1890, RG 59.

24. Chilton to Rockhill, February 11, 1897, Inspection Reports on Consulates, RG 59; George McAneny, "How Other Countries Do It," *Century* 57 (February 1899): 611; Mason to William R. Day, December 14, 1897, William R. Day Papers, LC. Mason was no doubt referring to consuls in Europe, particularly in his consular district. As noted above, the consuls in Europe were generally the better men in the service.

25. John B. Osborne, "The Glamour of a Consulship," *Atlantic Monthly* 91 (June 1903): 806; "Changes in the Consular Service," unsigned and undated memorandum, Consular Bureau Decisions and Precedents, RG 59; Lloyd Griscom, *Diplomatically Speaking* (New York, 1940), p. 46; Herbert W. Bowen, *Recollections, Diplomatic and Undiplomatic* (New York, 1926), p. 177.

26. John Sherman to Francis B. Loomis, March 16, 1893, Loomis Papers; Graham Stuart, *The Department of State*, p. 195; Hay to Robert R. Hitt, May 1, 1902, Hitt Papers; Hay to Whitelaw Reid, November 13, 1898, in NCSRL, *Report on the Foreign Service* (New York, 1919), pp. 130–31.

27. *Good Government* 20 (March 1903): 45; Hay to Whitelaw Reid, November 13, 1898, in NCSRL, *Report*, pp. 130–31.

28. Francis B. Loomis to William Loeb, November 19, 1904, Theodore Roosevelt Papers, LC; Heath to Hill, February 20, 1899, Hill Papers, University of Rochester.

29. Root to Andrew F. West, January 25, 1909, and Tracy Beecher to Root, January 6, 1906, copies in Philip C. Jessup Papers, LC; Charles M. Dickinson to John Hay, December 24, 1900, Hay Papers, LC; Truman DeWeese to William R. Day, July 7, 1897, Day Papers.

30. Leonard D. White, *The Republican Era, 1869–1901: A Study in Administrative History* (New York, 1958), p. 1; Gamble to Hill, February 13, 1902, Hill Papers, University of Rochester. See also Thomas E. Heenan, consul at Odessa, to Senator Knute Nelson, June 5 and August 19, 1902, Knute Nelson Papers, Minnesota State Historical Society, Saint Paul.

31. Department of State, *Instructions to Diplomatic Officers of the United States* (Washington, D.C., 1897), pp. 12–13, 17; Allan Nevins, *Henry White: Thirty Years of American Diplomacy* (New York, 1930), pp. 52–53.

32. The condition of consular buildings aroused little interest by comparison. Consuls and their offices could be housed in much less prepossessing quarters than the diplomats, who had extensive social obligations. Also, the dignity of the

nation was considered to be more at stake with embassies or legations, representing as they did the United States in foreign capitals. An important exception was the concern of American officials for better consular facilities in the Far East, where, according to Elihu Root, "appearances count for much more than they do with us." Root to Senator Shelby Cullom, May 8, 1906, Miscellaneous Letters Sent Regarding Consular Affairs, RG 59.

    33. *Diplomatically Speaking*, p. 47. Representing the United States in Great Britain from 1893 to 1897, Bayard was the first American to hold the rank of ambassador.

    34. Henry White to Francis Loomis, March 8, 1902, Loomis Papers; White to Root, October 14, 1905, Elihu Root Papers, LC.

    35. Milton Plesur, *America's Outward Thrust: Approaches to Foreign Affairs, 1865–1890* (DeKalb, Ill., 1971), pp. 36–37.

    36. See Robert A. Divine's forewords to his "America in Crisis" series, such as the volume by Daniel M. Smith, *The Great Departure: The United States and World War I* (New York, 1965), p. vii. C. Vann Woodward has termed the period in American history before 1940 as an "era of free security." "The Age of Reinterpretation," *American Historical Review* 66 (October 1960): 1–19.

    37. Root to J. St. Loe Strachey, September 9, 1905, letterbook, Root Papers; Griscom, *Diplomatically Speaking*, p. 26; Wilson to John V. A. MacMurray, December 21, 1905, John V. A. MacMurray Papers, Princeton University Library.

    38. Griscom, *Diplomatically Speaking*, pp. 46–47. See also Gaillard Hunt to James R. Garfield, April 12, 1889, JRG Papers, LC; Elihu Root to Andrew F. West, January 25, 1909, copy in Jessup Papers.

    39. Nicolson, *Diplomacy* (London, 1939), p. 218; William F. Sands, *Undiplomatic Memories* (New York, 1930), p. 47.

    40. Hay to Hill, August 4, 1902, Hill Papers, University of Rochester; Rockhill to James Harrison Wilson, May 14 and June 22, 1897, James H. Wilson Papers, LC.

    41. Root to Andrew F. West, January 25, 1909, copy in Jessup Papers; Ilchman, *Professional Diplomacy*, pp. 80–81.

    42. George W. Curtis, "Ten Years of Reform," *Proceedings of the NCSRL*, September 1891, p. 19; Department of State, *Register*, 1890s; Senator Henry Cabot Lodge to Jonathan A. Lane, December 24, 1894, letterbook, Henry Cabot Lodge Papers, Massachusetts Historical Society, Boston. There were three assistant secretaries of state in the department, ranked in numerical order. The second and third were called by their numbered titles, while the first was called simply "assistant secretary of state." The office of second assistant secretary of state did not change hands with every new administration. The incumbent from 1886 until his death in 1924 was Alvey Augustus Adee.

    43. Francis M. Huntington Wilson, *Memoirs of an Ex-Diplomat* (Boston, 1945), pp. 156, 51.

    44. National Archives, *Preliminary Inventory 157, General Records of the Department of State* (Washington, D.C., 1963), pp. 7–32; House, *Hearings on the LEJ* for 1899, December 1, 1897, p. 13; Wilson, *Memoirs*, pp. 57, 170.

    45. Department of State, *Register*, passim.

46. Wilson, *Memoirs*, pp. 82, 159–60; Griscom, *Diplomatically Speaking*, p. 199.

47. Wilson, *Memoirs*, pp. 159–60; Senate, Executive Document 53, 46th Cong., 3d sess., 1881; Department of State, *Register*, passim.

48. Sands, *Undiplomatic Memories*, p. 56; Wilson, *Memoirs*, pp. 159–60.

49. Childs, *American Foreign Service*, p. 7. For details of the nineteenth-century foreign service and attempts to improve it, see Ilchman, *Professional Diplomacy*, chapters 1 and 2; Barnes and Morgan, *Foreign Service*, chapters 5 through 17.

50. *Nation* 1 (November 2, 1865): 551–52, and 61 (September 26, 1895): 218; Carr, "American Consular Service," pp. 963, 902; Senate, Rept. 154, 40th Cong., 2d sess., 1868; address by A. E. Ingram, July 1, 1909, Lectures to Consular Officers, RG 59.

CHAPTER 2

1. Richard Hakluyt, *A Discourse concerning Western Planting*, excerpted in Merrill Jensen, ed., *English Historical Documents*, vol. 9 (New York, 1955), pp. 102–6; Ross M. Robertson, *History of the American Economy* (New York, 1964), p. 226.

2. U.S., Department of Commerce and Labor, *Statistical Abstract of Foreign Countries* (Washington, D. C., 1909), pp. 20–23, 42–45.

3. Robertson, *American Economy*, p. 331; Victor Metcalf, Secretary of Commerce and Labor, "American Trade and Commerce," in Robert M. LaFollette, ed., *The Making of America*, 10 vols. (Chicago, 1905), 4: 1; U.S., Department of Commerce, *Historical Statistics of the United States, Colonial Times to 1957* (Washington, D.C., 1960), pp. 544–45. Unless otherwise noted, export figures used in this study are expressed in the dollars of the period ("current dollars"), which is the way contemporaries almost always measured exports. The year refers to fiscal year. Except where the context clearly indicates otherwise, references to "manufactures" or "manufactured" products refer to finished or semifinished goods, excluding manufactured foodstuffs such as flour or prepared meat. Contemporaries generally included semifinished manufactures, such as lumber and pig iron, when they spoke of "manufactured" goods; they included prepared foodstuffs much less frequently. The government's statistical categories reflected and reinforced this usage, as noted in chapter 8.

4. Department of Commerce, *Historical Statistics* (1960), p. 44. The price inflation beginning in the late 1890s by itself accounted for a 23 percent rise in the value of all United States exports between 1900 and 1913. This was almost one-third of the 77 percent increase in exports over the same period as expressed in current dollars. But the inflation was distributed unevenly among the several kinds of products. Between 1900 and 1913, export prices of crude foodstuffs (such as wheat and corn) rose 34 percent and crude materials for use in manufacturing (chiefly raw cotton) 39 percent, while semifinished manufactures increased 12 percent and finished manufactures only 1 percent. Consequently, as government officials knew, the growth in exports of these two categories of manufactures relative to other products

was much more significant than even the current dollar figures showed them to be. Export prices of manufactured foodstuffs, on the other hand, increased 40 percent. Robert Lipsey, *Price and Quantity Trends in the Foreign Trade of the United States* (Princeton, N. J., 1963), pp. 142–43; U.S., Department of Commerce and Labor, *Foreign Commerce and Navigation of the United States, 1907* (Washington, D.C., 1908), pp. 18–22; Department of Commerce, *Foreign Commerce and Navigation, 1912*, p. 19.

5. David P. Thelen, "Social Tensions and the Origins of Progressivism," *Journal of American History* 61 (September 1969): 336; John Bassett Moore, diary entry for May 6, 1894, John Bassett Moore Papers, LC; Noyes, quoted in Thomas J. McCormick, *China Market: America's Quest for Informal Empire, 1893–1901* (Chicago, 1967), p. 30. For a valuable study of the frontier's impact in shaping American attitudes, see Henry Nash Smith, *Virgin Land: The American West as Symbol and Myth* (Cambridge, Mass., 1950).

6. Address by Hill, "The Expansion of Civilization," December 16, 1898, in Hill Papers, University of Rochester; Frye quoted in Walter LaFeber, *The New Empire: An Interpretation of American Expansion, 1860–1898* (Ithaca, N.Y., 1963), p. 366; Emory, "Review of the World's Commerce," in Department of State, *Commercial Relations during 1902* (Washington, D.C., 1903), 1: 24–27; Nelson in *Congressional Record*, 57th Cong., 1st sess., 1902, 35: 598; Hale, ibid., p. 914; Lodge to Day, June 6, 1898, Day Papers; Senate, *The Philadelphia Museums*, Rept. 1374, 56th Cong., 1st sess., 1900, p. 1.

7. Mira Wilkins, *The Emergence of Multinational Enterprise: American Business Abroad from the Colonial Era to 1914* (Cambridge, Mass., 1970), pp. 66, 72; Albert K. Steigerwalt, *The National Association of Manufacturers, 1895–1914: A Study in Business Leadership* (Grand Rapids, Mich., 1964), pp. 62–63; Kirby, "The Relation of Domestic Abuses to Our Foreign and Domestic Trade," *American Industries* 12 (January 1912): 12.

8. Emory Johnson et al., *History of Domestic and Foreign Commerce of the United States* (Washington, D.C., 1915), 2: 290; Department of C & L, *The Commercial Orient in 1905* (Washington, D.C., 1906), pp. 6, 12; McCormick, *China Market*, p. 130; Hitchcock to Secretary of State William Day, February 18, 1898, Day Papers; Emory, "Review of the World's Commerce," in Department of State, *Commercial Relations of the U. S. with Foreign Countries during 1900* (Washington, D.C., 1901), 1: 21.

9. Tom E. Terrill, *The Tariff, Politics, and American Foreign Policy, 1874–1901* (Westport, Conn., 1973), p. 16. Burton I. Kaufman has described this concern for new tools to promote exports in "Organizational Dimension," *Business History Review* 46: 19–22.

10. Formed by Congress in 1898 to investigate the nation's pressing economic and social problems, the Industrial Commission collected data and testimony sufficient to fill eighteen volumes in addition to its final report. An insider's account is S. N. D. North, "The Industrial Commission," *North American Review* 168 (June 1899): 708–19.

11. U.S., Industrial Commission, *Final Report* (Washington, D.C., 1902), p. 572; Beale to "John" (apparently John Addison Porter, President McKinley's pri-

vate secretary), October 20, 1897, Day Papers; U.S., *Statutes at Large*, 30: 768;
Ruth H. Hunter, *The Trade and Convention Center of Philadelphia: Its Birth and
Renascence* (Philadelphia, 1962), pp. 6–8.

12. An exception was raw cotton, of which, a government official asserted in
1909, "we can increase the supply almost indefinitely." Oscar P. Austin, Chief of the
Bureau of Statistics, Department of Commerce and Labor, address to new consuls,
July 21, 1909, in Lectures to Consular Officers, RG 59.

13. Fred A. Shannon, "A Post-Mortem on the Labor-Safety-Valve Theory,"
Agricultural History 19 (January 1945): 31–37; address by Skinner, *Proceedings of
the American Manufacturers Export Association*, September 1911, p. 137. Even the
New York Produce Exchange joined the chorus about the primacy of manufactured
exports: "If this country is to maintain its premier position in the world, we must look
to finished and not to crude products." *Proceedings of the National Board of Trade*,
January 1910, p. 189. For the similar views of government officials, see below, chapter 4, notes 14 and 15; address by Oscar P. Austin, *Proceedings of the National Board
of Trade*, January 1906, pp. 255–57; Austin to George B. Cortelyou, February 24,
1900, William McKinley Papers, LC; Assistant Secretary of State Huntington Wilson, "Increase of American Trade," n.d. but probably late 1912, F. M. Huntington
Wilson Papers, Ursinus College Library; DeWitt C. Poole, miscellaneous notes for a
lecture, March 1935, DeWitt C. Poole Papers, State Historical Society of Wisconsin,
Madison; U.S., Department of C & L, *Winning Foreign Markets: Containing
Suggestions for the Extension of Trade by American Manufacturers and Exporters*
(Washington, D.C., 1908), pp. 14–15.

14. See chapter 4, for Frederic Emory's shift in allegiance.

15. Department of C & L, *Winning Foreign Markets*, p. 15.

16. Two other categories of exports, semifinished manufactures and processed foodstuffs, also received considerable help from the Departments of State and
C & L. But semimanufactures were more descriptively termed "manufactures for
further use in manufacturing," and as such shared some of the greater accessibility to
foreign markets enjoyed by the unprocessed goods. Prepared foodstuffs, on the other
hand, shared a different characteristic with most raw goods—their increased domestic consumption. Address by Victor Metcalf, Secretary of C & L, in the *Proceedings
of the National Association of Manufacturers*, May 1905, pp. 295–314; O. P. Austin,
address to consuls, July 21, 1909, Lectures to Consular Officers, RG 59.

17. Wilson to American Diplomatic and Consular Officers, July 25, 1910,
file 164.1, RG 59.

18. Two exceptions were coal and, to a lesser extent, raw cotton. The Departments of State and C & L both rendered assistance to the powerful raw cotton
interests by demonstrating improved packing methods, one of the few ways the two
departments helped to sell agricultural goods. House, *Hearings on the LEJ* for 1913,
January 29, 1912, p. 99; *Congressional Record*, 62d Cong., 2d sess., 1912, 48: 7712.
For coal, see below, chapter 10, and also file 166.883, RG 59.

19. Jones, *Consular Service*, pp. 59–60; Poole, miscellaneous notes for a
lecture, March 1935, Poole Papers; Emory, "The New Department of Commerce
and Labor," *World's Work* 5 (April 1903): 3336.

20. House, *Promotion of Trade Interests*, Document 245, 58th Cong., 3d

sess., 1905, p. 94; Johnson et al., *History of Domestic and Foreign Commerce*, 1: 300–302. Although William Appleman Williams has stressed the importance of the agrarian sector's orientation toward foreign markets in the late nineteenth century, even he has acknowledged that during the 1890s the nation's foreign-policy makers worked from "an industrial conception of the economy and its needs." "The Vicious Circle of American Imperialism," *New Politics* 4 (Fall 1965): 48. See also his more recent and more elaborate statement, *The Roots of the Modern American Empire: A Study of the Growth and Shaping of Social Consciousness in a Marketplace Society* (New York, 1969). The picture is not completely clear, however. Consuls had standing instructions to report monthly on crop conditions for the Department of Agriculture's benefit, and their published reports contained occasional notices of local crop shortages. Although neither the State Department nor the consuls seem to have considered such reporting a very important responsibility, the Department of Agriculture probably did. Furthermore, Agriculture's annual reports for the 1890s and the very early 1900s indicate some trade promotion activity by that department, although the details of the work are vague. Yet in 1906 Congressman James A. Tawney of Minnesota, chairman of the House Appropriations Committee, declared flatly: "We don't give the Agriculture Department the money for the development of trade in foreign countries." House, *Hearings on the LEJ* for 1908, November 30, 1906, p. 319. An in-depth study is needed of the Agriculture Department's promotion of exports, to determine whether it translated agrarian foreign-markets rhetoric into institutional activity.

21. Department of Commerce, *Historical Statistics of the United States, 1789–1945* (Washington, D.C., 1949), p. 250; Department of C & L, *Statistical Abstract of the United States, 1907* (Washington, D.C., 1908), pp. 350–55; North, "The Industrial Situation," draft of speech, n.d. but apparently 1899 or 1900, S. N. D. North Papers, Cornell University Library.

22. The trade figures in the 1890s for all of Latin America south of the Rio Grande should not have been cause for much rejoicing among foreign trade advocates. Exports from the United States to that region increased by only 41 percent during that decade, well below both the overall increase of 63 percent and the 52 percent advance in goods which were bound for Europe. But their optimism was rewarded in the following decade. The value of exports to Latin America in 1910 was twice that of 1900 and rose from 9 percent to 15 percent of total American exports. During the same period, exports to Europe registered only a 9 percent increase, and Europe's share of total United States exports shrank from 75 to 65 percent. Department of Commerce, *Historical Statistics* (1949), pp. 250–51. In 1899, O. P. Austin used the favorable Central American statistics to demonstrate the bright future for exports to that region. U.S., Department of the Treasury, *Monthly Summary of Commerce and Finance* (June 1899), p. 3166. For signs of optimism in the 1890s about the future of United States trade with other parts of Latin America, which withstood the currently bleak statistical record, see House, *Commission to Study Commercial Conditions in China, Etc.*, Document 536, 55th Cong., 2d sess., 1898, p. 3; George H. Murphy to Wilbur Carr, August 30, 1899, Inspection Reports on Consulates, RG 59.

23. Loans could also be used to help gain a larger share, or even control, of

existing markets. Francis B. Loomis, diplomat, former consul, and future assistant secretary of state, wrote Secretary of State Day in 1898: "I think it our destiny to control more or less directly most all of the Latin American countries. It is possible to attain commercial ascendancy in them in much the same way that England does in China: that is, by lending them money and administering their revenues." Loomis to Day, June 20, 1898, Day Papers.

24. James Ragsdale in Saint Petersburg to Montgomery Schuyler, October 22, 1909, "Russia—Diplomatic," Foreign Service Posts records, RG 84; Charles M. Dickinson, consul-general at Constantinople, to David J. Hill, September 4, 1901, letterbook, Dickinson Papers.

For additional expressions about the primacy of markets in the less developed world, see Robert Chilton to Day, March 18, 1898, Day Papers; J. Hampton Moore, chief of the Bureau of Manufactures in the Department of C & L, to Kendall Banning, May 12, 1905, J. Hampton Moore Papers, Historical Society of Pennsylvania, Philadelphia; John G. A. Leishman, ambassador to Turkey, to Elihu Root, November 16, 1906, file 2866, RG 59; address by O. P. Austin, July 21, 1909, Lectures to Consular Officers, RG 59. Optimism based on the low standing of the United States in the import statistics of such countries may be found in Senate, *Commercial and Industrial Conditions of China and Japan*, Rept. 450, 56th Cong., 1st sess., 1900; Victor Metcalf, "American Trade and Commerce," in LaFollette, ed., *The Making of America*, pp. 5, 9–10, 15. An official statement containing both the strategy of increasing America's share of existing markets and that of development is Senate, *Foreign Trade and Treaty Relations*, Document 150, 61st Cong., 1st sess., 1909. David Novack and Matthew Simon conclude that the "American export community" began to stress the importance of these "third markets" after 1905. As noted here, however, some government officials had already been looking in that direction for several years. Novack and Simon, "Commercial Responses to the American Export Invasion, 1871–1914: An Essay in Attitudinal History," *Explorations in Entrepreneurial History*, 2d series, 3 (Winter 1966): 138, 146.

25. Adams, "Faults in Our Consular Service," *North American Review* 156 (April 1893): 462–63; *Proceedings of the National Board of Trade*, January 1900, p. 117; Chilton to William Rockhill, February 11, 1897, Inspection Reports on Consulates, RG 59.

26. For a more extensive summary of the material in the consular reports, see Jones, *Consular Service*, pp. 65–79.

27. Barnes and Morgan, *Foreign Service*, pp. 126–27; House, *Consular Service*, Executive Document 121, 48th Cong., 1st sess., 1884, pp. 10–11.

28. *Who Was Who*, Historical Volume, p. 540; *National Cyclopaedia of American Biography*, 8: 339; *Nation* 51 (July 24, 1890): 73; *Annals* 1 (October 1890): 292–93; Eugene Schuyler, *American Diplomacy*, pp. v–vi, 17, 30.

29. Frank H. Mason to William Rockhill, October 11, 1895, William W. Rockhill Papers, Houghton Library, Harvard University; Report of Convention of Consuls General and Treasury Agents at Paris, RG 59; John Karel to L. E. McGann, January 31, 1894; Philip B. Spence to James B. McCreary, June 16, 1894; and Claude Thomas to same, December 8, 1893, all in records of the Committee on Foreign Affairs, file 53A-F16.1, House records, RG 233; Consular Clerk Carl Hansmann

to William F. Wharton, June 30, 1890, Dispatches from Consular Clerks, RG 59.

30. Mason to Day, October 28, 1897, Day Papers; Dickinson to Alvey Adee, June 16, 1898, draft in Dickinson Papers; R. J. Gross to Secretary of C & L, July 12, 1904, file 26231, Commerce Department records, RG 40. See also Dickinson to David J. Hill, September 4, 1901, letterbook, Dickinson Papers.

31. *Boston Evening Transcript*, December 29, 1887, and December 16, 1892; Boston Merchants Association, "Index to Records and Resolutions, 1876–[sic]," in file 109-a, Boston Chamber of Commerce records, Baker Library, Harvard Business School; Boston Merchants Association, *Addresses Delivered at the Twelfth Annual Banquet* (Boston, 1893); Jonathan A. Lane to Robert Hitt, February 13, 1893, Hitt Papers.

32. Jonathan A. Lane, *The Appointments and Removals in the Consular Service* (Boston, 1893).

33. Boston Chamber of Commerce, *Annual Report*, 1894 (Boston, 1895), pp. 196–97; petition of Boston Chamber of Commerce, January 20, 1894, in Petitions, Memorials, and Resolutions to the Committee on Foreign Affairs, file 53A-H11.5, RG 233; National Board of Trade, executive council minutes, January 8, 1893, and January 23, 1894, in Philadelphia Board of Trade records, Historical Society of Pennsylvania.

34. *Proceedings of the National Board of Trade*, January 1894, pp. 89, 243.

35. *Good Government* 13 (April 15, 1894): 127; Senate, *Reorganization of the Consular and Diplomatic Service*, Rept. 1202, 56th Cong., 1st sess., 1900, p. 8; Chamber of Commerce of the State of New York, *Annual Report of the Corporation*, 1894, p. 2; House, *Journal*, and Senate, *Journal*, 53d Cong., 3d sess.

36. *Proceedings of the National Board of Trade*, January 1895, p. 31; Oscar Straus, "The Reform of the Consular Service," *Proceedings of the NCSRL*, December 1894, pp. 100–101.

37. Henry G. Chapman to George McAneny, May 18, 1906, George McAneny Papers, Princeton University Library; George W. Curtis, "Ten Years of Reform," *Proceedings of the NCSRL*, September 1891, p. 7; address by Elliot H. Goodwin to the New York Civil Service Association, 1909, NCSL Papers; *Nation* 46 (February 23, 1888): 148–49.

38. *Proceedings of the National Board of Trade*, January 1895, p. 31, and January 1896, pp. 60–61; Senate, *Reorganization of the Consular and Diplomatic Service*, p. 15; *Proceedings of the NCSRL*, December 1903, p. 72. For a general statement regarding businessmen's interest in civil service reform, see Seymour M. Lipset, "Bureaucracy and Social Reform," in Amitai Etzioni, ed., *Complex Organizations: A Sociological Reader* (New York, 1964), p. 261.

39. *Good Government* 20 (March 1903): 46, and 17 (May 15, 1900): 59; Goodwin to New York Civil Service Association, 1909, NCSL Papers.

40. *Proceedings of the National Board of Trade*, January 1894, pp. 93–99. Other bridges between civil service and business associations were the individuals who belonged to both. They included Harry Garfield, a leader in the National Municipal League and the Cleveland Chamber of Commerce; George McAneny, secretary of the NCSRL and member of the New York State Chamber of Commerce; Ansley Wilcox, active in the NCSRL and the Buffalo Merchants Exchange; John Ela, general

counsel for the National Business League and president of the Chicago Civil Service Reform League; and Oscar Straus, president of the New York Board of Trade and Transportation, who also was active in the NCSRL.

41. Gaillard Hunt to Harry A. Garfield, December 9, 1896, HAG Papers, LC; Wilbur Carr, "American Consular Service," p. 903; "Who's Who—And Why?" *Saturday Evening Post* 195 (January 27, 1923): 62; Crane, *Mr. Carr*, p. 54; August C. Radke, "John Tyler Morgan: An Expansionist Senator, 1877–1907" (Ph.D. diss., University of Washington, 1953), especially pp. 203–4; LaFeber, *New Empire*, pp. 354, 112.

42. *Good Government* 14 (September 15, 1894): 30; S. 1854, introduced April 3, 1894, in records of the Foreign Relations Committee, file 53A-F11, Senate records, RG 46.

43. S. 1854, April 3, 1894. An unprinted committee report on the bill detailed the principle of interchangeability between the department and the field, but not between the two field branches themselves. In draft form, dated the day before Morgan introduced the measure, it included a table showing corresponding grades for the departmental, consular, and diplomatic services. The draft report was probably written by Jones as well. See file 53A-F11, RG 46.

44. White to Morgan, May 23, 1894, Henry White Papers, LC; Nevins, *Henry White*, pp. 45–46, 103.

45. Morgan to White, May 29, 1894, White Papers.

46. Roosevelt to White, June 14 and December 12, 1894, White Papers.

47. Morgan to White, February 8, 1895, White Papers.

48. *Proceedings of the National Board of Trade*, January 1896, p. 56; *Congressional Record*, 53d Cong., 3d sess., 1895, 27: 1978–87; Senate, Rept. 1073, 54th Cong., 1st sess., 1896.

49. James D. Richardson, comp., *A Compilation of the Messages and Papers of the Presidents* (Washington, D.C., 1897), 11: 4922–23; Nevins, *Henry White*, p. 111.

50. Cleveland to Olney, September 12, 15, and 20, 1895, Olney to Cleveland, September 17, 1895, Faison to Olney, September 17, 1895, all in Richard Olney Papers, LC.

51. Olney to Cleveland and Faison to Olney, September 17, 1895, Olney Papers; undated typescript paper, ca. 1931, in Carr Papers.

52. Rockhill to Roosevelt, September 24, 1895, letterbook, Rockhill Papers; Roosevelt to Rockhill, September 25, 1895, and Rockhill to White, November 7, 1895, White Papers.

53. Undated comments by Wilbur Carr on Jessup's biography of Root, Philip C. Jessup Papers; Department of State, *Foreign Relations of the United States, 1896* (Washington, D.C., 1897), pp. xc–xci; Herbert C. Hengstler, "Hengstler Glances Back," *American Consular Bulletin* 4 (February 1922): 32.

54. Johnson et al., *History of Domestic and Foreign Commerce*, 2: 279; William Hunter to Arthur B. Wood, September 4, 1876, Miscellaneous Reports and Correspondence on Consular Inspections, RG 59; Hitt to Lane, quoted in *Proceedings of the National Board of Trade*, January 1895, p. 36 (emphasis in the origi-

nal); House, *Consular Service*, Executive Document 121, 48th Cong., 1st sess., 1884; Report on Convention of Consuls General, RG 59.

55. Uhl to Morgan, May 12, 1894, Consular Bureau Decisions and Precedents, RG 59; Senate, Rept. 209, 54th Cong., 1st sess., 1896, p. 2; *Proceedings of the National Board of Trade*, January 1897, pp. 66–67; Department of State, *Foreign Relations, 1896*, pp. xci–xcii.

56. *Proceedings of the National Board of Trade*, January 1897, pp. 68–69; House, Document 584, 57th Cong., 1st sess., 1902, p. 3; Straus, "The Reform of the Consular Service," *Proceedings of the NCSRL*, December 1894, pp. 100–101.

57. Murphy to Carr, July 22, 1899, and Mason, "Report of an Inspection of U.S. Consulates," May–June, 1899, Inspection Reports on Consulates, RG 59.

58. *Proceedings of the National Board of Trade*, January 1897, p. 74; House, *Journal*, 54th Cong., 1st and 2d sessions.

59. *Good Government* 16 (April 15, 1897): 49–50; George McAneny, "How Other Countries Do It," *Century* 57 (February 1899): 611.

60. Lodge to Lane, December 24, 1894, letterbook, Lodge Papers.

61. In 1899, an international commercial conference was held under the auspices of the Philadelphia Commercial Museum. The editor of the convention's official proceedings bemoaned the "difficulties and drawbacks incident to the organization of an enterprise of this kind at a time when American manufacturers were overwhelmed with orders at home." William M. Butler, ed., *Official Proceedings of the International Commercial Congress* (Philadelphia, 1899), preface, n.p.

CHAPTER 3

1. Gaillard Hunt to James R. Garfield, November 30, 1887, JRG Papers; Department of State, *Register*, 1908, p. 10, and 1887, p. 7; Hunt to Harry A. Garfield, October 26, 1890, HAG Papers.

2. Hunt to Lansing, January 21, 1916, Hunt Family Papers, LC; Hunt to J. Garfield, March 19, 1897, and September 15, 1897, and entry in Garfield's diary for April 2, 1904, all in JRG Papers.

3. Hunt to J. Garfield, March 19, March 28, and April 2, 1897, April 12 [1889], all in JRG Papers. Hunt's preoccupation with the spoils system also found expression in a series of articles on office-seeking during the early years of the American republic. See *American Historical Review* 1 (January 1896): 220–83, 2 (January 1897): 241–61, 3 (January 1898): 270–91.

4. Otis L. Graham, Jr., *The Great Campaigns: Reform and War in America, 1900–1928* (Englewood Cliffs, N.J., 1971), p. 16; Hunt to H. Garfield, December 6, 1896, HAG Papers.

5. Cleveland Chamber of Commerce, *Reports and Proceedings*, April 1895, pp. 49 and 65, and April 1897, p. 82; resolution of the Cleveland Chamber of Commerce, December 16, 1896, records of the Committee on Foreign Affairs, file 54A-F16.7, RG 233; E. A. Angell to H. Garfield, December 5, 1896, H. Garfield to Hunt and to Angell, December 7, 1896, both in letterbook, HAG Papers.

6. Hunt to H. Garfield, December 14, 1896, HAG Papers.

7. *National Cyclopaedia of American Biography*, 33: 154; "A New Princeton Professor," *Outlook* 75 (November 7, 1903): 570; E. A. Angell to H. Garfield, December 5, 1896, HAG Papers.

8. Cleveland Chamber of Commerce, *Reports and Proceedings*, April 1898, pp. 101–2; Hunt to H. Garfield, May 14 and October 6, 1898, and H. Garfield to J. Garfield, July 29, 1898, all in HAG Papers; J. Garfield, diary entry for April 16, 1898, JRG Papers.

9. Julius W. Pratt, *Expansionists of 1898: The Acquisition of Hawaii and the Spanish Islands* (Baltimore, Md., 1936), pp. 230–78; *Cleveland Plain Dealer*, May 18, 1898; Hunt to H. Garfield, July 15, [1898], HAG Papers. See also Hunt's article, "Our Place among the Nations," *World's Work* 1 (November 1900): 52–54. Wilbur Carr is the source for Hunt's authorship. Diary entry for October 25, 1900, Carr Papers.

10. H. Garfield to Lucretia R. Garfield, July 26, 1899, HAG Papers.

11. Thomas W. Cridler to H. Garfield, September 24, 1898, and H. Garfield to Hunt, September 17, 1898, letterbook, HAG Papers; Cleveland Chamber of Commerce, *Reports and Proceedings*, April 1899, pp. 70–71.

12. H. Garfield to Hunt, September 17, 1898, letterbook, Hunt to H. Garfield, September 19, October 6, and November 18, 1898, December 30 [1898], all in HAG Papers. Following Hunt's advice, Garfield approached McKinley late in 1898, but the president merely passed him on to Robert Chilton at the Consular Bureau.

13. Schwab to H. Garfield, December 6 and December 30, 1898, H. Garfield to Schwab, December 12 and December 17, 1898, both in letterbook, and H. Garfield to George McAneny, January 24, 1899, letterbook, all in HAG Papers; *Who Was Who*, 1: 1092.

14. Schwab to H. Garfield, December 28, 1898, Hunt to same, December 30, 1898; H. Garfield to Schwab, December 30, 1898, and January 24, 1899, both letterbook, and H. Garfield to George McAneny, January 24, 1899, letterbook, all in HAG Papers.

15. Cleveland Chamber of Commerce, *Reports and Proceedings*, April 1899, pp. 75–82; Hunt to H. Garfield, November 17, 1899, HAG Papers (emphasis in the original).

16. Hunt to H. Garfield, December 2 [1899], and H. Garfield to Schwab, December 28, 1899, letterbook, HAG Papers.

17. H. Garfield to Schwab, January 11, 1900, letterbook, and Schwab to H. Garfield, January 18, 1900, both in HAG Papers.

18. This provision is similar to today's civil service procedure. For most jobs in the federal civil service, the examining board sends three names from which the hiring agency may select its appointment. The names are taken from a list on which they have been ranked according to score.

19. Hunt's measure appears to have been the first consular bill to require knowledge of commercial resources as related to trade promotion.

20. H. R. 7097, introduced by Burton, January 23, 1900, records of the

Committee on Foreign Affairs, file 56A-F12.4, RG 233; McAneny to H. Garfield, March 13, 1900, and H. Garfield to A. A. Burnham, March 10, 1900, letterbook, HAG Papers.

21. H. R. 7097, file 56A-F12.4, RG 233; *Nation* 70 (February 8, 1900): 106; Harry Garfield, "The Remodeling of the Consular Service," *Independent* 52 (March 15, 1900): 658.

22. Harry Garfield, "The Business Man and the Consular Service," *Century* 60 (June 1900): 270.

23. H. Garfield to Henry Cabot Lodge, February 3, 1900, to Hamilton Holt, March 2, 1900, and to R. U. Johnson, March 5, 1900, all in letterbook, HAG Papers; *Nation* 70 (February 8, 1900): 106.

24. Volume of minutes, entries for February 15 and March 1, 1900, and docket volumes, entry for January 23, 1900, records of the Committee on Foreign Affairs, file 56A-F12.6, RG 233; H. Garfield to McAneny, February 7, 1900, and to Theodore E. Burton, March 1, 1900, both in letterbook, and Burton to H. Garfield, March 3, 1900, HAG Papers.

25. Senate, *Reorganization of the Consular and Diplomatic Service*, Rept. 1202, 56th Cong., 1st sess., 1900, pp. 9, 13–14, 17.

26. Ibid., pp. 14, 8, 25.

27. Ibid., pp. 13, 15.

28. Ibid., pp. 11, 23.

29. H. Garfield to George McAneny, January 24, 1899, and March 19, 1900, both in letterbook, HAG Papers; Hunt to H. Garfield, December 2 [1898], HAG Papers; Hunt, "Reform in the Consular Service," *Independent* 51 (October 26, 1899): 2882.

30. John Foster to H. Garfield, March 20, 1900, and Horace M. Sanford to same, April 11, 1900, HAG Papers.

31. H. Garfield to Schwab, December 28, 1899, and January 11, 1900, both in letterbook, HAG Papers.

32. H. Garfield to Corcoran Thom, January 18, 1902, letterbook, Schwab to H. Garfield, December 3, 1900, and F. A. Scott to same, November 25, 1900, all in HAG Papers.

33. Schwab to H. Garfield, May 29, 1901, Minutes of the Buffalo Meeting, June 27, 1901, and H. Garfield to Hunt, August 3, 1901, letterbook, all in HAG Papers.

34. H. Garfield to A. A. Burnham, November 9, 1901, letterbook, and Schwab to H. Garfield, October 24, 1901, HAG Papers.

35. Minutes of the National Committee on Consular Reorganization, December 11, 1901, HAG Papers.

36. Hunt to H. Garfield, December 20 and 30, 1901, H. Garfield to Corcoran Thom, January 18, March 14, and February 25, 1902, all in letterbook, HAG Papers.

37. Schwab to H. Garfield, January 16, 1902, E. G. Preston to H. Garfield, January 30, 1902, HAG Papers; H. Garfield to E. G. Preston, February 5, 1902, and to Hunt, February 10, 1902, both in letterbook, HAG Papers.

38. Washburn to H. Garfield, January 9, 1901, and Hunt to same, November 26, 1901, HAG Papers. Adams was reluctant to add an inspection provision to his bill, fearing that some of his colleagues might view it "as tending to create junketing positions." Ansley Wilcox to H. Garfield, February 24, 1902, HAG Papers.

39. See, for example, Henry Cabot Lodge to Jonathan Lane, December 24, 1894, letterbook, Lodge Papers.

40. As president, Theodore Roosevelt was more cautious and circumspect about many matters than he had been in his younger days. Despite his strong interest in foreign service reform during the mid-1890s, he did not play a leading role in consular reorganization. But he did give the reformers his moral support and included in his first annual message a plea for consular improvement (written by Gaillard Hunt). J. Garfield, diary entry for October 10, 1901, JRG Papers; Hunt to John Hay, January 3, 1902, David J. Hill Papers, University of Rochester.

41. William D. Foulke, "The Qualifications of a Consul," *Good Government* 19 (March 1902): 42–43; Wilcox to H. Garfield, February 18, 1902, HAG Papers; same to Roosevelt, November 14, 1905, copy in George McAneny Papers. It was in Wilcox's home that Roosevelt took the oath of office following McKinley's assassination in 1901. *National Cyclopaedia of American Biography*, 21: 201.

42. Elliot Goodwin to H. Garfield, July 7, 1902, HAG Papers.

43. *Good Government* 19 (October 1902): 153–55; H. Garfield to Schwab, June 6, 1902, letterbook, HAG Papers.

44. Thom to H. Garfield, July 15, 1902, and same to the National Committee on Consular Reorganization, December 9, 1902, HAG Papers; H. Garfield to Lucretia R. Garfield, included in J. Garfield to same, December 10, 1902, JRG Papers.

45. H. Garfield to Goodwin, January 31, 1903, and to Burnham, July 1, 1903, both in letterbook, and Goodwin to H. Garfield, January 28, 1903, HAG Papers; *Good Government* 20 (January 1903): 1; ibid. (February 1903): 23.

46. Thom to H. Garfield, July 17, 1903, McAneny to Cushing, October 11, 1903, H. Garfield to McAneny, October 24, 1903, letterbook, all in HAG Papers.

47. H. R. 11677, submitted by Adams, February 3, 1904, records of the Committee on Foreign Affairs, file 58A-F12.4, RG 233; H. Garfield to Ansley Wilcox, January 18, 1906, McAneny Papers.

48. Schwab to H. Garfield, January 19, 1900, Burnham to same, July 3 and June 24, 1903, resolution of the National Business League, adopted April 1, 1904, Burnham to H. Garfield, May 14, 1904, Adams to same, April 20 [1904], F. A. Scott to same, May 27, 1904, all in HAG Papers.

49. "A New Princeton Professor," *Outlook* 75 (November 7, 1903): 570; H. Garfield to J. Garfield, June 21, 1903, HAG Papers.

50. H. Garfield to J. Garfield, July 16, 1903, H. Garfield to Lucretia R. Garfield, July 15, 1903, and Hunt to H. Garfield, June 18, 1903, all in HAG Papers.

51. *National Cyclopaedia of American Biography*, 33: 154; *Outlook* 90 (October 17, 1908): 327.

52. *Who Was Who*, 1: 608; *National Cyclopaedia of American Biography*, 19: 81.

CHAPTER 4

1. James W. Foster, "The Author," in Frederic Emory, *Queen Anne's County, Maryland: Its Early History and Development* (Baltimore, 1950), p. vii.

2. Emory, *Queen Anne's County*, pp. 572, 527.

3. Foster, "The Author," in *Queen Anne's County*, p. vii; Emory to Thomas F. Bayard, December 19, 1890, Thomas F. Bayard Papers, LC; Emory, *Queen Anne's County*, p. 193; *Diplomatic and Consular Review*, May 21, 1896, clipping in Frederic Emory scrapbook, Columbus Memorial Library, Pan-American Union, Washington, D.C.; Miriam Strange, Archivist of St. John's College, to the author, March 1, 1974; Charles C. Tansill, *The Congressional Career of Thomas Francis Bayard, 1869–1885* (Washington, D.C., 1946), p. 234. Little is known about Emory before about 1890, and consequently this biographical sketch has many gaps.

4. Gerald W. Johnson et al., *The Sunpapers of Baltimore* (New York, 1937), pp. 148, 158, 164, 194, 196.

5. Emory to Bayard, January 28 and April 30, 1890, January 5 and August 25, 1891, February 11, 1892, Bayard Papers; Tansill, *Bayard*, p. 234.

6. Clipping from the *New York Times*, June 2, 1901, in Emory scrapbook; Emory to Bayard, July 1, 1892, and March 1, 1893, Bayard Papers.

7. Emory to Bayard, March 1, 1893, Bayard Papers. The month before his explicit request for government employment, Emory wrote an editorial for the *Philadelphia Public Ledger* boosting Bayard, in adulatory language, for secretary of state in Cleveland's new cabinet. He thoughtfully provided Bayard with a copy. Emory to Bayard, February 9, 1893, Bayard Papers.

8. The bureau had resulted from the first Pan-American Conference, held in Washington during the winter of 1889–1890, and its purpose was to gather, publish, and exchange commercial information to foster commerce and amity. Originally named the "Commercial Bureau of the American Republics," it was headquartered in Washington and affiliated with the State Department. In 1910 its name was changed to the Pan-American Union. John Barrett, *The Pan-American Union: Peace, Friendship, Commerce* (Washington, D.C., 1911), pp. 60–61.

9. Emory to Bayard, May 22 and September 4, 1893, Bayard Papers; Tansill, *Bayard*, p. 326. For an example of Emory's efforts, see Emory to Henry T. Thurber, February 13, 1894, Grover Cleveland Papers, LC; *Brooklyn Daily Eagle*, February 11, 1894.

10. Emory to Bayard, March 4 and April 17, 1894, Bayard Papers; clipping from the *Baltimore Sun*, April 17, 1894, Emory scrapbook.

11. DeWitt C. Poole, miscellaneous notes for a lecture, March 1935, Poole Papers; Barnes and Morgan, *Foreign Service*, pp. 79–80; address by John Osborne, July 27, 1909, Lectures to Consular Officers, RG 59; Carr, "American Consular Service," p. 907.

12. Barnes and Morgan, *Foreign Service*, pp. 79–80; address by John Osborne, July 27, 1909, Lectures to Consular Officers, RG 59; Johnson et al., *History of Domestic and Foreign Commerce*, 2: 291.

13. Johnson et al., *History of Domestic and Foreign Commerce*, 2: 291–92;

John Osborne, "The American Consul and American Trade," *Atlantic Monthly* 99 (February 1907): 161–64.

14. The quotations may be found in these articles by Emory: "The Uniting of American Society," *World's Work* 3 (March 1902): 1854–56; "The Greater America," ibid. 3 (December 1901): 1513–17; "Our Growth as a World Power," ibid. 1 (November 1900): 69.

15. The two paragraphs of quotations are from the following essays by Emory: "Our Growth as a World Power," p. 65; "Silver in Other Lands," *Baltimore Sun*, July 23, 1896; "Review of the World's Commerce," in Department of State, *Commercial Relations of the United States during 1902*, 1: 24–27. See also other articles by Emory: "The United States in the World's Markets," *Independent* 53 (July 4, 1901): 1543; "Causes of Our Failure to Develop South-American Trade," *Annals of the American Academy of Political and Social Science* 22 (July 1903): 154–55; "America as Peacemaker," *World's Work* 4 (May 1902): 2061; "Our New Horizon," ibid. 3 (January 1900): 1617; and the annual summary, "Review of the World's Commerce," in the *Commercial Relations* volumes published from 1896 to 1903 by the Department of State.

16. Emory, "Protection Break Up," *Baltimore Sun*, August 22, 1895; same, "A True American," ibid., December 14, 1895; Emory to Bayard, August 7, 1893, Bayard Papers (emphasis in the original); Emory, "The United States in the World's Markets," p. 1543.

17. Kaufman, "Organizational Dimension," *Business History Review* 46: 20–22; Emory, "Causes of Our Failure to Develop South-American Trade," pp. 154–55; "Review of the World's Commerce," in Department of State, *Commercial Relations during 1902*, 1: 24–27.

18. Ford to Emory, July 19, 1894, and Emory to Bayard, February 10, 1895, Bayard Papers.

19. Department of State, *Commercial Relations during 1894 and 1895*, p. 10; Department of State, *Foreign Relations, 1896* (Washington, D.C., 1897), p. xciii.

20. Emory to Chief Clerk Edward I. Renick, March 17, 1897, with a report of the Bureau of Statistics, in Report of the Chief Clerk, RG 59; "The Bureau of Statistics," *Diplomatic and Consular Review*, September 26, 1896, p. 9; House, *Hearings on the LEJ* for 1897, February 3, 1896, p. 11; Osborne, "American Consul and American Trade," pp. 161–62; Gaillard Hunt, *The Department of State of the United States, Its History and Functions* (New Haven, Conn., 1914), p. 142.

21. Emory to Bayard, December 14, 1895, December 23, 1896, February 10, 1895, Bayard Papers.

22. Henry Bryan to Bayard, August 23, 1896, and January 12, 1897, Emory to Bryan, December 28, 1895, Emory to Bayard, August 10, 1896, Bayard Papers.

23. William A. Williams, *The Roots of the Modern American Empire* (New York, 1969), pp. 41–42; Edward Younger, *John A. Kasson: Politics and Diplomacy from Lincoln to McKinley* (Iowa City, Iowa, 1955), pp. 366–67.

24. The *Baltimore Sun*, Emory's old newspaper, also broke with Bryan. The *Sun*'s position, and perhaps that of Emory and other gold Democrats as well, was reflected in an editorial prophesying that McKinley's election would produce only "a short reign of Protection," while the evils arising from the unlimited coinage of silver

would be much greater and last longer. Gerald W. Johnson et al., *Sunpapers of Baltimore*, pp. 191, 194, 196.

25. Bayard to Emory, quoted in Emory to Grover Cleveland, November 14, 1893, Cleveland Papers; Emory to Bayard, August 10 and October 25, 1896, Bayard Papers; Emory, "Republican Finance," *Baltimore Sun*, December 26, 1895; same, "Silver in Other Lands," ibid., July 23, 24, 25, 27, 28, 29, and August 1, 1896.

26. Emory to William Rockhill, November 23, 1896, and February 8, 1898, Rockhill Papers; U.S., *Statutes at Large*, 29: 590.

27. Bryan to Bayard, January 25 and February 2, 1897, Bayard Papers; "Our Foreign Trade," *Philadelphia Public Ledger*, January 26, 1897.

28. National Association of Manufacturers, *Methods of Extending Foreign Trade*, Circular of Information no. 15 (February 15, 1897), pp. 21–24.

29. Emory to Sherman, June 30 [1897], Emory scrapbook.

30. Emory to Day, November 18, 1897, Day Papers; Emory to Sherman, December 7, 1897, reprinted in *Consular Reports* 56 (January 1898): vi–vii; Memoranda on the History and Organization of the Office of the Economic Adviser, portion dated October 23, 1911, RG 59.

31. Osborne, "American Consul and American Trade," p. 162; Loomis, "On the Extension of American Trade through Diplomatic and Consular Officers," *American Industries* 3 (March 1, 1905): 9; U.S., *Statutes at Large*, 30: 273. In marked contrast to this innovation was the British method of publishing consular reports. After the reports were edited, they were returned to the consuls for proofreading. Emory to Sherman, December 7, 1897, in *Consular Reports* 56 (January 1898): iv–v.

32. Emory to Bayard, March 24, 1898, Bryan to Bayard, April 9, 1897, and May 2, 1898, Bayard Papers. Emory's close relations with the NAM and the Philadelphia Commercial Museum probably strengthened his position. William P. Wilson, the museum's director, spoke of Emory's "most eminent qualifications." Wilson to Don Joaquin Calvo, November 18, 1898, BAR records, Records Management Center, Organization of American States, Washington, D.C.; Emory to George R. Allen, April 19, 1898, BAR records.

33. See, for example, Emory to Day, January 9, 1900, Day Papers; Emory to Hay, October 18, 1900, Hay Papers.

34. Emory to Bayard, March 24, 1898, Bayard Papers. More than a year before, Emory had written an essay entitled "Britain as an Ally," contrasting the French and German policies of commercial exclusion in their overseas empires with the British open door. *Baltimore Sun*, January 11, 1897.

35. "American Trade in the Far East," clipping datelined New York, July 22, 1898, in Emory scrapbook; Emory, "Introduction to Review of the World's Commerce," April 25, 1898, in Department of State, *Commercial Relations during 1896 and 1897*, p. 21.

36. "American Trade in the Far East," July 22, 1898, Emory scrapbook; Emory, "John Hay and the Open Door," *Washington Post*, September 24, 1905, Emory scrapbook. Although noting the State Department's prior commitment to the open door in China, Emory did not minimize Hay's contribution.

Three months after Hay's message to the European powers and Japan, Emory's strong interest in a commercial mission to the Far East appears to have revived that project. Senator Jacob H. Gallinger of New Hampshire introduced the department-backed bill in December 1899; it passed the Senate early the next year, but died in the House. Emory to William Rockhill, December 16, 1899, Rockhill Papers; Senate, *Journal*, 56th Cong., 1st sess.

37. Emory to Bayard, March 24, 1898, Bayard Papers; Emory, *A Maryland Manor* (New York, 1901); Paul V. Siggers, a nephew of Emory's wife, to the author, September 13, 1971.

38. Emory to Theodore Roosevelt, January 6, 1903, Roosevelt Papers; Joaquin B. Calvo to Emory, March 3, 1898, BAR records; Emory to John A. Porter, April 9, 1898, McKinley Papers; Emory to Hay, December 17, 1898, and Hay to McKinley with Emory's report, December 30, 1898, records of the Committee on Foreign Affairs, file 55A-F13.2, RG 233; Emory, "What We Seek in South America," *Washington Post*, July 7, 1905, Emory scrapbook; Bureau of American Republics, *Monthly Bulletin*, January 1899, p. 1161; ibid., January 1900, p. 84.

39. Emory to John Bassett Moore, October 29, 1898, Moore Papers; Emory to Day, February 24 and April 26, 1899, Day Papers.

40. The Department of Commerce and Labor is discussed more fully in chapter 8.

41. *Congressional Record*, 57th Cong., 1st sess., 1902, 35: 601, 763.

42. Emory to Roosevelt, January 6, 1903, Roosevelt Papers; Emory to Day, January 9, 1903, Day Papers.

43. Emory to John Bassett Moore, May 18, 1903, Moore Papers.

44. Emory to Hay, May 19, 1903, in Memoranda on the History and Organization of the Office of the Economic Adviser, October 23, 1911 portion, RG 59.

45. James Garfield, diary entry for June 5, 1903, JRG Papers; William M. Collier to Secretary of C & L, May 21, 1903, file E102, RG 40; Memoranda on Office of Economic Adviser, October 23, 1911 portion, RG 59.

46. House, *Promotion of Trade Interests*, Document 245, 58th Cong., 3d sess., 1905; Emory, "Our Foreign Trade," *Philadelphia Public Ledger*, January 26, 1897; same to David J. Hill, March 5, 1901, Hill Papers, University of Rochester; same to William Rockhill, November 23, 1896, Rockhill Papers; Loomis to Senator Shelby Cullom, February 7, 1905, letterbook, Loomis Papers; Loomis to Day, November 5, 1897, Day Papers.

47. House, *Promotion of Trade Interests;* memorandum by Emory, February 1, 1905, in Loomis to Robert R. Hitt, February 8, 1905, records of the Committee on Foreign Affairs, file 58A-F12.3, RG 233. Roosevelt sent the plan to the Foreign Affairs and Foreign Relations committees, asking that it be incorporated into the annual diplomatic and consular appropriations bill.

48. House, *Promotion of Trade Interests*, pp. 3–14.

49. Emory to Elihu Root, December 30, 1905, Root Papers; Victor H. Metcalf to Roosevelt, June 16 and 26, 1904, and September 7, 1904, Roosevelt Papers.

50. Loomis to the Secretary of Commerce and Labor, August 1 and December 5, 1904, Victor H. Metcalf to Loomis, December 12, 1904, all in file 70801/11, RG 40; Emory to Metcalf, January 19, 1905, file 70332, RG 40; John Bassett Moore to Emory, February 11, 1905, and Emory to Moore, February 23, 1905, Moore Papers.

51. Emory to Moore, January 15, 1905, Moore Papers (emphasis in the original). A secondary reason for Emory's resignation may have been his growing pessimism about the Republican protectionist policy that had always been so abhorrent to him. He told Consular Bureau Chief Wilbur Carr late in 1904 that he feared possible revolution resulting in a monarchy, a dictatorship, or socialism if the administration continued a policy of protection that meant "capitalistic control of national affairs." Carr, diary entry for October 13, 1904, Carr Papers.

52. Hay to Emory, in *Washington Times*, January 6, 1905, enclosed in Emory to John Bassett Moore, January 15, 1905, Moore Papers; Emory articles: "Our Fettered Foreign Service," *Pittsburgh Dispatch*, June 18, 1905; "Congress as a Nursery of Graft," *Washington Post*, July 30, 1905; "John Hay and the Open Door," ibid., September 24, 1905; "What We Seek in South America," ibid., July 9, 1905, all in Emory scrapbook.

53. Maude S. Emory to Moore, March 3, 1909, Moore Papers; "Mr. Frederic Emory Dead," *Baltimore Sun*, September 21, 1908, in Emory scrapbook.

54. Emory to Elihu Root, October 24, 1905, and December 28, 1906, Root Papers.

CHAPTER 5

1. "Speech by Mr. Grew," *American Consular Bulletin* 6 (September 1924): 314; address by Major-General Charles G. Helmick at the dedication program for the Carr Memorial Library, Hillsdale College, June 2, 1951, Carr Papers. Both Jerry Israel and Waldo Heinrichs have published essays containing information about Carr. Israel, "A Diplomatic Machine," in Israel, ed., *Building the Organizational Society*, pp. 183–96; Heinrichs, "Bureaucracy and Professionalism," in Braeman et al., eds., *Twentieth-Century American Foreign Policy*, pp. 119–206.

2. Address by General Helmick, June 2, 1951, and biographical information from Carr's application for position of Chief of the Consular Bureau, n.d., Carr Papers; "Who's Who—And Why," *Saturday Evening Post* 195 (January 27, 1923): 26, 62; Crane, *Mr. Carr*, p. 8.

3. "Who's Who and Why," p. 26; biographical information from Carr's application, and Sevellon A. Brown, telegram to Carr, May 24, 1892, Carr Papers.

4. Crane, *Mr. Carr*, p. 49; memorandum by Faison, May 2, 1894, in Press Copies of Reports of the Consular Bureau, RG 59. For details of the 1894 legislation, see above, chapter 2.

5. Biographical information from Carr's application, Baldwin to Secretary of State, April 1, 1897, and Carr, diary entry for March 8, 1897, all in Carr Papers.

6. Carr, diary entry for January 1, 1901, Carr Papers.

7. Carr, diary entries for November 7, 1900, January 25 and April 26, 1901, Carr Papers. A study of latter-day federal executives likewise emphasizes the individual's yearning for recognition and for useful and interesting work. William Lloyd Warner et al., *The American Federal Executive: A Study of the Social and Personal Characteristics of the Civil and Military Leaders of the United States Federal Government* (New Haven, Conn., 1963), pp. 207–15. Historian Zara Steiner also demon-

strates the importance of this desire in the almost simultaneous reorganization of the British Foreign Office. Arthur Ponsonby's comment that he found the Foreign Office "absolutely unbearable," and that the "monotonous purely mechanical routine" was "quite intolerable," could have been borrowed from Wilbur Carr's diary. Steiner, *The Foreign Office and Foreign Policy, 1898–1914* (Cambridge, England, 1969), p. 228, and also pp. ix, 80–82, 154, 170, 222–26.

8. Chilton to John Hay, October 20, 1899, Hay Papers; Carr, diary entry for November 15, 1901, and undated entry immediately following, Carr Papers; Hunt to Hay, January 3, 1902, Hill Papers, University of Rochester. Chilton was later appointed consul at Toronto, where he remained until 1913.

9. See above, chapter 3.

10. Carr, diary entry for December 10, 1902, Carr Papers.

11. Hill to Andrew Carnegie, April 22, 1909, copy in David J. Hill Papers, Bucknell University Library; Scott, "A Review of President Roosevelt's Administration," *Outlook* 91 (February 13, 1909): 352–53; Elihu Root to W. N. Frew, September 26, 1905, letterbook, Root Papers; Carr, diary entry for April 26, 1901, Carr Papers.

12. Hay to Henry White, December 23, 1900, White Papers; Hay to Hill, September 24, 1900, Hill Papers, University of Rochester; Hay to Lodge, January 9, 1899, letterbook, Hay Papers; John Bassett Moore, diary entry for July 1, 1900, Moore Papers.

13. Jessup, record of conversation with Root, September 13, 1932, Jessup Papers; Henry B. Needham, "Mr. Root and the State Department," *World's Work* 11 (November 1905): 6835.

14. Samuel P. Huntington, *The Soldier and the State: The Theory and Politics of Civil-Military Relations* (Cambridge, Mass., 1957), pp. 270–73; "Address of Hon. Elihu Root to the Legislature of New York Accepting His Election to the United States Senate," January 28, 1909, Root Papers; Jessup, record of conversation with Root, n.d., Jessup Papers; "Military Preparation the Guaranty of Peace," address by Root to the Interstate National Guard Association of the United States, May 4, 1903, in Robert Bacon and James B. Scott, eds., *The Military and Colonial Policy of the United States* (Cambridge, Mass., 1916), p. 149. See also Root's speech to the Pennsylvania Society of New York, December 12, 1906, Root Papers. Root's address discussed the trend toward centralization in United States economic life, which required corresponding political changes to take regulatory control from the states and lodge it with the federal government. From his home on the Chester River, Frederic Emory wrote Root to praise the speech as containing Emory's own views. Emory to Root, December 28, 1906, Root Papers.

15. Root to Burnham, November 18, 1907, Jessup Papers. See also Root to Oscar Straus, in which he referred to "our efforts to induce Americans interested to be less apathetic and to adopt the vigorous methods of some of their foreign competitors." March 27, 1908, file 67288, RG 40.

16. Root to George W. Davis, July 20, 1905, letterbook, Root Papers; John B. Osborne, "The Reorganized American Consular Service as a Career," *Forum* 39 (July 1907): 122.

17. Jessup, record of conversation with Root, September 13, 1931, Jessup

Papers. Cf. Wilbur Carr's statement many years later, describing the pre-1905 field foreign service as "the football of ward politics." Carr, "Remarks on Occasion of Commencement of Work of Foreign Service School," September 30, 1927, Carr Papers.

18. Jessup, record of conversation with Carr, March 16, 1934, Jessup Papers; J. Garfield to H. Garfield, October 13, 1905, H. Garfield to J. Garfield, October 11, 1905, and H. Garfield to Lucretia R. Garfield, October 15, 1905, all in HAG Papers; J. Garfield, diary entry for November 15, 1905, JRG Papers; H. Garfield to George McAneny, November 27, 1905, and January 11, 1906, and Wilcox to Root, November 14, 1905, McAneny Papers.

19. Memoranda on the History and Organization of the Office of the Economic Adviser, RG 59; circular instruction to American Consular Officers, November 1, 1905, Dickinson Papers; notation dated October 27, 1905, file 54134, in subject index, RG 40; Carr, "American Consular Service," p. 909; Philip C. Jessup, *Elihu Root*, 2: 103; comments by Carr on Jessup manuscript, n.d., Jessup Papers.

20. Root to Lodge, October 25, 1905, and Jessup, miscellaneous notes, n.d., Jessup Papers; Carr, diary entry for December 12, 1905, Carr Papers; Robert J. Collier of *Collier's* to Root, December 15, 1905, Root Papers.

21. S. 1345, introduced by Lodge on December 11, 1905, Center for Research Libraries, Chicago (microfilm); Jessup, record of conversation with Root, September 13, 1931, Jessup Papers; Senate, *Reorganization of the Consular Service*, Rept. 112, 59th Cong., 1st sess., 1906, p. 1.

22. House, *Reorganization of the Consular Service*, pp. 28, 18; Senate, *Reorganization of the Consular Service*, p. 9.

23. Wilbur Carr believed Root's cultivation of Congress crucial to the success of consular legislation and possible because Root possessed qualities that Hay lacked. Pencil draft of an address, 1932, Carr Papers. See also Donald M. Dozer, "Secretary of State Elihu Root and Consular Reorganization," *Mississippi Valley Historical Review* 29 (December 1942): 339.

24. Senate, *Reorganization of the Consular Service*, pp. 40, 42.

25. J. Sloat Fassett, "Congress and the Consular Service," *Review of Reviews* 33 (May 1906): 555–57; Ansley Wilcox to Francis V. Greene, quoting Senator Thomas Platt, January 25, 1906, copy in McAneny Papers; *Congressional Record*, 59th Cong., 1st sess., 1906, 40: 1756. For the constitutional argument, see above, chapter 3.

26. Hunt to H. Garfield, February 8 [1906], Schwab to same, January 15 and February 1, 1906, HAG Papers; H. Garfield to Wilcox, January 18, 1906, copy in McAneny Papers; Chamber of Commerce of the State of New York, *Annual Report*, 1906, pp. 103–4.

27. House, *Reorganization of the Consular Service*, pp. 17–18.

28. Carr, diary entries for January 29 and February 26, 1906, Carr Papers; Denby to Root, March 20, 1906, and Root to Denby, letterbook, March 22, 1906, Root Papers.

29. Root to Lodge, December 18, 1905, and Lodge to Root, December 19, 1905, Jessup Papers; *Proceedings of the National Board of Trade* (January 1906), p. 148; F. A. Scott to H. Garfield, January 24, 1906, HAG Papers; "The Consular Ser-

vice as It Should Be," *Outlook* 82 (March 24, 1906): 622; Thomas G. Paterson, "American Businessmen and Consular Service Reform," *Business History Review* 40: 91–92; Loomis, "Three Years of Consular Reform," unpublished manuscript, n.d., but apparently written in the spring of 1909, Loomis Papers; *Washington Post*, March 14, 1906.

30. Carr, diary entry for March 30, 1906, Carr Papers; *Congressional Record*, 59th Cong., 1st sess., 1906, 40: 3968.

31. Volume of Minutes, entry for March 1, 1906, records of the Committee on Foreign Affairs, file 59A-F14.5, RG 233; *Good Government* 23 (April 1906): 50; *Congressional Record*, 59th Cong., 1st sess., 1906, 40: 3975; Denby to Root, March 20, 1906, and Root to Denby, March 22, 1906, letterbook, Root Papers.

32. *New York Times*, June 6, 1906, p. 1; U.S., *Statutes at Large*, 34: 288.

33. Root to George W. Wickersham, May 17, 1919, NCSL Papers; Root's undated order convening the board, Dickinson Papers; *American Consular Bulletin* 4 (June 1922): 159. Other board members were Edward Ozmun, George Murphy, Charles Dickinson, and Robert Chilton, Jr., Carr's former chief and currently consul at Toronto.

34. The copy of the report I have seen used the figure $100, but this was doubtless a typographical error.

35. Report of the Consular Reorganization Board, June, 1906, Dickinson Papers. (See above, chapter 2, for information about the 1890 conclave.) Although Mason and his colleagues were quick to minimize the importance of invoice certification, they did favor greater official attention to the import trade. Not only were import duties the largest source of federal revenues, but the board also recognized that "successful export of our own products requires return cargoes from foreign countries." This testimony to the significance of imports was exceptional (although Frederic Emory would have been delighted), and the department ignored the advice. See below, chapter 10.

36. For practical reasons, chiefly financial, this requirement did not apply to the subordinate grades—vice-consuls, deputy consuls, consular agents, and clerks at the consulates. But if these officers wished to rise higher in the service, to a position of consul or consul-general, they had to take the examination. Subordinates in consulates would naturally gain experience that was valuable for passing the test.

37. Carr, diary entry for June 24, 1906, Carr Papers; Roosevelt, executive order, June 27, 1906.

38. Carr, diary entry for June 24, 1906, Carr Papers; Roosevelt, executive order, June 27, 1906.

39. Carr, diary entry for February 9, 1906, Carr Papers.

40. Carr, diary entries for February 9, 1906, March 3–4, May 8, September 12, and November 27, 1907, Carr Papers. With Carr's elevation in 1907, Herbert C. Hengstler was promoted to chief of the Consular Bureau, continuing as Carr's chief subordinate. The two men worked together closely for decades. Hengstler retired in 1941, after serving for many years as chief of the Division of Foreign Service Administration. Department of State, *Register*, 1942, p. 273.

41. Crane, *Mr. Carr*, pp. 147, 7; address by General Charles Helmick,

June 2, 1951, and Carr, diary entry for February 1, 1912, Carr papers; Carr to Robert W. Belcher, October 1, 1913, NCSL Papers.

42. Carr, diary entries for February 5, 1897, and November 10, 1914, and undated entries in scrapbooks, Carr Papers.

43. Undated note in "Immigration Measures" folder, Carr Papers. See also Carr, "American Consular Service," p. 891, and Lejeune Cummins, "The Origins and Development of Elihu Root's Latin American Diplomacy," (Ph.D. diss., University of California, Berkeley, 1964), p. 1.

44. Huntington Wilson, "Regulations Covering Examinations," in Paul Reinsch, ed., *Readings on American Federal Government* (Boston, 1909), pp. 674–75. The initial draft was Report of the Board of Examiners to the Assistant Secretary of State, December 11, 1905, file 1592/16-24, RG 59.

45. A. A. Burnham to Root, May 23, 1907, file 1592/25, RG 59; Root to Shaw, March 23, 1907, file 1592/8a, RG 59; Chief Clerk Charles Denby to John H. Foster, July 23, 1906, Letters Sent by the Chief Clerk, RG 59.

46. Jessup, record of conversation with Carr, March 16, 1934, Jessup Papers; Jessup, *Root*, 2: 105; "Recapitulation" chart for the consular service, n.d., but early 1913, in Reports of Consular Service Entrance Examinations, RG 59.

47. Jessup, record of conversation with Carr, March 16, 1934, Jessup Papers; *Nation* 82 (May 10, 1906): 380.

48. *Congressional Record*, 59th Cong., 1st sess., 1906, 40: 3973; Jessup, record of conversation with Carr, March 16, 1934, Jessup Papers.

49. "Consular Bureau: Duties and Functions," n.d., but probably 1911, in Reports of Clerks and Bureau Officers, RG 59; Root to George Wickersham, May 17, 1919, NCSL Papers; Philander Knox to Senator Shelby Cullom, February 18, 1911, file 122.1/179H, RG 59; Jessup, record of conversation with Root, September 13, 1931, Jessup Papers. The 1911 figures applied only to appointments as "consul" and did not cover the less numerous consular assistant or student interpreter positions (see below), for which the department did not use the quota system.

50. John Osborne, "Education for the New Consular Career," *North American Review* 188 (October 1908): 553–54; Charles Nagel to Philander Knox, December 9, 1910, letterbook, November 11 and November 28, 1910, Charles Nagel Papers, Yale University Library; William Phillips to Knox, March 22, 1909, Reports of Consular Service Entrance Examinations, RG 59.

51. House, *Improvement of the Foreign Service*, Hearings on H.R. 20044, March 27, 1912, p. 78; Crane, *Mr. Carr*, p. 98; George T. Keyes, memorandum, June 17, 1918, NCSL Papers; *Good Government* 29 (March 1912): 46.

52. Herbert Hengstler, "Hengstler Glances Back," *American Consular Bulletin* 4 (February 1922): 32; Huntington Wilson to E. T. Williams, December 21, 1907, Edward T. Williams Papers, University of California, Berkeley, Library; House, *Improvement of the Foreign Service*, Rept. 2008, 61st Cong., 3d sess., 1911, p. 7; Gottschalk to Hengstler, February 15, 1909, Miscellaneous Reports and Correspondence on Consular Inspections, RG 59.

53. Richard Harlan to Root, March 3 and May 24, 1907, Root Papers; *Nation* 88 (March 4, 1909): 220; Root to Hengstler, April 1908, file 2108/56, RG 59.

54. Franz Boas to George McAneny, September 11, 1907, and McAneny to Gustav Schwab, September 14, 1907, McAneny Papers; Melvin T. Copeland, *And Mark an Era: The Story of the Harvard Business School* (Boston, 1958), pp. 4–8; National Business League, *American Universities, American Foreign Service, and an Adequate Consular Law* (Chicago, 1909), pp. 54–55.

55. Adee to Carr, September 19, 1907, file 2108/21, RG 59; Philander Knox to William H. Douglas, January 3, 1911, file 120.1, RG 59.

56. Speech by Carr, "The Merit System in the United States Consular Service," June 22, 1912, Carr Papers; Osborne, "The American Consul and American Trade," p. 160.

57. Address by Hengstler, July 1, 1909, Lectures to Consular Officers, RG 59; Huntington Wilson to American Consular Officers, January 30, 1907, file 4341, RG 59.

58. Address by Hengstler, July 1, 1909, Lectures to Consular Officers, RG 59.

59. Ibid.; Jessup, record of conversation with Root, n.d., Jessup Papers; Carr, "The Merit System in the Consular Service," June 22, 1912, Carr Papers.

60. Root to Nicholas Murray Butler, April 10, 1908, file 2108/54, RG 59; Root to George Wickersham, May 17, 1919, NCSL Papers.

61. Carr, diary entry for March 30, 1906, Carr papers; Report of the Consular Reorganization Board, June 1906, Dickinson Papers; Carr to Horace L. Washington, September 25, 1906, Instructions to Consuls General and Inspectors, RG 59; Thomas Morrison, Chief of the Bureau of Accounts, "Statement of Accounts Expended . . . ," n.d., Reports of the Bureau of Accounts, RG 59. The first five inspectors were: Fleming D. Cheshire (Far East), Richard M. Bartleman (South America), George H. Murphy (North America), Charles M. Dickinson (Middle East and Africa), and Horace Lee Washington (Europe). Kent C. Carter, "Development of the Foreign Service Inspection System," *Foreign Service Journal* (January 1974), pp. 18–20, 25. Carter's fine account has some interesting details about the consular inspections.

62. Gottschalk to Hengstler, December 22, 1909, Miscellaneous Reports and Correspondence on Consular Inspections, RG 59; Department of State, *Register*, 1924, p. 55, and 1925, p. 53.

63. Inspection form for Consul-General William Michael at Calcutta, January 29, 1907, Dickinson Papers; Crane, *Mr. Carr*, pp. 92–93.

64. Carr to Horace L. Washington, March 9, 1908, Instructions to Consuls General and Inspectors, RG 59; Carr to Consuls-General-at-Large, July 16, 1912, file 122.41/29, RG 59; address by Hengstler, July 1, 1909, Lectures to Consular Officers, RG 59.

65. Dickinson to Carr, December 9 and July 8, 1907, Carr to Dickinson, July 31, 1907, Dickinson to Washington, October 8, 1907, all in Dickinson Papers; Gottschalk to Hengstler, January 26, 1909, Miscellaneous Reports and Correspondence on Consular Inspections, RG 59.

66. Dickinson to Carr, July 8, 1907, and Carr to Dickinson, July 31, 1907, Dickinson Papers.

67. Carr to Root, September 23, 1907, file 2108/47, RG 59; Senate, *Amend-*

ing Act for Reorganization of Consular Service, Rept. 256, 60th Cong., 1st sess., 1908, pp. 2–10; House, *Hearings on the Dip/Cons* for fiscal 1909, January 20, 1908, p. 6; same for fiscal 1913, January 22, 1912, p. 65.

68. Root to Butler, December 21, 1907, Jessup Papers.

69. Report of Convention of Consuls General and Treasury Agents, August 1890, RG 59; Report of the Consular Reorganization Board, June 1906, Dickinson Papers; Root to E. F. Baldwin, November 18, 1905, Miscellaneous Letters Sent regarding Consular Affairs, RG 59; House, *Hearings on the Dip/Cons* for fiscal 1913, January 22, 1912, pp. 69–70.

70. Address by Hengstler, July 1, 1909, Lectures to Consular Officers, RG 59; memorandum by Consular Reorganization Board [June 1906], Consular Bureau Decisions and Precedents, RG 59; Loomis, "Three Years of Consular Reform," Loomis Papers; U.S., *Statutes at Large,* 35: 181.

71. McAneny, "How Other Countries Do It," p. 611; Carr, comments on Jessup's manuscript, n.d., Jessup Papers; House, *Hearings on the Dip/Cons* for 1913, January 22, 1912, pp. 69–70; same for 1909, January 20, 1908, pp. 4–5; Department of State, *Register,* 1912; U.S., *Statutes at Large,* 37: 696.

72. Cridler to Foster, January 25, 1901, records of the Committee on Appropriations, file 56A-F2, RG 46; order by the Secretary of State, July 18, 1902, General Records of the Board of Examiners, RG 59; McAneny, "Report of the Committee on Consular Reform," *Proceedings of the NCSRL,* November 1906, pp. 79–80.

73. Wilson to Straight, April 28, 1908, Willard Straight Papers, Cornell University Library; *Proceedings of the National Board of Trade,* January 1909, p. 218.

74. Draft of Hunt's bill, n.d., HAG Papers; Root to Chairman, Foreign Relations Committee, December 20, 1905, miscellaneous notes, Jessup Papers; Carr to Burnham, July 25, 1908, file 2108/63, RG 59. The next chapter deals extensively with the geographic divisions.

75. Halstead to Assistant Secretary of State, January 30, 1907, file 7442, and same to same, September 5, 1907, file 8365, RG 59; Carr to Root, September 23, 1907, file 2108/47, RG 59. Only one week before Halstead wrote his January dispatch, a similar proposal had briefly surfaced in a memorandum from Third Assistant Secretary of State Huntington Wilson to Root. Its source was a paper scheduled for delivery to a foreign trade convention in Washington and forwarded to the department by the Director of the Philadelphia Commercial Museum. William P. Wilson to Root, January 21, 1907, and Huntington Wilson to Root, January 23, 1907, file 2108/10, RG 59. As noted above in chapter 3, Gaillard Hunt's consular bill had contained a provision to accomplish this purpose.

76. For the effects of the panic see Robert Wiebe, *Businessmen and Reform: A Study of the Progressive Movement* (Cambridge, Mass., 1962), pp. 68–72, and passim; Wiebe, *The Search for Order, 1877–1920* (New York, 1967), pp. 201, 211; memorandum of an address presented to President Roosevelt by representatives of commercial bodies from the Midwest, "1908," John C. O'Laughlin Papers, LC; Root to Whitelaw Reid, May 22, 1908, letterbook, Root Papers.

77. Ozmun to Assistant Secretary of State, December 9, 1907, and Root to

Oscar Straus, December 28, 1907, file 10654, RG 59. John G. A. Leishman, ambassador to Turkey, had expressed similar warnings to Root a year earlier. Leishman to Root, November 16, 1906, file 2866, RG 59.

78. Root to the Secretary of the Treasury, January 2, 1908, in House, *Explanations as to Estimate for Foreign Intercourse, 1909*, Document 498, 60th Cong., 1st sess., 1908, p. 14; H. F. Temple to Root, January 23, 1908, file 2108/30, RG 59; Carr to American Consuls in the Far East, January 25, 1908, file 11425, RG 59; Carr to Root, April 29, 1908, file 13511/1, and same to same, May 26, 1908, file 13511, RG 59.

79. Hengstler to Carr, April 25, 1908, file 13511, RG 59; speech by Carr to the Saint Louis Businessmen's League, April 1910, Carr Papers.

80. Lay, quoted in a London newspaper, August 1, 1908, in Frank D. Hill, consul-general at Barcelona, to State Department, August 21, 1908, file 2108/74, RG 59.

81. Hengstler to Carr and Carr to Hengstler, December 6, 1908, file 16866, RG 59; C. S. Donaldson, "Government Assistance to Export Trade," *Annals* 34 (November 1909): 558–59; Consul-General Thomas Sammons at Yokohama to Secretary of State, October 14, 1912, file 160.1 Sa/2, RG 59; Carr to George T. Coppins of the NAM, April 14, 1913, file 122.1/218, RG 59; Lee S. Smith, quoted in *Pittsburgh Post*, n.d., clipping in "Comment on the Addresses of Mr. James E. Dunning, American Consul at Havre, at Manufacturing Centers of the United States in Favor of Foreign Trade Extension," n.d., Consular Bureau Decisions and Precedents, RG 59.

82. Carr to S. C. Mead, December 3, 1909, and Carr, "Rough Notes for an Address," 1911, Carr Papers; Carr to Root, October 14, 1908, file 121.56, RG 59.

CHAPTER 6

1. J. Garfield, diary entry for November 1, 1905, JRG Papers.

2. Wallace J. Young to Chandler Hale, October 29, 1912, General Records of the Board of Examiners, RG 59; Collier to Root, April 26, 1907, Root Papers. According to one source, the average expenditures of a diplomatic secretary, for living expenses alone, were between $5,000 and $12,000 annually. The maximum salary was $3,000. Childs, *American Foreign Service*, pp. 10–11.

3. Collier to Root, April 26, 1907, Root Papers; Henry P. Fletcher to "Emily," October 31, 1905, and August 4, 1904, and to his uncle, September 12, 1904, Henry P. Fletcher Papers, LC (emphasis in the original).

4. Henry White to Senator John Morgan, May 23, 1894, White Papers; *Congressional Record*, 61st Cong., 2d sess., 1910, 45: 3033.

5. Henry L. Nelson, "The Need of Trained Diplomats and Consuls," *Harper's Weekly* 45 (June 15, 1901): 599; Hunt to H. Garfield, October 6, 1898, HAG Papers; Fletcher to "Emily," September 29, 1907, Fletcher Papers. Even President Roosevelt, at least a cautious champion of consular reform, was much less impressed with the necessity for reform in the diplomatic service. See Alfred L. P. Dennis,

"The Foreign Service of the United States," *North American Review* 219 (February 1924): 178; Joseph C. Grew, *Turbulent Era: A Diplomatic Record of Forty Years* (Cambridge, Mass., 1952), 1: 13; Jessup, *Root*, 2: 108.

6. Roosevelt, executive order, November 10, 1905; Root, department order, November 10, 1905, General Records of the Board of Examiners, RG 59; Francis B. Loomis, "The Proposed Reorganization of the American Consular Service," *North American Review* 182 (March 1906): 358.

7. Scott, "A Review of President Roosevelt's Administration," *Outlook* 91 (February 13, 1909): 353; MacMurray to John Bassett Moore, May 21, 1907, Moore Papers. Ilchman, *Professional Diplomacy*, pp. 91–93, has a more critical account of the first examination system.

8. House, *Estimates for Foreign Intercourse for Year Ending June 30, 1907*, Document 54, 59th Cong., 1st sess., 1905, pp. 1–3; House, *Hearings on the Dipl Cons* for 1908, December 18, 1906, p. 29.

9. Jessup, miscellaneous notes, Jessup Papers; Root to Ambassadors and Ministers of the United States, June 19, 1908, file 14336, RG 59.

10. U.S., *Statutes at Large*, 34: 288–89, and 35: 174; Thomas Morrison, chief of the Bureau of Accounts, to William Phillips, May 4, 1909, file 19641, RG 59.

11. Ilchman, *Professional Diplomacy*, pp. 72–73; Huntington Wilson to Philander Knox, February 2, 1909, Huntington Wilson Papers, Ursinus College Library.

12. Root to W. N. Frew, September 26, 1905, letterbook, Root Papers; House, *Hearings on the LEJ* for 1908, November 28, 1906, p. 110, and for 1907, February 8, 1906, p. 151. Although many Americans residing abroad were missionaries, I have not found a single instance where State Department officers, either privately or publicly, even mentioned that group as among the beneficiaries of a reorganized foreign service. Missionaries may have often received a sympathetic hearing from the department. But when government officials thought about reshaping the foreign affairs machinery, missionary interests apparently did not constitute even a peripheral factor.

13. Wilson, *Memoirs*, pp. 45–47, 88; Walter V. and Marie V. Scholes, *The Foreign Policies of the Taft Administration* (Columbia, Mo., 1970), p. 15.

14. Wilson, *Memoirs*, p. 107; Griscom, *Diplomatically Speaking*, p. 225; Lucy Wilson to Taft, August 10, 1911, William Howard Taft Papers, LC; Archibald Butt, *Taft and Roosevelt: The Intimate Letters of Archie Butt, Military Aide*, 2 vols. (New York, 1930), 2: 770–71. When Lloyd Griscom was expounding Wilson's virtues for Root in December 1905, Root interrupted to say, "My gracious! he has a pretty wife, hasn't he." Griscom to Wilson, December 28, 1905, Wilson Papers.

15. Moore to J. Reuben Clark, November 17, 1915, Wilson Papers; Wilson, *Memoirs*, pp. 234–35; Wilson, diary entries for February 28, March 3, 11, and 26, all 1904, Wilson Papers (emphasis in the original); Jessup, record of conversation with Root, September 13, 1931, Jessup Papers; Jessup, *Root*, 1: 457. The wording of Moore's compliment makes it clear that Wilson was not universally admired. Taft once expressed a desire to "sit on Wilson once and mash him flat," certainly an awesome threat. Butt, *Taft and Roosevelt*, 1: 371. But see also Roosevelt to Root,

July 13, 1907, Root Papers, where the president praises "Wilson's admirable memorandum on the Japanese situation." For a good description of Wilson, see Scholes and Scholes, *Foreign Policies of the Taft Administration*, pp. 15–17.

16. Carr, diary entries, between June 24 and August 15, 1906, after August 15, 1906, March 1, March 14–15, and May 8, 1907, Carr Papers.

17. Wilson, *Memoirs*, p. 129; same, "The American Foreign Service," *Outlook* 82 (March 3, 1906): 499–504.

18. As noted in chapter 2, the Jones bill in 1894 contemplated the same sort of classification and mobility.

19. Wilson to Root, October 5, 1906, file 11200/3, RG 59; same to same, October 29, 1906, and Wilson, copy of reorganization proposal, Wilson Papers.

20. "Hearing of Mr. Sydney Y. Smith, Chief of Diplomatic Bureau," August 31, 1905, in file 210.31, PCEE records, in records of the Bureau of the Budget, RG 51; House, *Hearings before the Committee on Expenditures in the State Department*, May 10, 1911, pp. 6–7; House, *Hearings on the LEJ* for 1912, November 29, 1910, pp. 37–38; "Address of Mr. Huntington Wilson," July 3, 1909, Wilson Papers.

21. Wilson had made a significant reversal since writing his *Outlook* article the year before. At that time, he had recommended retaining the Diplomatic and Consular bureaus but dividing them along geographic lines. Now he was advocating the creation of new geographic divisions and dividing them along diplomatic and consular lines. "American Foreign Service," p. 501.

22. Copy of reorganization proposal and accompanying memorandum, July, August, September, 1906, Wilson Papers.

23. Ibid.; Carr, diary entry following June 24, 1906, Carr Papers.

24. Jessup, record of conversation with Carr, March 16, 1934, Jessup Papers; Wilson, *Memoirs*, p. 153, and *The Peril of Hifalutin'* (New York, 1918), pp. 14–15; Carr, diary entry following June 24, 1906, Carr Papers.

25. Thomas J. McCormick, *China Market*; "The Consular Service and the Spoils System," *Century* 26 (June 1894): 311; William Phillips, "Reminiscences," Columbia University Oral History Project, pp. 35, 38; Carr, diary entry for May 8, 1907, Carr Papers; Wilson to Carr, July 21, 1931, Wilson Papers; House, *Hearings before the Committee on Expenditures in the State Department*, May 10, 1911, p. 6. Chief Clerk Charles Denby, who had lived in China for twenty years, served informally as a one-man Far Eastern division while he was in the department during 1906 and early 1907. His departure for a consular post in 1907 might have helped Root decide in favor of a more explicit structural innovation. For Denby's role, see some of the earlier items in file 785, and also Denby to Diplomatic Bureau, November 11, 1906, file 2112/1, RG 59.

26. Wilson to Robert J. Tracewell, May 14, 1907, and Tracewell to Wilson, May 20, 1907, file 6536, RG 59; Phillips, *Ventures in Diplomacy* (Boston, 1952), pp. 32–34; Phillips, "The Geographical Divisions," *American Consular Bulletin* 4 (December 1922): 346. Although Phillips's memoirs report his initial appointment as a messenger, the 1907 department *Register* lists him as a clerk.

27. Wilson to Bacon, July 10, 1907, file 21669, RG 59; Wilson to T. John Newton, July 31, 1907, file 11200/9, RG 59; Bacon to Root, August 6, 1907, Root

Papers; Bacon, department order, August 14, 1907, Departmental Orders, RG 59; Phillips, *Ventures*, p. 34.

28. Memorandum by Root, n.d., but shortly after July 10, 1907, file 21669/1, RG 59; Wilson to Root, October 23, 1907, file 11200/19, RG 59. While Carr genuinely approved of Wilson's plan, it is not impossible that his helpfulness was spurred by an additional consideration: without his geographical division, Wilson might turn his attention back to Carr's consular service for something to do.

29. Root, department order, March 20, 1908, Departmental Orders, RG 59; Wilson to Straight, March 23, 1908, Straight Papers.

30. Phillips, "Reminiscences," p. 36; O'Brien to Root, June 28, 1908, file 18476/7, RG 59; House, *Estimates for Foreign Intercourse*, Document 1193, 60th Cong., 2d sess., 1908, pp. 2–3; comments by Carr on Jessup manuscript, n.d., Jessup Papers.

31. Egan to David J. Hill, May 7, 1902, Hill Papers, University of Rochester; Wilson, "American Foreign Service," p. 502; House, *Hearings before the Committee on Expenditures in the State Department*, May 11, 1911, p. 12.

32. Copy of reorganization proposal and accompanying memorandum, July, August, September, 1906, Wilson Papers.

33. Straus, "Our Diplomacy with Reference to Our Consular and Diplomatic Service," *Journal of Social Science* 40 (1902): 10; Mark A. DeWolfe Howe, *George von Lengerke Meyer* (New York, 1920), pp. 220–21.

34. Griscom to Wilson, March 30, 1906, Wilson Papers; Denby, memorandum to Root, January 10, 1906, Miscellaneous Correspondence of the Chief Clerk, RG 59.

35. House, *Hearings on the LEJ* for 1907, February 8, 1906, pp. 151–52. Root received the appropriation for the two clerks, but for unknown reasons did not establish the proposed system. Thomas Morrison to Carr, April 13, 1908, Reports of the Bureau of Accounts, RG 59.

36. Wilson to Ransford Miller, December 1, 1909, file 21669/6–7, RG 59; Phillips to Bacon, February 26, 1908, Adee to same, February 27, Root's department order, February 27, Wilson to Emmett C. Hall, February 28, and instructions to London, Paris, Berlin, Saint Petersburg, Peking, and Tokyo, February 29, all in file 18476, RG 59; Bacon to Phillips, July 3, 1908, file 18476/4, RG 59.

37. O'Brien to Root, June 28, 1908, file 18476/7, RG 59; Schuyler to Root, April 11, 1908, file 18476/3, RG 59.

38. House, *Hearings on the LEJ* for 1907, February 8, 1906, p. 151.

39. For a detailed study of the State Department's various filing systems, see H. Stephen Helton, "Recordkeeping in the Department of State, 1789–1956," *National Archives Accessions*, no. 56 (November 1961), pp. 1–24.

40. National Archives, *Preliminary Inventory 157*, p. 49; Department of State, *Manual for Classification of Correspondence, Department of State*, 4th ed. (Washington, D.C., 1939).

41. Carr, diary entry for November 27, 1907, Carr Papers.

42. House, *Hearings on the LEJ* for 1907, February 8, 1906, pp. 151–52, and for 1908, November 28, 1906, pp. 112–14.

43. Emory to Root, October 24, 1905, and December 28, 1906, and Root to Emory, January 9, 1907, letterbook, Root Papers. Emory apparently overlooked Root's initial efforts to coordinate the State Department's commercial work with that of other departments.

44. Department of State, *Register*, 1905. From 1897 until 1906, a Reciprocity Commission under John Kasson's direction was attached to the State Department. Kasson negotiated a number of reciprocity treaties, but the Senate confirmed only one of them, and the commission slowly withered away. Its secretary, Chapman Coleman, was appointed to the consular service in 1906. Edward Younger, *John A. Kasson*, pp. 365–66; Richard C. Baker, *The Tariff under Roosevelt and Taft* (Hastings, Nebr., 1941), pp. 20, 23, 29.

45. House, *Hearings on the LEJ* for 1909, January 11, 1908, pp. 44–45.

46. Baker, *Tariff under Roosevelt and Taft*, p. 72. For the State Department's view that manufactured products were more vulnerable to "hostile tariffs," see Department of State, *Outline of the Organization and Work of the Department of State* (Washington, D.C., 1911), p. 10, and the section discussing raw and finished goods, above, chapter 2. Although not particularly concerned about promoting the foreign sale of raw products, the department did attempt to protect all American exports, of whatever character, from foreign tariffs, sanitary regulations, or administrative practices that discriminated against American goods and in favor of other nations.

47. House, *Hearings on the LEJ* for 1910, December 5, 1908. See also S. N. D. North to Samuel S. Dale, July 1, 1907, copy in North Papers; Henry Cabot Lodge to S. O. Bigney, September 21, 1906, Lodge Papers.

48. Carr to Root, September 23, 1907, file 2108/47, RG 59; House, *Explanations as to Estimate for Foreign Intercourse, 1909*, Document 498, 60th Cong., 1st sess., January 14, 1908, p. 6. Chapter 8, below, discusses C & L's special agents.

49. Carr to Root, October 14, 1908, Phillips to Root, October 14, 1908, and Bureau of Trade Relations to Root, October 13, 1908, all in file 121.56, RG 59.

50. Crane, *Mr. Carr*, p. 79.

CHAPTER 7

1. Root to Whitelaw Reid, November 23, 1908, letterbook, Root Papers; Jessup, record of conversation with Root, September 15, 1930, Jessup Papers; Root to James B. Scott, March 17, 1909, James Brown Scott Papers, Special Collections Division, Georgetown University Library.

2. Lodge to White, January 12, 1909, White Papers; Jessup, record of conversation with Root, September 15, 1930, Jessup Papers.

3. Jessup, record of conversation with Root, September 15, 1930, Jessup Papers; undated memorandum, apparently by Wilbur Carr, outlining the legislative history of the undersecretary provision, Huntington Wilson Papers; Wilson, *Memoirs*, p. 176.

4. House, *Estimates for Foreign Intercourse*, Document 1193, pp. 2–3; Wilson, *Memoirs*, p. 173; Jessup, record of conversation with Root, September 13,

1931, Jessup Papers; Phillips to Senator Henry Cabot Lodge, January 25, 1909, and supporting memoranda, in Papers Accompanying H. R. 27523, 60th Cong., RG 46.

5. House, *Hearings on the Dip/Cons* for 1910, January 6, 1909, pp. 14–16; Phillips to Lodge, January 25, 1909, and supporting memoranda, and Knox to the Senate Foreign Relations Committee, February 9, 1909, in Papers Accompanying H. R. 27523, 60th Cong., RG 46.

6. Jessup, record of conversation with Root, September 13, 1931, Jessup Papers; Taft to Knox, December 23, 1908, Philander C. Knox Papers, LC. Taft explained to a friend that "with Knox as Secretary of State I shall have to put in Beekman Winthrop as Assistant Secretary." It is unclear why Taft believed he had to do so. Taft to John C. O'Laughlin, December 22, 1908, O'Laughlin Papers.

7. W. A. Day to Knox, December 29, 1908, Knox Papers.

8. James B. Scott to J. M. Dickinson, January 4 [1909], Scott Papers; Wilson, memorandum of conversation with Knox, n.d., but probably early in 1912, Wilson Papers.

9. Wilson to Knox, February 2 and 24, 1909, clipping from *Chicago Tribune*, February 10, 1909, and Wilson, "Under Sec'y argument," 1909, all in Wilson Papers; Wilson, *Memoirs*, pp. 175–77; Jessup, record of conversation with Root, September 13, 1931, Jessup Papers.

10. House, *Hearings before the Committee on Expenditures in the State Department*, February 9, 1910, p. 3. The complex story of the tariff's relationship to foreign policy in the decades before World War I requires a book-length study. Tom Terrill has made a beginning with *The Tariff, Politics, and American Foreign Policy, 1874–1901* (Westport, Conn., 1973). See also Lewis L. Gould, "Tariffs and Markets in the Gilded Age," *Reviews in American History* 2 (June 1974): 266–71.

11. Senate, *Expenses in Connection with Foreign Trade Relations with the Orient and Latin America*, Document 139, 61st Cong., 1st sess., July 26, 1909, pp. 1–2.

12. Senate, *Foreign Trade and Treaty Relations*, Document 150, 61st Cong., 1st sess., July 31, 1909, pp. 4–5.

13. Ibid.

14. William Phillips, "Reminiscences," pp. 44–45.

15. Wilson, *Memoirs*, p. 181; Tawney to Knox, July 23, 1909, file 1995/16, RG 59; *Congressional Record*, 61st Cong., 1st sess., July 31, August 2, and August 4, 1909, 44: 4673, 4681, 4828–33, 4907–9. While the new "maximum-minimum" scheme could serve as a handy lever against other nations, it left little room for flexibility in negotiations. A nation's products were subject either to the maximum rate or the minimum, and in later years department officers advocated a more flexible sliding scale to allow more room for negotiation. By March 1910, when the new schedules were to take effect, only two countries remained beyond the pale; Taft declared in April that the minimum rates were universally applied. "Notes on the Payne Tariff Bill," n.d., and Knox to Congressman Oscar Underwood, December 13, 1911, Wilson Papers. For an indication of the new schedule's inflexibility, see Tariff Board Chairman Henry C. Emery to John G. Foster, March 14, 1910, John Gilman Foster Papers, University of Vermont Library. For discussion of the sliding scale, see the extensive material in file 611.003, RG 59.

16. See, for example, the remarks of Congressman James R. Mann of Illinois, *Congressional Record*, 61st Cong., 2d sess., 1910, 45:3032–33.

17. Department of State, *Outline of Organization*, pp. 12–13; Stuart, *Department of State*, pp. 212–13.

18. The solicitor, the department's legal officer for many years, dealt with questions of municipal and international law, claims of United States citizens against foreign governments and of foreign citizens or subjects against the United States, applications for extradition of criminals, and matters involving international arbitrations. Report on the State Department's organization, file 141.21, PCEE records, RG 51.

19. Department of State, *Outline of Organization*, pp. 8–9; John Bassett Moore to William J. Bryan, March 13, 1913 and undated memorandum, Moore Papers; Knox to Senator Francis Warren, February 12 and August 2, 1912, Miscellaneous Letters Sent by the Secretary of State, RG 59. During the Taft administration, the counselor's office negotiated such agreements as the arbitration treaties with England and France and handled some diplomatic negotiations involving treaty interpretations and foreign commerce. Undated memorandum from the counselor's office, Chandler P. Anderson Papers, LC.

20. Department of State, *Outline of Organization*, p. 28; House, *Hearings on the LEJ* for 1913, January 29, 1912, pp. 111–12; Department of State, *Register*, 1909, 1910; *National Cyclopaedia of American Biography*, 13: 512.

21. Knox, department orders of November 19 and December 13, 1909, in Departmental Orders, RG 59; memorandum by Carr, April 13, 1909, file 111.22, RG 59.

22. "Statement of Persons Employed," December 7, 1909, Knox Papers; Senate, *Hearings on the LEJ* for 1913, May 23, 1912, p. 316; report on the State Department's organization, file 141.21, PCEE records. The organization underscores the department's comparative indifference to European developments. Contrast this situation with that prevailing in the 1930s, when Graham Stuart remarked that the Division of Western European Affairs, as "might be expected," was the largest geographic division in the department. Stuart, *American Diplomatic and Consular Practice*, p. 93.

23. See, for instance, Osborne's "Expansion Through Reciprocity," *Atlantic Monthly* 88 (December 1901): 721–31, and "Reciprocity in the American Tariff System," *Annals* 23 (January 1904): 55–83.

24. House, *Hearings on the LEJ* for 1909, January 29, 1908, p. 451; *National Cyclopaedia of American Biography*, 22: 133; Charles M. Pepper, *Guatemala: The Country of the Future* (Washington, D.C., 1906); Pepper, *Panama to Patagonia: The Isthmian Canal and the West Coast Countries of South America* (Chicago, 1906); Dick to Taft, August 8, 1909, Taft Papers; Charles Nagel to Knox, August 18, 1909, Nagel Papers; Pepper to Taft, August 31, 1909, Taft Papers.

25. Thomas Morrison to Carr, April 13, 1908, Reports of the Bureau of Accounts, RG 59; Carr to John C. O'Laughlin, February 1, 1909, file 18476/9, RG 59; Phillips to Robert Bacon, February 6, 1909, file 18476/8, RG 59; *Congressional Record*, 60th Cong., 2d sess., 1909, 43: 3253; Wilson to diplomatic officers, June 22,

1909, file 18476/11a, RG 59; Knox, department order, July 28, 1909, Departmental Orders, RG 59; Stuart, *Department of State*, p. 217.

26. Acting Secretary Alvey Adee, department order, August 31, 1909, file 11200/21, RG 59; "Division of Information: Duties and Functions," n.d., but probably 1911, Reports of Clerks and Bureau Officers, RG 59; Knox to Secretary of the Treasury, December 7, 1909, Knox Papers; report on the State Department's organization, file 141.21, PCEE records, RG 51.

27. Department of State, *Outline of Organization*, p. 26; Stuart, *Department of State*, p. 214; memoranda by Wilson, Carr, and Herbert Hengstler, May 1911, file 111.08/7, RG 59; Wilson to Knox, August 12 and September 15, 1910, Wilson Papers.

28. Knox to Congressman James B. Perkins, June 22, 1909, file 20345, RG 59; Wilson to Fred Carpenter, June 29, 1909, and "Address by Mr. Huntington Wilson," July 3, 1909, Wilson Papers; *Good Government* 26 (July 1909): 73.

29. Young to Wilson, June 5, 1909, General Records of the Board of Examiners, RG 59; Knox to Taft, November 26, 1909, Knox Papers.

30. Taft, executive order, November 26, 1909; Knox to editor, *New York Herald*, November 29, 1909, file 22629, RG 59.

31. Joseph C. Grew, *Turbulent Era: A Diplomatic Record of Forty Years* (Cambridge, Mass., 1952), 1: 63; "Report of the Special Committee on Consular Reform," *Proceedings of the NCSRL*, December 1909, p. 100, and December 1911, p. 135.

32. Miles Shand to Hiram Bingham, November 1, 1910, General Records of the Board of Examiners, RG 59; Knox to Congressman D. T. Morgan of Oklahoma, February 21, 1911, file 120.1/13, RG 59; "Recapitulation of Examinations, Diplomatic Service," n.d., in Reports on Diplomatic Service Entrance Examinations, RG 59; Knox to Ansley Wilcox, December 4, 1911, file 122.1/192, RG 59.

33. An American Diplomat, "The Diplomatic Service—Its Organization and Demoralization," *Outlook* 106 (March 7, 1914): 536; Phillips, "The Geographical Divisions," *American Consular Bulletin* 4: 364; House, *Hearings on the Dip/Cons* for 1915, December 17, 1913, pp. 54–55; Taft, executive order, November 26, 1909; report on the State Department's organization, file 141.21, PCEE records, RG 51.

34. James B. Scott to Phillips, May 5, 1909, file 19641, RG 59; U.S., *Statutes at Large*, 33: 918, 35: 675, and 36: 1030; Wilson, *Memoirs*, p. 232; Barnes and Morgan, *Foreign Service*, pp. 174–77; *Congressional Record*, 61st Cong., 3d sess., 1911, 46: 2098–102.

35. Root to Reid, May 11, 1907, letterbook, Root Papers; Stuart, *Department of State*, p. 223; Hugh Wilson, *The Education of a Diplomat* (London, 1938), pp. 9–10; Knox, department order, June 13, 1910, Departmental Orders, RG 59; J. Reuben Clark to John Bassett Moore, December 7, 1938, Moore Papers; Carr, diary entries for April 17 and November 1, 1911, Carr Papers.

36. White to Henry Cabot Lodge, May 4, 1909, Lodge Papers; Wilson, *Memoirs*, pp. 179–80; Carr, draft of a 1932 address, Carr Papers; Jessup, *Root*, 2: 109–10.

37. Wilson to Elbert F. Baldwin, December 21, 1909, Wilson Papers.

38. Gibson to his mother, March 2, 9, 16, and December 4, 1910, Hugh Gibson Papers, Hoover Institution on War, Revolution, and Peace, Stanford, California.

39. Wilson to Knox, January 18 and September 20, 1910, and Wilson, memorandum of conversation with Knox, n.d., but early 1912, all in Wilson Papers; Wilson to Knox, January 7, 1912, Knox Papers.

40. Wilson, *Memoirs*, p. 244; Wilson to Knox, January 7, 1912, Knox Papers; Wilson, memorandum of conversation with Knox, n.d., but early 1912, Wilson Papers. For the outlines of Wilson's utopia, see his *Memoirs*, especially chapters 41–46; *Save America: An Appeal to Patriotism* (New York, 1914); *Peril of Hifalutin'*, chapter 6, note 24; speech of May 15, 1915, and "The War of the Unborn," n.d., Wilson Papers.

In 1917, avidly seeking a staff position in the army, Wilson jotted the following lines to himself: "To be useful, one must be heeded & respected. After the war, one's *standing*, as a means to do any good, will depend upon the public view of one,—and that will be measured, above all, by the popular prejudiced judgment of what one did during the war." Miscellaneous notes, 1917, Wilson Papers (emphasis in the original).

41. Wilson, *Memoirs*, p. 165; Hugh Wilson, *Education*, p. 10; Gibson to his mother, March 2, 1910, Gibson Papers; MacMurray to Wilson, July 24, 1942, Wilson Papers.

42. Unsigned memorandum, probably prepared in the Bureau of Trade Relations, October 6, 1909, Knox Papers; Wilson to Taft, February 22, 1910, Wilson Papers.

43. Wilson to American Diplomatic and Consular Officers, July 25, 1910, file 164.1, RG 59; Wilson to George T. Coppins, April 21, 1911, General Records of the Board of Examiners, RG 59; James D. Richardson, comp., *A Compilation of the Messages and Papers of the Presidents*, 15: 7421; House, *Hearings on the Dip/Cons* for 1913, January 22, 1912, p. 69. For a fuller discussion of diplomats and trade promotion, see below, chapter 10, and Charles S. Donaldson, "Government Assistance to Export Trade," *Annals* 34 (November 1909): 556.

44. A. E. Ingram to Carr, December 31, 1909, Carr Papers.

45. Address by Hengstler, July 1, 1909, Lectures to Consular Officers, RG 59; Phillips, memorandum for Knox, May 10, 1909, Knox Papers; Nagel to Taft, October 31, 1911, Nagel Papers; "History, Organization, and Activities of the Bureau of Trade Relations," May 1912, file 111.26, RG 59.

46. Barnes and Morgan, *Foreign Service*, p. 356; Department of State, *Register*, 1913; U.S., *Statutes at Large*, 33:926–27, 35:681, and 37:696. A $50,000 annual increase for clerk hire resulted when the State Department and Congress arranged early in 1911 to divert that amount from the fund for consular contingent expenses. House, *Estimates for Foreign Intercourse*, House Document 1133, 61st Cong., 3d sess., 1910, pp. 10–11.

47. Speech by Carr in *Nation's Business*, February 17, 1913, copy in Knox Papers; House, *Improvement in the Foreign Service*, Hearings on H. R. 20004, March 27, 1912, p. 77; "Recapitulation" chart for the consular service, n.d., but early 1913, Reports of Consular Service Entrance Examinations, RG 59; James Dunning,

"Young Americans in the Consular Service," in James R. Garfield, ed., *Public Service* (Boston, 1911), p. 202; Lewis R. Freeman, "Trade Scouts Who Capture Millions," *World's Work* 26 (June 1913): 205.

48. Undated chronology of developments in the Bureau of Trade Relations, in Memoranda on the History and Organization of the Office of the Economic Adviser, RG 59; "Report of the Bureau of Trade Relations: Duties and Functions," n.d., but probably 1911, in Reports of Clerks and Bureau Officers, RG 59; John B. Osborne, interview with Mr. Choate, October 3, 1905, file 210.31, PCEE records, RG 51.

49. "History, Organization, and Activities of the Bureau of Trade Relations," May 1912, file 111.26, RG 59; DeWitt C. Poole, "Reminiscences," Columbia Oral History Project, p. 142. The bureau's library contained 7,000 books and pamphlets concerning statistics of commerce and navigation throughout the world, 2,000 dealing with tariffs, and 6,800 concerning various industries. "History, Organization, and Activities of the Bureau of Trade Relations," May 1912, file 111.26, RG 59.

50. Ibid.; "Address of Hon. John Ball Osborne," to the American Manufacturers Export Association, September 29, 1911, in *Pan American Union Bulletin* 33 (December 1911): 1136; House, *Hearings on the LEJ* for 1912, November 29, 1910, pp. 40–41.

51. Senate, *Hearings on the LEJ* for 1913, May 23, 1912, p. 325; Morse to Huntington Wilson, May 21, 1911, file 160./10, RG 59. My computations for the exports are taken from figures in Department of Commerce, *Historical Statistics* (1960), p. 544. See chapter 10 for additional expressions of businessmen's appreciation, as well as other examples of the work of the Bureau of Trade Relations.

52. In an almost simultaneous reorganization of the British Foreign Office, more individuals were allowed to engage in important drafting work. But in London it was Foreign Office clerks, not men from the field, who filled the new slots. Steiner, *Foreign Office*, p. 79.

53. Wilson, "Memorandum regarding Necessity for an Under Secretary," n.d., and Wilson to Elbert F. Baldwin, December 21, 1909, Wilson Papers; House, *Hearings on the LEJ* for 1912, November 29, 1910, pp. 34ff.

54. Phillips to Rockhill, September 19, 1908, Rockhill Papers; Heintzleman to Henry P. Fletcher, February 18, 1910, Fletcher Papers; Heintzleman to J. V. A. MacMurray, March 22, 1910, MacMurray Papers.

55. Memorandum of a departmental meeting, March 24, 1911, Wilson Papers; House, *Hearings before the Committee on Expenditures in the State Department*, May 10, 1911, p. 11; Miller to Carr, December 23, 1909, file 16704/12, RG 59.

56. Memoranda by Evan Young, June 8 and 9, 1911, and W. T. S. Doyle to Chandler Hale, November 29, 1910, file 160./12, RG 59; Charles Pepper, "State Department and Foreign Trade Extension," June 7, 1911, file 160., RG 59.

57. For the basic goals of the Taft administration's foreign policy, see Wilson, *Memoirs*, pp. 214–15, and Wilson's memorandum, marked "confidential—file," n.d., but apparently February 1913, Wilson Papers.

58. Wilson, memorandum marked "confidential—file," and Wilson to Knox, December 23, 1910, Wilson Papers.

59. Gibson to his mother, June 15, August 6, and August 11, 1910, Gibson

Papers; MacMurray, diary entry for September 23, 1911, MacMurray Papers; Wilson to Dawson, January 7, 1910, file 1070/161, RG 59.

60. William Phillips to Willard Straight, September 9, September 16, and October 9, 1908, Straight Papers; Phillips to Rockhill, July 16 and September 19, 1908, and January 8, 1909, Rockhill Papers. For interpretations emphasizing the continuity of United States Far Eastern policy, see Helen Dodson Kahn, "The Great Game of Empire: Willard D. Straight and American Far Eastern Policy" (Ph.D. diss., Cornell University, 1968), chapter 8; Michael H. Hunt, *Frontier Defense and the Open Door: Manchuria in Chinese-American Relations, 1895–1911* (New Haven, Conn., 1973), pp. 262–63. Charles Neu provides a recent dissent in "1906–1913," in Ernest R. May and James C. Thomson, eds., *American–East Asian Relations: A Survey* (Cambridge, Mass., 1972), pp. 155–72. Raymond A. Esthus occupies a middle ground in "The Changing Concept of the Open Door, 1899–1910," *Mississippi Valley Historical Review* 46 (December 1959): 434–54.

61. Copies of Wilson's campaign speeches are in the Wilson Papers. For additional examples of the department's efforts to minimize pre-1909 trade promotion, see Knox to Senator Eugene Hale, December 20, 1910, file 113./27A, and Knox to J. B. Doan, May 27, 1912, file 120.1/28, RG 59.

While the exigencies faced by the administration spurred on its rhetoric about reorganization and trade promotion, it was not necessarily a rhetoric divorced from perceived reality. Taft thought that Senator Elihu Root was "a bit sore" at his administration for improving the State Department since Root had never gotten around to doing it himself. Surprisingly, Root's biographer accepted Taft's opinion as fact. Taft to Knox, December 18, 1913, Knox Papers; Jessup, *Root*, 2:109.

CHAPTER 8

1. Senate, *Department of Commerce and Industries*, Rept. 321, 56th Cong., 1st sess., 1900; *Congressional Record*, 57th Cong., 2d sess., 1903, 36: 858, 911–12.

2. Senate, *Journal*, and House, *Journal*, 46th–57th congresses; Kirk H. Porter and Donald B. Johnson, comps., *National Party Platforms* (Urbana, Ill., 1966), p. 124.

3. Chamber of Commerce of the State of New York, *Annual Report*, 1901; NAM, *A Department of Commerce and Manufactures*, circular of information no. 4 (Philadelphia, 1896), and *A New Federal Department*, circular of information no. 36 (Philadelphia, 1900); Cleveland Chamber of Commerce, *Reports and Proceedings*, 1897, p. 81; Edward R. Wood of the National Board of Trade to Senator Knute Nelson, June 26 and August 11, 1902, and A. A. Burnham to Nelson, June 23, 1902, Nelson Papers.

4. Robert Wiebe, *Businessmen and Reform*, p. 44.

5. Senate, *A Department of Commerce and Industries*, Document 205, 55th Cong., 2d sess., 1898; House, *Hearings on Senate Bill 569, and House Bills 14, 95, and 2026* (Washington, D.C., 1902); U.S. Industrial Commission, *Final Report*, 575–76; NAM, *Department of Commerce and Manufactures* and *New Federal De-*

partment; Burnham to H. Garfield, April 7, 1902, HAG Papers; *Congressional Record*, 57th Cong., 1st sess., 1902, 35: 598.

6. For some legislators, including Nelson, the "and Labor" was largely an afterthought, added to demonstrate a supposed affinity between capital and labor. The new department absorbed the Department of Labor, a statistical agency without cabinet status, despite opposition from the American Federation of Labor and most labor spokesmen. Although organized labor had no particular objection to a Commerce Department, it preferred an independent Department of Labor. House, *Hearings on Senate Bill 569, and House Bills 14, 95, and 2026*, pp. 18–19, 33, 104.

7. *Congressional Record*, 57th Cong., 1st sess., 1902, 35: 862, 910, and 1903, 36: 867, 875, 945–46.

8. "Summary of the Laws Affecting the Bureau of Foreign and Domestic Commerce," January 30, 1938, file 160, records of the Bureau of Foreign and Domestic Commerce, RG 151.

9. "Proceedings of the Committee on Statistical Reorganization," October 10, 1907, file 66651, RG 40; address by Oscar P. Austin, July 21, 1909, Lectures to Consular Officers, RG 59. The statistical categories adopted in 1906 provided a better description of the export and import trade than the categories they replaced. In 1905, for example, the last year under the old classification, "Agriculture" accounted for an impressive 55 percent of total exports. But in 1906, the new system revealed that in 1905 crude foodstuffs had accounted for only 8 percent of total exports. The remainder of the "Agriculture" exports had been processed foodstuffs and raw materials for use in manufacturing, principally cotton. The improved classification resulted in an immediate net increase of more than $68,000,000 (or 13 percent) in favor of semi-finished and finished manufactured exports. *Statistical Abstract of the United States, 1905*, p. 303, and *1906*, p. 330; E. Dana Durand, Director of the Census, to Secretary of Commerce and Labor, April 3, 1911, file 218.01, PCEE records, RG 51.

10. "Proceedings of the Committee on Statistical Reorganization," October 1907, file 66651, RG 40; House, *Hearings on the LEJ* for 1913, February 10, 1912, p. 735, and same for 1903, January 28, 1902, pp. 132–37.

11. "Meeting of the Interdepartmental Committee for the Revision of Statistics of Foreign Commerce," October 9, 1911, file 218.01, PCEE records, RG 51; John M. Carson to Oscar Straus, February 17, 1909, file 66651, RG 40. Part of the problem was ameliorated in 1916 when new Treasury regulations placed greater responsibility for declarations of exports upon the shippers themselves. The shippers presumably would know the ultimate destination of the goods, while representatives of transportation companies or other agents might not. Lawrence F. Schmeckebier and Gustavus A. Weber, *The Bureau of Foreign and Domestic Commerce: Its History, Activities, and Organization* (Baltimore, Md., 1924), p. 33; Frank R. Rutter, "Statistics of Imports and Exports," *Publications of the American Statistical Association* 15 (March 1916): 23–24.

12. House, *Hearings on the LEJ* for 1911, January 27, 1910, p. 300. My reading of the export figures, including the prepared and partly prepared foodstuffs category, gives manufactures about 10 percent less of the export trade than Carson did. See *Statistical Abstract, 1909*, p. 450. Nevertheless, his point was well taken, because even my total is almost 20 percent higher than the figure usually ascribed to

exports of manufactures by contemporaries and historians alike. Although Carson was unsatisfied, the Bureau of Statistics had in fact adopted the new foreign trade classification in 1906 partly to demonstrate the real importance of manufactures in the export trade. If the bureau had consistently labeled the category "manufactured" instead of "prepared" foodstuffs, it might have eliminated much confusion. The Commerce Department changed the category's designation to "manufactured foodstuffs" in 1924. Department of Commerce and Labor, *Exports of Manufactures from the United States and Their Distribution by Articles and Countries* (Washington, D.C., 1907), p. 7; *Statistical Abstract, 1924*, p. 425.

13. *National Cyclopaedia of American Biography*, 24: 157–58; address by Austin, July 21, 1909, Lectures to Consular Officers, RG 59; Austin to Charles D. Hilles, August 19, 1912, and to William Howard Taft, June 8, 1912, Taft Papers.

14. Austin to Hilles, August 19, 1912, Taft Papers; same to Theodore Weed, January 2, 1909, file 67010, RG 40.

15. *Proceedings of the National Board of Trade*, January 1906, pp. 255–57; House, *Hearings on the LEJ* for 1912, December 2, 1910, p. 243; address by Austin, July 21, 1909, Lectures to Consular Officers, RG 59.

16. Some expressions of Austin's attitudes may be found in his published essays, which include: "Colonial Systems of the World," *National Geographic* 10 (January 1899): 21–26; "Our New Possessions and the Interest They Are Exciting," ibid. 11 (January 1900): 31–32; "Problems of the Pacific—The Commerce of the Great Ocean," ibid. 13 (August 1902): 313–18; "The Relations of Commerce to Geography," ibid. 15 (December 1904): 503; "Does Colonization Pay?" *Forum* 28 (January 1900): 621–31; "Why Not Three Hundred Million People?" ibid. 31 (January 1901): 165–74; "Our Growing Dependence on the Tropics," ibid. 33 (June 1902): 400–408.

17. Department of Commerce and Labor, *The Commercial Orient in 1905* (Washington, D.C., 1906), pp. 6, 12; House, *Hearings on the LEJ* for 1906, December 2, 1904, p. 202; *Statistical Abstract, 1913*, pp. 328–63.

18. *Congressional Record*, 57th Cong., 2d sess., 1903, 36: 945–46, and same for 57th Cong., 1st sess., 1902, 35: 761, 765, 865; "History, Organization, and Activities of the Bureau of Manufactures," n.d., but early 1912, file 142, PCEE records, RG 51. The departmental hearings of 1907 contain the best single source for the bureaucratic infighting. See file 66651, RG 40.

19. Austin to George B. Cortelyou, June 27, 1903, file 66651, RG 40.

20. Both North and Wright, statisticians like Austin, shared the broad consensus among bureaucrats at State and C & L about the need for foreign markets. See Wright's "The Relation of Production to Productive Capacity," *Forum* 24 (November 1897): 290–302. For North, see "The Industrial Situation," unpublished manuscript, n.d., but apparently 1899 or 1900, and North to Samuel S. Dale, July 1, 1907, North Papers.

21. North to Cortelyou, May 25 and 26, 1903, and Cortelyou to North, May 23, letterbook, George B. Cortelyou Papers, LC; Report of the Subcommittee to the Statistical Commission, n.d., in "Proceedings of the Committee on Statistical Reorganization," file 66651, RG 40.

22. J. Garfield, diary entry for June 10, 1903, same to Lucretia R. Garfield, June 25, 1903, and 1903 plan of reorganization, all in JRG Papers.

23. Press release for publication on May 10, 1903, Cortelyou Papers; Department of Commerce and Labor, *Address of Secretary Cortelyou at Banquet of Merchants' Club in Chicago* (March 12, 1904), p. 24; Austin to Taft, June 8, 1912, Taft Papers.

24. George W. Seadley to Secretary of C & L, December 31, 1904, J. Hampton Moore Papers.

25. Moore to Metcalf, February 7, 1905, and Metcalf to Moore, February 11, 1905, file 42219, RG 40; W. M. Collier to Metcalf, February 15, 1905, file 67006, RG 40; Moore to W. V. Smith, of the Philadelphia Drug Exchange, January 21, 1905, letterbook, and to William H. Pfahler of the Metal Trades' Association, March 1, 1905, J. H. Moore Papers.

26. Moore to an unidentified editor, April 29, 1905, Moore Papers; Department of Commerce and Labor, *Reports* (Washington, D.C., 1906), pp. 63–64.

27. Moore to Senator Boies Penrose, May 5, 1905, Moore Papers; *New York Times*, September 30, 1912, p. 13; James Harrison Wilson to Theodore Roosevelt, November 1, 1901, James H. Wilson Papers; "Writers in the December *Forum*," *Forum* 32 (December 1901): 511.

28. "Proceedings of the Committee on Statistical Reorganization," November 6, 1907, file 66651, RG 40; House, *Hearings on the LEJ* for 1908, November 30, 1906, p. 319, and same for 1911, January 27, 1910, p. 299.

29. Donaldson, memorandum to Oscar Straus, May 3, 1907, file 70328, RG 40; transcript of conference of bureau chiefs, n.d., but probably February 1907, file 68699, RG 40. The recording secretary wrote "pisgar."

30. North to Cortelyou, May 7, 1903, Cortelyou Papers; House, *Hearings on the LEJ* for 1905, December 17, 1903, pp. 256–57, 280, and same for 1906, December 2, 1904, pp. 201ff.

31. House, *Hearings on the LEJ* for 1912, December 2, 1910, p. 229, and same for 1913, February 9, 1912, pp. 664–66; Senate, *Hearings on the LEJ* for 1909, February 28, 1908, p. 11, and same for 1913, May 22, 1912, pp. 194, 201.

32. House, *Hearings on the LEJ* for 1911, January 27, 1910, p. 297, and same for 1909, January 29, 1908, p. 450; Metcalf, circular instruction to special agents, June 30, 1905, and Straus to Carson, February 7, 1907, file 64934, RG 40.

33. Department of Commerce and Labor, *Reports*, 1907, p. 55; House, *Hearings on the LEJ* for 1908, November 30, 1906, p. 319, and same for 1909, January 29, 1908, p. 466.

34. House, *Hearings on the LEJ* for 1912, December 2, 1910, p. 229, and same for 1913, February 9, 1912, pp. 662–63; Senate, *Hearings on the LEJ* for 1909, February 28, 1908, p. 11.

35. James Tawney to the Cincinnati Milling Machine Company, December 11, 1906, James A. Tawney Papers, Minnesota State Historical Society, St. Paul; House, *Hearings on the LEJ* for 1909, January 29, 1908, pp. 451–53, 467; A. L. Goetzmann to Straus, April 18, 1908, Oscar Straus Papers, LC. Providing an agent to conduct investigations for flour was probably more of a political move than were other special agent assignments. Straus was obviously infatuated with the importance of the millers as a powerful interest group and probably expected their support for his department. Particularly revealing is Oscar Austin's statement the following year to a

group of consuls that they should not bother to promote the foreign sale of processed foodstuffs, flour included, because such products would be increasingly consumed at home. Address by Austin, July 21, 1909, Lectures to Consular Officers, RG 59.

36. Austin to Cortelyou, June 15, 1903, file 66651, RG 40; same to same, August, 1903, and to Metcalf, November 22, 1904, file 47134, RG 40; Department of Commerce and Labor, *Reports*, 1906, pp. 63–64, and 1907, p. 53; circular letter to "Manufacturers and Exporters," ca. March 5, 1907, file 66651, RG 40; Carson to John Osborne, March 12, 1908, file 166./9, RG 59.

37. Emory to Robert Chilton, July 21 and 26, 1894; Renick to Emory (2) (emphasis in the original) and Rockhill to Renick, all n.d., but in late July 1894; Chilton to Renick, July 27, 1894; memorandum by Emory, n.d., but ca. July 1895. All citations are from Consular Bureau Decisions and Precedents, RG 59.

38. Huntington Wilson to Carpenter, Baggot and Company, February 6, 1907, file 4006, RG 59; Carr to Paul Beich Company, July 7, 1911, file 160./15, RG 59; same to Cardwell Machine Company, April 29, 1910, Consular Bureau Decisions and Precedents, RG 59.

39. Wilson to R. D. Douglass, quoting Carr, June 6, 1910, Consular Bureau Decisions and Precedents, RG 59; Carr to Dun and Company, October 28, 1911, file 163./32b, RG 59.

40. Carr to Illinois Malleable Iron Company, March 10, 1908, file 12222, RG 59; same to Charles N. Butler, November 11, 1910, file 163./24, RG 59; same to National Association of Credit Men, August 10, 1912, file 164.1/48, RG 59; same to Cardwell Machine Company, April 29, 1910, Consular Bureau Decisions and Precedents, RG 59; same to Paul Beich Company, July 7, 1911, file 160./15, RG 59; Osborne to Carr, November 9, 1911, file 163./32, RG 59. In 1909 Carr asked the United States ambassadors in Great Britain, Germany, France, and Austria-Hungary about the policy of their host governments on this issue. He was informed that the French and British consuls usually supplied the data. The German imperial consular authorities decided whether the inquirer was sufficiently reliable to exclude possible misuse of the information. Like the Americans, the British accompanied the names of the firms with the warning that the government could accept no responsibility for statements about commercial standing. Carr to Sydney Smith, January 20, 1909, Henry White to Secretary of State, March 13, 1909, translations of replies from the Austrian and German Foreign Offices, "Extract" describing British policy, all in file 17643, RG 59.

41. "Memoranda for Circular Letter to Consular Officers," ca. February 14, 1908, file 11773/1, RG 59; Carson to Osborne, June 29, 1908, file 14663, RG 59; address by Carson, July 19, 1909, Lectures to Consular Officers, RG 59; Burnham to Congressman Michael F. Conry, February 17, 1910, records of the Committee on Interstate and Foreign Commerce, file 61A-H13.7, RG 233.

42. Carson, "To Manufacturers and Merchants of the United States," April 25, 1910, and same to Tawney, May 11, 1910, records of the Committee on Appropriations, file 61A-F2.5, RG 233.

43. Carr to consular officers, June 4, 1910, file 11773/126, RG 59; James A. McKibben, Secretary of the Boston Chamber of Commerce, form letters, June 28 and August 17, 1910, file 327-49, Boston Chamber of Commerce records; "History,

Organization, and Activities of the Bureau of Manufactures," file 142, PCEE records, RG 51.

44. Address by John Osborne, July 27, 1909, Lectures to Consular Officers, RG 59; "History, Organization and Activities of the Bureau of Manufactures," file 142, PCEE records, RG 51; House, *Hearings on the LEJ* for 1909, January 29, 1908, p. 464; Nahum I. Stone, memorandum to Oscar Straus, April 19, 1907, file 66151, RG 40.

45. John Osborne, "The American Consul and American Trade," p. 169; Mason to department, April 6, 1905, and Thackara to department, December 9, 1905, Consular Despatches, Berlin, RG 59; Halstead to Assistant Secretary of State, January 30, 1907, and Wilson to Carr, February 13, 1907, file 7442, RG 59; Sammons to Assistant Secretary of State, February 23, 1907, and Wilson to Carr, March 6, 1907, file 5039, RG 59; Carr to Secretary of C & L, November 30, 1907, file 1615/49a, RG 59; Straus to Root, December 10, 1907, file 1615/52, RG 59; Root to Straus, March 7, 1908, file 67006/1, RG 40.

46. Austin to Secretary of C & L, October 10, 1905, file E1408, RG 40; Schmeckebier and Weber, *Bureau of Foreign and Domestic Commerce*, p. 27; Charles Donaldson, memorandum to Straus, May 3, 1907, file 70328, RG 40; Osborne, "American Consul and American Trade," p. 170; E. J. Gibson to Straus, September 27, 1907, file 65209, RG 40; address by Carson, July 19, 1909, Lectures to Consular Officers, RG 59.

47. Sammons to Secretary of State, August 11, 1911, file 161.3/6, RG 59; undated confidential circulars in file 161.7, RG 59; confidential circular no. 38, October 22, 1910, 161.7/92; confidential circular no. 116, July 17, 1909, file 18691/9, RG 59; Benjamin Cable to Secretary of State, September 6, 1912, file 68109/16, RG 40.

48. "History, Organization, and Activities of the Bureau of Manufactures," file 142, PCEE records, RG 51; Johnson et al., *History of Domestic and Foreign Commerce*, 2: 292; Charles Nagel to Philander Knox, October 11, 1911, file 161./15, RG 59; Department of Commerce and Labor, *Reports*, 1910, p. 381, and 1911, p. 64; Baldwin, report on the Bureau of Manufactures in Material relating to the President's Commission on Economy and Efficiency, Box 7, RG 40; Thackara to Secretary of State, August 31, 1912, 161.4/3, RG 59. The system could also be used to warn American firms of impending political crises in areas of the world where they did business. For one such instance see A. H. Baldwin to John Osborne, October 6, 1910, file 161.7/89, RG 59.

49. Transcripts of conferences of bureau chiefs, April 11, 1907, and September 19, 1907, file 68699, RG 40; Department of Commerce and Labor, *Statistical Reorganization* (Washington, D.C., 1908); Lawrence Murray to Nagel, June 16, 1909, file 67407, RG 40; memorandum by Straus, March 1, 1909, file 66651, RG 40.

50. *National Cyclopaedia of American Biography*, 16: 356–57; clipping from the *Minneapolis Journal*, July 27, 1909, Knox Papers; Nagel, *Federal Control of Corporations* (Chicago, 1910); Department of Commerce and Labor, *Views of the Department of Commerce and Labor on the Bill to Regulate Corporations Engaged in Interstate and Foreign Commerce* (Washington, D.C., 1911); address by Nagel to the Boston Chamber of Commerce, February 2, 1912, file 104-1, Boston Chamber of Commerce records; Nagel to Taft, October 31, 1911, Taft Papers.

51. Herbert Knox Smith to Nagel, May 19, 1909, file 69253/57; Lawrence O. Murray to Nagel, June 16, 1909, file 67407; Nagel to Comptroller of the Treasury, July 14, 1909, file 66651; R. J. Tracewell to Nagel, July 27, 1909, file 69253/57; Nagel to George W. Wickersham, August 4, 1909, and Wade H. Ellis to Nagel, August 18, 1909, file 66651. All these files are in RG 40.

52. Nagel to Foster, March 9, 1910, file 69253/57, RG 40.

53. Nagel to Taft, July 8 and November 8, 1910, Taft Papers; same to Carson, July 8, 1910, and to Lodge, October 11, 1910, Nagel Papers; Nagel to Baldwin, January 23, 1911, file 67006/9, RG 40.

54. "History, Organization, and Activities of the Bureau of Manufactures," file 142, PCEE records, RG 51; House, *Hearings on the LEJ* for 1913, February 10, 1912, p. 687, and same for 1914, November 25, 1912, p. 280; Baldwin to Carr, November 2, 1911, and Carr to American Consular Officers, November 10, 1911, file 164.1/21, RG 59; Benjamin Cable to Senator Reed Smoot, December 20, 1911, file 67028/1, RG 40.

55. House, *Hearings on the LEJ* for 1911, January 27, 1910, pp. 286–87, 299, same for 1912, December 2, 1910, pp. 229–30, and same for 1913, February 9, 1912, pp. 662–63; "History, Organization, and Activities of the Bureau of Manufactures," file 142, PCEE records, RG 51.

56. Nagel to Charles D. Hilles, December 17, 1911, letterbook, Nagel Papers; *Proceedings of the American Manufacturers Export Association*, September 1911, p. 10; House, *Hearings on the LEJ* for 1913, February 10, 1912, p. 687.

57. Hunt to H. Garfield, n.d., HAG Papers; Emory to John Bassett Moore, May 18, 1903, Moore Papers.

58. Ozmun to Assistant Secretary of State, January 16, 1908, file 12478, RG 59; Albert Halstead to Secretary of State, November 3, 1910, file 161./1, RG 59; House, *Hearings on the Dip/Cons* for 1909, January 30, 1908, p. 12.

59. Iddings to Assistant Secretary of State, May 25, 1907, and Carr to same, May 31, 1907, file 6900, RG 59; Department of Commerce and Labor, *Reports*, 1907, pp. 248–49; Osborne to Baldwin, July 13, 1911, Baldwin's reply of July 17, 1911, and undated statement of complaints against the State Department, in file 210.39, PCEE records, RG 51.

60. Knox to Nagel, July 1, 1909, Consular Bureau Decisions and Precedents, RG 59; Osborne, memorandum for Secretary Root, October 13, 1908, file 121.56, RG 59; unidentified (but probably Hengstler) to Carr, June 23, 1909, Consular Bureau Decisions and Precedents, RG 59.

61. Seeger to Assistant Secretary of State, November 19, 1906, and Murray to Secretary of State, December 11, 1906, file 1615/2, RG 59; Roosevelt to Straus, January 11, 1907, file 65209, RG 40.

62. Gibson to Straus, September 25, 1907, file 65209, RG 40; Straus to Root, September 26, 1907, file 1615/39, and same to Carson, September 30, 1907, file 1615/41, RG 59. The subject was sufficiently important to be discussed at a cabinet meeting. Memorandum by Straus, January 15, 1907, file 65209, RG 40.

63. Murray to Secretary of State, September 6, 1907, and Adee to Murray, September 26, 1907, file 1615/37, RG 59; Murray to Adee, September 30, 1907, file 1615/40, RG 59; Gibson to Straus, October 1, 1907, file 65209, RG 40.

64. Carr to Secretary of C & L, November 30, 1907, file 1615/49a, RG 59; Root to same, March 7, 1908, file 67006/1, RG 40.

65. Austin to Secretary of C & L, October 10, 1905, file E1408, RG 40; House, *Hearings on the LEJ* for 1911, January 27, 1910, pp. 295–96; National Business League, resolution adopted January 23, 1908, in file 2108/35, RG 59; A. A. Burnham to Congressman Frank Lowden, January 29, 1908, Frank O. Lowden Papers, University of Chicago; Straus to Root, June 11, 1907, file 7171, RG 59; Nagel to Knox, August 22, 1911, file 110.78/4, RG 59.

66. Carr to Root, February 4, 1908, file 121.56, RG 59; Osborne to Carr, June 12, 1907, with copy of his March 8, 1906, memorandum, "In Re Control of Consular Service," file 7171, RG 59; same to same, September 18, 1907, file 8363, RG 59; Metcalf to his bureau chiefs, March 28, 1906, file 65225, RG 40; Carr to Charles Donaldson, December 30, 1909, file 7171, RG 59.

67. Hunt to H. Garfield, n.d., HAG Papers.

68. "Confidential Memorandum: Criticism on the Publication of the Daily Consular and Trade Reports," n.d., file 110.78, RG 59; Charles P. Bryan to Secretary of State, February 2, 1911, file 600.1117/1, RG 59; extract from Foreign Trade Opportunity, November 29, 1911, in file 218.01, PCEE records, RG 51; Washburn, "A Plea for Consular Inspection," *Forum* 30 (October 1900): 32; Osborne to Hengstler, July 19, 1912, file 162./26a, RG 59 (emphasis in the original).

69. Osborne to Carr, October 25, 1911, file 161./15, same to same, February 8, 1912, file 161./28, same to same, April 20, 1912, file 161./29, Nagel to Knox, October 11, 1911, file 161./15, same to same, February 29, 1912, file 161./20, all in RG 59; Baldwin to Chief Clerk of C & L, December 27, 1910, Material relating to the President's Commission on Economy and Efficiency, Box 5, RG 40.

70. "Confidential Memorandum: Criticism on the Publication of the Daily Consular and Trade Reports," n.d., file 110.78, RG 59; memorandum by Osborne, May 20, 1912, file 111.26, RG 59 (emphasis in the original).

71. Speech by Carr in Saint Louis, 1910, and clipping from the *St. Louis Times*, April 12, 1910, Carr Papers.

72. "Confidential Memorandum: Criticism on the Publication of the Daily Consular and Trade Reports," n.d., file 110.78, RG 59.

73. Undated memorandum from the Bureau of Manufactures, file 210.39, PCEE records, RG 51; House, *Hearings on the LEJ* for 1913, February 10, 1912, pp. 688–89; Baldwin, memorandum to Nagel, June 22, 1911, file 69253/57, RG 40; same to Chief Clerk of C & L, December 27, 1910, Material relating to the PCEE, Box 5, RG 40 (emphasis in the original); Carson to Straus, December 17, 1908, file 67954, RG 40; Senate, *Hearings on the LEJ* for 1913, May 22, 1912, pp. 193 ff.

CHAPTER 9

1. Walter O. Jacobson, "A Study of President Taft's Commission on Economy and Efficiency and a Comparative Evaluation with Three Other Commissions" (M.A. thesis, Columbia University, 1941), pp. 9–10; Senator Jonathan Bourne, "How to Spend a Billion Dollars," *Outlook* 93 (October 9, 1909): 297–302.

2. *Congressional Record*, 61st Cong., 2d sess., 1910, 45: 1503, 1518–19, 7656–58.

3. Ibid., pp. 7656–58.

4. Bess Glenn, "The Taft Commission and the Government's Record Practices," *American Archivist* 21 (July 1958): 277; Gustavus A. Weber, *Organized Efforts for the Improvement of Methods of Administration in the United States* (New York, 1919), p. 85; Frederick A. Cleveland, "Causes of Waste and Inefficiency in National Government," *Review of Reviews* 45 (April 1912): 468–69.

5. Taft to Knox, December 23, 1908, Knox Papers; Jacobson, "President Taft's Commission," pp. 12, 79.

6. Glenn, "Taft Commission," p. 284; *Congressional Record*, 62d Cong., 2d sess., 1912, 48: 6039.

7. Baldwin, memorandum to Nagel, June 22, 1911, file 69253/57, RG 40.

8. Nagel to Knox, June 29 and August 22, 1911, Knox to Nagel, August 18 and October 13, 1911, file 110.78/4, RG 59; Nagel to Knox, October 11, 1911, file 161./15, RG 59.

9. Carr to Wilson, November 21, 1911, file 161./15, RG 59.

10. Ibid., Wilson's marginal comment; Carr to Osborne, December 8, 1911, file 161./15, RG 59.

11. Nagel to Charles D. Hilles, February 29, 1912, and to Congressman F. H. Gillette, March 4, 1912, file 69253/57, RG 40.

12. Knox to Nagel, August 18, 1911, file 110.78/4, RG 59; Wilson to Nagel, March 20, 1912, and to Taft, February 27, 1912, file 69253/57, RG 40; House, LEJ, Rept. 633, 62d Cong., 2d sess., 1912, pp. 5, 9–10.

13. *Congressional Record*, 62d Cong., 2d sess., May 9 and 10, 1912, 48: 6178–90, 6231.

14. Minutes of the PCEE for April 22, 1911, and May 25, 1912, file 017.12, PCEE records, RG 51; Glenn, "The Taft Commission," p. 282; Nagel to Taft, March 29, 1911, letterbook, Nagel Papers.

15. A year earlier, another member of the commission had urged Willoughby to moderate his tone when criticizing inefficiency in the government departments. Frank J. Goodnow to Willoughby, April 24, 1911, Frank J. Goodnow Papers, Eisenhower Library, Johns Hopkins University.

16. PCEE to Taft, May 28, 1912, file 218.01, PCEE records, RG 51. Beginning in October 1910, Willoughby met with Cleveland several times to discuss methods of improving efficiency in the Census Bureau and other executive agencies. Impressed with Willoughby's work, Cleveland arranged for his appointment to the commission weeks before it was formally organized; the other three commissioners were selected later. It is not unreasonable to assume that Willoughby's opinions carried a good deal of weight with the commission's chairman. See Cleveland, summary of daily activities, October 26 and December 12, 1910, January 19, 20, 21, March 8, 1911, Taft to Willoughby, February 20 and March 16, 1911, all in Taft Papers; Taft to Frank J. Goodnow, April 20, 1911, Goodnow Papers.

17. PCEE to Taft, May 28, 1912, file 218.01, PCEE records, RG 51.

18. Merritt Chance to House Appropriations Committee, February 1, 1912,

records of the Committee on Appropriations, file 62A-F1.4, RG 233; Jacobson, "President Taft's Commission," p. 51; Nagel to Hilles, February 28, 1912, file 69253/57, RG 40; Fitzgerald to Nagel, March 8, 1912, and Nagel's March 9 reply, file 66651, RG 40; *Congressional Record*, 62d Cong., 2d sess., May 4, May 7, and May 9, 1912, 48: 5896–97, 6034, 6039–40, 6178–90; Oscar W. Underwood to Wilson, July 12, 1912, file 113./45, RG 59.

Even before the Cleveland Commission's formal establishment early in 1911, Charles Nagel had cultivated good relations with Cleveland. Cleveland, summary of daily activities, November 15, 1910, March 1 and 2, 1911, Taft Papers.

19. House, *Hearings on the LEJ* for 1913, January 29, 1912, p. 117; Senate, *Hearings on the LEJ* for 1913, May 23, 1912, p. 324; Taft to Knox, December 15, 1910, file 113./25, RG 59.

20. *Congressional Record*, 61st Cong., 2d sess., 1910, 45: 3063, 3033, and 62d Cong., 2d sess., 1912, 48: 7709.

21. *Congressional Record*, 61st Cong., 2d sess., 1910, 45: 3066–67, and 62d Cong., 2d sess., 48: 7708.

22. Wilson, draft of memorandum, May 11, 1912, Wilson Papers; unsigned memorandum to the House Appropriations Committee, May 25, 1912, records of the Committee on Appropriations, file 62A-F1.4, RG 233; Wilson to Knox, May 29, 1912, Wilson Papers.

23. Wilson to "Gentlemen," May 14, 1912, file 120.1/32A, RG 59; Phillips to Wilson, May 22, 1912, file 120.1/30, RG 59; Wilson to Knox, June 7, 1912, Wilson Papers; Senate, *Hearings on the LEJ* for 1913, May 23, 1912, p. 317.

24. Knox to Rudolph Forster, chief clerk of the White House staff, June 15, 1912, Taft to Senator Francis Warren, June 15, 1912, and Nagel to Taft, January 10, 1913, Taft Papers; Knox to Wilson, August 3, 1912, Wilson Papers; U.S., *Statutes at Large*, 37:372–73, 407–8. The senators likewise came to the aid of other government agencies whose appropriations the House had cut. See the *Washington Evening Star*, June 1, 3, and 4, 1912.

25. Nagel to Taft, May 15, 1912, Taft Papers; Charles Earl to Nagel, May 18, 1912, file 69253/57, RG 40; Nagel to Senator Francis Warren, May 31, 1912, file 66651, RG 40; Senate, *Hearings on the LEJ* for 1913, May 22, 1912, p. 202.

26. Wilson to Knox, May 29, 1912, Wilson Papers (emphasis in the original).

27. Pepper, memorandum, August 8, 1912, McNeir to Wilson, August 14, 1912, and Carr to Wilson, August 29, 1912, file 162./27, RG 59.

28. Carr to Wilson, August 29, 1912, file 162./27, RG 59.

29. William McNeir to Chiefs of Bureaus and Divisions, September 12, 1912, Departmental Orders, RG 59; Pepper, memorandum, August 8, 1912, file 162./27, RG 59; Wilson to Pepper, August 26, 1912, Memoranda on the History and Organization of the Office of the Economic Adviser, RG 59. The State Department no longer received appropriations for a chief of the commercial bureau, and that same August John Osborne was appointed consul at Havre. Commercial adviser Mack Davis died in 1912.

30. Wilson, order dated September 30, 1912, Departmental Orders, RG 59; Carr to Baldwin, December 9, 1912, Clarence E. Gauss to Hengstler, December 7,

1912, and Hengstler's appended comment, file 161./24a, RG 59; Carr to Wilson, August 29, 1912, file 162./27, RG 59; Roger Tredwell to Carr, August 18, 1913, and unsigned memorandum from the Office of Foreign Trade Advisers, February 1916, file 111.26, RG 59.

31. Senate, *Hearings on the LEJ* for 1913, May 22, 1912, pp. 200, 204.

32. Austin to Congressman Joseph Johnson, May 6, 1912, records of the Committee on Appropriations, file 62A-F1.4, RG 233; Austin to Nagel, May 23 and June 6, 1912, file 69253/57, RG 40.

33. Austin to John F. Lacey, June 26 and July 2, 1912, John F. Lacey Papers, Iowa State Department of History and Archives, Des Moines (I am indebted to Professor Lewis Gould of the University of Texas for copies of Austin's letters to Lacey); Congressman Joseph W. Fordney of Michigan to Taft, June 11, 1912, Grosvenor to Mrs. Taft, June 12, 1912, Charles Needham to Taft, July 6, 1912, Austin to Taft, June 8 and 10, 1912, and Austin to Charles D. Hilles, August 19, 1912, all in Taft Papers; Austin to Roosevelt, July 22 and 29, 1912, Roosevelt Papers.

34. In April 1912 the Commerce and Labor Department, with the assistance of a few businessmen, organized the Chamber of Commerce of the United States. Nagel and Baldwin desired a permanently mobilized constituency among the organized businessmen, for reasons involving more widespread participation in the export trade, rivalry with the State Department, and the political fortunes of the Taft administration. See the material in files 66419 and 70503, RG 40.

35. Conant to Taft, August 12, 1912, and Fahey to Congressman John W. Weeks of Massachusetts, July 16, 1912, enclosed in Weeks to Taft, July 18, 1912, Taft Papers.

36. Nagel to Taft, August 23, 1912, Taft Papers; House, *Hearings on the LEJ* for 1914, November 25, 1912, p. 279.

37. For details about this continuing rivalry after 1912, see my article, "Selling the Foreign Service: Bureaucratic Rivalry and Foreign Trade Promotion, 1903–1912," *Pacific Historical Review* 45 (May 1976), and also Burton Kaufman, *Efficiency and Expansion*, pp. 79–80, 218–20.

CHAPTER 10

1. North, "The Industrial Situation," n.d., but apparently 1899 or 1900, North Papers.

2. Robert P. Skinner to Francis B. Loomis, July 5, 1910, Loomis Papers; Beale to "John" (apparently John A. Porter, President McKinley's secretary), October 20, 1897, Day Papers.

3. In 1911 the Supreme Court handed down decisions ordering the dissolution of the Standard Oil and American Tobacco companies. Although the Roosevelt administration had initiated these cases, Taft's Justice Department followed with suits against other giants in the export trade—United States Steel and International Harvester. Henry Pringle, *The Life and Times of William Howard Taft*, 2 vols. (New York, 1939), 2: 659–75.

4. Nagel to Taft, October 31, 1911, Nagel Papers. See also above, chapter 9, n. 34.

5. Charles Pepper, *American Foreign Trade: The United States as a World Power in the New Era of International Commerce* (New York, 1919), p. 316; William A. Neumann to Knox, January 3, 1911, file 160./2, RG 59; Kelsey to the State Department, May 17, 1912, file 120.1/30, RG 59; Steven de Cseznak, "The Export Situation," *American Industries* 12 (May 1912): 26.

6. Marilyn Blatt Young has urged scholars to address themselves to this important question. "American Expansion, 1870–1900: The Far East," in Barton Bernstein, ed., *Towards a New Past: Dissenting Essays in American History* (New York, 1967), pp. 178–79.

7. Department of Commerce, *Statistical Abstract, 1916*, pp. 180–81; same, *Historical Statistics* (1960), p. 544; Lipsey, *Price and Quantity Trends*, p. 58.

8. William H. Becker, "American Manufacturers and Foreign Markets, 1870–1900: Business Historians and the 'New Economic Determinists,'" *Business History Review* 47 (Winter 1973): 478, 480; Evan B. Metcalf, "Secretary Hoover and the Emergence of Macroeconomic Management," *Business History Review* 49 (Spring 1975): 60–80; Galen Reid Fisher, "The Chamber of Commerce of the United States and the Laissez-faire Rationale, 1912–1919" (Ph.D. diss., University of California, Berkeley, 1960), particularly pp. 29–30, 34, 206; Chamber of Commerce of the United States, *Balancing Production and Employment through Management Control* (Washington, D.C., 1930), pp. 58–59. See also Alfred D. Chandler, Jr., *Strategy and Structure: Chapters in the History of the Industrial Enterprise* (New York, Anchor Books, 1966), pp. 35–36, 476–87.

9. One who did foresee this development was the veteran commissioner of labor, Carroll D. Wright. He believed that in time, through both general and industrial education, American labor would earn higher wages and thus form a domestic market sufficient to handle the nation's growing productive capacity. Meanwhile, however, it was the federal government's duty "in order to supply remunerative employment to the greatest number of citizens, to take every step possible toward the extension of our foreign trade." Wright, "The Relation of Production to Productive Capacity," *Forum* 24 (November 1897): 671–74.

10. S. N. D. North, *Seventy-five Years' Progress in Statistics: The Outlook for the Future* (Concord, N.H., 1914), p. 25; Albert Rees, *Real Wages in Manufacturing, 1890–1914* (Princeton, N.J., 1961), p. 125.

11. Department of Commerce, *Thirteenth Census* (Washington, D.C.), 1: 53–54; Lipsey, *Price and Quantity Trends*, pp. 142–43; Department of Commerce, *Historical Statistics* (1960), p. 544. In order to help the trade balance, imports could theoretically have been reduced by raising the tariff wall still higher, above the 1897 Dingley rates. But political realities took precedence over theoretical economics, as they so often do. After the turn of the century, public sentiment increasingly favored lower tariffs, not higher. The failure of the 1909 Payne-Aldrich act to lower duties helped shatter the Republican party during Taft's presidency.

12. John G. A. Leishman to Root, November 16, 1906, file 2866, RG 59.

13. Paul Varg, "The Myth of the China Market, 1890–1914," *American*

Historical Review 73 (February 1968): 742–43; J. A. Thompson, "William Appleman Williams and the 'American Empire,' " *Journal of American Studies* 7 (April 1973): 95.

14. "Meeting of the Statistics Committee," April 28, 1911, file 218.01, PCEE records, RG 51.

15. According to export statistics, in 1903 Europe purchased 40 percent of America's finished manufactures; ten years later the figure was 31 percent. The share bought by countries of North America (which according to the statistical categories included Canada, Mexico, Central America, and the Caribbean islands) rose from 29 to 39 percent. South America increased its share from 8 to 13 percent, while Asia's portion declined from 11 to 8 percent. Semifinished manufactures underwent a less marked change in the same direction. In 1903 Europe purchased 77 percent of these exports, North America 14 percent, South America 3 percent and Asia 1½ percent. Ten years later Europe received two and a half times as many such products from the United States, but its share had declined to 64 percent. North America received 23 percent, South America 7 percent, and Asia 2 percent. *Statistical Abstract, 1909*, pp. 450–51, and *1913*, pp. 410–11. Foreign affairs bureaucrats did neglect, relatively, the growing importance of the Canadian market.

16. See above, chapter 8.

17. Consular Bureau to Emory, January 28, 1901, Consular Bureau Decisions and Precedents, RG 59; address by Osborne, July 27, 1909, Lectures to Consular Officers, RG 59.

18. Address by Hengstler, July 1, 1909, Lectures to Consular Officers, RG 59; Osborne to Carr, October 31, 1911, and Carr's notation, file 164.11/8, RG 59; Osborne to Hengstler, May 20, 1908, and Hengstler's appended comment, file 3943/128–129, RG 59.

19. Carr to David R. Birch, April 16, 1908, file 3943/88, RG 59; same to George Hotschick, February 3, 1909, file 3943/470, RG 59. On several occasions, Carr and Hengstler were willing to allow the consuls to go past what Osborne considered proper limits. See Osborne to Carr, December 30, 1909, and Carr to Osborne and Hengstler, December 31, 1909, file 22678, RG 59; Clarence E. Gauss to Hengstler, January 18, 1912, file 164.11/15, RG 59.

20. Acting Attorney-General Henry Hoyt to the Secretary of State, March 30, 1905, Consular Bureau Decisions and Precedents, RG 59; Paul F. Beich Co. to Carr, May 18, 1911, Davis to Carr, May 26, 1911, and Carr to Paul F. Beich Co., July 7, 1911, file 160./15, RG 59.

21. See, for instance, House, *Promotion of Trade Interests*, Document 245, 58th Cong., 3d sess., 1905, pp. 8–9, 83, 90, 189. Harold Nicolson, the noted diplomatist, mentions the prevalence of this attitude among his older colleagues in the British service. Nicolson, *The Evolution of Diplomatic Method* (London, 1953), pp. 80–81.

22. Acting Secretary Bacon to John Hicks, November 11, 1906, copy in Jessup Papers; Department of State, *Foreign Relations of the United States, 1897* (Washington, D.C., 1898), p. 56. The 1906 instruction was drafted by Adee and approved by Root.

23. Grevstad to Secretary of State, March 8, 1912, same to same, telegram, April 8, 1912, Wilson, telegram to Grevstad, April 9, 11, 12, Osborne to Seth L. Pierrepont in the Latin American division, April 13, same to Henry Janes, chief of the Latin American division, April 11, all in files 166.033-166.033/23, RG 59.

24. Grevstad to Secretary of State, April 20, and consul Frederick Goding to same, May 7, 1912, both ibid.

25. Albert Halstead to Secretary of State, November 3, 1910, file 161./1, RG 59; Charles S. Thorne to Carr, February 19, 1913, file 164.1/67, RG 59.

26. Carr to A. E. Ingram, May 13, 1912, file 164.2, RG 59; Report of the Consular Reorganization Board, June 1906, Dickinson Papers; Young and Pepper to Carr, June 4, 1913, and Carr's marginal comment, file 164.22/17, RG 59.

27. A. E. Ingram to Secretary of State, April 18, 1912, file 164.2, RG 59; Poole, notes for a lecture, March 1935, Poole Papers (emphasis in the original).

28. A valuable study of this phenomenon is Mira Wilkins, *The Emergence of Multinational Enterprise: American Business Abroad from the Colonial Era to 1914* (Cambridge, Mass., 1970). See also Robert B. Davies, " 'Peacefully Working to Conquer the World': The Singer Manufacturing Company in Foreign Markets, 1854–1899," *Business History Review* 43 (Autumn 1969): 299–325.

29. Chilton to Secretary of State, June 24, 1896, Miscellaneous Reports and Correspondence on Consular Inspections, RG 59; Davies, "The Singer Manufacturing Company," p. 304.

30. Herbert Peirce to American Consular Officers, April 30, 1906, Circulars to Consular Officers, RG 59; Huntington Wilson to Carr, n.d., and Oscar Straus to Elihu Root, March 11, 1907, file 3943/3–9, RG 59; address by John Carson, July 19, 1909, Lectures to Consular Officers, RG 59; Carr to H. D. Van Sant, December 14, 1909, Consular Bureau Decisions and Precedents, RG 59.

31. Osborne to Anderson, April 5, 1911, Anderson to Clark, April 7, 1911, Van Dyne to Osborne, April 14, Clark to Anderson, April 18 (emphasis in the original), Anderson to Osborne, April 18, Clark to Bureau of Trade Relations and to Carr, April 26, Carr to Caraconda Brothers, May 5, 1911, all in file 164.12/21, RG 59.

32. Peirce to American Consular Officers, April 30, 1906, Circulars to Consular Officers, RG 59; James Worman to Assistant Secretary of State, February 6, 1907, file 3943/3–9, RG 59; Carr to H. D. Van Sant, December 14, 1909, Consular Bureau Decisions and Precedents, RG 59; Carr to Osborne, n.d., but apparently late November, 1909, file 164.21/1, RG 59; Van Sant to State Department, December 27, 1909, file 24220/4, RG 59; Theodosius Botkin to Assistant Secretary of State, March 3, 1910, file 24220/6, RG 59.

33. E. W. McCullough to the State Department, March 19, 1912, file 661.1112/5, RG 59; C. S. Funk to Secretary of State, April 22, 1910, file 164.21 In 8/7, RG 59. Details about the visits of McCormick and other Harvester officials to Russia between July 1909 and April 1910 are in the records of the United States Embassy at Saint Petersburg, volumes designated "Russia-Diplomatic," RG 84. For a description of McCormick's interviews, see the memoranda dated June 28, July 5, 6, and 7, 1909, box 52, Nellie Fowler McCormick Papers, State Historical Society of Wisconsin, Madison. For Harvester's requests of the State Department, see George

Perkins to Knox, February 14, 1910, file 23549, and Perkins to Wilson, February 24, 1910, file 164.21 In 8/2, RG 59; E. A. Bancroft to Post Wheeler, April 26, 1910, "Russia-Diplomatic," RG 84.

34. Wilson, memorandum of March 10, 1910, file 164.21 In 8/9, RG 59; Knox to American Diplomats and Consuls, March 24, 1910, file 164.21, RG 59; Baldwin to Osborne, December 7, 1910, file 164.21/25, RG 59.

35. Rockhill to Secretary of State, April 2, 1910, file 164.21 In 8/5, RG 59; Snodgrass to same, October 5, 1910, file 164.21 In 8/12, RG 59.

36. Osborne to Wilson, April 23, 1910, Wilson to Osborne, May 2, 1910, and C. S. Funk to Secretary of State, April 22, 1910, all in file 164.21 In 8/5, RG 59; E. A. Bancroft to Post Wheeler, April 26, 1910, "Russia-Diplomatic," RG 84.

37. For a synopsis of the ad hoc approach, see Pepper, *American Foreign Trade*, pp. 294–95. See also Pepper to Hengstler, June 6, 1910, file 24121/6, and Carr to Spencer Kellogg and Sons, October 9, 1912, file 164.21/36, RG 59.

38. Hitt to William L. Scruggs, January 8, 1899, letterbook, Hitt Papers; Hill to Consul-General William M. Osborne at London, July 20, 1899, letterbook, Hill Papers, University of Rochester; House, *Hearings on the Dip/Cons* for 1911, January 17, 1910, pp. 102–3; Carr, diary entry for January 29, 1913, Carr Papers; Senate, *Reorganization of the Consular Service*, p. 26.

39. *American Consular Bulletin* 1 (October 1919): 4. For the recurring complaints of foreign service personnel, see also Eugene Schuyler, *American Diplomacy*, pp. 17, 25–27; Huntington Wilson, *Memoirs*, p. 156; William Phillips, *Ventures in Diplomacy*, p. 45; Hugh Gibson to his mother, June 11 and 15, 1910, Gibson Papers; J. V. A. MacMurray, diary entry for May 3, 1911 and to his mother, July 6, 1912, MacMurray Papers; Pepper, *American Foreign Trade*, pp. 312, 316–18; Tracy H. Lay, *The Foreign Service*, pp. ix, 93, 378–79; DeWitt C. Poole, *The Conduct of Foreign Relations under Modern Democratic Conditions* (New Haven, Conn., 1924), p. 129; Jessup, *Elihu Root*, 2: 108; Henry S. Villard, *Affairs at State* (New York, 1965), pp. 10, 47.

40. Consul-General Julius Lay, quoted in a London newspaper, August 1, 1908, in Frank D. Hill, consul-general at Barcelona, to State Department, file 2108/74, RG 59; Edward Ozmun to Assistant Secretary of State, December 9, 1907, file 10654, RG 59; Sammons to Rockhill, May 15, 1908, Rockhill Papers; Loomis, "Three Years of Consular Reform," Loomis Papers.

41. Francis E. Rourke, *Bureaucracy, Politics, and Public Policy* (Boston, 1969), p. 56; D. C. M. Platt, *Finance, Trade, and Politics in British Foreign Policy, 1815–1914* (Oxford, England, 1968), p. xxx; Steiner, *Foreign Office*, p. x.

42. A classic study of this genre is Charles S. Campbell, *Special Business Interests and the Open Door Policy* (New Haven, Conn., 1951). Other examples include Paul A. Varg, *Missionaries, Chinese, and Diplomats: The American Protestant Missionary Movement in China, 1890–1952* (Princeton, N.J., 1958), chapter 8; and Joan H. Wilson, *American Business and Foreign Policy* (Lexington, Ky., 1971).

43. Paul M. Hirsch, "Organizational Analysis and Industrial Sociology: An Instance of Cultural Lag," *American Sociologist* 10 (February 1975): 3–12; Charles Perrow, *Complex Organizations: A Critical Essay* (Glenview, Ill., 1972), p. 199.

44. Wiebe, *Search for Order*, p. 227; Chilton to William Rockhill, February 1, 1899, Rockhill Papers.

45. Transcript of conference of bureau chiefs, September 19, 1907, file 68699, RG 40; Chamber of Commerce of the State of New York, *Annual Report* (November 1912), pp. 103–4.

46. Carr to Root, September 23, 1907, file 2108/47, RG 59; Wilson, form letter, March 11, 1912, 120.1/21c, RG 59; Knox to Congressman William Sulzer, February 12, 1912, file 120.1/17a, RG 59.

47. Straight to Carr, August 6, 1909, Carr Papers.

48. Franklin Johnston to Carr, November 22, 1911, and Carr to Johnston, December 5, 1911, file 122.1/205, RG 59; article by Joseph Keegan in the *Far Eastern Review*, March 1908, enclosed in William Rockhill to the department, April 30, 1908, file 13375, RG 59; Consul-General John H. Snodgrass to Secretary of State, October 24, 1910, with editorial from *Fur Trade Review*, October 1910, file 161., RG 59; Gottschalk to Hengstler, May 6, 1910, Miscellaneous Reports and Correspondence on Consular Inspections, RG 59 (emphasis in the original); Carr, undated note, Carr Papers; *Proceedings of the National Board of Trade*, January 1911, pp. 288–89; Poole, notes for a lecture, March 1939, Poole Papers.

49. A decade ago, Samuel Haber called attention to the mutuality of perceived self-interest and national interest. Haber, *Efficiency and Uplift: Scientific Management in the Progressive Era, 1890–1920* (Chicago, 1964), p. xii. See also Otis Graham, *The Great Campaigns*, p. 16; Wiebe, *Search for Order*, p. 168.

50. *American Consular Bulletin* 4 (January 1922): 18–19; Poole, notes for a lecture, March 1935, Poole Papers (emphasis in the original).

51. MacMurray to Huntington Wilson, July 24, 1942, Wilson Papers; Herbert Croly, *Willard Straight* (New York, 1925), p. 267. See also Waldo H. Heinrichs, Jr., *American Ambassador: Joseph C. Grew and the Development of the United States Diplomatic Tradition* (Boston, 1966), p. 9; Charles N. Neu, "1906–1913," in Ernest R. May and James C. Thomson, eds., *American-East Asian Relations: A Survey* (Cambridge, Mass., 1972), pp. 158–59.

52. For a look at this same phenomenon in America's post–World War II foreign affairs bureaucracy, see Richard Barnet, *Intervention and Revolution: The United States in the Third World* (Cleveland, Ohio, 1968), p. 263 and passim. For a lengthier statement, see E. A. J. Johnson's revealing memoir, *American Imperialism in the Image of Peer Gynt: Memoirs of a Professor-Bureaucrat* (Minneapolis, Minn., 1971).

CHAPTER 11

1. For the problems in the diplomatic corps, see Alfred L. P. Dennis, "The Foreign Service of the United States," *North American Review* 219 (February 1924): 179; William Phillips to Secretary of State, May 8, 1922, file 121.31/19, RG 59; H. F. Arthur Schoenfeld, chargé at Bucharest, to Ellery C. Stowell, Ellery C. Stowell Papers, LC.

2. Here I refer to the beginnings of a systematic interchange between Washington and the field, and of a working relationship between diplomats and consuls in the geographic divisions to be consummated by later steps in foreign service reorganization.

3. National Archives, *Preliminary Inventory 157*, p. 51.

4. See above, chapter 9, note 34.

5. *National Cyclopaedia of American Biography*, vol. "A": 50–51; William C. Redfield, *With Congress and Cabinet* (New York, 1924), chapter 1. For an extensive study of the government's foreign trade organization during the Wilson administration, see Burton Kaufman, *Efficiency and Expansion*.

6. Baldwin to Redfield, March 17, 1913, and Redfield to Senator Thomas Gore, March 22, 1913, file 70801/8, RG 40.

7. Baldwin to Redfield, April 16, 1913, file 70801/46, RG 40.

8. Redfield to Wilson, July 15, 1913, records of the Committee on Appropriations, file 63A-F2.4, RG 233; *Washington Star*, October 16, 1913, clipping in file 70801/46, RG 40; Elliot H. Goodwin to Richard H. Dana, September 25, 1919, Stowell Papers; Schmeckebier and Weber, *Bureau of Foreign and Domestic Commerce*, pp. 40–41.

9. Senate, *Hearings on the LEJ* for 1915, April 29, 1914, p. 57; House, *LEJ*, Rept. 485, 63d Cong., 2d sess., 1914, pp. 44–45; same, Rept. 1221, 63d Cong., 3d sess., 1914, p. 38; same, Rept. 652, 66th Cong., 2d sess., 1920, pp. 47–48.

10. "Reorganization of the Department of Commerce," n.d., in file 74801, RG 40; Redfield to Frank Polk, counselor of the State Department, February 21, 1916, file 74014, RG 40.

11. Henry P. Fletcher to William G. McAdoo, February 1, 1913, Fletcher Papers; Willard Straight to Edwin Morgan, January 8, 1913, Straight Papers.

12. Crane, *Mr. Carr*, p. 147; Gottschalk to Hengstler, February 5, 1913, Miscellaneous Reports and Correspondence on Consular Inspections, and Carr to Gottschalk, February 24, 1913, Correspondence of Inspector Alfred L. M. Gottschalk, RG 59; Straight to Carr, April 15, 1913, and Carr to Bacon, May 1, 1913, Carr Papers.

13. "The Diplomats of Democracy," *North American Review* 199 (February 1914): 161; Seward W. Livermore, "Woodrow Wilson and the Foreign Service" (unpublished manuscript, May 10, 1945, in Historical Office of the Department of State), p. 1; Thomas Hardwick to Bryan, April 3, 1913, General Records of the Board of Examiners, RG 59; *Good Government* 30 (June 1913): 58; C. Vann Woodward, *Origins of the New South* (Baton Rouge, La., 1951), pp. 456–81. While some members of Congress from the South were unhappy with what they considered the low proportion of southerners in the consular service, the State Department's adherence to a quota system had brought results sufficient to satisfy others. See *Congressional Record*, 62d Cong., 2d sess., 1912, 48: 6189.

14. Straight to Morgan, January 8, 1913, Straight Papers; Carr, diary entry for February 25, 1913, Carr Papers; Gibson to his mother, January 8, 1913, Gibson Papers.

15. *Good Government* 30 (June 1913): 58; Wiebe, *Businessmen and Reform*, pp. 37–38; Elliot H. Goodwin to Woodrow Wilson, May 14, 1913, General Records

of the Board of Examiners, RG 59; William McAdoo to Henry Fletcher, December 27, 1912, Fletcher Papers; Livermore, "Woodrow Wilson and the Foreign Service."

Howard Bliss, president of the Syrian Protestant College at Beirut, likewise urged retention of the merit system in letters to President-elect Wilson and to Cleveland Dodge, a close mutual friend. William Coffin, consul at Jerusalem, to Carr, October 15, 1912, Carr Papers; Livermore, "Woodrow Wilson and the Foreign Service," p. 2. Livermore has published a shorter version of his manuscript as "'Deserving Democrats': The Foreign Service under Woodrow Wilson," *South Atlantic Quarterly* 49 (Winter 1970): 144–60.

16. "The Evolution of the Organization of the Foreign Service . . . ," undated draft of a speech, Carr Papers; *Proceedings of the NCSRL*, December 1913, pp. 115–17.

17. Livermore, "Woodrow Wilson and the Foreign Service," pp. 11–13; Straight to Fletcher, May 28, 1913, Straight Papers. The following year Long was replaced by William Heimke, a diplomat with seventeen years of experience at Latin American posts. Department of State, *Register*, 1914, p. 83.

18. Wilson to Moore, July 22, 1913, Moore Papers; Livermore, "Woodrow Wilson and the Foreign Service," p. 2; "Diplomats of Democracy," pp. 161–74.

19. Livermore, "Woodrow Wilson and the Foreign Service," p. 2; Aubrey L. Parkinson, "David Jayne Hill" (Ph.D. diss., University of Rochester, 1961), p. 434; Carr, diary entry for April 18, 1911, Carr Papers.

20. Carr, diary entry for February 10, 1913, Carr Papers; House, *LEJ*, Rept. 485, 63d Cong., 2d sess., 1914, p. 20; same, Rept. 1221, 63d Cong., 3d sess., 1914, p. 16; *Diplomatic and Consular Appropriation Bill*, House Rept. 545, 63d Cong., 2d sess., 1914, p. 1; same, House Rept. 1324, 63d Cong., 3d sess., 1915, p. 1.

21. Ilchman, *Professional Diplomacy*, pp. 102–11.

22. Bryan to Senator William J. Stone, May 18, 1914, Phillips to same, May 19, 1914, and copy of S. 5614, all in records of the Committee on Foreign Relations, file 63A-F8, RG 46; Carr, diary entry for December 8, 1914, Carr Papers; Phillips, "Reminiscences," p. 46; Bryan to Stone, August 21, 1914, file 120.1/48c, RG 59; copy of H.R. 16680, introduced by Henry Flood, Henry D. Flood Papers, LC; House, *Hearings on H.R. 16680*, September 2, 1914, pp. 7–12.

23. U.S., *Statutes at Large*, 38: 805–7. When Congress demonstrated its continued unwillingness to mandate a merit system for the foreign service, the State Department judiciously eliminated sections of the bill that spelled out the composition of the Boards of Examiners and some of the examination subjects. Unpublished draft of hearings on H.R. 16680, records of the Committee on Foreign Affairs, file 63A-D7, RG 233.

24. "Hail to the Chief," *American Consular Bulletin* 4 (June 1922): 155; "The American Consular Association," 1919 memorandum in Stowell Papers; memorandum from "RJT" to Hengstler, "1918," with circular letter of the new American Consular Association, Consular Bureau Decisions and Precedents, RG 59; Carr, diary entry for January 10, 1915, and Carr to Chilton, June 23, 1922, Carr Papers; Crane, *Mr. Carr*, pp. 38, 268.

Following World War I, Carr expected that consuls would devote less time to gathering statistics and trade information, and more to "creating an atmosphere on the one hand which encourages trade, and facilitating on the other hand the carrying on of trade and protecting it by discovering and laying bare the facts to the American diplomatic representatives in the country." In this manner, the two field branches would continue both their real and their apparent usefulness to American trade, while their work would draw closer together. Such a development would take time, however, and the department continued its prewar emphasis on trade promotion as the consuls' most important task. On the average, consuls spent about 40 percent of their time on it, and they flooded the Commerce Department with four times as many reports as it could circulate. Carr, undated memorandum, but apparently 1919, Carr Papers; "Remarks of Mr. Wesley Frost, Acting Foreign Trade Adviser . . . at Conference of Council on Foreign Relations," *American Consular Bulletin* 2 (June 1920): 2–4.

25. Despite the benefits to their branch, it was the diplomats who fought amalgamation. They tended to look down on the consuls as a distinctly lower order, and an observer noted that they were "up in arms" over proposed consolidation. Ellery Stowell, memorandum, December 29, 1919, Stowell Papers. For an account of the diplomats' agitation and their attempts to frustrate amalgamation, see Heinrichs, "Bureaucracy and Professionalism," pp. 119–206.

26. Carr to Huntington Wilson, July 29, 1931, Wilson Papers; Barnes and Morgan, *Foreign Service*, pp. 205–9.

27. Barnes and Morgan, *Foreign Service*, pp. 215–17, 256–62, 272–85.

28. Joseph Grew's foreword to James R. Childs, *American Foreign Service* (New York, 1948), p. vi; Givon Parsons, "Foreign Service People and Their Constituents," *Newsletter of the Department of State*, no. 35 (March 1964), pp. 12–13; "New Communications with Grass Roots America," ibid., no. 41 (September 1964), pp. 7–9.

29. Address by Carroll L. Wilson, April 14, 1941, file 160, RG 151 (emphasis in the original).

SELECTED
BIBLIOGRAPHY

The bibliography is complete for the manuscript and archival collections that are cited in the notes, reflecting their paramount importance as source material for this study. The remainder of the list contains only the most important published sources and secondary works.

UNPUBLISHED SOURCE MATERIALS

United States Government Archives, National Archives, Washington, D.C.
Bureau of Foreign and Domestic Commerce Records, Record Group 151
Commerce Department Records, Record Group 40
Foreign Service Posts Records (Russia—Diplomatic), Record Group 84
House of Representatives Records, Record Group 233
President's Commission on Economy and Efficiency Records, in Records of the
      Bureau of the Budget, Record Group 51
Senate Records, Record Group 46
State Department Records, Record Group 59
      Consular Bureau Decisions and Precedents
      Consular Dispatches (Berlin)
      Correspondence of Inspector Alfred L. M. Gottschalk
      Decimal Files, 1910 and following
      Departmental Orders
      Dispatches from Consular Clerks
      General Records of the Board of Examiners
      Inspection Reports on Consulates
      Instructions to Consuls General and Inspectors
      Lectures to Consular Officers
      Letters Sent by the Chief Clerk
      Memoranda on the History and Organization of the Office of the Economic
            Adviser
      Miscellaneous Correspondence of the Chief Clerk
      Miscellaneous Letters Sent by the Secretary of State

Miscellaneous Letters Sent regarding Consular Affairs
Miscellaneous Reports and Correspondence on Consular Inspections
Numerical Files, 1906–1910
Press Copies of Reports of the Consular Bureau
Report of Convention of Consuls General and Treasury Agents at Paris,
          August, 1890
Report of the Chief Clerk
Reports of Clerks and Bureau Officers
Reports of Consular Service Entrance Examinations
Reports of the Bureau of Accounts
Reports on Diplomatic Service Entrance Examinations

Private Papers and Other Manuscript Collections (Unless otherwise noted,
collections are located at the Manuscripts Division, Library of Congress.)
Chandler P. Anderson
Thomas F. Bayard
Boston Chamber of Commerce Records (Baker Library, Harvard Business School,
          Boston, Mass.)
Bureau of American Republics Records (Records Management Center, Organization
          of American States, Washington, D.C.)
Wilbur J. Carr
Robert S. Chilton, Jr. (Duke University Library, Durham, N.C.)
Grover Cleveland
George B. Cortelyou
William R. Day
Charles M. Dickinson
Frederic Emory Scrapbook (Columbus Memorial Library, Pan-American Union,
          Washington, D.C.)
Henry P. Fletcher
Henry D. Flood
John G. Foster (University of Vermont Library, Burlington)
Harry A. Garfield
James R. Garfield
Hugh Gibson (Hoover Institution on War, Revolution, and Peace, Stanford, Cal.)
Frank J. Goodnow (Eisenhower Library, Johns Hopkins University, Baltimore, Md.)
John Hay
David J. Hill (Bucknell University Library, Lewisburg, Pa., and University of
          Rochester Library, Rochester, N.Y.)
Robert R. Hitt
Hunt Family
Philip C. Jessup
Philander C. Knox
Henry Cabot Lodge (Massachusetts Historical Society, Boston)
Francis B. Loomis (Department of Special Collections, Stanford University Li-
          braries, Stanford, Cal.)
Frank O. Lowden (University of Chicago Library, Chicago, Ill.)

George McAneny (Princeton University Library, Princeton, N.J.)
Nellie Fowler McCormick (State Historical Society of Wisconsin, Madison)
John V. A. MacMurray (Princeton University Library, Princeton, N.J.)
John Bassett Moore
Joseph Hampton Moore (Historical Society of Pennsylvania, Philadelphia)
Charles Nagel (Yale University Library, New Haven, Conn.)
National Civil Service League (Pendleton Room, U.S. Civil Service Commission
    Library, Washington, D.C.)
Knute Nelson (Minnesota State Historical Society, St. Paul)
Simon N. D. North (Cornell University Libraries, Ithaca, N.Y.)
John C. O'Laughlin
Richard Olney
Philadelphia Board of Trade Records (Historical Society of Pennsylvania, Philadel-
    phia)
DeWitt C. Poole (State Historical Society of Wisconsin, Madison)
William W. Rockhill (Houghton Library, Harvard University, Cambridge, Mass.)
Theodore Roosevelt
Elihu Root
James Brown Scott (Special Collections Division, Georgetown University, Wash-
    ington, D.C.)
Ellery C. Stowell
Willard Straight (Cornell University Libraries, Ithaca, N.Y.)
Oscar Straus
William H. Taft
James Tawney (Minnesota State Historical Society, St. Paul)
Henry White
Edward T. Williams (University of California, Berkeley, Library)
James H. Wilson
Huntington Wilson (Myrin Library, Ursinus College, Collegeville, Pa.)

PUBLISHED SOURCE MATERIALS

United States Government Documents

Congress. *Congressional Record.*
Congress. House of Representatives. *Estimates for Foreign Intercourse.* Document
    1193, 60th Cong., 2d sess. 1908.
_____. *Explanation as to Estimate for Foreign Intercourse, 1909.* Document 498,
    60th Cong., 1st sess. 1908.
_____. *Hearings before the Committee on Expenditures in the State Department.*
_____. *Hearings on the Diplomatic and Consular Appropriations Bill.*
_____. *Hearings on the Legislative, Executive and Judicial Appropriations Bill.*
_____. *Promotion of Trade Interests.* Document 245, 58th Cong., 3d sess. 1905.
_____. *Reorganization of the Consular Service.* Rept. 2281, 59th Cong., 1st sess.
    1906.

Congress. Senate. *Expenses in Connection with Foreign Trade Relations with the Orient and Latin America.* Document 139, 61st Cong., 1st sess. 1909.

———. *Foreign Trade and Treaty Relations.* Document 150, 61st Cong., 1st sess. 1909.

———. *Hearings on the Legislative, Executive and Judicial Appropriations Bill.*

———. *Reorganization of the Consular and Diplomatic Service.* Rept. 1202, 56th Cong., 1st sess. 1900.

———. *Reorganization of the Consular Service.* Rept. 112, 59th Cong., 1st sess. 1906.

Department of Commerce. *Historical Statistics of the United States, 1789–1945.* Washington, D.C., 1949.

———. *Historical Statistics of the United States, Colonial Times to 1957.* Washington, D.C., 1960.

———. *Statistical Abstract of the United States.*

Department of Commerce and Labor. *Reports of the Department of Commerce and Labor.*

———. *The Commercial Orient in 1905.* Washington, D.C., 1906.

———. *Foreign Commerce and Navigation of the United States.*

———. *Monthly Summary of Commerce and Finance.*

———. *Statistical Abstract of the United States.*

Department of State. *Commercial Relations of the United States with Foreign Countries.*

———. *Monthly Consular Reports.*

———. *Outline of the Organization and Work of the Department of State.* Washington, D.C., 1911.

———. *Register of the Department of State.*

———. *Regulations Prescribed for the Consular Service of the United States.* Washington, D.C., 1896.

United States. *Statutes at Large.*

Books, Articles, and Pamphlets

Adams, Robert. "Faults in Our Consular Service." *North American Review* 156 (1893): 461–66.

Austin, Oscar P. "Does Colonization Pay?" *Forum* 28 (1900): 621–31.

———. "Our Growing Dependence on the Tropics." *Forum* 33 (1902): 400–408.

———. "Why Not Three Hundred Million People?" *Forum* 31 (1901): 165–74.

Bacon, Robert, and Scott, James B., eds. *The Military and Colonial Policy of the United States: Addresses and Reports by Elihu Root.* Cambridge, Mass., 1916.

Carr, Wilbur J. "The American Consular Service." *American Journal of International Law* 1 (1907): 891–913.

Donaldson, Charles S. "Government Assistance to Export Trade." *Annals of the American Academy of Political and Social Science* 34 (1909): 555–62.

Emory, Frederic. "The Greater America." *World's Work* 2 (1901): 1320–25, and 3 (1901): 1513–17.

———. "Our Foreign Trade." *Philadelphia Public Ledger*, January 26, 1897.

_____. *Queen Anne's County, Maryland: Its Early History and Development.* Baltimore, Md., 1950.

_____. "The Uniting of American Society." *World's Work* 3 (1902): 1854–56.

Garfield, Harry A. "The Business Man and the Consular Service." *Century* 60 (1900): 268–71.

_____. "The Remodeling of the Consular Service." *Independent* 52 (1900): 657–59.

Griscom, Lloyd. *Diplomatically Speaking.* New York, 1940.

Hunt, Gaillard. "Reform in the Consular Service." *Independent* 51 (1899): 2881–82.

_____. "To Reorganize the Consular Service." *World's Work* 3 (1902): 1606–13.

Lane, Jonathan A. *The Appointments and Removals in the Consular Service.* Boston, 1893.

Lay, Tracy H. *The Foreign Service of the United States.* New York, 1925.

McAneny, George. "How Other Countries Do It: An Inquiry into the Consular Systems of Other Nations." *Century* 57 (1899): 604–11.

National Association of Manufacturers. *Methods of Extending Foreign Trade.* Circular of Information, no. 15, 1897.

National Civil Service Reform League. *Report on the Foreign Service.* New York, 1919.

Osborne, John B. "Alternative of Reciprocity Treaties or a Double Tariff." *North American Review* 181 (1905): 731–44.

_____. "The American Consul and American Trade." *Atlantic Monthly* 99 (1907): 159–70.

Pepper, Charles M. *American Foreign Trade: The United States as a World Power in the New Era of International Commerce.* New York, 1919.

Phillips, William. "The Geographical Divisions." *American Consular Bulletin* 4 (1922): 345–47, 362–66.

_____. "Reminiscences." Columbia Oral History Project. 1951, © 1972.

Schuyler, Eugene. *American Diplomacy and the Furtherance of Commerce.* New York, 1886.

"Who's Who—and Why." *Saturday Evening Post,* January 27, 1923, pp. 26, 62.

Wilson, Francis M. Huntington. *Memoirs of an Ex-Diplomat.* Boston, 1945.

Wilson, Huntington. "The American Foreign Service." *Outlook* 82 (1906): 499–504.

_____. *The Peril of Hifalutin'.* New York, 1918.

_____. *Save America: An Appeal to Patriotism.* New York, 1914.

Wright, Carroll D. "The Relation of Production to Productive Capacity." *Forum* 24 (1897): 290–302.

Periodicals and Proceedings

American Consular Bulletin.

American Foreign Service Journal.

Chamber of Commerce of the State of New York. *Annual Report of the Corporation.*

Cleveland Chamber of Commerce. *Reports and Proceedings.*

Good Government.

National Board of Trade. *Proceedings.*

National Civil Service Reform League. *Proceedings.*

SECONDARY MATERIALS

Barnes, William, and Morgan, John H. *The Foreign Service of the United States: Origins, Development, and Functions*. Washington, D.C., 1961.

Barnet, Richard. *Intervention and Revolution: The United States in the Third World*. Cleveland, Ohio, 1968.

Chandler, Alfred D., Jr. *Strategy and Structure: Chapters in the History of the Industrial Enterprise*. New York, Anchor Books, 1966.

Crane, Katherine. *Mr. Carr of State: Forty-seven Years in the Department of State*. New York, 1960.

Galambos, Louis. "The Emerging Organizational Synthesis in Modern American History." *Business History Review* 44 (1970): 279–90.

Graham, Otis L. *The Great Campaigns: Reform and War in America, 1900–1928*. Englewood Cliffs, N.J., 1971.

Haber, Samuel. *Efficiency and Uplift: Scientific Management in the Progressive Era*. Chicago, 1964.

Hays, Samuel P. "Political Parties and the Community-Society Continuum." In *The American Party Systems: Stages of Political Development*, edited by William N. Chambers and Walter D. Burnham, pp. 152–81. New York, 1967.

Heinrichs, Waldo H., Jr. "Bureaucracy and Professionalism in the Development of American Career Diplomacy." In *Twentieth-Century American Foreign Policy*, edited by John Braeman et al., pp. 119–206. Columbus, Ohio, 1971.

Hirsch, Paul M. "Organizational Analysis and Industrial Sociology: An Instance of Cultural Lag." *American Sociologist* 10 (1975): 3–12.

Huntington, Samuel P. *The Soldier and the State: The Theory and Politics of Civil-Military Relations*. Cambridge, Mass., 1957.

Ilchman, Warren F. *Professional Diplomacy in the United States, 1779–1939: A Study in Administrative History*. Chicago, 1961.

Israel, Jerry. "A Diplomatic Machine: Scientific Management in the Department of State, 1906–1924." In *Building the Organizational Society: Essays on Associational Activities in Modern America*, edited by Israel, pp. 183–96. New York, 1972.

Jessup, Philip C. *Elihu Root*. 2 vols. New York, 1938.

Johnson, Emory, et al. *History of Domestic and Foreign Commerce of the United States*. 2 vols. Washington, D.C., 1915.

Jones, Chester L. *Consular Service of the United States*. Philadelphia, 1906.

Kaufman, Burton I. *Efficiency and Expansion: Foreign Trade Organization in the Wilson Administration, 1913–1921*. Westport, Conn., 1974.

―――. "The Organizational Dimension of United States Foreign Economic Policy, 1900–1920." *Business History Review* 46 (1972): 17–44.

LaFeber, Walter. *The New Empire: An Interpretation of American Expansion, 1860–1898*. Ithaca, N.Y., 1963.

Leuchtenburg, William E. "The New Deal and the Analogue of War." In *Change and Continuity in Twentieth-Century America*, edited by John Braeman et al., pp. 81–143. New York, 1966.

Lipsey, Robert M. *Price and Quantity Trends in the Foreign Trade of the United States*. Princeton, N.J., 1963.

Livermore, Seward W. "Woodrow Wilson and the Foreign Service," May 10, 1945. Unpublished article in Historical Office of the Department of State.

McCormick, Thomas J. *China Market: America's Quest for Informal Empire, 1893–1901*. Chicago, 1967.

_____. "The State of American Diplomatic History." In *The State of American History*, edited by Herbert J. Bass, pp. 119–41. Chicago, 1970.

Merton, Robert K. *Social Theory and Social Structure*. New York, 1957.

Metcalf, Evan B. "Secretary Hoover and the Emergence of Macroeconomic Management." *Business History Review* 49 (1975): 60–80.

Nevins, Allan. *Henry White: Thirty Years of American Diplomacy*. New York, 1930.

Paterson, Thomas G. "American Businessmen and Consular Service Reform, 1890s to 1906." *Business History Review* 40 (1966): 77–97.

Perrow, Charles. *Complex Organizations: A Critical Essay*. Glenview, Ill., 1972.

Rees, Albert. *Real Wages in Manufacturing, 1890–1914*. Princeton, N.J., 1961.

Schmeckebier, Lawrence F., and Weber, Gustavus A. *The Bureau of Foreign and Domestic Commerce: Its History, Activities, and Organization*. Baltimore, Md., 1924.

Scholes, Walter V., and Scholes, Marie V. *The Foreign Policies of the Taft Administration*. Columbia, Mo., 1970.

Shannon, Fred A. "A Post-Mortem on the Labor-Safety-Valve Theory." *Agricultural History* 19 (1945): 31–37.

Steiner, Zara S. *The Foreign Office and Foreign Policy, 1898–1914*. Cambridge, England, 1969.

Stuart, Graham H. *American Diplomatic and Consular Practice*. New York, 1936.

_____. *The Department of State*. New York, 1949.

Thelen, David P. "Social Tensions and the Origins of Progressivism." *Journal of American History* 61 (1969): 323–41.

Wiebe, Robert. *Businessmen and Reform: A Study of the Progressive Movement*. Cambridge, Mass., 1962.

_____. *The Search for Order, 1877–1920*. New York, 1968.

Williams, William A. *The Tragedy of American Diplomacy*. New York, 1962.

INDEX